INTERNATIONAL DEVELOPMENT IN FOCUS

Fiscal Policies for Development and Climate Action

Miria A. Pigato, Editor

WORLD BANK GROUP

1818 H Street NW, Washington, DC 20433
Telephone: 202-473-1000; Internet: www.worldbank.org

1 2 3 4 22 21 20 19

ISBN: 978-1-4648-1358-0
DOI: 10.1596/978-1-4648-1358-0

Cover photo: ARTappler/iStock by Getty Images. Used with the permission of iStock by Getty Images. Permission required for reuse.
Cover design: Debra Naylor / Naylor Design Inc.

Contents

Boxes

Figures

Maps

Tables

Foreword

The world is in the early stages of a transition to a post-carbon economy. The impact of climate change is already upon us and is projected to worsen. For developing countries, climate damages threaten to derail steady progress toward the Sustainable Development Goals and will likely trigger significant losses to the gross domestic product. Policy decisions in developing countries—where aggregate emissions now exceed emissions in developed countries—are critical to tackling climate change. Recent developments are encouraging: politicians, policymakers, and business leaders around the world increasingly recognize the urgency of the climate change threat and the benefits of proactive action.

This book is a call to take charge. In the past, climate policy was the exclusive domain of sector and environment ministries. But as this report demonstrates, finance ministries can and must become the linchpin of effective climate action. Fiscal policy reforms are the most powerful lever to reduce climate emissions in a cost-efficient manner and serve as a foundation to deliver on important development goals. The most pressing fiscal reforms needed to achieve broader development goals are increasingly indistinguishable from reforms needed to mitigate and adapt to climate change.

The book shows that there is a striking chasm between current levels of taxation on activities that have a significant negative impact on the environment (environmental taxation) and the level that would be optimal for enhancing both development and climate action. Environmental tax reforms designed to close energy price gaps would raise substantial revenues, and at lower cost than raising other taxes. While there is no single solution for using revenues from environmental taxes, there are many options. For instance, governments could use these revenues to reduce preexisting taxes that inhibit growth, increase spending on education and other public goods, or to help the economy to adapt to climate change.

In developing countries with large informal sectors and dependence on distortionary taxes in formal sectors, the benefits of environmental tax reforms are especially pronounced. For example, using environmental tax revenues to reduce formal-sector taxes on labor and capital could enable a "double dividend" of lower emissions and higher employment and growth. The report also brings new empirical evidence that should be encouraging to fiscal policymakers:

environmental tax reforms need not be a strain on competitiveness and can, in fact, lead to increased firm productivity and investment.

While no country can be completely prepared for the sudden ecological and economic impacts of climate disasters, fiscal policy can and should serve as a protective buffer. Preventive investments in adaptation will go a long way to making the economy more resilient to climate change. In addition to the use of insurance, finance ministries can gradually build fiscal buffers that can support countries' preparedness to climate shocks.

In the coming months and years, politicians and economic policymakers will be seeking the most effective ways to deliver on their country's Nationally Determined Contributions to the Paris Agreement as well as their commitments to Sustainable Development Goals. These efforts will require the highest-quality evidence base, cross-national knowledge sharing, and expert technical guidance in crafting winning solutions.

It is my hope that this book will serve as an essential reference for the cohort of finance ministers that will pioneer the next generation of climate-smart fiscal reforms. There is no time to waste. The time to act is now.

Ceyla Pazarbasioglu-Dutz
Vice President, Equitable Growth,
Finance and Institutions
The World Bank

Acknowledgments

Fiscal Policies for Development and Climate Action was prepared by a World Bank team led by Miria Pigato and comprising Dirk Heine, Simon Black, Antoine Coste, Massimiliano Calì, Nicola Cantore, Lorenzo Forni, Michele Catalano, Emilia Pezzolla, Philip Schuler, Luiz Edgard Oliveira, Gianluca Mele, and Matias Antonio. The team worked under the overall guidance of Carlos Felipe Jaramillo.

Grzegorz Peszko provided detailed inputs and advice to chapter 1. Substantive inputs were also provided by Goran Dominioni and Sanaz Ettehad. The team is grateful to reviewers Annela Anger-Kraavi, Sebastian Gechert, Tuan Minh Le, and Michael Mehling. The empirical analysis of chapter 2 was based on three background papers prepared jointly by Massimiliano Calì and Nicola Cantore, with Massimiliano Mazzanti, Giovanni Marin, and Francesco Nicolli. Taufik Hidayat and Giorgio Presidente contributed to the Indonesia case study, and Leonardo Iacovone, Mariana De La Paz Pereira Lopez, and Julio Valle Pereña to the Mexico case study. Feedback was received from Ana Fernandes, Jun Rentschler, and Michael Mehling. The team is grateful to William F. Maloney for his insightful comments and suggestions on this chapter. Feedback on chapter 3 was received from Yannis Dafermos, Sudarshan Gooptu, and Willi Semmler.

The team also benefited from comments and advice provided by John Roome, Paloma Anos Casero, John Panzer, Carter Brandon, Kevin Carey, Maria de Los Angeles Cuqui Gonzalez Miranda, Sudarshan Gooptu, Michael Grubb, Wei-Jen Leow, Marcelo Mena, Klaus Oppermann, Ian Parry, Leela Raina, Mike Toman, Mathew Verghis, Gregor Schwerhoff, and Marinus Verhoeven. The team is grateful to Ivana Ticha and Patricia Mendez for their assistance during the preparation of the report.

About the Editor and Contributors

ABOUT THE EDITOR

Miria A. Pigato is a Lead Economist and Climate Lead in the World Bank's Macroeconomics, Trade, and Investment Global Practice. Prior to assuming this position in 2016, she served as Practice and Sector Manager of the Macroeconomics and Fiscal Management Global Practice. She led senior policy dialogue on growth, climate, macro, fiscal, and trade policies and supervised more than 60 development policy operations for Africa, the Caribbean, Central Asia, Eastern Europe, the Middle East, and South Asia. Currently, Pigato coleads the Climate Action Peer Exchange, a capacity-building forum for peer-to-peer knowledge sharing and advisory support for Finance Ministries. She holds a master's degree in economics at the London School of economics and a PhD in Economics at University College, London.

ABOUT THE CONTRIBUTORS

Matias Antonio is a mathematician and macroeconomist with experience in institutional investing and macroeconomic policy. Antonio has been involved in the development and deployment of tactical and strategic asset allocation models to manage $25 billion at the World Bank Pension Fund, and in the successful reconstruction and management of a $2 billion emerging market equities portfolio at the same Fund. He has also participated in various World Bank and International Monetary Fund (IMF) macroeconomic stabilization programs.

Simon Black is an Economist with the Global Climate Change Research and Analytics (GCCRA) team at the World Bank. Previously, he was a Fast Stream Diplomatic Service Economist at the United Kingdom's Foreign and Commonwealth Office and a member of the U.K. delegation to the United Nations Framework Convention on Climate Change in the run-up to the Paris Agreement. He holds a master's degree in international political economy from the London School of Economics and a master's degree in development economics from Harvard University, where he was a Frank Knox Fellow.

Massimiliano Calì is a Senior Economist in the Jakarta office of the World Bank, where he leads the Bank's advisory and lending work on trade and investment in Indonesia. Previously he was an Economist in the World Bank's Trade and Competitiveness Global Practice working on ways to use trade and trade policy to reduce poverty and conflict. Prior to joining the Bank, he served as an Economic Advisor to the Palestinian Ministry of National Economy, as a Research Fellow with the Overseas Development Institute, and as an Economist with the Italian embassy in Bolivia. He has published on various topics in development economics in journals such as *Journal of Economic Geography, World Bank Economic Review, Review of International Economics,* and *Labour Economics*. He holds a PhD in economic geography from the London School of Economics; a master's degree in development economics from the University of East Anglia, England; and a bachelor's degree in economics from the University of Pavia, Italy.

Nicola Cantore holds a PhD in environmental economics and management from the University of York and a PhD in economics from the Universita' Cattolica del Sacro Cuore in Milan. He worked as a Junior Researcher at the Fondazione ENI Enrico Mattei in Milan, as a Senior Researcher at the Department of Agricultural Economics and Engineering of the University of Bologna, and as a Research Fellow at the Overseas Development Institute in London. He is currently a Researcher at the Department of Policy Research and Statistics of the United Nations Industrial Development Organization in Vienna.

Michele Catalano is an Economist at the Prometeia Associazione think tank in Bologna. He received a PhD in economics from the University of Pisa, Italy. He is responsible for long- and short-run projections with structural equilibrium models for the Italian and world economy.

Antoine Coste is an Economist in the Environment and Natural Resources (ENR) Global Practice of the World Bank, working in the South Asia Region and based in Washington, D.C. He focuses on sustainable private sector development, resource efficiency and cleaner production, pollution management, and green competitiveness. Previously, he worked for six years in the Finance, Competitiveness and Innovation (FCI) Global Practice, in the Africa and East Asia and Pacific Regions. Coste holds a master's degree in development studies from the London School of Economics, as well as a master's degree in political science and an undergraduate degree in economics, both from Panthéon-Sorbonne University in Paris.

Luiz Edgard Oliveira is a former World Bank Group Analyst with the Macroeconomic, Trade, and Investment Global Practice, focusing on areas including economic growth, fiscal policy, and debt sustainability in the Latin America and Caribbean Region. He was formerly a Research Assistant at the IMF, focusing on fiscal revenue mobilization. He is currently an Associate Economist at the Federal Reserve Bank of San Francisco, where he is primarily responsible for producing U.S. economic forecasts.

Lorenzo Forni is a Professor of economic policy at the University of Padua, Italy, and is Head of the Prometeia Associazione think tank in Bologna. He worked at the IMF from 2010 to 2016, and before that he worked at the Bank of Italy. He received a master's degree in political economy and a PhD in economics from Boston University, and he was a visiting scholar at Harvard University in 2005/2006. His research interests include the economic impact of fiscal policy, sovereign debt restructuring, credit cycles and, recently, climate change.

Dirk Heine is an Economist in the World Bank's Macroeconomics, Trade, and Investment Global Practice, Global Macro and Debt Unit. Previously, Heine was an Economist in the Division for Structural Issues of Tax Policy in the Economics Department of the German Finance Ministry, and he coauthored several IMF publications on environmental tax policy, including the book *Getting Energy Prices Right*. Publications that he coauthored on taxation and development have received the IMF Management Award, the European Association for Law and Economics' Deloitte Award, and three prizes from the Massachusetts Institute of Technology Climate CoLab. Passionate about issues of fiscal policy, Heine believes that building robust public finance is at the heart of economic development. Since 1998, Heine has used his free time to volunteer for sustainable development projects.

Gianluca Mele is a Senior Economist at the World Bank. He currently serves on the advisory team of the World Bank Chief Executive Officer, focusing on economic matters. Prior to this position, he served as a Senior Country Economist in charge of the macroeconomic policy dialogue with various Caribbean and Sub-Saharan African countries. Before joining the World Bank, he worked at the International Trade Centre and at the United Nations in Geneva as an investment and trade expert. He has published extensively on macroeconomic, fiscal, competitiveness, and environmental policies with the United Nations and the World Bank, and he has cooperated with the Columbia University Press. Mele holds a PhD in Economics and Statistics, and a master's degree in international relations. He has led official missions to over 25 low- and middle-income countries and is fluent in 5 languages.

Emilia Pezzolla is an Economist at the Prometeia Associazione think tank in Bologna. She received a master's degree in markets analysis and local development and a PhD in economics from the University of Lecce, Italy. Previously, she was a Teaching Assistant in econometrics at the University of Lecce and a Coworker and Visiting Fellow at the Institute for Empirical Research in Economics, University of Zurich.

Philip Schuler has worked at the World Bank since 2001 and is currently Lead Economist for East Africa in the Macroeconomic and Fiscal Management Global Practice. Schuler led the World Bank's Systematic Regional Diagnostic for the Eastern Caribbean, and in Jamaica and other Caribbean countries he led several World Bank lending operations that were designed to increase the fiscal and macroeconomic resilience of those countries.

Executive Summary

MIRIA A. PIGATO AND SIMON BLACK

INTRODUCTION

Climate change is one of the greatest threats to economic development

Climate change is already occurring and will worsen over time. According to the United Nations' Intergovernmental Panel on Climate Change, the increase in global carbon emissions caused by human activity will result in "severe, pervasive, and irreversible impacts for people and ecosystems" (IPCC 2014). These impacts include increasingly frequent weather-related disasters, alongside gradual but potentially devastating processes of ocean acidification and sea-level rise. Climate change is intensifying pressure on communities and ecosystems worldwide. In the past year alone, storms, fires, and hurricanes in the Caribbean and the United States, mudslides in Colombia, monsoonal flooding in Bangladesh, and tropical cyclones in Asia have inflicted a catastrophic economic and human toll. Avoiding a disastrous increase in global temperatures will require a dramatic reduction in emissions growth in both developed and developing countries. If the Paris Agreement's overarching goal of limiting global warming to well below 2 degrees Celsius is not achieved, climate-induced natural disasters will become increasingly frequent and costly.

But, even if the goal is reached, climate change will continue to disproportionately affect developing countries. Countries that are less developed, as indicated by lower Sustainable Development Goals Index (SDG Index) scores, are more exposed to the negative effects of climate change (maps ES.1 and ES.2). These countries are also the least responsible for global greenhouse gas (GHG) emissions and the least prepared to adapt to a changing climate.

As a result, while mitigation is essential, adaptation policies are also necessary. Climate change will continue to increase both the frequency and severity of natural disasters. In addition to human loss, such disasters can destroy commercial and private property, damage infrastructure, reduce agricultural yields, and slow economic growth. Moreover, lost tax revenues and increased public spending for relief and reconstruction can strain governments' budgets. Without proactive policies, such costs could stymie or reverse development gains made to date.

MAP ES.1

Less-developed countries...

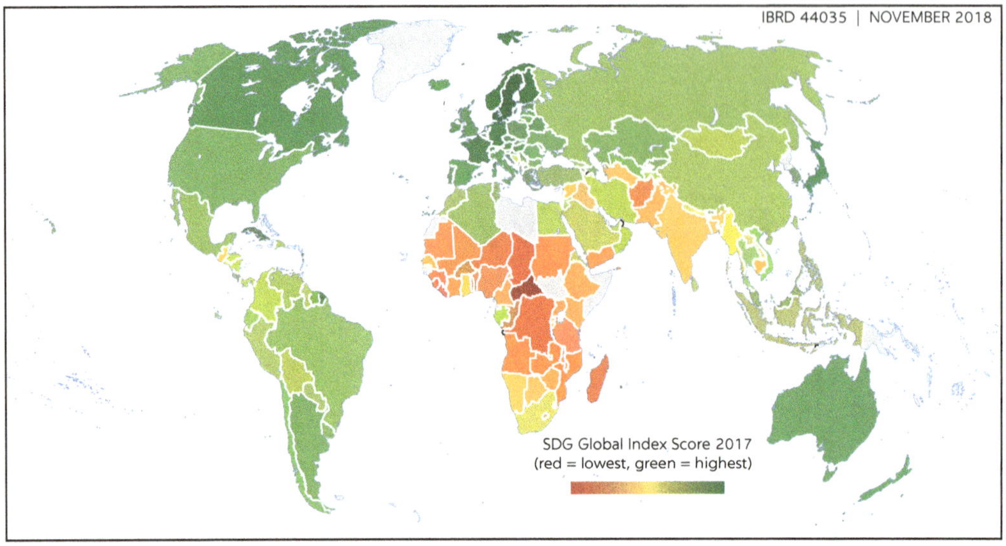

Source: World Bank map using data from SDSN 2017.
Note: Shows Sustainable Development Goal (SDG) Global Index scores in 2017 (from 0 to 100; higher scores indicate higher levels of development). Colors range from dark red for the lowest score (37) to dark green for the highest (86).

MAP ES.2

...are more vulnerable to climate change

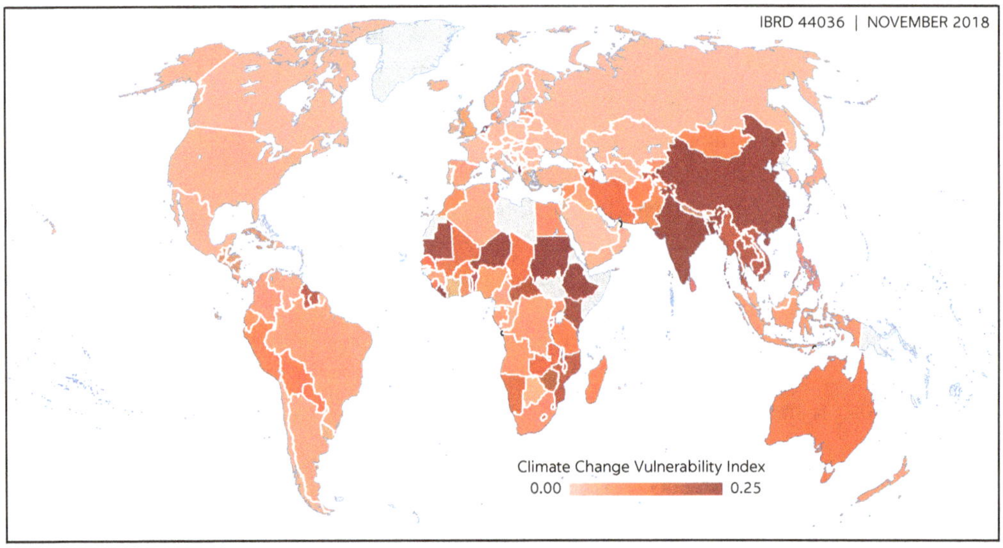

Source: World Bank map using data from HCSS 2014.
Note: Climate Change Vulnerability Index scores are based on vulnerability to weather-related natural disasters, sea level rise, and loss of agricultural productivity. Scores range from light red for least vulnerable (0.01) to dark red for most vulnerable (0.43).

Other environmental hazards continue to hamper development efforts

Beyond the costs of climate change, other environmental hazards continue to hamper development efforts. Notably, air pollution and road accidents inflict enormous costs to well-being and growth in developing countries. Air pollutants like black carbon and PM2.5[1] arising from fossil fuel combustion are a leading cause of illness and death. Each year, an estimated 9 million people die prematurely because of pollution; 92 percent of these premature deaths are in low- and middle-income countries (Lancet Commission 2017).[2] These deaths account for annual welfare losses of US$4.6 trillion, or 6.2 percent of global gross domestic product (GDP) (Lancet Commission 2017). Moreover, safe and efficient mobility remains a rich-world good. Severe congestion and road accidents disproportionately affect people living in poorer countries. Developing countries account for a staggering 90 percent of the 20–30 million injuries and the 1.3 million deaths that occur on the world's roads each year (WHO 2015). Left unaddressed, these costs are expected to become increasingly concentrated in developing countries, holding back development.

Well-designed fiscal policies can mitigate climate change while raising welfare

This report argues that fiscal instruments are among the most effective means to fight climate change while raising human welfare. Environmental taxes are taxes whose base "is a physical unit (or a proxy of it) that has a proven specific negative impact on the environment" (OECD 2018a). Taxes can include those on energy, transportation, pollution, and resources. These taxes leverage price signals to discourage the burning of fossil fuels and other environmentally damaging activities while promoting innovation and investment in cleaner, more efficient sources of energy. In addition, the revenue generated by environmental taxes can be used to reduce other, preexisting taxes or to finance spending on health, education, social protection, and public infrastructure to increase the economy's resilience to climate change.

Environmental tax reform (ETR) combines environmental taxes with reductions in other taxes (tax shifts), expenditure policies, and supplementary policies. By raising upstream taxes on fossil fuels and using revenues to reduce labor taxes or increase public investment and social spending, ETR can help developing countries mitigate climate change while raising welfare. For example, an ETR could comprise a tax on the import or extraction of coal, with revenues funding expansions of public infrastructure, supplemented with targeted compensation for poorer households.

ETR can help countries mitigate climate change while accelerating their social and economic development, yielding multiple benefits for well-being (figure ES.1). These benefits include reduced climate risks, "development co-benefits" such as cleaner water and safer roads, and helping fund important public goods like energy access, health, and education. In addition, in circumstances more common in developing countries, ETR can yield net benefits for economic activity, such as expansions in output and employment or improvements in productivity. As a result, ETR can help countries reap a "triple dividend": cutting pollution, generating and funding development co-benefits and public goods, and raising economic activity.

But few countries have shaped their fiscal policies to reflect the realities of climate change

Although the governments of developing countries are increasingly aware of the social and economic costs of climate change and other environmental hazards, finance ministries have thus far mostly remained at the periphery of climate action. This is understandable: "environmental policies" have traditionally fallen

FIGURE ES.1

Environmental tax reform can help raise welfare directly and indirectly

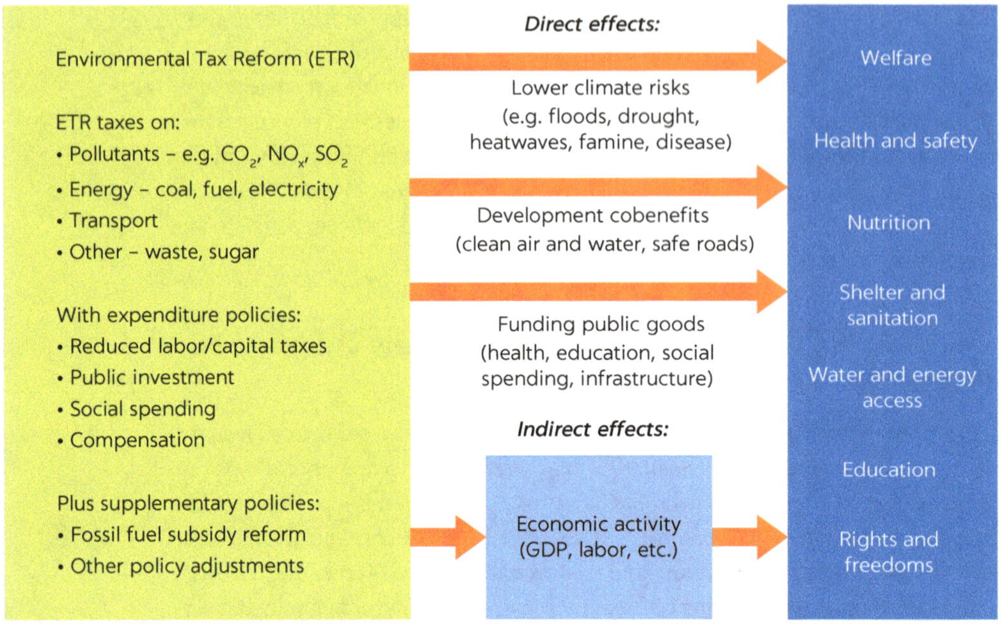

Note: ETR can have direct effects (by reducing climate externalities, generating "development co-benefits," and funding public goods) and indirect effects (through changes in economic activity) on human welfare. CO_2 = carbon dioxide; GDP = gross domestic product; NO_x = nitrogen oxides; SO_2 = sulfur dioxide.

under the purview of line ministries. However, mounting evidence of the effectiveness of environmental fiscal policy and the consequences of environmental degradation underscores the key role of finance ministries. For example, fossil fuels are subject to large and pervasive "environmental tax gaps" because consumer prices are far below the efficient price levels implied by externalities. These gaps are due partly to direct financial subsidies on energy but mostly to the externalized costs of energy. Both factors tend to be especially large in developing countries (figure ES.2). Coal, which accounts for almost half of global carbon emissions, is typically taxed at low rates or not taxed at all. Gasoline, diesel, and natural gas, which account for most of the remaining GHG emissions, also tend to be taxed well below efficient levels, or even subsidized directly.

However, mitigation policies must not come at the expense of development. In addition to limiting global warming to well below 2 degrees Celsius by the end of the century, in 2015 countries committed to achieving 16 other Sustainable Development Goals (SDGs). The goals include eliminating poverty and hunger, achieving gender equality, raising educational achievement, and raising water quality, among others. This report argues that fiscal reforms for climate mitigation and adaptation are the foundation for achieving both the Paris commitments and the SDGs. Although ETRs are vital to help mitigate climate change and increase welfare, fiscal instruments can also raise environmental resilience and manage the economic risks associated with natural disasters.

This study is both a clarion call and a road map for implementing fiscal policies to combat climate change

This report responds to a growing demand from client countries for insights into how fiscal policy can advance development objectives in areas outside of the

FIGURE ES.2

Global environmental tax gaps on fossil fuels are large

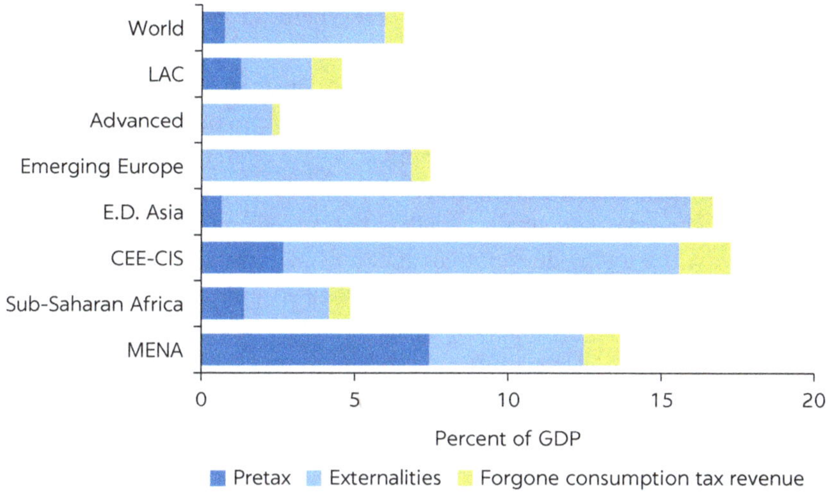

Source: Data from Coady et al. 2017.
Note: The figure shows that global environmental tax gaps on fossil fuels (coal, diesel, gasoline, and natural gas) are large (7 percent of gross domestic product [GDP]) but have large regional variations. "Pretax" gap includes financial subsidies to fossil fuels. "Externalities" include costs from underpriced fuel to climate change, local air pollution, road accidents, and congestion. "Forgone consumption tax revenue" is the value of revenues that would have been collected from households if fossil fuels faced the same rate of value added tax or goods and services tax as consumer goods. CEE-CIS = Central and Eastern Europe & Commonwealth of Independent States; E.D. Asia = Emerging and Developing Asia; LAC = Latin America and the Caribbean; MENA = Middle East and North Africa.

World Bank's traditional scope. The report is designed to build the capacity of client countries and World Bank staff to use fiscal instruments to mitigate and adapt to climate change. It does so by filling knowledge gaps on the economic, well-being, distributional, and competitiveness implications of ETR in developing countries, alongside the use of fiscal policy to manage increasing economic risks of climate change. Crucially, the report provides actionable advice on how to design and implement fiscal policies for both development and climate action.

The report is organized into four chapters. The first chapter, "Benefits beyond Climate: Environmental Tax Reform," argues that well-designed environmental taxation is especially valuable in developing countries, where it can reduce emissions, increase domestic revenues, and generate positive welfare effects. The second chapter, "Staying Competitive: Productivity Effects of Environmental Taxes," discusses the potential impacts of environmental taxation on competitiveness in emerging economies. It analyzes new empirical evidence from Indonesia and Mexico regarding the relationship between productivity and changes in energy prices, which are used as a proxy for changes in environmental taxation. The third and fourth chapters, "Increasing Resilience: Fiscal Policy for Climate Adaptation" and "Managing the Fiscal Risks Associated with Natural Disasters," discuss the role of fiscal policy in strengthening resilience to climate change. The report's key findings and policy recommendations are summarized below.

Space constraints have necessarily limited the scope of analysis. First, discussion is limited to domestic fiscal policy reforms: this report does not analyze non-fiscal environmental instruments such as national emissions trading systems or international emissions trading, for example. Second, the first chapter mostly presumes an ETR combining upstream energy taxes with revenue recycling through reduced labor taxes or increases in social spending and public infrastructure. Third, this report is not an implementation road map: fiscal systems vary significantly around the world, so specific reforms should be seen, designed, and implemented in the context of the overall fiscal, economic, political, and administrative systems of each particular country. Fourth, competitiveness effects are examined through the impact of energy prices on firm-level productivity: the report does not conduct a formal examination of the link between firm productivity and international competitiveness. Fifth and finally, chapters three and four are modeling exercises and therefore make assumptions that may not apply to all contexts.

KEY FINDINGS

The benefits of environmental tax reform are considerable, extending beyond environmental goals

ETR has three attributes that make it desirable for all countries. First, ETR is likely to generate efficiency gains by ensuring that market prices reflect all costs of goods and services, including the social cost of environmental externalities. Second, ETR can minimize the economic costs (or raise economic activity) of cutting pollution across different firms and industries in the economy by realigning price incentives. Third, ETR can raise domestic revenues at a lower cost than other taxes (see also OECD 2018b). The revenues produced by ETR can finance investment in climate change mitigation and adaptation, offset the social impact of other forms of pollution, and accelerate the transition toward safer, more efficient infrastructure and cleaner technologies. Given its considerable benefits, ETR should be an integral part of all modern fiscal systems.

For developed countries, evidence suggests ETR has a neutral or positive impact on employment and output. Although empirical evidence is limited, a large body of theoretical literature has examined the potential effects of ETR on output and employment in developed countries. ETR studies in the late 1990s and early 2000s suggested that reforms could sharply reduce pollution and increase employment but that their impact on output was ambiguous (Bosquet 2000; Patuelli, Nijkamp, and Pels 2005). Later studies found strong effects on emissions but inconclusive effects on employment and output. The few existing empirical studies of ETR in developed contexts—including research conducted in Canada, Denmark, and the United Kingdom—suggest negligible or positive effects on output and employment.

ETR is particularly desirable in developing countries

For developing countries, two factors make ETR especially desirable. First, ETR is more likely to increase economic activity while cutting emissions in developing countries. The benefits of ETR reflect several features that are common in developing countries, including (i) large informal sectors, which create opportunities to increase employment and output by using ETR revenues to reduce formal-sector taxes; (ii) inefficient tax systems, which create opportunities for

ETR to reduce tax distortions, broaden the tax base, and tax rents rather than profits; and (iii) low levels of domestic taxation, which create opportunities for ETR to mobilize domestic resources to fund growth-enhancing public investment. These factors make it likely that ETR will raise measures of economic activity (for example, output and employment) more in developing countries than in developed countries.

Second, "development co-benefits"—direct gains to welfare—also tend to be larger in developing countries. In addition to its positive effects on employment and growth, ETR can directly improve welfare. By discouraging pollution-intensive activities, environmental taxation can promote improvements in air quality and public health, alleviate costly traffic congestion, and reduce the frequency of road accidents. GHGs, for example, are largely co-emitted with sources of local pollution, meaning that abatement of GHGs through ETR can help reduce local pollution as well. Meanwhile, the revenue from environmental taxes can help the economy to adapt to climate change and fund increased spending on education, infrastructure, social services, and other public goods.

These co-benefits can be substantial, in most cases justifying unilateral environmental taxes. These co-benefits are particularly large in developing countries, often significantly dwarfing the benefits of reduced climate risks. As a result, co-benefits alone may justify the use of ETR in developing countries, even before the benefit of climate mitigation is considered.

Well-designed ETR policies can have positive effects on poverty and equity

ETR policies must be tailored to avoid negative welfare effects on lower-income households. Environmental taxation in developing countries can have a negative impact on the income of poorer households. Although wealthier households are very likely to bear a larger absolute amount of the total costs of environmental taxation, the costs borne by the poor may represent a greater portion of their household income. However, poorer households in developing countries tend to spend a smaller share of their income on pollution-intensive goods and services—such as automobiles and electricity—than do poorer households in wealthy countries. As a result, taxes on hydrocarbon fuels are more likely to be progressive in developing countries (Parry, Mylonas, and Vernon 2017). Policies that encourage the use of cleaner energy in poor communities could preserve the progressivity of fuel taxes as access to automobiles, electricity, and other modern technologies expands.

Moreover, failing to tax environmental externalities can make fiscal policy more regressive. The environmental tax gap for fossil fuels disproportionately benefits wealthier households, which consume a larger share of underpriced fuel. Meanwhile, the welfare costs of environmental externalities, such as ill health due to local air pollution, are heavily concentrated among the poor. By addressing the unequal distribution of benefits and costs, ETR can help to improve welfare and promote shared prosperity.

In certain contexts, however, ETR may entail income losses to lower-income households; in these cases, compensation is required. In developed countries, 6 to 12 percent of the revenue from a carbon tax would be sufficient to compensate households in the lowest income quintile (Vivid Economics 2012; Dinan 2015). In developing countries, where environmental taxation tends to be more progressive, compensating the poorest households would likely require an even smaller share of revenues. Appropriate compensation policies will vary depending on the unique circumstances of lower-income households in each country. Compensatory mechanisms can include targeted transfers to poorer households, for example through an existing cash-transfer system. Alternatively, policy makers can increase public spending on policies that disproportionately benefit the poor, such as housing support or public health care.

ETR policies can be administratively simple and easy to implement

ETR is a broad category of policies that can be tailored to any country context. Key decisions with ETR design include the tax base, current and future pathways of tax rates, and, crucially, how to allocate environmental revenues. These can be tailored to each country's specific context. Importantly for developing countries, ETR designs can be simple, making them well suited to contexts with limited administrative capacity. For example, imposing downstream taxes on a small number of major polluters or altering existing upstream fuel taxes can yield gains comparable to those generated by a more complex reform package. It is therefore possible in most countries to implement simple forms of ETR through adjustments to existing fiscal systems for fuel pricing. With no need for entirely new administrative systems, countries will find it easier to get started.

In some cases, ETR may not be the best instrument to achieve environmental goals

Other policies may be more effective at achieving specific environmental goals. Uniform environmental taxes, such as a carbon tax linked to carbon content, are most useful for addressing large-scale global pollutants with multiple sources, such as carbon dioxide. For other environmental externalities, direct regulations may be more pragmatic and cost-effective, especially when the revenues from taxation would be low and the costs of administering market-based instruments would be high. For example, countries could reduce the environmental costs of plastic bags by establishing minimum prices among retailers, as Ireland and several Organisation for Economic Co-operation and Development (OECD) countries have done, or by simply banning them, as Kenya, Uganda, and almost 30 other countries have done. Regulations are also preferable if the policy objective is to eradicate the pollutant rather than to reduce it—so countries outlaw asbestos but tax pollution from motor fuels.

In addition, broad political support is crucial to the effectiveness of ETR

Building and maintaining political support is vital to ensure the efficacy and durability of ETR. Despite the various economic, well-being, environmental, and fiscal benefits of ETR outlined in this report, public support tends to be low. Because of the concentration of costs among certain classes of firms and consumers and the diffusion of benefits across society, opposition to ETR is easier to mobilize than support. Moreover, the costs of environmental taxation—that is, higher prices for energy and fuel, among other things—tend to be more visible than the benefits, which include cleaner air, safer roads, reduced climate risks, and increased social spending. Addressing public support is therefore critical to ensuring ETRs are implemented and sustained.

Policy makers can draw on strategies informed by behavioral economics to build support for ETR. Holding public forums that include both net winners and net losers from the reform, along with trusted national experts, can raise the profile of ETR benefits. Ensuring that compensation mechanisms are in place before the reform takes effect can help defuse opposition. For example, the government of the Islamic Republic of Iran transferred funds to dedicated bank accounts to compensate citizens before raising energy costs, unfreezing these accounts on the date of the reform. Strategies such as these can help policy makers build and sustain support for ETR.

Governments may be concerned about the potential impact of ETR on international competitiveness…

Governments in developing countries may hesitate to adopt ETR because of its perceived negative impact on the international competitiveness of domestic firms. In theory, environmental taxes adopted unilaterally may undermine cost-competitiveness if foreign firms do not face equivalent cost increases. Higher energy prices could make it harder for domestic firms to compete in both foreign and domestic markets, especially in energy-intensive tradable sectors. The impact of environmental taxation on competitiveness could also push some industries to relocate production to countries with lower environmental tax rates or no environmental taxes at all, resulting in an unintended increase in GHG emissions via the so-called carbon leakage effect.

However, there are also reasons to suspect that environmental taxes may not harm competitiveness. Energy represents a relatively small share of production costs in most (but not all) industries. Firms, even in energy-intensive sectors, may be able to deal with such cost increases by substituting inputs, seeking efficiency gains, or innovating. Cost is also just one of several dimensions on which firms compete, although it is key for commodity producers. Moreover, impacts are unlikely to be uniform, and competitiveness losses for some types of firms or sectors may be more than offset by gains in others.

Existing literature, focused on high-income countries, has found little evidence of adverse competitiveness effects from ETR. Any adverse competitiveness effects tend to be small and concentrated in a few energy-intensive and trade-exposed (EITE) sectors. Likewise, there is little empirical evidence of significant carbon leakage. Most analysts also agree that negative impacts can be minimized by good tax design and complementary measures, without undermining the environmental goals of ETR. However, few studies have considered how environmental taxes affect firm performance in developing countries, a knowledge gap this report contributes to filling.

…but new empirical evidence suggests ETR can raise firm productivity and hence competitiveness in developing economies…

This report includes new empirical analysis of the effects of ETR on competitiveness measures, using detailed firm-level data. The second chapter of the report analyzes the effects of ETR on competitiveness by proxying ETR with exogenous changes in energy prices faced by firms over time. First, it uses a panel of firms in the World Bank Enterprise Survey across 11 upper-middle-income countries in Latin America and Eastern and Central Europe. It relies on the changes in energy prices at the country and country-sector levels over time to test for the impact of such changes on firms' performance. Second, it conducts country-specific analyses using large sets of panel data for manufacturing plants in two large developing economies that have highly subsidized fuel prices—Indonesia (1990–2015) and Mexico (2009–2015). These within-country analyses distinguish between the changes in prices of different energy sources, particularly electricity and fuels, exploiting the variation in price of other plants in the same regions or region-sectors.

The empirical findings suggest that increases in fuel prices improve firms' performance. Increases in energy prices faced by firms in the 11 countries are associated with firm-level improvements in labor productivity and profitability. This result holds even for energy-intensive firms and is not affected by other firm characteristics, such as size and type of ownership. It also does not appear to be explained by the substitution of labor for energy. In both Indonesia and Mexico, the empirical analysis confirms that higher energy prices improve plant-level performance, a result entirely driven by fuel prices. By contrast, the price of electricity is negatively related to performance in both countries, in line with recent empirical studies in other contexts.

...as firms upgrade their machinery in response to increased fuel (but not electricity) prices

This surprising result for fuel prices is explained by firms' adopting more productive and energy-efficient capital rather than increasing output prices in response to fuel price hikes. Empirical evidence is consistent with this mechanism. First, fuel price increases incentivize plants' purchase of new machinery and scrapping of old, fuel-based machinery. Second, plants become more energy efficient and use more electricity in response to fuel price increases, consistent with changes in the technical efficiency of production. Third, the negative effects of electricity price increases on performance are consistent with the idea that electricity-powered machines tend to be closer to the efficiency frontier than fuel-powered machines and hence the price increase reduces their performance. Fourth, performance is less affected by fuel price increases in larger and foreign-owned firms, consistent with the idea that these firms operate closer to the technological frontier than small, domestic firms, and therefore have less room to adopt new machinery. This result is again less consistent with the output price increase hypothesis because larger firms typically have a higher market power than small firms.

A plausible interpretation of these results is that, in developing countries with low fuel prices and far from the efficiency frontier, firms use their fuel inputs inefficiently. A rise in fuel prices incentivizes investment in information that brings firms closer to the efficiency frontier through innovation. This interpretation is consistent with the strong version of the Porter hypothesis (Porter 1980), according to which more stringent environmental policy can result in innovation that enables companies to improve their productivity, thereby more than offsetting compliance costs. Firms in developing countries are more likely to be far from the efficiency frontier as management quality tends to be lower. As a result, these firms have more room to upgrade to more energy-efficient (and productive) technology because management quality is positively correlated with energy efficiency. In addition, poorly managed firms are unlikely to change technology on their own, even if doing so yields net positive returns, because they lack information on their true managerial quality and the potential for improvement. Hence an external incentive—such as an input price increase—could help incentivize investment in information and eventually in new capital adoption.

In the short term, protection can be designed to help especially vulnerable industries to adapt

Several policy instruments can mitigate any remaining competitiveness risks, but policy makers should understand the trade-offs. Although this report finds that higher fuel prices may not hurt competitiveness in developing countries, there may still be adjustment costs and competitive pressures in the short term, especially for energy intensive trade exposed (EITE) sectors. Policy options to protect vulnerable industries have several trade-offs including price signal strength, administrative complexity, and cost. Exemptions, despite their frequent use, appear the least efficient way to preserve competitiveness and may be counterproductive in the longer run. By contrast, reductions in corporate taxes, output-based rebates, support for resource efficiency, border-tax adjustments, and consumption-based taxes may be more desirable. Each of these policies can protect EITE industries while retaining price signals and encouraging innovation. However, these measures should also be time-limited, be reviewed regularly, and balance short-term relief for industries with long-term incentives to adapt.

Fiscal policy is an effective instrument to help countries adapt to climate change

Climate change entails gradual effects that intensify slowly over time and extreme events that inflict large damages in a short period. Both effects have repercussions for fiscal policy. The third chapter of this report uses modeling to assess the effectiveness of different fiscal policies in addressing the gradual effects of climate change as well as the impact of climate-related extreme events. It adopts a model of an open economy with overlapping generations and perfect foresight in which climate change manifests itself through gradual increases in the rate of depreciation of the capital stock, and extreme weather events that swiftly and dramatically reduce the capital stock. Under the baseline scenario, the government makes no effort to adapt to climate change—a circumstance that is all too common in the real world. Against this baseline, the chapter evaluates the implications for growth and debt sustainability of two different strategies: (i) preventive action, under which policy makers implement adaptation measures designed to anticipate the effects of climate change, and (ii) remedial action, under which policy makers focus solely on responding to effects that have already occurred.

Early action through proactive investments is the optimal strategy for climate-resilient fiscal policy

Modeling indicates that early investments in adaptation yield better economic outcomes than delaying, focusing on remedial actions, or doing nothing. Preventive investment in adaptation reduces the rate of depreciation of the capital stock; the earlier actions are taken, the greater the cumulative benefit.

By contrast, remedial action is both costlier and less effective at protecting economic output. Taking no action at all entails the largest economic losses. The best results are achieved when early investment in adaptation is funded through taxation or spending cuts rather than with deficit financing, which increases the debt stock and reduces the scope for external borrowing in response to extreme events.

In addition, to prepare for extreme weather events, fiscal buffers need to be increased. Extreme weather events damage the capital stock and cause a sharp drop in economic output. Recovery is slow, because of adjustment costs, and depends partly on the availability of financing. The financing required to rebuild the capital stock could exceed both available domestic resources and the country's external borrowing capacity. Preventive spending in adaptation bolsters the resilience of the capital stock, reducing the severity of the damage and the economic losses from disasters, but cannot fully shield it. As a result, the optimal strategy is to combine early investment in adaptation with measures to increase fiscal space. Such measures could include reducing the debt stock to create more borrowing space or accumulating resources in a contingency savings fund before a disaster strikes.

But few developing countries are fiscally prepared for climate change

Governments around the world rarely invest in preventive adaptation measures or adjust their savings and debt policies to prepare for climate change. This is partly because the costs of climate change—and its effects on individual countries—are subject to significant uncertainty and partly because of the trade-offs between spending on mitigation or adaptation and other development priorities such as health and education, which compete for limited fiscal resources. In addition, the presumed availability of donor assistance could weaken incentives for governments, firms, and households to take preventive action. Indeed, donor engagement tends to focus far more on relief than preparedness, although donor support has often been insufficient to cover reconstruction costs. Finally, domestic political economy considerations also tend to favor relief over preparedness; voters are more likely to reward politicians who show leadership in the wake of a disaster rather than politicians who show foresight in preparing for one.

Even with preparation, fiscal policy cannot eliminate all climate fiscal risks, especially for island nations

Climate change exposes governments to fiscal risks arising from the disruption of economic activity and damages to both public and private assets. Small island states are especially vulnerable to these risks because of their greater degree of economic specialization—often in weather-sensitive sectors such as tourism, fishing, or agriculture. On average, the annual cost of disasters for small states is more than four times that for larger countries, a reflection of both a higher frequency of natural disasters (many small states are islands that face frequent tropical cyclones) and small countries' greater vulnerability to natural hazards. Adaptation efforts can reduce climate risks, but they cannot eliminate those risks entirely.

Chapter 4 uses a stochastic fiscal sustainability analysis (FSA) model to assess the behavior of key fiscal variables in the face of climate-related shocks and under alternative strategies for financing responses to these shocks. The model is applied to two middle-income island countries: the Dominican Republic, which has enjoyed relatively rapid economic growth and low debt, and Jamaica, a highly indebted country with a history of low and volatile GDP growth.

The results suggest that the Dominican Republic is highly vulnerable to fiscal risks brought about by potential natural disasters. For example, the fiscal impact of a natural disaster of historical proportions would be large, resulting in a sharp deterioration of the primary balance and an increase in the debt-to-GDP ratio to 70 percent (compared to 40 percent in the baseline). The application of the FSA tool to Jamaica finds that a similar event would push the fiscal balance well off its target, and the downward trajectory of debt to GDP would reverse unless the government is able to run larger primary fiscal surpluses. However, the deterioration in the debt-to-GDP ratio can be avoided if the government can arrange sufficient contingent financing in anticipation of the event. This result highlights the importance of contingent financing instruments in enabling governments to respond more quickly with recovery and reconstruction.

POLICY IMPLICATIONS

The four chapters that underpin this report yield five major policy implications for finance ministries in developing countries and their partners.

1. Finance ministries should use ETRs to "get prices right"

Finance ministries in developing countries should seek to implement ETR as soon as possible. Environmental tax gaps and the welfare opportunities offered by ETR tend to be greatest in developing countries. Although most environmental policies are the purview of environment ministries, implementing ETR requires the active engagement of finance ministries. Given the crucial role of price incentives throughout the economy, and the potential for substantial direct and indirect welfare gains, environmental taxation should be an integral component of all modern national fiscal systems.

Using ETR to "get energy prices right" is especially important. All countries should strive to align energy prices with the social costs of carbon emissions, local air pollution, and other negative externalities. Failing to close the environmental tax gap for fossil fuels incentivizes overuse and contributes to a range of negative social and economic outcomes. Moreover, subsidizing fuel or electricity is a highly inefficient strategy for transferring welfare benefits to poor households, which typically use the least fuel and electricity and suffer the most from their negative externalities. It is also a highly inefficient industrial policy because it interferes with managerial decisions by distorting input prices rather than rewarding output. Taxes are not the only set of instruments that achieve environmental objectives; however, in many cases, environmental taxation will be critical for getting energy prices right.

2. ETRs should be tailored, transparent, and politically viable

Taxing upstream activities in the energy value chain may be especially effective. Taxing fossil fuels at the point of extraction or importation, as opposed to the point of combustion, minimizes the administrative burden, and covers the entire economy, including the informal sector. As the firms handling the fuel upstream incorporate the tax in the prices at which they sell the fuel to downstream consumers, the environmental tax incidence is passed forward through the supply chain. This means that the tax can be implemented where it is easiest (upstream) without diminishing the incentive to cut emissions where the fuel is burned (downstream).

Experience with energy price reform in developing countries suggests that reforms need to be transparent and inclusive. There is no "one-size-fits-all" ETR. However, experience from developing countries that have reduced or eliminated fossil fuel subsidies, as well as the smaller number that have implemented carbon taxes, suggest *how* reforms are implemented is critical to their effectiveness. Outreach strategies, such as targeted informational campaigns or broad consultations (which include "winners" as well "losers"), are crucial for raising and sustaining the political support for ETR.

The design of environmental taxes should maximize their political acceptability. Public knowledge of environmental taxation is often limited, and voters tend to be risk-averse. Governments should implement sophisticated public outreach strategies that emphasize the environmental, social, and economic benefits of ETR and thoroughly explain the trade-offs involved, along with any planned mitigation or compensatory measures. Special attention should be drawn to popular benefits that might otherwise be overlooked, such as reductions in other taxes. Sound policy design and an effective outreach strategy increase the chances that the public, and even affected industries, will accept the new tax. The implementation of the tax should be gradual and predictable to allow firms to adapt their investment plans. Finally, the government should clearly communicate how the expected benefits of ETR compare to those of alternative policies.

3. Affected firms should be compensated only where necessary

ETR policies do not necessarily reduce competitiveness and can promote firm-level efficiency gains. The evidence from Indonesia and Mexico suggests that raising fuel prices can—in certain circumstances—foster firm-level efficiency gains by encouraging energy efficiency and incentivizing investment in modern equipment. These gains in efficiency and productivity can, in turn, make firms more competitive internationally.

Some sectors will have difficulty adapting to higher energy prices, but support should be provided only if there is clear evidence of a significant negative impact on competitiveness. A rigorous country-specific assessment could identify which industries and firms will be positively or negatively affected by ETR. This assessment should analyze (i) anticipated impacts in the short, medium, and long term; (ii) the scope for efficiency gains across industries and sectors; (iii) potential competitiveness losses in vulnerable industries and sectors; and (iv) the relative importance of these industries and sectors to domestic output, exports, and employment compared to those that will benefit from the reforms.

When support measures are used to preserve competitiveness, they must be carefully targeted and appropriately calibrated. According to an in-depth review of various policy options, the government should identify the most cost-effective instrument or combination of instruments to mitigate adverse competitiveness impacts. In addition to administrative and legal considerations, policy makers should strive to preserve incentives for firms in protected sectors to adopt more energy-efficient and environmentally responsible technologies and processes. The amount of support should be proportionate to the negative effect on competitiveness, and it should decrease over time as domestic industries adapt to higher energy prices and international competitors adopt similar ETR policies.

4. Preventive investments and expanded fiscal buffers are needed to strengthen climate resilience

Finance ministries should support climate change adaptation efforts. Early, preventive investments in adaptation are effective in fighting the gradual impacts of climate change and in preparing the economy for extreme weather events if combined with policies to maintain fiscal space and ease borrowing constraints. Finance ministries can also bolster climate resilience by mainstreaming climate change considerations into the design, appraisal, and selection of public investment projects and encouraging private investment in adaptation. Contingent plans should allow for the scaling-up of existing safety nets in the event of a disaster. Rules for triggering public interventions, including the size of relief transfers to households, and responsibilities for administering different programs should be defined in advance on the basis of clear criteria.

Governments should incorporate and quantify climate change risks into the fiscal risks statements that accompany the budget presentation. This would start with conducting a hazard and vulnerability analysis to develop probability distributions of damages and losses from different types of climate-related shocks. Governments should also incorporate forward-looking assessments of the expected type, frequency, and intensity of future climate shocks (such as from IPCC 2014) into their scenario analysis.

Establishing a robust fiscal responsibility framework would help minimize fiscal risks from climate shocks. Credible fiscal rules, accompanied by measures to constrain the growth of the wage bill and other spending components that are rigid in the short run, can help governments avoid procyclical policies that would magnify these shocks. Credible fiscal rules would also provide the discipline to gradually build fiscal buffers, such as a contingency savings fund. One challenge for the fiscal authority is to decide on the size of this fund, determine the trade-offs in maintaining it, and assess how savings can be increased if the buffer falls short. Contingent lines of credit offered by international financial institutions and market-based instruments, such as catastrophe bonds, enable governments to quickly mount relief, recovery, and reconstruction efforts needed for the economy to rebound from natural disasters. In the case of highly indebted countries, these financial instruments may also have a secondary effect of giving capital markets confidence that a natural disaster will not push a government into debt distress, which in turn could reduce borrowing costs.

Finally, governments need to seek ways to transfer risks to markets and to pool risks across countries. They are less likely to be called upon to cover private losses from natural disasters if firms and households are covered by affordable insurance policies. Governments that self-insure public buildings and infrastructure may want to consider pursuing market-based insurance for these assets. Private or sovereign insurance systems and regional catastrophe insurance schemes—such as the Caribbean Catastrophe Risk Insurance Facility

(CCRIF), which was created in 2007 to provide ex ante disaster-risk financing, and the African Risk Insurance Company Limited, have played a role in helping countries manage climate risks. However, the CCRIF and other regional schemes suffer from the problem that members largely face the same risks. Finding ways to broaden risk pools is critical.

5. Donor support for ETR and fiscal policies for adaptation needs to be broadened and deepened

Donors should increase their support for ETR policies in developing countries. The signing of the Paris Agreement and the establishment of the SDGs ushered in a new era in international development. Instruments that had become widespread under the Kyoto Protocol, such as emissions-trading systems and offsetting mechanisms, are no longer as relevant as they once were. Environmental taxation can help countries meet their Nationally Determined Contributions while sustaining robust economic growth. However, the international experience with ETR and other relatively new instruments is limited, and the existing structures for facilitating access to the emissions trading systems of developed countries are not designed to enable developing countries to implement ETR. Donors should step forward to fill gaps in both the analytical underpinnings of ETR and the mechanisms for implementing it.

The analytical toolkit for evaluating ETR policies is incomplete, and gaps in the literature must be narrowed or closed. Existing models often miss key contextual factors that are especially important in developing countries, such as how public policy interacts with the informal sector. In addition, existing models do not capture direct welfare benefits that are crucial for a full appraisal of ETR. Although the need to increase environmental taxation is a matter of consensus in the literature and across multilateral development institutions, several specific issues have yet to be conclusively resolved. Inconsistent definitions cause disparities in estimates of fossil fuel subsidies, external costs, corrective taxes, and implicit carbon prices; and conceptual ambiguity can weaken the effectiveness of policy advice. Addressing these gaps in the literature could forge a shared understanding of the nexus between fiscal and environmental policy and thereby increase the credibility, consistency, and value of policy advice.

Key tools for incorporating climate risks into our fiscal modeling should be improved. The FSA tool used in this report is useful for assessing risks from climate events that have transitory effects. The model assumes that GDP converges over time to its long-run potential, which in turn is based on the country's endowments of land, labor, and capital, and on the productivity of using these factors of production. However, climate change is expected to affect these underlying endowments, and therefore potential GDP. In some countries, for example, climate change may permanently destroy or degrade natural assets, or is likely to induce substantial cross-border labor migration. Thus, risks of changes to long-run potential GDP due to climate change need to be incorporated into macroeconomic models and medium-term projections.

Finally, donor coordination efforts must be strengthened to cope with the increasing frequency and severity of climate-related natural disasters.

Donor financing is vital to support investment in climate change adaptation and to provide the emergency funding necessary to recover from a natural disaster. A variety of existing risk-transfer schemes could be expanded, including private or sovereign insurance, multilateral risk-sharing mechanisms, and catastrophe insurance schemes. Coordination mechanisms should include multilateral institutions, bilateral donors, the national authorities, and civil society.

CONCLUSIONS

The four chapters that underpin this report contribute to an emerging body of knowledge on the role of fiscal policies in supporting climate mitigation and adaptation, alongside broader development goals. They are linked by a common thread—that fiscal policies can make a crucial contribution to climate mitigation and economic development while safeguarding future prosperity. This report is intended to inform the ongoing dialogue on the evolving role of macro-fiscal management in the context of a changing climate and warming world. The report is also designed to better equip finance ministries in developing countries with the tools to understand, appraise, and implement ETR policies and climate change adaptation and risk-management strategies.

The key final messages of this report are the following:

- The agenda for combatting climate change is now indistinguishable from the broader international development agenda. Eliminating extreme poverty and promoting shared prosperity will require that all economies—developing, emerging, and advanced—shift toward a sustainable, low-carbon growth model. Considering this challenge, fiscal policies must not only advance macroeconomic objectives but also reinforce environmental sustainability and directly raise human well-being.
- Fiscal instruments can lay the foundation upon which developing countries can build low-carbon growth models. Fiscal policy instruments can help developing countries achieve their Nationally Determined Contributions under the Paris Agreement while advancing the economic and social development objectives enshrined in the SDGs. ETR and climate change adaptation and risk-management strategies are core components of a successful low-carbon growth model. By following the recommendations presented in this report, finance ministers can more effectively raise human well-being while protecting development from one of its greatest threats.

NOTES

1. PM2.5 refers to atmospheric particulate matter (PM) that has a diameter of less than 2.5 micrometers and can therefore permeate the lungs. PM2.5 causes asthma and respiratory inflammation, jeopardizes lung functions, and causes lung cancer and even ischemic heart disease and strokes (Lancet Commission 2017).
2. Of these 9 million deaths, 6.5 million accrue to air pollution and 1.8 million to water pollution.

REFERENCES

Bosquet, Benoît. 2000. "Environmental Tax Reform: Does It Work? A Survey of the Empirical Evidence." *Ecological Economics* 34 (1): 19–32. https://doi.org/10.1016/S0921-8009(00)00173-7.

Coady, David, Ian Parry, Louis Sears, and Baoping Shang. 2017. "How Large Are Global Fossil Fuel Subsidies?" *World Development* 91 (March): 11–27. https://doi.org/http://dx.doi.org/10.1016/j.worlddev.2016.10.004.

Dinan, Terry. 2015. "Offsetting a Carbon Tax's Burden on Low-Income Households." In *Implementing a US Carbon Tax*, edited by Ian Parry, Adele Morris, and Roberton Williams III. Abingdon: Routledge.

HCSS (The Hague Centre for Strategic Studies). 2014. "Climate Change Vulnerability Monitor." The Hague: The Hague Centre for Strategic Studies. http://projects.hcss.nl/monitor/70/.

IPCC (Intergovernmental Panel on Climate Change). 2014. *Climate Change 2014: Synthesis Report. Contribution of Working Groups I, II and III to the Fifth Assessment Report of the Intergovernmental Panel on Climate Change.* Cambridge: Cambridge University Press. http://www.ipcc.ch/pdf/assessment-report/ar5/syr/AR5_SYR_FINAL_SPM.pdf.

Landrigan, Philip, et al. 2017. "The Lancet Commission on Pollution and Health." *The Lancet*, October 19. http://www.thelancet.com/commissions/pollution-and-health.

OECD (Organisation for Economic Co-operation and Development). 2018a. "OECD Glossary of Statistical Terms." https://stats.oecd.org/glossary/.

——. 2018b. "Taxing Energy Use 2018: Companion to the Taxing Energy Use Database." Paris: OECD Publishing. https://one.oecd.org/document/23201804/en/pdf.

Parry, Ian, Victor Mylonas, and Nate Vernon. 2017. *Reforming Energy Policy in India: Assessing the Options*. Washington, DC: Internatonal Monetary Fund. https://doi.org/10.5089/9781475595734.001.

Patuelli, Roberto, Peter Nijkamp, and Eric Pels. 2005. "Environmental Tax Reform and the Double Dividend: A Meta-Analytical Performance Assessment." *Ecological Economics* 55 (4): 564–83. http://www.sciencedirect.com/science/article/pii/S092180090500008X.

Porter, Michael. 1980. *Competitive Strategy: Techniques for Analyzing Industries and Competitors*. New York: Free Press.

SDSN (Sustainable Development Solutions Network). 2017. "SDG Index and Dashboards Report 2017." https://doi.org/10.1016/S0140-6736(09)61513-0.

Vivid Economics. 2012. "Carbon Taxation and Fiscal Consolidation: The Potential of Carbon Pricing to Reduce Europe's Fiscal Deficits." Brussels.

WHO (World Health Organization). 2015. *Global Status Report on Road Safety*. Geneva. https://doi.org/http://www.who.int/violence_injury_prevention/road_safety_status/2015/en/.

Abbreviations

AE	advanced economies
BTA	border tax adjustment
CBT	consumption-based taxation
CCRIF	Caribbean Catastrophe Risk Insurance Facility
CDM	Clean Development Mechanism
CFE	Comisión Federal de Electricidad
CGE	computable general equilibrium
CPI	Cleaner Production Institute
DRM	domestic resource mobilization
DSGE	dynamic stochastic general equilibrium
EITE	energy-intensive and trade-exposed
EMMIE	emerging and middle-income economies
ETR	environmental tax reform
ETS	emissions trading systems
EU	European Union
FSA	fiscal sustainability analysis
GATT	General Agreement on Tariffs and Trade
GDP	gross domestic product
GE	general equilibrium
GHG	greenhouse gas
IAM	integrated assessment models
IEA	International Energy Agency
IET	International Emissions Trading
ITC	induced technological change
LIDC	low-income developing countries
NAICS	North American Industry Classification System
NDC	nationally determined contributions
NFA	net foreign assets
OBR	output-based rebating
OECD	Organisation for Economic Co-operation and Development
OLG	overlapping generations
PIT	personal income tax
PPP	purchasing power parity
R&D	research and development

RECP	resource efficiency and cleaner production
RTFP	revenue total factor productivity
SCEPA	Schwartz Center for Economic Policy Analysis
SDG	Sustainable Development Goal
SME	small and medium enterprises
SOE	state-owned enterprises
TFP	total factor productivity
UN	United Nations
UNEP	United Nations Environment Programme
UNFCCC	United Nations Framework Convention on Climate Change
UNIDO	United Nations Industrial Development Organization
VAT	value added tax
WBES	World Bank Enterprise Survey

1 Benefits beyond Climate: Environmental Tax Reform

DIRK HEINE AND SIMON BLACK

INTRODUCTION

Ending poverty while managing climate change are the defining challenges of this century. In recent years, these twin objectives have become enmeshed normatively and enshrined institutionally. In the last three years, 193 countries committed to achieving 17 Sustainable Development Goals (SDGs)—from tackling poverty, hunger, and gender disparities to improving health, energy access, and education. In addition, 195 countries committed in the Paris Agreement to limit global warming to "well below" 2 degrees Celsius by the end of this century. Notably, over 130 developing countries committed to national emissions abatement (Nationally Determined Contributions, NDCs), for the first time. As a result, these countries need policy instruments to help them achieve their SDGs and NDCs.

Environmental tax reform (ETR) has been proposed as a potential solution. This chapter argues that ETR can help developing countries reap substantial benefits, far beyond those of climate action. Building on more than two decades of research in development and environmental economics, it argues that the welfare of ETR effects are likely to be more positive in developing countries than is commonly understood. In developing contexts, ETR is more likely to yield a "double dividend": cutting pollution while raising economic activity. Further, development co-benefits, such as direct improvements in human health, are often larger than in developed countries. ETR can also help finance ministries raise much-needed domestic funds for expanding public expenditure. Last, low administrative capacity and political support need not hinder reform efforts: ETR can be simple to design and implement. In short, ETR can be the fiscal foundation upon which developing countries achieve both the SDGs and their NDCs.

The argument in this chapter proceeds as follows. There is a strong need for mitigating climate change while raising development, especially in developing countries ("Why 'climate action'?" and "Why 'beyond climate'?"). ETR can help foster market efficiency, cost-effectively mitigate climate change, and raise domestic resources ("Why ETR?"). However, large gaps in environmental tax levels persist globally ("How large is the environmental tax gap?"). Closing these gaps is especially desirable for developing countries, where co-benefits of ETR tend to be higher and effects on economic activity more positive than in developed countries ("What is ETR's effect on development and welfare?"). Further, competitiveness and poverty objectives can be protected ("What is ETR's effect on equity, poverty, and competitiveness?"). The final three sections of the chapter highlight ETR's suitability and ease of implementation for developing countries compared with other environmental policies and the important policy implications of these findings.

This chapter is necessarily limited in scope. The discussion is restricted to reforms to domestic fiscal policy, notably variants of ETR that raise energy taxes upstream (at the point of import or extraction of fossil fuels) and recycle revenues through reduced labor taxes or increased social spending and public investment. It does not assess other forms of ETR, such as those with taxes on vehicles or forestry, or the international linking of domestic policies, such as emissions trading systems (ETSs) or taxes. Across the range of individual effects that ETR can have on well-being (for example, by reducing local air pollution or improving the economic efficiency of the tax system), there are conceivably other policies that can achieve that single objective more effectively. This chapter, however, considers and assesses the combined effects of ETR against a baseline of no change in other policies.

WHY "CLIMATE ACTION"?

There is broad scientific consensus on climate change. "It is extremely likely [95–100 percent] that human influence has been the dominant cause of the observed warming since the mid-20th century. For the warming over the last century, there is no convincing alternative explanation supported by the extent of the observational evidence" (USGCRP 2017). More broadly, the United Nations' (UN) body of climate experts (Intergovernmental Panel on Climate Change, IPCC) finds that a large body of evidence supports the existence, causes, and ramifications of climate change. In its latest compendium, the IPCC (2014) states that climate change

- **Is happening**—the planet is warming rapidly, well above historical averages (figure 1.1, panel a);
- **Is caused by human activity**—emissions of greenhouse gases (GHGs), especially carbon dioxide (CO_2) from fossil fuels (figure 1.1, panel b), are extremely likely to have caused these global temperature increases;
- **Will continue to worsen over the 21st century**—resulting in "severe, pervasive and irreversible impacts for people and ecosystems," including heat waves, flooding, ocean acidification, and sea level rise; and
- **Will amplify and create new risks for natural and human systems**—damages and the risk of these changes being abrupt or irreversible rise as the magnitude of warming increases.

The economic costs of climate change are likely to be substantial and disproportionately concentrated in developing countries. There is significant uncertainty about the economic effects of climate change. How the effects of a warming world will affect economic activity is not as well understood as how it will impact chemical, biological, and ecological processes. Nevertheless, the economic costs of climate change could be substantial. A central estimate is that, without

FIGURE 1.1

Relation of temperature increases to emissions

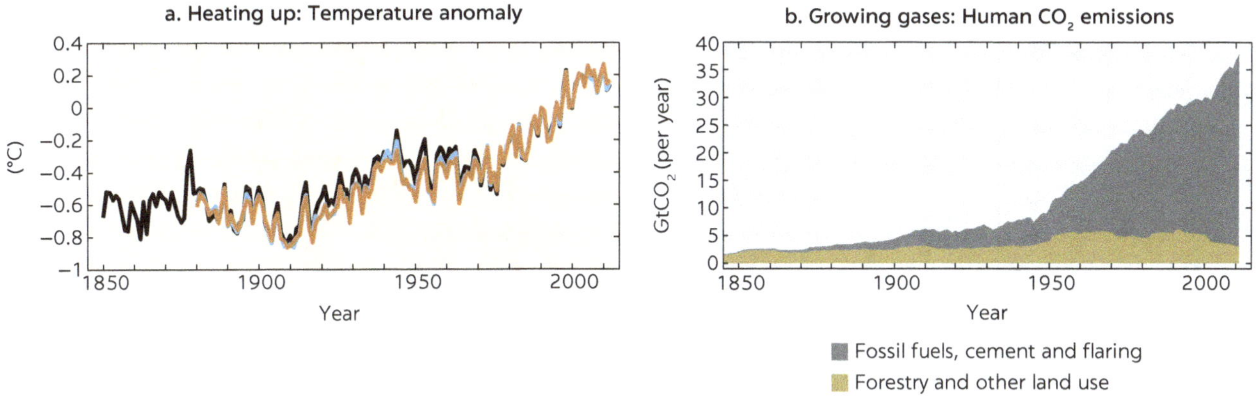

Source: IPCC 2014.
Note: Panel a shows average temperature anomaly (relative to 1986–2005 baseline); colors indicate different data sets. Panel b shows contribution of anthropogenic carbon dioxide (CO_2) emissions (1850–2010). $GtCO_2e$ = gigatons of CO_2 equivalent.

MAP 1.1

Warming world: Projected temperature changes to 2100

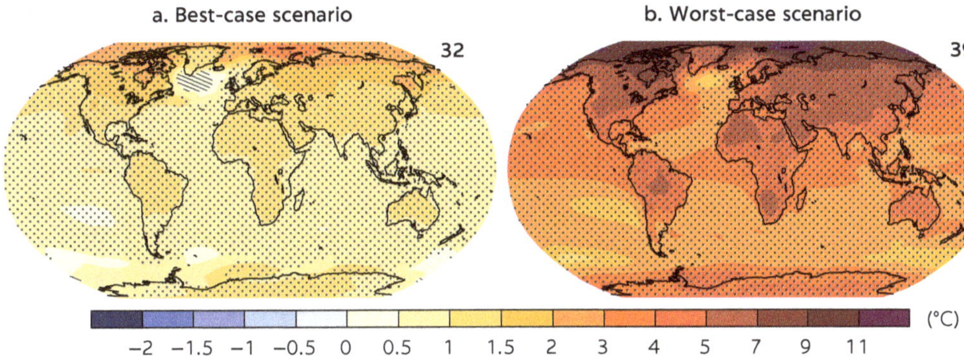

Source: IPCC 2014.
Note: Map shows projected change in average surface temperature (2018–2100 compared to 1986–2005): Best-case (high mitigation) scenario in panel a and worst-case (low mitigation) in panel b.

mitigation, by 2100 costs to global gross domestic product (GDP) could be 23 percent or more (Burke, Hsiang, and Miguel 2015), but even these estimates understate the risks. In addition, the costs of global warming are likely to be disproportionately concentrated in developing countries. This is due in part to higher average temperature changes (map 1.1) alongside greater exposure to natural disasters, temperature variability (Bathiany et al. 2018), and sea level rise. As a result, these countries are more vulnerable to the negative effects of climate change (map 1.2).

Without substantive mitigation efforts now, the world could be risking "climate ruin." Despite consensus on the causes and broad consequences of climate change, there is pervasive uncertainty about how damaging it could be. Numerous "known unknowns" and "unknown unknowns" about climate change could entail pervasive risks to human systems (Weitzman 2011). Crossing critical thresholds ("tipping points") could have potentially catastrophic consequences[1]—such as if global warming triggers the mass release of methane from permafrost

MAP 1.2

Developing countries are more vulnerable to climate change

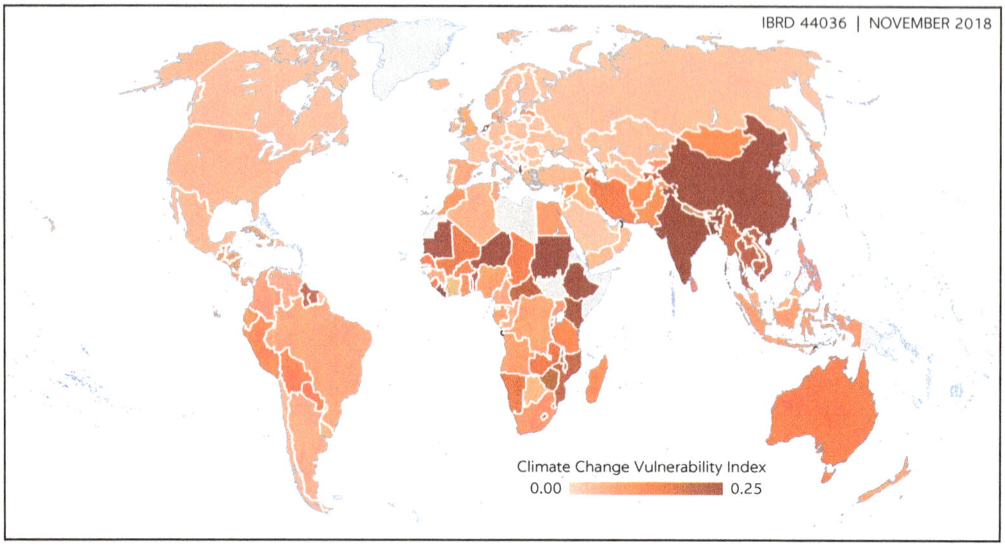

Source: World Bank map using data from HCSS 2014.
Note: Index scores are based on vulnerability to weather-related natural disasters, sea level rise, and loss of agricultural productivity due to climate change. Scores range from light red for least vulnerable to dark red for most vulnerable.

and if climate change triggers domino effects like mass migration (Rigaud et al. 2018) and debt crises (Bovari, Giraud, and McIsaac 2018). These and other uncertainties are not well understood and hence are poorly reflected in existing cost estimates (Stern 2016). However, such risks are likely to increase in probability with higher cumulative global GHG emissions (IPCC 2014). Mitigation efforts are therefore justified both to minimize the costs of known likely damages from climate change and the risks of extreme events that could lead to climate ruin (Bettis, Dietz, and Silver 2017).

Climate mitigation through emissions abatement is urgently needed, including by developing countries. The international community, negotiating under the auspices of the UN's climate change body (United Nations Framework Convention on Climate Change, UNFCCC), has set an objective of limiting warming to well below 2 degrees Celsius above preindustrial levels, with an aspiration of limiting it to 1.5 degrees. Low- and middle-income countries have, in general, contributed less to the problem of climate change than developed countries. High-income countries have higher per capita emissions ("personal carbon footprints" as seen in figure 1.2, panel a) and account for most historical CO_2 emissions (figure 1.2, panel b). However, middle-income countries have a larger and growing share of total annual emissions compared to high-income countries (figure 1.3). Without significant abatement efforts, this rapid emissions growth is expected to continue.

If emissions growth continues unchecked in middle-income countries, the international objectives for controlling global warming will fail, irrespective of action taken by high-income countries. "Staying below a 2°C temperature increase implies that the global carbon budget has to be limited to 800 $GtCO_2$ [gigatons of CO_2 equivalent]. This means that by 2050 almost 90% of coal, half of gas, and two-thirds of oil reserves have to remain unburnt" (Edenhofer et al. 2017), which is impossible without significant climate action also in

FIGURE 1.2

Contributions to climate change

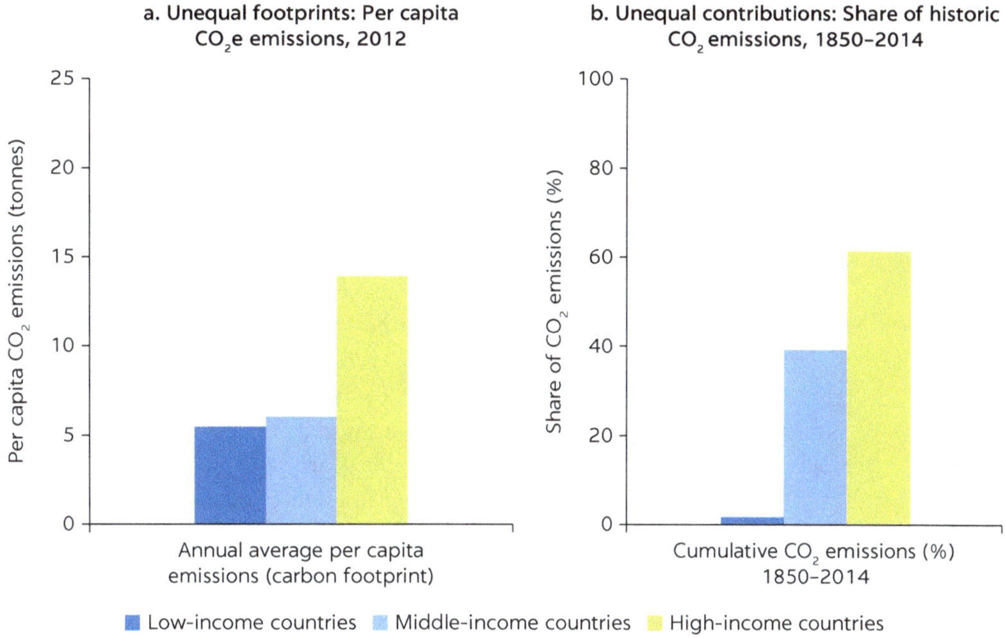

Source: Created using data from EDGAR 2014, UNDESA 2017, and WRI 2017.
Note: Panel a shows that per capita CO_2 emissions (excluding land use) were higher among developed countries in 2012. Panel b shows that high-income countries accounted for most cumulative CO_2 emissions between 1850 and 2014. CO_2e = carbon dioxide (CO_2) equivalent.

FIGURE 1.3

Overtaken: Annual greenhouse gas emissions in middle-income countries exceed those of high-income countries, 1970–2012

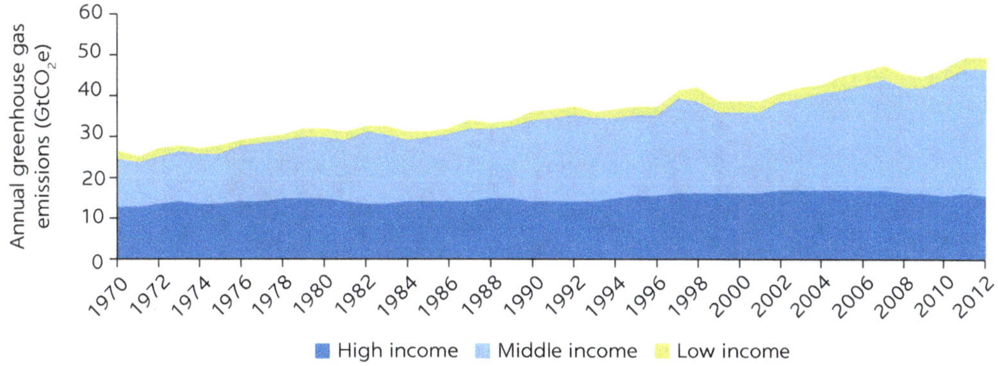

Source: Created using data from EDGAR 2014.
Note: Shows annual emissions of greenhouse gases (all anthropogenic CO_2, CH_4, N_2O sources, and F-gases) in gigatons of CO_2 equivalent ($GtCO_2e$) by income levels. CH_4 = methane; CO_2 = carbon dioxide; F-gases = fluorinated gases; N_2O = nitrous oxide.

developing countries. Recognizing the necessity for global mitigation, in 2015 all countries committed to mitigate climate change by slowing or reversing emissions growth to keep global warming to well below 2 degrees Celsius above preindustrial levels. This included 130 developing country signatories to the Paris Agreement: these countries published and committed to national plans to abate GHG emissions (NDCs), most for the first time.

However, despite the wide adoption of targets among developing countries, few have experience with mitigation policies, including economy-wide measures like carbon pricing (carbon taxes and ETSs). Crucially, mitigation must not come at the expense of development. Knowledge is therefore needed on the most economically desirable methods for achieving mitigation in developing countries.

WHY "BEYOND CLIMATE"?

Meanwhile, countries have committed to achieving 16 other SDGs, in addition to tackling climate change. These range from confronting poverty, hunger, and gender disparities to improving health, energy access, and education—all by 2030.

However, large gaps in achieving these goals, and thus in human development, persist. Scores against SDGs can be measured to assess development levels across countries in aggregate and for specific goals.

In aggregate, countries have very uneven levels of development (map 1.3). Sub-Saharan Africa and South Asia tend to have the lowest SDG Index scores, followed by Latin America, East and Southeast Asia, Eastern Europe and Central Asia, North America, and finally Western Europe.

On specific SDGs, the gaps vary across income category, especially on SDGs 1 to 9 (figure 1.4). Upper-middle-income countries tend to lag high-income countries on hunger, economic growth, and innovation and infrastructure SDGs. Lower-middle-income countries tend to lag upper-middle-income countries on health and well-being, water and sanitation, energy access, economic growth, and innovation and infrastructure SDGs. Lower-income countries tend to score significantly below other countries across SDGs 1 to 9. For the remaining SDGs, median scores do not vary as significantly across income categories.[2]

MAP 1.3

Unequal development: SDG global index scores, 2017

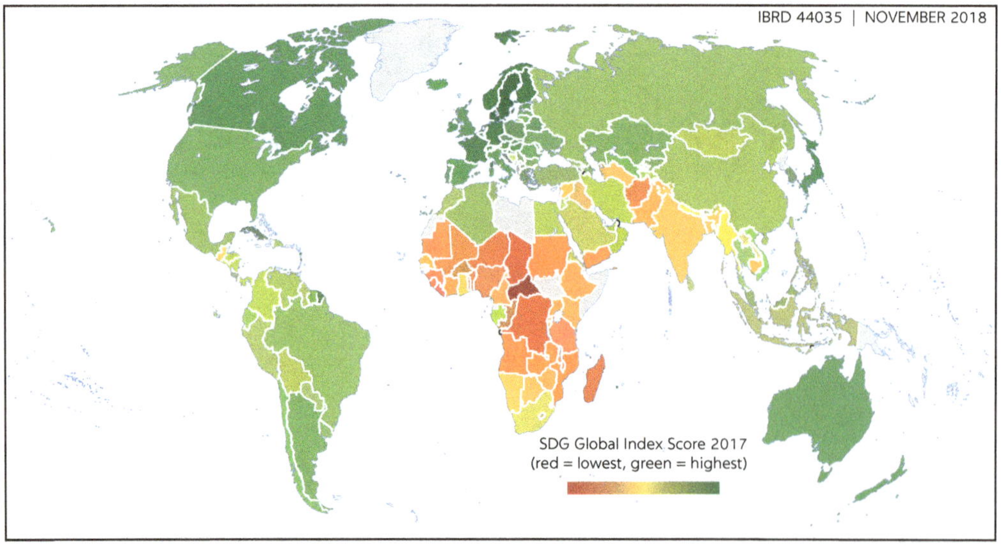

Source: Data from SDSN 2017.

Note: Map shows Sustainable Development Goal (SDG) Index Scores in 2017 (from 0 to 100, with a higher score indicating higher levels of development). Colors range from dark red for the lowest score (Central African Republic, 37) to dark green for the highest (Sweden, 86).

FIGURE 1.4

Human development varies by income level: SDGs 1–9 scores, 2017

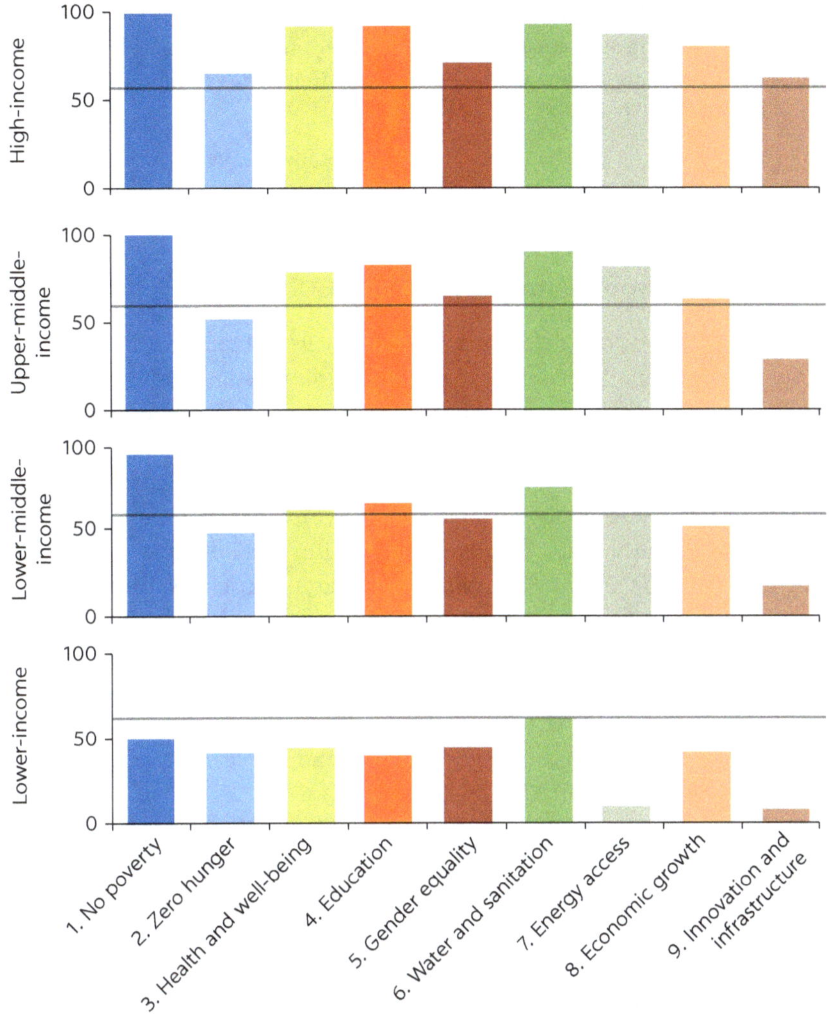

Source: Created using data from SDSN 2017.
Note: Figure shows median SDG Index scores across country income categories for Sustainable Development Goals (SDGs) 1 to 9 for 2017. Grey bar shows median score across all countries and SDGs (61).

Solutions are therefore required to help countries achieve mitigation and other development goals simultaneously. Numerous scholars have argued that environmental taxation, when part of a reform package which includes expenditure policies can achieve the environmental and development objectives such as raising output or employment (Fullerton 2001; Acemoglu et al. 2012; UNEP 2015). However, the literature on ETR has focused on applications in developed countries, with comparatively less discussion about ETR's prospects for helping developing countries achieve sustainable development.

This chapter argues that ETR can be the fiscal foundation for developing countries to achieve their NDCs and their SDGs jointly. The study supplements efforts by the World Bank Group to increase support to developing countries on ETR. Complementary initiatives include the Climate Action Peer Exchange of Finance Ministries, which helps developing countries align fiscal and climate policy; the Partnership for Market Readiness, which provides support for building the next generation of carbon markets; and the Carbon Pricing Leadership Coalition, which promotes public–private collaboration on carbon taxation and emissions trading. These efforts, and this chapter, seek to assist developing countries to achieve sustainable development, including by meeting their NDC and SDG targets.

WHY ETR?

What are environmental taxation and ETR?

Environmental taxation refers to a range of fiscal "instruments that can raise revenue, while simultaneously furthering environmental goals" (World Bank 2005).[3] Environmental taxes include fees/charges and taxes/duties[4] which have a base that "is a physical unit (or a proxy of it) that has a proven specific negative impact on the environment" (OECD 2018a). For example, environmental taxes could be levied on emissions of CO_2 and other pollutants (for example, carbon, nitrous oxide, and sulfur dioxide/acid rain taxes); energy generation and consumption (coal, coke, electricity, kerosene, petroleum, diesel, and natural gas duties); vehicles (road taxes, vehicle registration taxes, and congestion charges); air transport (airport duties, air passenger duties, and aviation fuel duties); shipping (fuel oil and port taxes); water and sanitation (water, wastewater, and effluent charges); general waste (charges on batteries, solvents, plastic bags, and other nonrecyclables); sugar (sugar taxes); and many others.[5]

Data on environmental revenues in developing countries are limited. But, among Organisation for Economic Co-operation and Development (OECD) countries, environmental tax revenues grew between 1994 and 2014 (from US$420.7 billion to US$785.2 billion), but declined as a share of total tax revenues (6.2 percent to 5.2 percent) and GDP (1.9 percent to 1.6 percent) (figure 1.5).

Environmental tax reforms (ETRs) are packages of policies that combine environmental taxes with expenditure policies, alongside various supplementary policies. ETR seeks to improve "alignment of taxes and tax-like instruments with environmental damages, coupled with socially productive ways of using revenues raised" (OECD 2017).[6] In doing so, ETR can achieve numerous environmental and nonenvironmental benefits, resulting in direct and indirect effects on measures of human welfare (figure 1.6). For example, revenues from increasing environmental taxes can be used for pursuing development objectives, by, for example, raising health and education spending. Revenues could also be used to reduce other preexisting taxes ("revenue recycling"), potentially increasing output or employment.

Overall, there are many reasons for implementing ETR. Three are notable: market efficiency, cost-effectiveness, and raising domestic resources. These are rooted, respectively, in the desire for optimal economic, environmental, and fiscal policies, and are described below.

Reason 1: Achieving market efficiency

First, from the perspective of economic policy, a principal rationale for environmental taxation is *market efficiency*. Efficient markets require that prices reflect

FIGURE 1.5

Environmental tax revenues have declined as a proportion of GDP and total taxation in OECD countries, 1994–2014

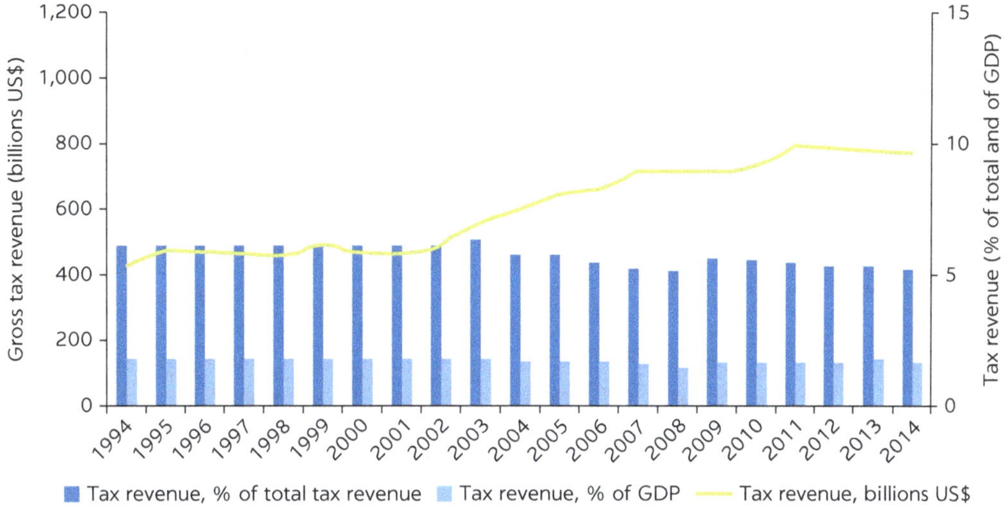

Source: Created using data from OECD PINE Database, https://pinedatabase.oecd.org/.
Note: The line (left axis) shows gross tax revenue in Organisation for Economic Co-operation and Development (OECD) countries increased from 1994 to 2014, but the bars (right axis) show revenues declined as a proportion of gross domestic product (GDP) and total tax revenues.

FIGURE 1.6

Environmental tax reform has direct and indirect effects on welfare

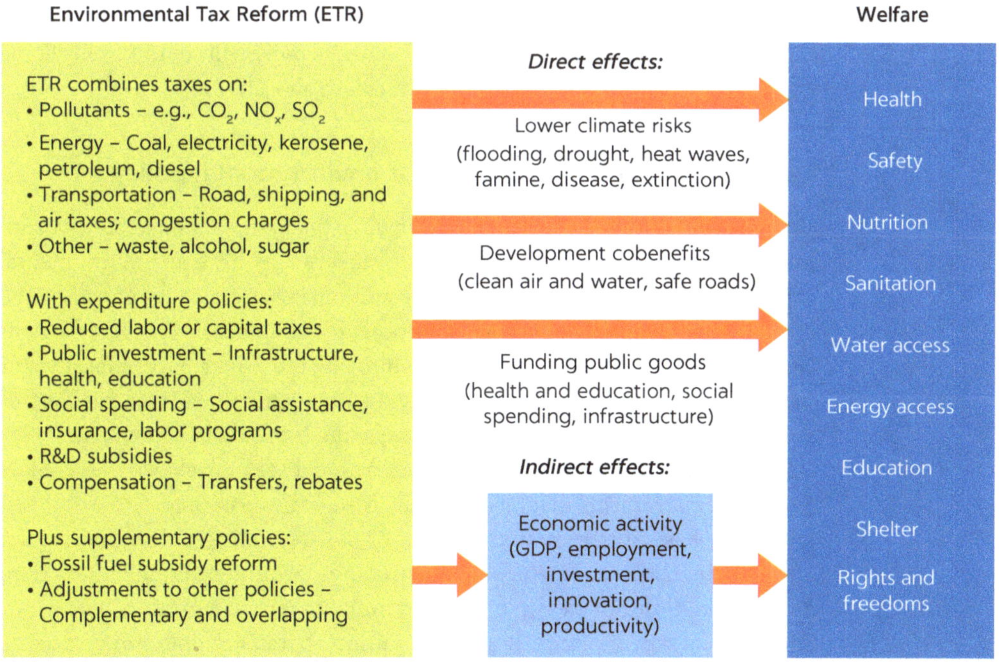

Note: Figure shows that ETR is a combination of taxes, expenditure policies, and supplementary policies. ETR can have direct effects (by reducing climate externalities, providing "development cobenefits," and funding public goods) and indirect effects (through changes in economic activity) on human welfare. CO_2 = carbon dioxide; GDP = gross domestic product; NO_x = nitrogen oxides; R&D = research and development; SO_2 = sulfur dioxide.

all costs of a good or service, including costs imposed on third parties ("negative externalities").

Most economists agree on the need for government intervention to address negative externalities. Production by firms and consumption by households can have unintended, indirect effects that harm other agents in an economy without their consent. Left alone, market prices may not reflect these external costs. But government intervention does not mean eliminating negative externalities entirely. From the perspective of efficiency, the aim should be to restore a socially desirable equilibrium. This equilibrium balances the costs of reducing the externality, borne by its producers, with the costs of harm inflicted on those affected by that externality. In the absence of well-defined property rights, there is a case for government intervention through "Pigouvian taxation" on efficiency grounds (see box 1.1).[7]

The market efficiency objective of environmental taxation is rooted in theoretical economics. The idea of third parties bearing costs of private activities is antithetical to the philosophical underpinnings of free markets. As Adam Smith argued, "It is unjust that the whole of society should contribute towards an expense of which the benefit is confined to a part of the society" (Smith 1776). In more technical terms, the First Fundamental Theorem of Welfare Economics states that free markets can generate a Pareto-efficient competitive equilibrium only if external costs are internalized into prices (see also Lerner 1934; Lange 1942; Arrow 1951). Pigou (1932) derived how tax policy can be used to manage such external costs. "Total welfare of society is maximized by continuing a production activity until social marginal benefit falls to the level of social marginal costs" (Eskeland and Devarajan 1996). Accordingly, "a Pigouvian tax on emissions that is equal to external damages would generally be the first-best policy description" (Eskeland and Devarajan 1996).

By internalizing external costs into prices, ETR can help countries achieve a more socially efficient allocation of resources. The market efficiency objective of ETR seeks not to *stop* the polluting activities but rather to *internalize the marginal external costs* of those activities. As a result, the activity will continue only at the level that is socially desirable, helping to achieve allocative efficiency.

Reason 2: Minimizing the costs of environmental policy

Second, from the perspective of environmental policy, the rationale for environmental taxes is *cost-effectiveness*. Policy makers may have an environmental objective that they want to achieve while minimizing any negative effects on the economy. This could include reducing local air pollutants such as fine particulate matter (PM2.5), cutting acid rain, improving the drinkability of local water supplies, improving sanitation, and reducing litter. Most relevant for this chapter are developing countries' mitigation targets under the Paris Agreement. Policy makers should keep in mind welfare concerns and seek to achieve these objectives using instruments that minimize any costs to the economy.

Market-based instruments (taxes or ETSs) are, in many cases, more cost-effective instruments for achieving broad environmental objectives than direct regulation. For example, the government may wish to cut down on CO_2 produced by power plants. But this pollution abatement does not come free of charge. Implementing direct regulatory measures, such as performance standards or mandated use of specific technologies standards, has costs for firms, such as the costs of adopting the required technology or improving existing equipment. These costs will vary across plants and firms.

BOX 1.1

Externalities and Pigouvian taxation

Economists have long suggested taxing activities that have undesirable effects on others, and whose effects are not reflected in market prices and transactions (negative externalities). Adam Smith argued, for example, that carriages in England should be taxed in proportion to the damage they cause to roads and therefore other road users (Smith 1776). Later, Arthur Pigou argued that governments should tax producers of externalities at a rate equal to marginal external costs at the efficient level of output (Pigouvian taxation; Pigou 1932).

One way of illustrating the desirability of Pigouvian taxation is through a simplified model economy with "complete economic allocation" (figure B1.1.1). Firms produce private goods consumed by households. Firms and households have some demand for public goods and contribute resources equal to the benefit they gain from them ("Lindahl taxes"; Lindahl 1958). Assume that production and consumption result in externalities that are currently unpriced. Firms and consumers have some demand for externalities or their absence, but there is no market or price for them (a "missing market"). The externalities are therefore either oversupplied if they are negative (for example, pollution) or undersupplied if they are positive and with a public good element (for example, knowledge spillovers from investment). This is an instance of incomplete economic allocation, also known as market failure. By implementing Pigouvian taxation through an ETR, the external costs of consumption and production can be internalized into prices. Assuming market clearance, this equilibrium will be closer to an efficient, and complete, economic allocation.

When externalities inflict costs on other firms (for example, a power plant polluting water used by a farm downstream), this new allocation may entail increased overall output (more private goods), cleaner water (more public goods), and a shift to socially efficient levels of production of externalities (less pollution, that is, another public good). Internalizing externalities through higher prices results in reductions in demand for polluting private goods, which may or may not dominate the increased demand for cleaner private goods. However, welfare losses from reduced private goods consumption can be more than offset by welfare gains from an improved environment (Mirrlees 2011), that is, increased public goods and reduced externalities.

This simplified model masks numerous complex interactions (with, for example, factor markets, international trade, transboundary and intergenerational impact of pollution, uncertainty, human behavior, and other tax policies). In addition, it ignores the costs of government intervention. As public choice theorists note, governments as well as markets can fail (see, for example, Tullock, Brady, and Seldon 2002). However, if the costs of intervention are outweighed by the potential gains, Pigouvian policies such as environmental taxation can lead to substantial welfare gains.

FIGURE B1.1.1

Theoretical complete economic allocation

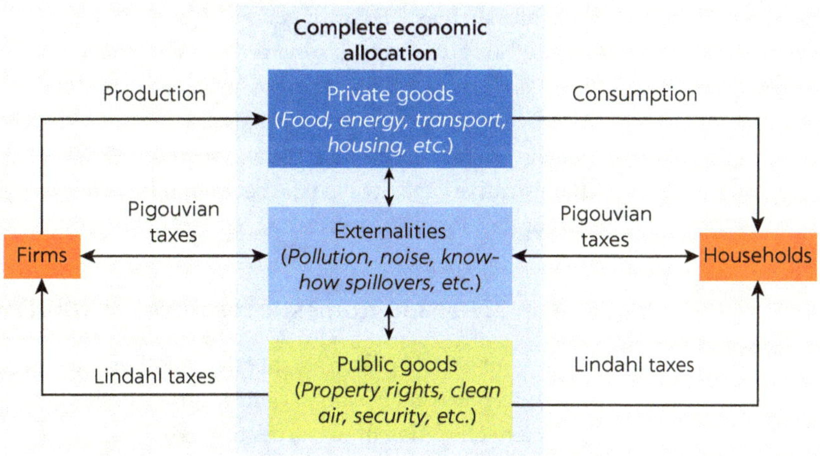

Source: Based on Hammond 1998.
Note: The figure excludes factor markets.

For example, because of scale economies, a large power plant may find it cheaper to abate each unit of pollutant than a smaller plant would because of scale economies.

The government's objective should be to minimize the total costs across firms to minimize the costs to the economy of cutting pollution. Hence, the government should seek to minimize the sum of abatement costs across all firms in a jurisdiction. More abatement should take place where it is cheaper to do so—among larger plants in the example in the previous paragraph. However, the government may not know which firms face cheaper abatement opportunities. As a result, direct regulation—such as the requirement to install scrubbers on smokestacks to limit emissions—may force larger plants to cut emissions less, and smaller plants more, than would be desirable economically.[8]

In a case like this, market-based instruments like taxes are more likely to result in lowest-cost abatement. Facing the same per-unit-of-CO_2 tax, plants that have cheaper abatement opportunities (that would prefer to abate than pay the tax) will cut pollution relatively more than plants facing high abatement costs (that would prefer to simply pay the tax). Taxes can therefore achieve the same reduction in CO_2 emissions at a lower cost to firms. Hence, in a static sense, taxes are more cost-effective than direct regulatory measures like technology mandates.

Environmental taxes are also more cost-effective than regulation in a dynamic sense. Taxes send price signals not just to exploit abatement opportunities but also to create cheaper ways of abating through innovation. By contrast, technology mandates or performance standards provide much weaker incentives for firms to innovate.[9] As a result, by incentivizing both least-cost abatement and innovation, environmental taxes can be more cost-effective than regulations for achieving environmental objectives.

Note, however, that ETR is not always the most cost-effective or feasible policy for achieving specific environmental objectives (refer to appendix A for detail). In certain circumstances, alternative environmental policies such as regulations or ETSs may be better at achieving the desired objective. For example, where the potential tax revenues are small relative to the costs of administering the tax, such as for plastic bags, regulations or outright bans may be more cost-effective than environmental taxes. In addition, there is an ongoing debate about the relative desirability of ETSs versus environmental taxes for abating emissions such as GHGs. In general, quantity instruments such as ETSs are expected to give firms, governments, and households more certainty over future emissions levels, whereas price instruments such as environmental taxes give more certainty over prices. However, environmental taxes tend to be simpler to administer than ETSs and so may be preferable in contexts with low administrative capacity (see the section in this chapter titled "How suitable is ETR for developing countries?").

Reason 3: Raising domestic resources to fund public goods

Third, from a fiscal policy perspective, another reason for ETR can be raising *domestic resource mobilization* (DRM). Fiscal policy has three broad objectives: (i) efficient allocation of resources through provision of public goods and internalizing externalities; (ii) raising revenues to fund government priorities like redistribution; and (iii) stabilization (Musgrave 1959). In addition to helping achieve economic efficiency (objective i), ETR can also help finance ministries achieve the second objective. For developing countries, the revenue-raising potential of ETR may be its most attractive aspect.

Tax revenue as percentage of GDP tends to be lower in developing than developed countries. For example, in 2016, government revenues were on average 27.3 percent of GDP in high-income countries but only 17.5 percent of GDP in middle-income and 16.2 percent of GDP in low-income countries (figure 1.7). As a result, developing countries struggle to provide basic services such as transport infrastructure, health care, and social safety nets.

Lower DRM not only holds back the provision of basic services but may also constrain economic growth. New research suggests that 15 percent of GDP is needed to fund these basic services (World Bank 2018). But 30 of the 75 poorest countries fall below this threshold. In addition, there may be a "tipping point" in tax-to-GDP ratios: A threshold beyond which growth and development significantly accelerate. This tipping point has been estimated at approximately 12.75 percent (Gaspar, Jaramillo, and Wingender 2016a, 2016b); however, 17 of the 75 poorest countries are below this threshold.

Raising DRM in developing countries is therefore a development priority. As the World Bank (2016) argues, "a country's ability to collect domestic taxes and spend those resources effectively lies at the crux of financing for development." In addition, domestic resources have desirable properties relative to foreign sources of finance such as overseas aid. As Oxfam argues, compared with overseas aid, domestic resources tend to be "more stable, aligned with government priorities . . . and easier to implement than donor-funded spending" (Martin and Walker 2015) Achieving the SDGs therefore requires "a massive step up in domestic resource

FIGURE 1.7

Tax revenues among low- and middle-income countries lag advanced economies

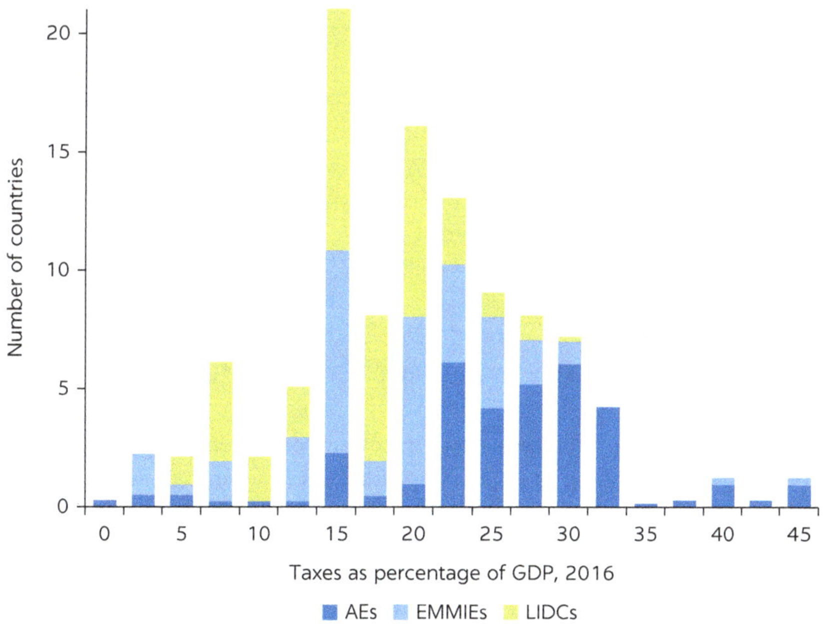

Source: IMF 2017.
Note: Histogram shows the number of countries, grouped by income level, that achieve different levels of tax revenue as percentage of gross domestic product (GDP). Country groups are low-income developing countries (LIDCs, green), emerging and middle-income economies (EMMIEs, light blue), and advanced economies (AEs, dark blue).

mobilization" (Martin and Walker 2015). Last, raising tax-to-GDP ratios can be an important part of efforts to raise the quality of political and administrative institutions (Gaspar, Jaramillo, and Wingender 2016a). Along with economic growth, improving these institutions is crucial for raising well-being (Pritchett 2016).

Evidence suggests that environmental taxation is a cost-effective way of raising revenues. Environmental taxes can raise additional revenue at lower cost than other, more broad-based taxes (OECD 2010a, 2018b) because marginal economic costs of tax distortions tend to be lower for environmental revenues. As a result, environmental taxation could be a cost-effective way of increasing DRM. Countries with very high debt-to-GDP ratios could especially benefit: using increased environmental taxes for debt reduction can be an efficient use of revenues (Carbone et al. 2014). That said, as with all tax changes, distributional consequences need to be considered. In this case, raising domestic tax revenues to pay off debt benefits future generations at the expense of current generations (Carbone et al. 2013), and using revenues to invest in public infrastructure has ambiguous distributional effects (Siegmeier et al. 2017).

For developing countries, which tend to have lower levels of DRM, funding public investments and services through environmental taxation may or may not be desirable (Siegmeier et al. 2015). Environmental taxes are less distortionary to collect than other taxes and, as this chapter will argue, can help countries reap substantial, direct development co-benefits. Raising DRM through environmental taxation, however, may not always raise well-being. As with any tax, before considering the effect of revenue use, the expected effect on output is likely to be contractionary because of distortionary effects. How governments use revenues is therefore a crucial factor in determining the social desirability of raising taxes through environmental taxation.

Improper use of revenues (for example, siphoning off through corrupt practices) would clearly render ETR undesirable. Likewise, increases in undesirable public investments—for example, in services that would have otherwise been provided by the private sector—are unlikely to raise welfare. By contrast, increasing public spending—for example, in road infrastructure, education, health, or social safety nets—could more than compensate for any welfare costs from a larger tax burden and increased prices for polluting goods (Oueslati 2013).

Overall, as with many facets of ETR, the desirability of using it as a tool for raising revenue depends on a variety of country-specific factors, notably existing levels of taxation and the government's ability to effectively direct revenues toward socially desirable ends.

HOW LARGE IS THE ENVIRONMENTAL TAX GAP?

Globally, there is a large gap between current and socially efficient levels of environmental taxation. Despite different approaches to measuring this gap, there is consensus that some gap exists. The two main approaches to estimating optimal tax rates, and hence for determining the gap, are market efficiency and cost-effectiveness estimates.

Market efficiency estimates

The first approach, based on market efficiency, seeks to quantify external damages to equate tax rates with marginal social costs. Optimal Pigouvian taxation entails internalizing all external costs of production and consumption into prices. For gasoline consumption, these external costs would include pollution's effect on the health of residents, increased road accidents due to the overconsumption of cars and motorcycles, increased congestion, and increased risks of climate change due to the emission of CO_2.

These costs can be estimated and used to calculate corrective taxes. Figure 1.8 offers an illustrative example using gasoline consumption. A consumer purchases 1 liter of gasoline for $0.80 (item 1). The government subsidizes fuel directly through $0.10 of financial support (pre-tax subsidy, item 2) and indirectly by forgoing value added tax (VAT) of $0.10 normally charged on goods (item 3). The total ($1.00) is the private cost of gasoline, but there are also social costs (externalities) of gasoline consumption. Burning fossil fuels increases pollution-related deaths and health disorders, costs that can be estimated ($0.30, item 4). Underpricing fuel also incentivizes inefficient car use, with welfare and efficiency costs from increased congestion ($0.20, item 5). Last, the global warming costs from emitting CO_2 can be derived by estimating the social cost of carbon ($0.10, item 6). Total private and social costs ($1.50) equal the socially optimal price of fuel.

The gap between social costs and the private price paid by the consumer at the pump ($0.80) has been called post-tax subsidies,[10] but this definition of fossil fuel subsidies is not universally adhered to.[11] Policies and reforms designed to close this gap in part or in full include energy price reform, fossil fuel subsidy reform, and carbon pricing.[12] In this chapter, the difference between optimal and

FIGURE 1.8

Illustrative example of corrective tax on gasoline

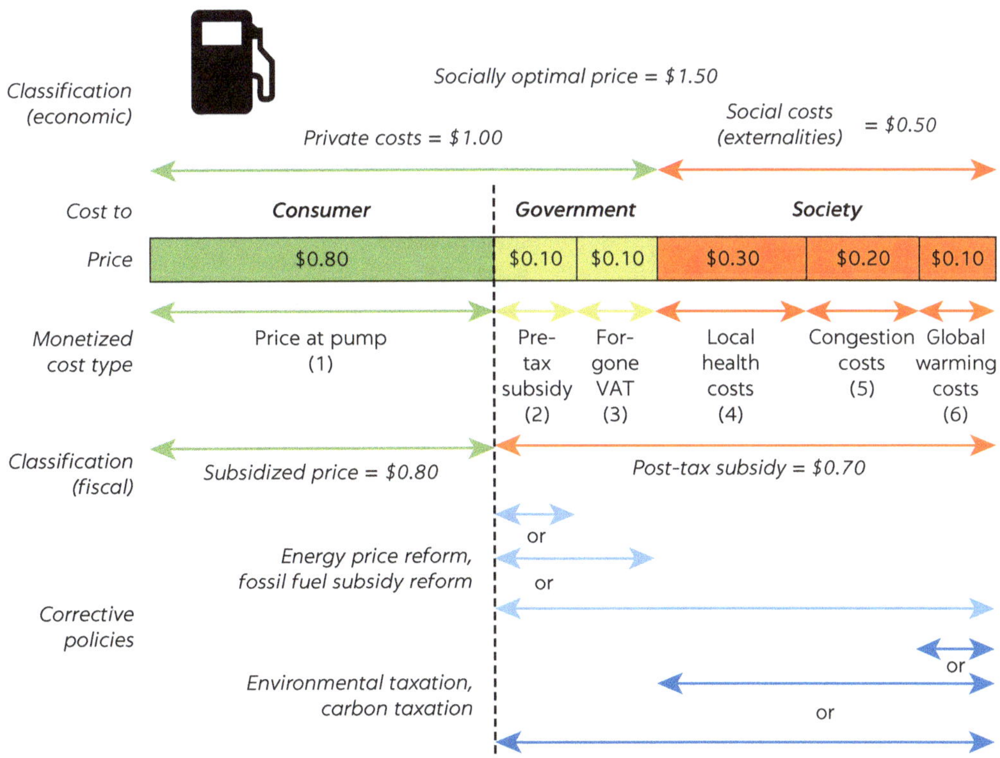

Note: Figure shows the potential divergence between private costs for 1 liter of gasoline and socially optimal prices due to negative externalities. All estimates are fictional. $ = U.S. dollars. VAT = value added tax.

current consumer prices is considered the full environmental tax gap. Closing this gap entails specific corrective taxes.

Because of differences in external costs, estimates of optimal corrective taxes on gasoline vary substantially by country (figure 1.9). For example, in South Africa, climate externalities might justify a corrective tax of $0.08 per liter of gasoline. However, this is dwarfed by the corrective tax justified by the external costs of accidents ($0.30 per liter) and congestion ($0.50), while the tax justified by local pollution costs is modest ($0.02). By contrast, for Indonesia, the nonclimate externality contributions from congestion ($0.09 per liter) and accidents ($0.24), are still larger than climate ($0.08) and local pollution ($0.02) externalities, but are not as large as in South Africa. Both countries, however, have large gaps between the optimal gasoline tax and current taxes ($0.50 and $0.44 per liter gap, respectively).

Large environmental tax gaps exist worldwide between consumer prices and prices implied by market efficiency (map 1.4). Efficient prices for gasoline, diesel,

FIGURE 1.9

Corrective taxes on gasoline by externality type, select countries, 2014

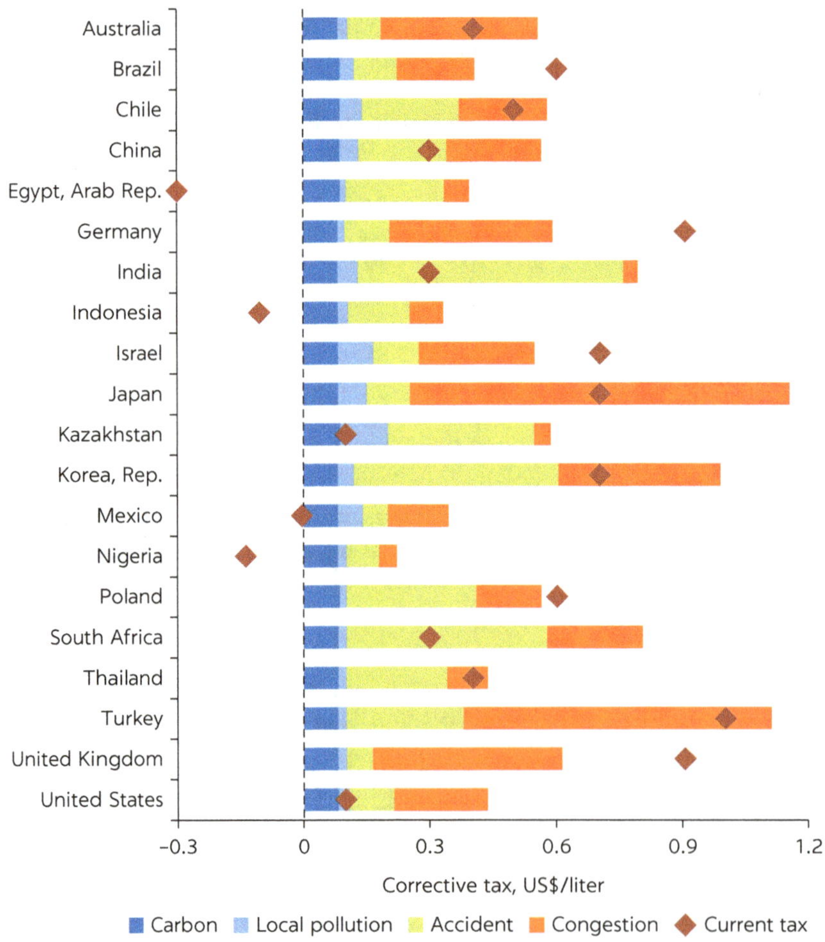

Source: Parry et al. 2014.
Note: Figure shows optimal tax on gasoline per liter by externality (bars) and current tax level (diamonds). The gap is the difference between optimal and current taxes, which in some cases (for example, Germany and the United Kingdom) is negative. The figure uses an illustrative social cost of carbon of US$35 per tonne of carbon dioxide equivalent.

MAP 1.4

Global environmental tax gaps, 2015

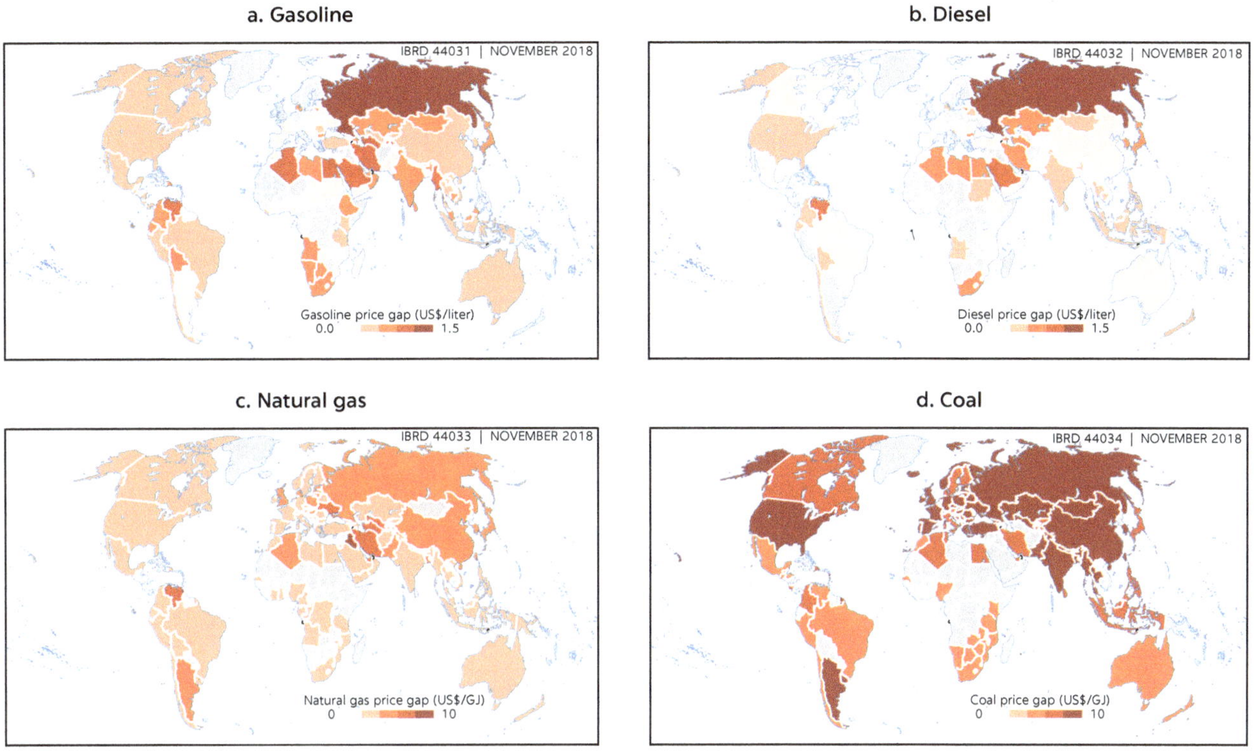

Sources: Created using data from Coady et al. 2017.
Note: Map shows that gaps exist between consumer prices and lower-bounds estimates for efficient energy prices implied by external costs (including local pollution, traffic congestion and road accidents, and climate change). It shows only countries where consumer prices were below efficient prices in 2015. Countries not shown had either negative price gaps (for example, much of Europe with diesel) or missing data (parts of Africa on diesel and coal). Price gaps on gasoline and diesel are expressed in US$/liter, with the dark red (1.5) group including all countries with gaps greater than US$1.5/liter. Gaps for natural gas and coal are expressed in US$ per Gigajoule (GJ) energy produced, with the dark red (10) group including all countries with gaps greater than US$10/GJ.

natural gas, and coal tend to be well below efficient prices implied by internalizing externalities.

The market efficiency approach can also be used to estimate the global environmental tax gap for energy. A study by the International Monetary Fund finds that, in 2015, the gap between existing fuel prices and the levels justified by their environmental damages amounted to US$5.3 trillion, or 6.5 percent of global GDP, having grown from US$4.1 trillion or 4.9 percent of global GDP in 2011 (figure 1.10, panel a).[13] The gap is due partly to direct financial subsidies on energy (pre-tax subsidies), but mostly and increasingly to the externalized costs of energy. This gap is also unevenly distributed around the world, with larger absolute and relative gaps in East Asia and Eastern Europe than in Latin America and Sub-Saharan Africa, for example (figure 1.10, panel b).

But these are lower-bound estimates: the tax gap may be even larger. Other external costs from using fossil fuels could be substantial, but these costs have been excluded from estimation because they are difficult to measure. They include any damages to human health and productivity from air pollution's adverse effects on human morbidity, environmental impacts from upstream fuel extraction and transportation, energy security, indoor air pollution, and terms of

FIGURE 1.10
Global environmental tax gap

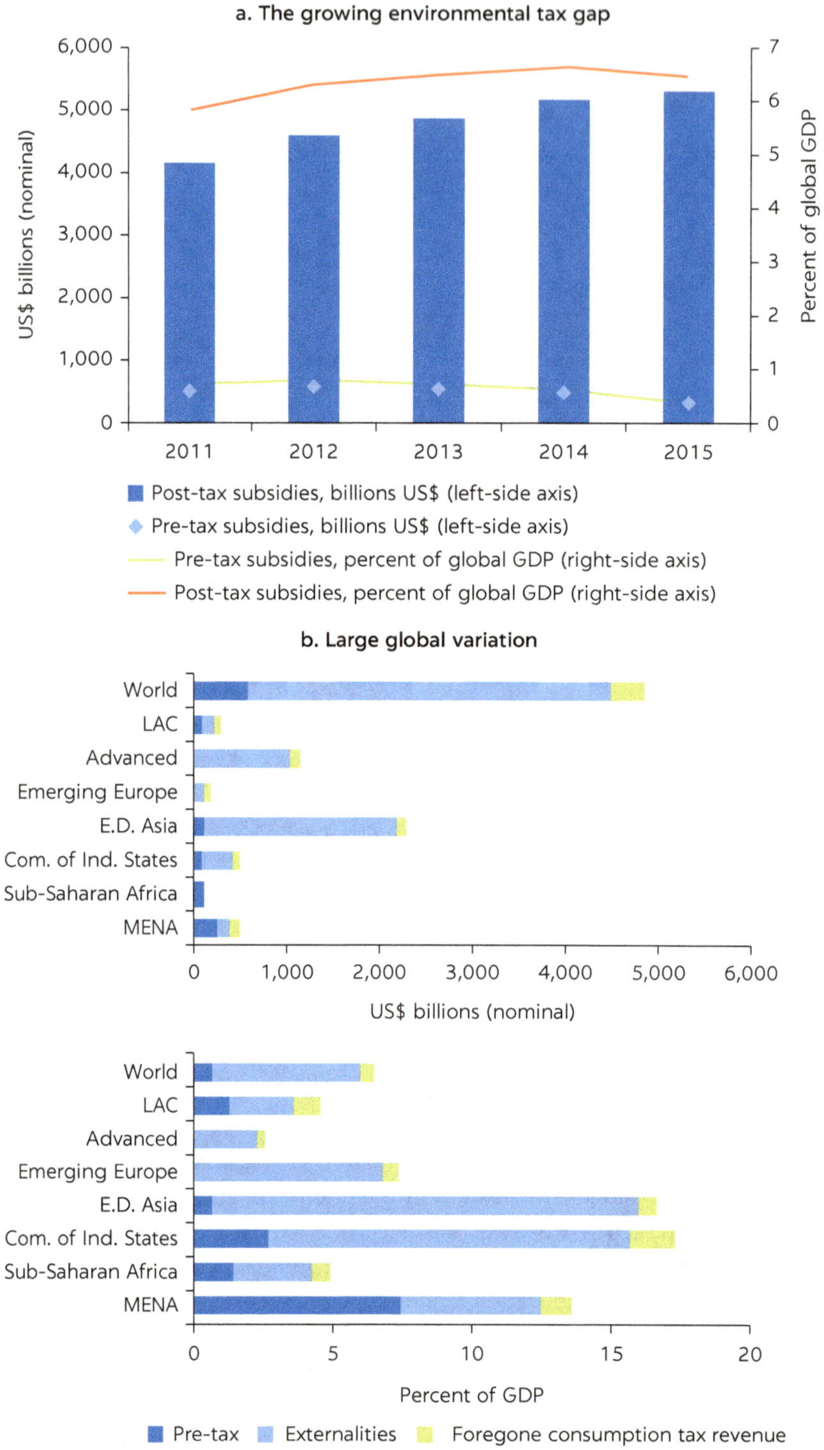

Source: Coady et al. 2017.
Note: The global environmental tax gap (termed post-tax subsidies; panel a) has grown in absolute terms (left axis) and relative to GDP (right axis). But there is large variation in the gap (panel b), both in absolute terms (top axis) and as a share of GDP (bottom axis). CEE-CIS = Central and Eastern Europe and Commonwealth of Independent States; E.D. Asia = Emerging and Developing Asia: GDP = gross domestic product; LAC = Latin America and Caribbean; MENA = Middle East and North Africa.

trade effects (Parry, Veung, and Heine 2015). If the estimation included these costs, energy price and environmental tax gaps would be even wider. Even when not considering these damage categories, this method suggests the gap is large and growing.

Cost-effectiveness estimates: Climate mitigation

The second approach to estimating the tax gap focuses on the *cost-effectiveness* of achieving a specific environmental objective, for example, meeting a country's NDC as part of an international effort to mitigate climate change. Achieving the objective of the Paris Agreement—of limiting global warming to below 2 degrees Celsius by the end of the century, and pursuing efforts towards limiting it to below 1.5 degrees—implies a number of pathways for cost-effective environmental tax rates, expressed as carbon prices over time.

In 2017, an assembly of eminent economists reviewed the literature to estimate the price of carbon required for implementing the Paris Agreement. They found that lower-bound estimates of the needed global carbon price consistent with cost-effectively achieving the Paris Agreement are US$40–80 per tonne of CO_2 (tCO_2) by 2020 and US$50–100/$tCO_2$ by 2030 (CPLC 2017). They also cautioned that higher carbon prices (in the range of US$80–100/$tCO_2$ in the period 2020–30) could be needed if the improvement of technology and tightening of other environmental policies are weaker than assumed. At present, the world is far from the lower-bound estimates of needed carbon prices to cost-effectively mitigate climate change even at the 2-degree level. This implies that there is currently a huge global environmental tax gap.

Coverage of emissions remains pervasively low. The number of jurisdictions around the world that use some form of carbon pricing, either carbon taxation or emission trading schemes, has significantly increased (World Bank and Ecofys 2018). These policies started in Northern Europe but have since grown in region and size. However, the proportion of global emissions covered by carbon pricing is low: 15 percent in 2018.

Even where emissions are priced, actual prices tend to be low (figure 1.11). In 2018, the carbon price of most mechanisms is below the US$40–80/$tCO_2$ lower bound estimated as being required by 2020 to meet the Paris Agreement. Only the carbon taxes of Finland, Liechtenstein, Sweden, and Switzerland are within this range. But even these taxes do not cover most of their jurisdictions' emissions. As a result, adjusted for coverage, only Sweden's carbon tax is within the range needed to meet the Paris Agreement.[14]

Another approach is to estimate *effective carbon tax rates* (the total of implicit and explicit carbon prices) for fuel taxes, comparing them to what is needed to achieve the Paris Agreement. This methodology converts fuel taxes into carbon taxes by dividing the tax rates on fuels by their carbon content. For example, the OECD estimates effective tax rates in 42 developed and emerging economies that jointly account for 80 percent of global energy consumption (OECD 2018b).

However, this "effective carbon tax rate" approach runs the risk of understating the environmental tax gap. Fuels are taxed for many more environmental reasons than just climate change, and the *efficient* tax should incorporate all external costs beyond the social cost of carbon. By focusing on *effective* carbon taxes, the many nonclimate externalities from energy consumption can be missed.[15] This approach therefore finds a smaller gap compared to the

FIGURE 1.11

Explicit carbon prices around the world, 2018

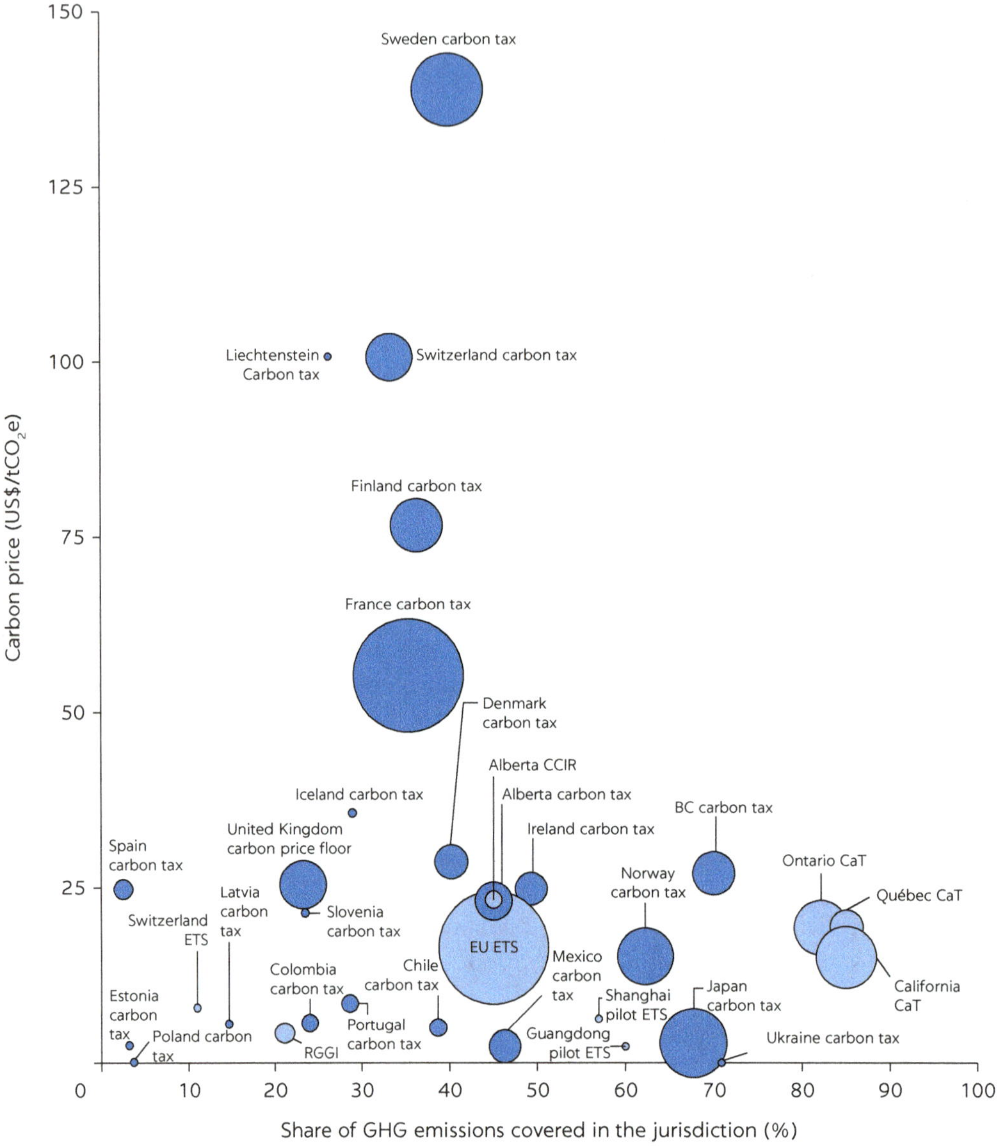

Source: World Bank and Ecofys 2018.

Note: Figure shows carbon prices by mechanism and proportion of a jurisdiction's emissions covered. The size of the circles is proportional to the amount of government revenues except for initiatives with government revenues below US$100 million in 2017 (which have equal size). Light blue circles show pricing based on emissions trading schemes; dark blue circles represent carbon taxes. BC = British Columbia; CaT = Cap and Trade; CCIR = Carbon Competitiveness Incentive Regulation; ETS = emissions trading system; EU = European Union; GHG = greenhouse gas; RGGI = Regional Greenhouse Gas Initiative; tCO_2e = tonnes of carbon dioxide equivalent.

efficiency approach, which includes consideration of nonclimate externalities. However, the OECD nonetheless finds a large and growing gap: "almost all taxes are too low from an environmental point of view," and "taxes continue to be poorly aligned with environmental and climate costs of energy use, across all countries. . . . Apart from some modest steps forward in a couple of countries, there is little evidence of better use of taxes on energy use to address the mounting global environmental and climate challenges. Instead, real tax rates are gradually eroded by inflation in most countries, suggesting indifference to the environmental efficacy of taxes" (OECD 2018b).

Overall, there are many ways to estimate the environmental tax gap. The plethora of definitions of concepts and approaches to measuring them is itself undesirable, in that it can dilute the message to policy makers. For example, a variety of definitions exist for fossil fuel subsidies (such as whether external costs are included), and ways of estimating implicit effective carbon prices (such as whether to net out nonclimate external costs). This problem underpins the need for economists to harmonize approaches to estimating efficient and cost-effective environmental taxes. Such disparities, although theoretically difficult, need to be addressed. To better support client countries, economists should seek to harmonize approaches to environmental taxes, fossil fuel subsidies, and implicit carbon taxes.

That said, the broad message for policy makers remains the same: countries are not sufficiently taxing environmental externalities, to meet either social costs or what is needed to achieve the Paris Agreement. Countries are not "getting energy prices right": They are systematically pricing fuels too low.

WHAT IS ETR'S EFFECT ON DEVELOPMENT AND WELFARE?

Having established the existence of large global environmental tax gaps and the rationale for closing them, a key question arises: What effect does using ETR to close the gap have on development and welfare in developing countries? This section summarizes the large and growing empirical and theoretical literature examining the welfare effects of ETR in developed and, increasingly, developing countries. This section argues that ETR can be welfare-enhancing for developing countries, on two fronts.

First, ETR can improve well-being *indirectly* by expanding economic activity. In general, expanding economic activity metrics, such as GDP per capita and employment, can be expected to raise measures of well-being, such as those manifest in the SDGs. Across 128 countries, measures of national development (GDP per capita, political rights, and effective bureaucracy) are positively correlated with measures of well-being, including access to nutrition, medical care, water and sanitation, shelter, personal safety, education, and other SDG indicators (Pritchett 2016).[16] ETR can expand economic activity either by reducing the net costs (excess burden) of the tax system through revenue-neutral recycling of revenues or by facilitating increases in domestic resources used for public investment. Existing empirical evidence on these effects is limited. But what evidence does exist does not support concerns that ETR will adversely affect economic activity in general. In fact, as will be shown, there are firm theoretical reasons to suspect that economic effects may be positive in developing countries.

Second, ETR can raise well-being *directly*. By facilitating reductions in pollution, ETR can directly reduce welfare losses from environmental externalities. Depending on the market structure of the good or service (price and income elasticities), polluting activities should be reduced relative to a situation without environmental taxation. Further, because many pollutants are emitted together as part of the same process, the positive effect may not be limited to the pollutant or externality of interest. For example, coal combustion simultaneously produces CO_2 (which contributes to global warming) and PM2.5 (which adversely affects public health). A tax on coal reduces welfare costs from both of these pollutants.

Figure 1.12 provides an illustrative example of an ETR in the form of an upstream tax on coal, combined with increased expenditure on energy access and removal of other fossil fuel subsidies. As a result, this ETR can yield direct climate benefits: incentivizing a reduction in coal consumption (through switching to cleaner natural gas or renewables and improving energy efficiency by diffusion of existing or new innovations) can reduce CO_2 and methane emissions. This type of ETR can help countries achieve their NDCs and, in so doing, contribute to the achievement of the Paris Agreement through substantive emissions abatement while helping foster more ambitious reductions in emissions. This ETR can also have direct benefits on human health. As noted, reductions in coal combustion also mean reductions in numerous other pollutants entering air and water supplies—yielding substantial health benefits from reduced mortality and morbidity. In addition, the increased spending on energy infrastructure can more than compensate for any loss of energy from a likely increase in electricity prices.

Similarly, ETRs can foster other development co-benefits. Notably, in the case of motor fuel taxes, this includes reductions in congestion and road accident rates because of reduced vehicle use. Modeling techniques used to appraise ETR often miss these co-benefits (see box 1.2), which can be substantial, justifying high environmental tax rates even if a country does not consider climate benefits (Parry, Veung, and Heine 2015). For example, one study estimates that the value of air pollution co-benefits for avoided mortality alone amounts to US$50–380/$tCO_2$, levels that exceed estimated marginal abatements costs through 2050 (West et al. 2013). In studies of post-tax subsidies on energy, the monetized value

FIGURE 1.12

ETR and development cobenefits: An example

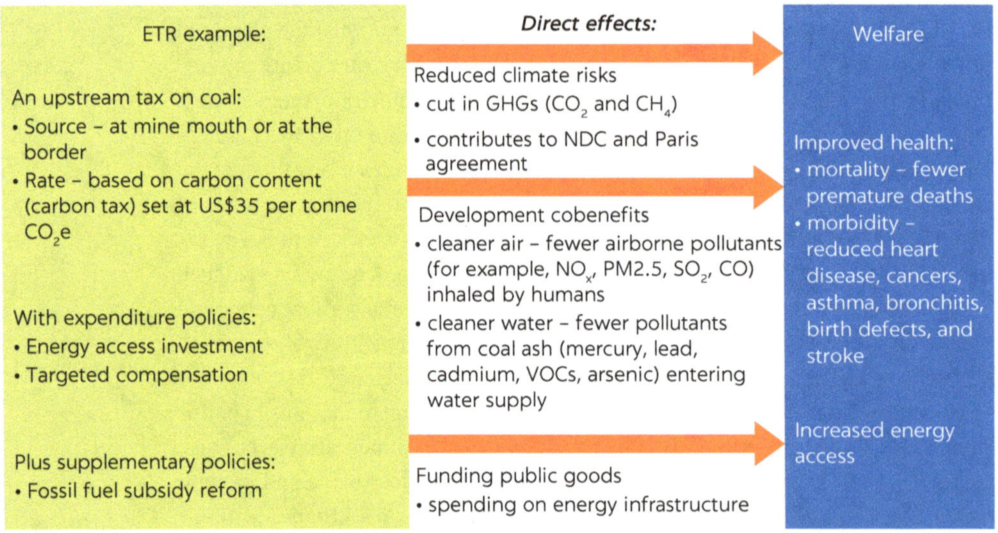

Note: The figure shows an illustrative example of an environmental tax reform (ETR) that combines taxes on coal extraction or import with expenditure and supplementary policies. This ETR has direct effects on welfare by helping foster numerous development cobenefits in addition to climate benefits and helping fund public goods. CH_4 = methane; CO = carbon monoxide; CO_2 = carbon dioxide; CO_2e = carbon dioxide equivalent; GHG = greenhouse gas; NDC = Nationally Determined Contribution; NO_x = nitrogen oxides; PM2.5 = fine particulate matter with diameter of less than 2.5 micrometers; SO_2 = sulfur dioxide; VOC = volatile organic compound.

BOX 1.2

Analytical tools for appraising and evaluating ETR

Economists and policy makers have a broad range of tools for assessing ETR, both before and after implementation. In practice, most analyses focus on estimating ETR's effects on economic activity rather than development co-benefits, though the latter can be substantial. For ex ante appraisal of ETR, analytical tools include the following:

- *Qualitative analysis* can be used to appraise *nonmonetizable welfare co-benefits*, such as a government's desire to increase energy independence. Without a clear way of quantifying these benefits, however, balancing the costs and benefits on objectives (such as output) can be difficult.
- *Partial equilibrium analyses* can be used to quantify direct, first-order effects on well-being such as *monetizable co-benefits* like improvements in health due to reduced local pollution. However, because ETR affects prices throughout the economy (particularly through energy prices), second-order effects will be large and mostly missed by partial equilibrium analyses.
- *General equilibrium (GE) analyses* (for example, computable general equilibrium [CGE] and dynamic stochastic general equilibrium [DSGE]) can be used to analyze and quantify potential economy-wide effects of a tax perturbation on economic activity, notably on output, employment, unemployment, and consumption. The main strength of such models is that they permit analysis of sectoral adjustments (Taylor 2016). Such models are sensitive to inputs such as demand and supply elasticities of labor and relative elasticities of substitution between energy, labor, and capital. Appendix A identifies several structural features of many developing economies, which are especially important to incorporate into such models when appraising ETR's effects in developing countries. GE analyses also compute a single, unique (usually interpreted as long-run) equilibrium, whereas ETR should, ex ante, entail a distribution of probable outcomes.
- *Macroeconometric analyses* use statistical correlations to predict future pathways for economic variables. This analytical technique includes consideration of short-run adjustments (which are less important in CGE models). However, a critique of these approaches is that they are not based on theory, and relationships may change over time, rendering predictions unreliable.
- *Input-output models* model interdependencies between sectors of the economy and can be useful for understanding effects across sectors as well as regions. Most CGE, DSGE, and macroeconometric models use input-output models as part of their framework.
- *Endogenous growth models* can capture induced innovation and positive externalities/spillovers compared with CGE and DSGE models to analyze ex ante potential effects on long-run economic activity. But these models are less aggregated and may not capture important sectoral shifts from ETR.

For ex post evaluation of ETR, tools include the following:

- *Econometric analyses*—methods such as regression analyses, complemented with instrumental variable approaches (see, for example, Martin et al. 2009)—can help isolate the effects of ETR on the environment, economic activity, and other metrics. However, because ETR has economy-wide, second-order diffused effects that emerge over time, isolating causation can be difficult.
- *Qualitative surveys*—such as surveys of business opinion (see, for example, National Audit Office 2007)—can give insights into the effectiveness of environmental taxes and the potential adjustments that can be made. However, responses from affected firms need to be balanced against other forms of evidence because emitters have some incentive to overstate negative effects, whereas ETR tends to benefit low-carbon entrants that may not yet be represented in surveys.

of reducing nonclimate externalities tends to substantially dominate climate benefits, providing a strong impetus to ETRs (Parry et al. 2014; Parry, Veung, and Heine 2015).[17] Therefore, proper consideration of development co-benefits is crucial for determining ETR's effects on welfare.

Empirical studies of ETR: Impacts on output, growth, employment, innovation, and competitiveness

The economic effects of a particular version of ETR depend on several factors. These factors include tax design (for example, scope of tax base, tax rates, upstream versus downstream), timing (phased versus sudden), and, perhaps most important, the use of revenues (for example, revenue-neutral ETR—recycling revenues through reduced taxes on labor or capital—and revenue-raising ETR—funding expansion of public expenditure on investment and public goods).

There is a strong need for an improved empirical evidence base on ETR's economic effects, for both developed and developing countries (Withana et al. 2014). Few countries have experience with ETR, and those that do tend to be developed countries. Partly as a result of this, many more academic studies have focused on ex ante (that is, theoretical) appraisal than on ex post (that is, empirical) evaluation of ETR policies (refer to box 1.2 on methods for appraising and evaluating ETR). Nevertheless, the small number of ex post studies on ETR in developed countries offer some indication of potential effects in developing countries, including impacts on GDP growth, employment, innovation, and international competitiveness.

For output and growth, there is a widespread expectation that environmental measures, including ETR, will have negative effects on economic growth. However, empirically, ETR appears to have had zero or slightly positive effects on GDP (an "output dividend") despite some negative experiences (IEEP 2013):

- Denmark's carbon tax had a near-zero effect on GDP (negative 0.03 percent) between 2000 and 2005, while managing to substantially reduce emissions (IEEP 2013).
- British Columbia's carbon tax was expected by its government to have a small negative effect on GDP. However, later empirical analyses find GDP growth was slightly higher or unaffected, whereas emissions were cut by 5–15 percent (Elgie and McClay 2013; Murray and Rivers 2015).
- The United Kingdom's carbon tax has had no detectable effect on output, but it substantially increased energy productivity of covered firms (Martin et al. 2009; Bassi and Duffy 2016).

With respect to employment, ETR can be expected to shift employment from polluting to nonpolluting industries. If revenues are used to reduce taxes on labor, this shift may result in a net increase in employment (an "employment dividend"). Fewer empirical studies have looked at employment effects, but those that do find the following:

- British Columbia's carbon tax increased employment overall. Employment in the most carbon-intensive industries fell but was more than offset by increases in clean service industries, and net employment rose 0.74 percent between 2007 and 2013 (Beck et al. 2015).
- The United Kingdom's carbon tax had a small positive or undetectable effect on employment (Martin et al. 2009; Ekins and Speck 2011).

- Germany's ETR did not significantly affect employment upward or downward (Ekins and Speck 2011).

In terms of innovation, ETR incentivizes firms to adopt or invent more efficient technologies. There is some empirical evidence:

- In Sweden, taxes on nitrogen oxides (NO_x) rapidly reduced emissions by dramatically increasing the adoption of existing abatement technologies. A tax resulted in a 35 percent reduction in NO_x emissions in transport, industry, and power sectors within 20 months. This was due to rapid uptake of existing abatement technologies: from 7 percent to 62 percent of firms adopted the abatement technology within a year (OECD 2010c). Ensuring a well-designed policy that recycled revenues back to affected firms also made the tax more politically acceptable (OECD 2013).
- The United Kingdom's carbon tax appeared to stimulate innovation among the most affected firms. A carbon tax (the Climate Change Levy) on fossil fuels and electricity increased patents among firms subject to the higher rate of tax compared with those subject to the lower (one-fifth) rate (OECD 2010c).
- In general, however, the link between innovation and ETR remains empirically ambiguous. For example, on fuel taxes, one cross-country study found a strong connection between higher fuel prices and clean innovations (Aghion et al. 2016), whereas another, albeit earlier, cross-country study was inconclusive (OECD 2010c).[18] It should be noted that no evidence suggests that ETR *reduces* innovation.

For international competitiveness effects, ETR can be expected to disadvantage "dirty" industries while advantaging "clean" industries, and could also induce technological innovation (see chapter 2). The balance of effects on aggregate economic competitiveness is therefore ambiguous ex ante. Overall, current empirical literature does not suggest that ETR hinders competitiveness:

- In the United Kingdom, carbon taxes and other climate policies "appear to have had no detectable impact on competitiveness to date" (Bassi and Duffy 2016).
- Across OECD and select middle-income countries, environmental policies over the 1990s–2000s advantaged clean industries at the expense of dirty industries but had no significant effect on overall trade in manufactured goods (Koźluk and Timiliotis 2016).
- In Indonesia and Mexico, increases in fuel prices raised labor productivity without affecting profits among firms (see chapter 2 for a detailed discussion).

Theoretical studies: Output and employment

Although empirical evidence is lacking, a large body of theoretical literature examines ETR's potential effects on output and employment. Debates in environmental economics commenced in the 1990s on the question of whether ETR could yield a "double dividend": simultaneously achieving environmental objectives such as emissions abatement (first dividend) while raising economic output or employment (second dividend). Some contended that, by recycling revenues raised from environmental taxes to reduce other, more distortive taxes like those on formal sector employment, ETR could improve the environment while expanding economic activity. Shifting the tax burden from formal sector employment to polluting activities could reduce the net excess burden of taxation (economic losses due to distortions imposed by the tax system). This reduction in the net excess burden could increase the labor supply (because of lower income taxes paid by workers) or labor demand (because of lower payroll taxes falling on firms). But, by raising the price level, this tax switch also lowers real wages and therefore labor supply. The net effect of ETR on economic activity (the second dividend) could therefore be positive or negative.

More than two decades of modeling suggests that ETR can reduce emissions while raising employment, but effects on output remain ambiguous (figure 1.13). Literature reviews of early ETR studies indicated that reforms would reduce pollution sharply and increase employment, but that effects on output were ambiguous (Bosquet 2000; Patuelli, Nijkamp, and Pels 2005). Later studies variably found strong effects on reducing emissions while increasing employment (Anger, Böhringer, and Löschel 2010), or on reducing emissions while increasing both employment and output (Heady et al. 2000; Markandya 2012). A more recent literature review found strong effects on emissions but inconclusive effects on employment and output (Freire-González 2017).

FIGURE 1.13

Simulations of developed countries suggest that ETR can cut emissions while increasing employment, but effects on output are ambiguous

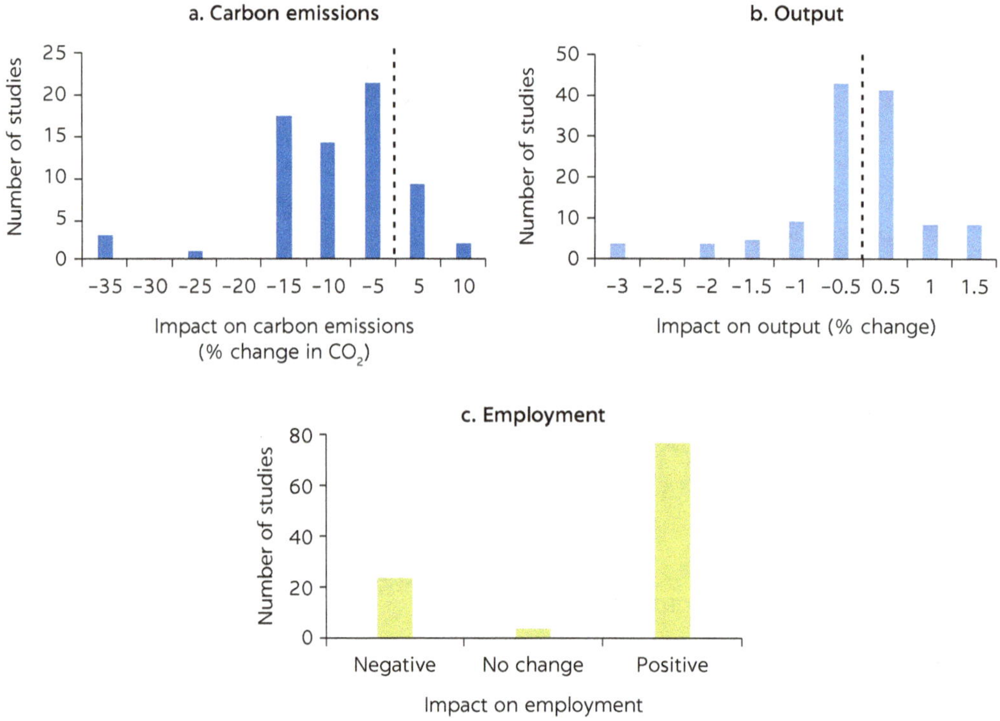

Source: Bosquet 2000.

Note: Panels show the number of studies (y axis) that find effects (x axis) on carbon emissions (panel a), output (panel b), and employment (panel c). Emissions and output results are organized into classes—for example, the "1.5 percent" class on output includes all simulations resulting in a 1.25 percent or greater positive effect on output. Total simulations were 131 from 56 studies from 1996 to 2000. Panel a shows 64 simulations (67 did not return data; 1 outlier was excluded). Panel b shows 120 simulations (7 did not return data, 4 outliers excluded), and panel c shows 103 simulations (28 did not return data). Dotted lines represent zero.

The hundreds of ex ante economic simulations, predominately in the form of CGE analyses calibrated on developed countries, have failed to resolve the double dividend debate. In fact, as early critics pointed out, the issue is not resolvable as a general matter: positive effects on employment and output generally emerge for certain key parameters (Fullerton and Gravelle 1998). Notable among these are the numerous response elasticities (for example, income elasticities of energy demand) that vary substantially across countries and are weakly associated to national income (Huntington, Barrios, and Arora 2017).

However, existing studies may understate ETR's potential positive effects on economic activity in developing countries. In addition to general issues arising from ex ante modeling (see box 1.2), most simulations have until now been calibrated to developed countries. As a result, prior findings of ETR studies may reveal less about likely effects of ETR on developing countries. More recent studies have revealed several contextual factors (or channels) that are likely to determine whether ETR results in a double dividend. Many of these channels are important in developing countries (for details refer to appendix A), and the most important are large informal sectors and highly distortive tax systems.

Informal sector interactions

The informal sector, or "shadow economy," tends to be relatively untaxed compared with the formal sector. Agents in the informal sector avoid paying certain direct taxes like income taxes; in fact, avoidance of taxes is an important motivation for informality (La Porta and Shleifer 2014).[19] The presence of the informal sector increases the costs of generating revenue through direct taxes (Piggott and Whalley 2001). If a government has a fixed revenue requirement, informality increases the rates of tax required on the formal sector by reducing the overall tax base. This imbalance exacerbates welfare losses associated with the tax system.

Informality is a drag on growth. The disincentive from direct taxes for workers and firms to join the formal sector poses many challenges to countries' development. Informal firms face a disincentive to take on additional workers because they fear attracting the tax authorities' attention. Informality also prevents the effective use of liability systems, and contract and property law, thus constraining business transactions, which in turn creates a drag on output (see, for example, Acemoglu, Johnson, and Robinson 2000). Informality also prevents the economy from allocating resources optimally because, in the presence of informality, "allocation is determined not by productivity but by "fiscally effective" productivity" (Markandya, González-Eguino, and Escapa 2013). Each of these factors means that countries could see large gains by rebalancing the burden of taxation from the formal to the informal sector.

ETR creates the opportunity for countries to do so. In shifting the tax burden from the formal to the informal sector, ETR reduces the relative opportunity costs of formality. In addition, this broadening of the tax base improves the efficiency of the tax system (see the discussion in "Distortive tax systems") while boosting the functioning and the neutrality of the VAT system, effects that are further enhanced when the ETR is designed as an upstream tax with downstream rebates (refer to appendix A for detail). These effects stimulate the growth of the formal sector, and therefore of the economy.

Evidence from simulations suggests that the effect on economic activity can be substantial, including in developed countries. In the United States, where the informal sector accounts for just 9 percent of GDP, incorporating the above effects reduced the estimated costs of mitigation by 62 percent (Bento, Jacobsen, and Liu 2017). In Spain, where informality accounts for 20 percent of GDP, the inclusion of informal sector interactions in one study resulted in an estimated 7 percent rise in GDP and a 3 percent decrease in unemployment (Markandya, González-Eguino, and Escapa 2013).

Effects are likely to be even greater in developing countries, which tend to have larger informal markets. Accordingly, recent simulations for China, India, and the Islamic Republic of Iran—which include consideration of informal sector interactions—suggest that ETR can increase GDP (Carson, Jacobsen, and Liu 2014; Bento, Jacobsen, and Liu 2017; Mirhosseini, Mahmoudi, and Valokolaie 2017). This finding undermines the perception of a trade-off between environmental and economic objectives, particularly in developed countries. Reducing informality could make ETR economically desirable for many developing countries, even *before* considering effects on the environment and other welfare co-benefits.

Distortive tax systems

ETR also presents opportunities to improve the tax system in developing countries, which can raise economic activity. In general, prospects for ETR to generate positive effects on economic activity are stronger where preexisting tax systems are more distortive. For example, the costs of raising an additional unit of revenue (marginal costs of public funds) tend to rise as the tax base becomes narrower. Developing countries tend to have narrower tax bases and, as a result, more distortive and economically costly tax systems (the excess burden of taxation is higher because of larger deadweight losses). Expanding tax bases through environmental taxation and using revenues to reduce more distortive taxes can reduce the overall macroeconomic cost of public funds (welfare losses due to taxation). Reducing these losses improves the economic efficiency of the tax system, and hence economic activity.

ETR also creates the opportunity to implement two policies long known in the economics of optimal taxation to be economically desirable: Ramsey taxation and taxing Ricardian rents. The efficiency of the tax systems increases if rates are higher for goods that are demanded inelastically (*Ramsey taxation*). Because the price elasticity of demand for many polluting products such as fuel is low compared to other goods, environmental taxation can be a way to implement Ramsey taxation without high administration costs, thereby increasing the efficiency of the tax system. In addition, environmental taxes can allow governments to capture a portion of the rents from natural resource extraction. *Ricardian rents* are windfall gains not due to the risk-taking efforts of firms, unlike economic profits that are earnings arising from risk-taking efforts. In an efficient economy, rent-seeking activities (where there is no effort to incentivize) would be discouraged relative to profit-seeking activities (which generate output but require effort). Accordingly, the optimal taxation literature suggests that rents should be taxed at higher rates than profits. Natural resource extraction tends to have a larger proportion of Ricardian rents than other economic activities; environmental taxes can capture a portion of the rents from natural resource extraction, which is possible irrespective of the point of tax (upstream or downstream) or point of extraction (domestic or overseas). Environmental taxes can therefore reduce economic distortions by encouraging profit-seeking activities compared to rent-seeking activities (see "Channels affecting output and employment effects of ETR" in appendix A for more detail).

Last, ETR can help improve the efficiency of the tax system by tackling tax evasion while reducing compliance costs for firms and households. Environmental taxes tend to be much easier to collect than many other taxes, especially direct income taxes; therefore, shifting from income taxes to environmental taxes can reduce the costs of tax evasion. As a result, the costs of environmental taxation are drastically smaller in countries with larger preexisting tax evasion. For example, taking into account tax evasion effects, Liu (2013) finds that "in countries with high levels of pre-existing tax evasion, a carbon tax will pay for itself through improvements in the efficiency of the tax system." In addition, environmental taxes can be levied on a small number of taxpayers, especially upstream taxes on fossil fuel extraction or import. Reducing the number of taxpayers can reduce the overall costs of compliance of the tax system.

Other channels

In addition to informality and tax system optimization opportunities, several other channels increase the likelihood that ETR will have positive effects on economic activity (see "Channels affecting output and employment effects of ETR" in appendix A for more detail).

For developing countries these channels include the following:

- **Low labor market skills:** Demand and supply for unskilled labor are more elastic than for skilled labor. Countries with relatively more unskilled labor should see a larger response from reduced labor taxes—especially social security contributions—and therefore stronger prospects for employment and output dividends.
- **Improved energy efficiency and productivity:** Environmental taxation encourages energy efficiency enhancements among firms and households. This can raise factor productivity, foster more cost-competitive industries, and enhance growth.

Additionally, the following channels may make double dividends more likely for both developed and developing countries:

- **Involuntary unemployment:** Unemployment can be, in part, *involuntary*, for example because of deficiencies in labor demand. With involuntary unemployment, a cut in labor taxes paid by firms (for example, social security contributions or other payroll taxes) would reduce the cost of labor and may therefore increase overall employment.
- **Induced technological change and competitiveness:** Environmental taxation increases innovations among affected firms. These innovations are additional and may allow firms to reap scale economies, improving productivity and international competitiveness. However, as noted above, the empirical evidence for strong innovation and competitiveness effects from ETR in developed countries is mixed. The effects in developing countries are less clear, although chapter 2 provides encouraging empirical evidence.
- **Imperfect competition in goods markets:** In perfectly competitive markets input cost shocks (such as an environmental tax) are fully passed through to prices (because firms are price-takers and make zero profits). In markets with imperfect competition, pass-through may be less than one because firms with market power must consider the effect of price changes on demand. As a result, capital absorbs part of the costs, reducing the cost to labor of an environmental tax, potentially raising consumer welfare.

Welfare co-benefits

As noted above, ETR can have direct effects on measures of human well-being along with indirect effects via increased economic activity. These so-called co-benefits are often overlooked, but they can be large. In the case of GHG emissions abatement, co-benefits can in many cases dwarf the benefits of reduced climate risks.

Improved air quality

The burning of fossil fuels can result in large amounts of local air pollution, with costs to health and productivity. In addition to the emissions of GHGs, localized pollutants such as PM2.5 and black carbon can damage human health, raising morbidity and mortality risks. These and other localized pollutants are disproportionately concentrated in developing countries, and their costs can be monetized and included when setting optimal environmental tax rates (see "Market efficiency estimates," above).

The effect on air quality co-benefits of optimal corrective taxes can be substantial. A meta-analysis finds that incorporating air quality co-benefits raises optimal carbon tax rates by an average of US\$49/tCO_2 (Nemet, Holloway, and Meier 2010). The authors argue that, "because policy debates are framed in terms of cost minimization, policy makers are unlikely to fully value air quality co-benefits." Crucially, they find that development co-benefits from improved air quality are larger in developing countries (figure 1.14).

Despite the above findings, few double dividend or climate change mitigation studies include the indirect effects of improved air quality. Those that do find that co-benefits shift the way ETR is appraised. Markandya, González-Eguino, and Escapa (2012), for example, find a small gain or loss in welfare from ETR, but

FIGURE 1.14

Air quality cobenefits tend to be larger in developing countries

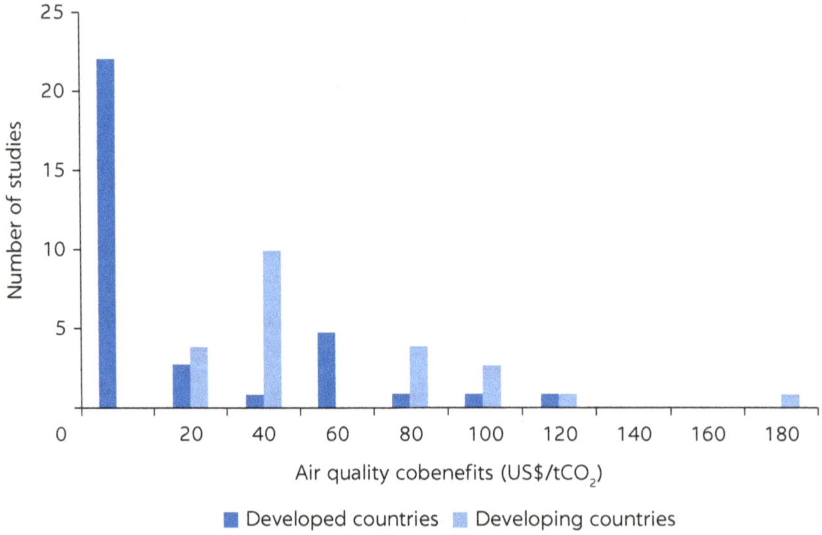

Source: Nemet, Holloway, and Meier 2010.
Note: Histogram shows the number of studies finding different values of the monetized benefits of environmental tax reform from improved local air quality (for example, through health improvements). Cobenefits are expressed as the value in US\$/tCO_2 (US\$ per tonne of CO_2) abated.

this rises to a large (2–3 percent) increase in welfare when including indirect effects from reduced local air pollution. As with assuming perfect labor markets or no informal economy, excluding air quality co-benefits from studies of ETR systematically biases welfare effects estimates downward in general and for developing countries.

Reduced congestion and road accidents

In a rapidly urbanizing world, with over half of the population living in cities, congestion has become a major economic problem. The mispricing of motor fuels, lack of availability of low-cost public transportation, and underfunding of transport infrastructure mean that overconsumption of private car transportation affects firms and households. For firms, congestion effectively shrinks business markets, reduces the agglomeration economies of businesses operating in urban areas, and raises production costs (Weisbrod, Vary, and Treyz 2003). These factors can create a significant drag on growth.

In addition to its effects on the economy, congestion significantly impedes consumer welfare. For households, congestion extends effective commuting distance, negatively affecting measures of happiness (decreased energy, increased stress, and higher illness-related work absences [Hansson et al. 2011]), and worsening physical health (raised blood pressure, lower physical activity, and increased risk of obesity [Hoehner et al. 2012]). For road users and pedestrians, the overconsumption of private car transport due to underpriced gasoline and the absence of corrective taxes imposes costs in the form of road accidents. The numerous economic costs of these accidents include increased medical expenses, legal and court costs, police and fire services costs, property damage, economic output losses, and grief and suffering imposed on victims, families, and friends (Santos et al. 2010). In theory, these costs can be internalized if they are covered by private risk-based insurance. In the United States, however, only about half of these costs are covered by private insurance (Blincoe et al. 2002), and coverage is likely to be even less in developing countries, where motor insurance penetration is low (HERE and Swiss Re 2015). As a result, few of the social costs of road accidents are likely to be internalized in developing countries, which is a significant development problem.

Developing countries have significantly higher incidences of road deaths and injuries (figure 1.15). Lower- and middle-income countries suffer 90 percent of both the 1.25 million worldwide road traffic deaths and the 20 million to 30 million nonfatal road crash injuries, despite having only half the world's motor vehicles (WHO 2015). In 2013, low- and middle-income countries had significantly worse road death rates per capita than high-income countries (figure 1.15). Some 48 of the 50 worst-scoring countries were developing countries. Most of these were in Africa, which had the highest fatality rate (at 26.6 per 100,000 of population), compared to Europe, which had the lowest (9.3) (WHO 2015). With increasing rates of motorization and urbanization, the problem is likely to get worse.

Besides the negative direct effects on human welfare, evidence shows that these road deaths and injuries indirectly affect welfare in developing countries by holding back economic growth. As a World Bank report notes, developing countries are less able to finance improvements in road design, maintenance, and traffic enforcement. However, "road safety is a prerequisite for stable and sustainable economic development" (World Bank

FIGURE 1.15

Road death rates are higher in developing countries, 2013

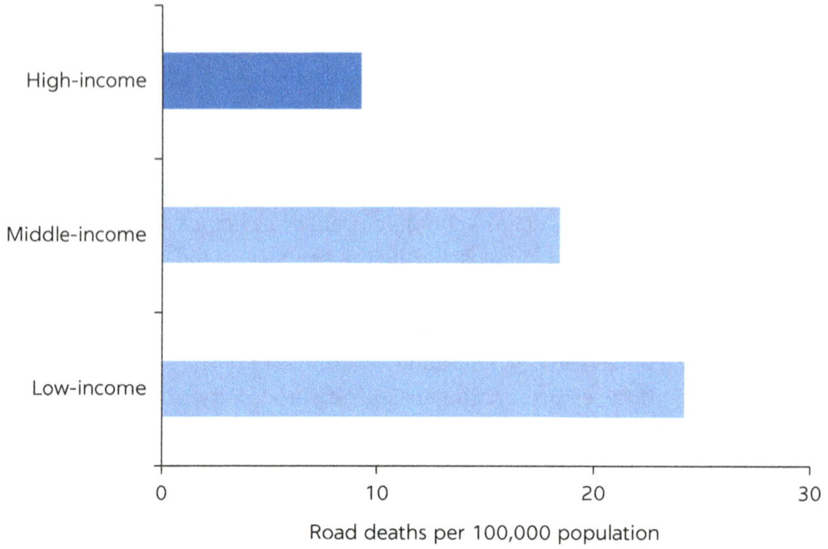

Source: WHO 2015.

Group 2017). Because road accidents disproportionately affect people in their most productive years, the costs from accidents have ripple effects across the economy, "well beyond the cumulative effect on households" (World Bank Group 2017). Cutting road deaths and injuries could therefore yield large increases in output by increasing labor productivity and labor supply, enhancing the ability of people to acquire education and skills, and freeing up savings for investment into physical and intellectual capital. For example, halving road deaths over a 24-year period could result in a 7.1 percent increase in GDP in Tanzania, 7.2 percent in the Philippines, and 14 percent in India (World Bank Group 2017).

One method for potentially reducing costly road injuries and fatalities is the use of corrective motor fuel taxes. The difference between road death rates in developing and developed countries is principally due to the inability of the developing countries to finance improvements in road design, maintenance, and traffic enforcement (World Bank Group 2017). Low motor fuel prices play a role in this problem. By incentivizing more efficient levels of road use (through decreased mileage), corrective taxes can reduce the risks of accidents on roads.[20]

International evidence suggests that fuel prices and road death rates are strongly correlated (figure 1.16). Controlling for other variables, one study of 144 countries finds a causal[21] link between the two: a 10 percent increase in gasoline pump prices reduces road fatalities by between 3 and 6 percent (Burke and Nishitateno 2015).[22] Given that 90 percent of road accident fatalities occur in developing countries, this finding suggests that a 10 percent increase in gasoline prices could save approximately 34,000 to 68,000 lives per year in developing countries, sparing perhaps several hundreds of thousands more from injuries. The direct co-benefits of "getting fuel prices right" through ETR could therefore be substantial, both by cutting congestion and reducing costly road accidents.

FIGURE 1.16

Road deaths are strongly associated with gasoline prices, 2010

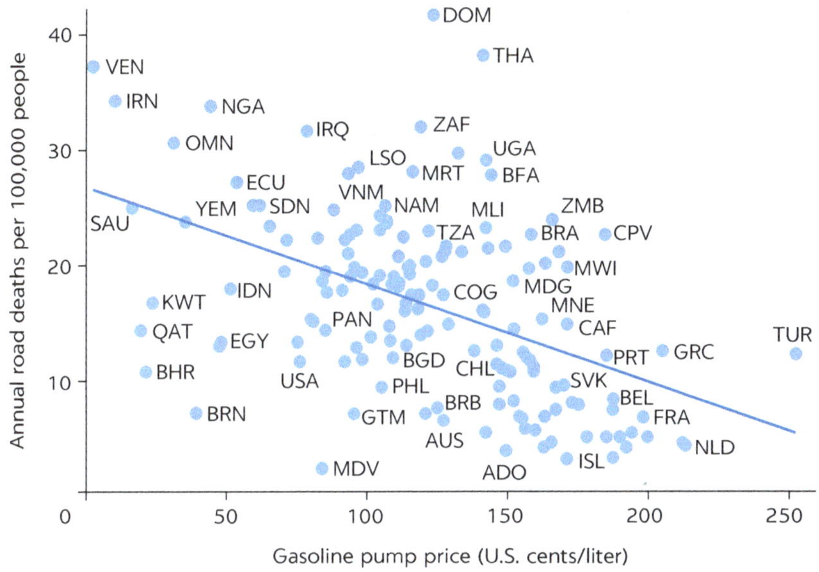

Source: Burke and Nishitateno 2015.
Note: Figure shows the negative association between gasoline prices (x axis) and annual rates of road deaths (y axis) across countries (R-squared not available).

How big are the effects of these channels?

This chapter has identified many channels through which ETR may positively affect welfare in developing countries. This includes channels that affect estimates from simulations (involuntary unemployment, informal sector interactions, tax optimization opportunities, imperfect goods competition, labor skills composition, and induced technological change) as well as co-benefits channels (improved air quality and health, and reduced congestion and road accidents). Studies comparing the effects of these various channels in general, or for developing countries, are lacking at present.

Figure 1.17 is a first attempt at illustrating quantitatively the potential effects of these various channels. Under several simplifying assumptions, the figure shows the range of estimates of the impact of these channels on welfare (blue bars) as well as a best-guess estimate of the likely average impact for developing countries. These estimates give a rough indication of the potential individual effects these channels could have on welfare (for notes on construction of the chart, see "Estimated effects of channels" in appendix A).

Some channels appear to be more important for welfare in general and for developing countries in particular. The informal sector, the possibility of taxing natural resource (Ricardian) rents, and air quality improvements appear to be more significant for developing countries. Given the potentially larger effects from these channels, policy makers evaluating ETR should pay close attention to them. Goods market competition, labor skills competition, and induced technological change are comparatively less important for developing countries but are nonetheless likely to positively affect welfare estimates. The key point is that excluding these channels from appraisals, such as those incorporating CGE models, is likely to bias estimates of ETR's welfare effects downward.

FIGURE 1.17

Channels that impact estimated welfare effects of ETR: Range of estimates from studies and possible effects for developing countries

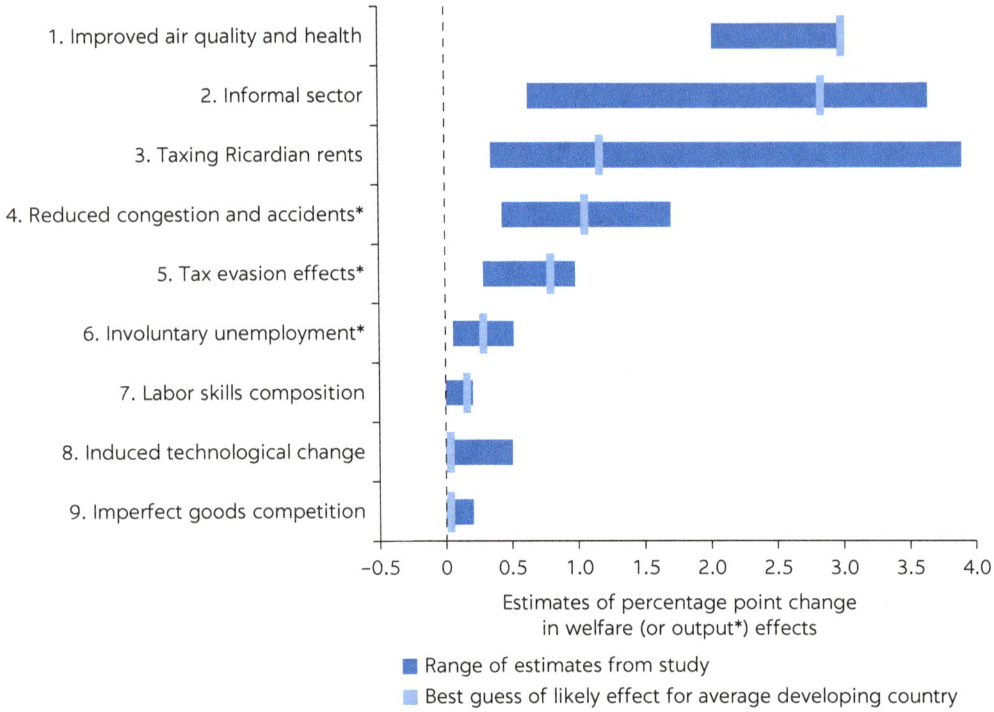

Sources: Based on data from Bento and Jacobsen 2007; Markandya, González-Eguino, and Escapa 2012; Liu 2013; Orlov, Grethe, and McDonald 2013; Burke and Nishitateno 2015; Pereira, Pereira, and Rodrigues 2016; Liu and Yamagami 2017; Bento, Jacobsen, and Liu 2017; World Bank Group 2017.
Note: Refer to "Estimated effects of channels" in appendix A for detailed sources and notes. Dark blue bars display the range of potential effects of channels discussed in this chapter of ETR's impact on output or consumer welfare (* indicates the effect is measured in terms of output). Light blue bars give a rough indication (best guess) of likely effect for an average developing country, depending on characteristics discussed in studies (for example, size of informal sector). All estimates have a high degree of uncertainty. ETR = environmental tax reform.

Note, however, that figure 1.17 does not include channels for which estimates were unavailable—such as preexisting tax system distortions, broadening tax bases, taxing leisure higher than labor, improving the tax neutrality of the VAT system, Ramsey efficiency, improved energy efficiency among firms and households, domestic resource mobilization, increased energy security, and other governmental objectives not explicitly related to output or welfare. Some of these channels could be estimated using existing or new models, whereas others will require a qualitative assessment on behalf of policy makers.

In addition, questions remain about the combined impact of these various effects. Determining how big that impact is on estimated output and welfare effects of ETR depends partly on the relationship between effects—how they interact to amplify or reduce the combined estimated economic effect. Few studies have examined this issue or sought to combine a number of these channels into one cohesive model, but the studies identified here can aid in understanding the likely impact on modeling estimates for other developing countries (table 1.1). Because few studies combine more than one of the

TABLE 1.1 **Findings of studies that incorporate multiple effects**

STUDY	COUNTRY	CHANNELS COMBINED	FINDINGS
Marsiliani and Renström (2000)	Italy	Imperfect goods market competition and imperfect labor markets	Find a strong double dividend that increases with the degree of assumed goods and labor market imperfections.
Markandya, González-Eguino, and Escapa (2012)	Spain	Involuntary unemployment, labor skills composition, informal sector, and cobenefits from reduced local air pollution	Find a gain in employment of 3.5 percent and a small loss or gain in consumer welfare, rising to a large increase (2–3 percent) in welfare when including the benefits of reduced local pollutants. Find welfare effects would be even higher with imperfect goods market competition.
Carson, Jacobsen, and Liu (2014)	China and the United States	Taxing Ricardian rents, tax evasion, and informal sector interactions	Find a strong double dividend (negative economic costs) in both countries for a large range of emissions reductions. They also find the gains are higher for China, and argue that the results extend to many other developing countries
Pereira and Pereira (2016)	Portugal	Involuntary unemployment and labor skills composition	Find a strong double dividend and argue that ignoring these labor market effects leads to "systematic underreporting" of the economic gains from environmental tax reform.

effects discussed in this chapter, it is not currently possible to quantify whether interactions between various effects are summative, dilutive, or synergistic, and what the combined effect will be. However, the sign of combined effects appears to be maintained when considering multiple channels.

Key mechanisms, assumptions, and uncertainties on the effects of ETR on development and welfare are described in detail in appendix A. But, combined, these channels suggest that prospects for expanded economic output and raised welfare in developing countries are stronger than in developed countries.

WHAT IS ETR'S EFFECT ON EQUITY, POVERTY, AND COMPETITIVENESS?

Environmental taxation and ETR can affect other government objectives beyond the environment, output, and employment. Notable are distributional equity, poverty, and international competitiveness.

Distributional equity and poverty

In certain circumstances, environmental taxation can have regressive effects on income distribution. Many studies in developed countries, in particular for North America, have found that environmental taxation negatively affects poorer households more than it does wealthier households—as a proportion of their incomes (OECD 2006). Although wealthier households are likely to bear a larger *absolute portion of the burden of taxation*, in certain circumstances the poor may be more affected *relative to their own income.*

However, the reality is complex (see box 1.3). Consumption patterns vary across a country's income distribution. Accordingly, the effects of environmental taxes on equity depend on a variety of factors, notably the type of tax (for example, taxes on fuels, electricity, forestry, transport, waste, sanitation, and so on) and country characteristics (for example, consumer preferences and assets such as car ownership). Effects also vary across tax bases. For example, the poor in some countries consume different fuels than

BOX 1.3

Factors determining the distributional effects of ETR

Distributional effects (across income groups and generations) of environmental taxes vary significantly across countries and tax types because of a variety of factors. These factors include the following:

- *Definitions of income*: Different proxies for well-being give different distributional results. Consumption-based measures, which are arguably better proxies for well-being than reported annual income, tend to show more progressive effects (Metcalf and Hassett 2012).
- *Time*: Distributional effects (on current generations) tend to be more progressive in the long term. Given the credit constraints of the poor, it can take them longer to adjust than richer households. For example, the poor may be more locked into high-energy capital purchased on the basis of low fuel prices (Cockburn, Robichaud, and Tiberti 2017).
- *Development levels*: Poor households in rich countries tend to spend a larger portion of their income on polluting goods than poor households in relatively poorer countries (Sterner 2012).
- *Demand responses*: In cases where the elasticity of demand for fuel is greater for poor households than for richer ones, environmental taxes are more distributionally progressive (Stolper 2016).
- *Factor incomes*: Environmental taxes can affect factor returns, predominately affecting upper-income groups (Dissou and Siddiqui 2014; Beck et al. 2015; Metcalf and Hassett 2012; Rausch, Metcalf, and Reilly 2011). Taxes should therefore be more progressive in countries with higher concentrations of factor ownership or where capital returns are a small portion of income for the poor.
- *Industrial structure*: Pollution tends to be concentrated in capital-intensive industries. Environmental taxation can then cause a shift toward labor-intensive production (as shown in chapter 2), creating opportunities for the poor.
- *Distribution of averted damages*: The costs of environmental degradation (like local air pollution or depletion of common natural resources) and environmental risks (like damages from climate change) tend to be heavily concentrated on the poor (World Bank 2005). The benefits from averting these damages and mitigating risks tend to be socially progressive.
- *Tax bases*: Some fuels that pose greater health risks tend to be consumed more, as a proportion of income, by the poor (for example, kerosene and charcoal) than others (for example, diesel and natural gas) (IEA 2016). Taxes that internalize health costs may therefore disproportionately affect the prices of goods consumed by the poor. By contrast, environmental taxes on the extraction of large natural resource assets such as oil reserves are generally progressive. This is also because the benefits of extraction tend to accrue to larger producers that are often foreign-owned. By contrast, taxes on small-scale extraction like small-scale timber or fisheries can be regressive (World Bank 2005).
- *Revenue usage*: The biggest determinant of ETR's overall effect on distribution is revenue usage. A portion of revenues can be used to compensate low-income groups by reducing labor taxes on low-income earners (social security and payroll) or through lump sum rebates. Using ETR revenues to lower capital taxes is regressive, and reducing national debt tends to favor later generations at the expense of current generations. Redistributing revenues through lump sum transfers can result in substantial reductions in inequality (Guillaume, Zytek, and Reza Farzin 2011; Sdralevich et al. 2014; Böhringer et al. 2017; Metcalf and Hassett 2012; Horowitz et al. 2017).

Because of these factors, environmental taxes tend to be more progressive in developing countries than developed countries. However, circumstances vary significantly. As a result, while all appraisals of ETR should consider context, distributional analyses need to be carefully tailored to country and tax design circumstances.

the wealthy. In China, the poorest spend a larger share of income on coal-powered electricity whereas the wealthy spend more on fuel (Jiang, Ouyang, and Huang 2015). In Ghana, those in the poorest quintile spend a larger share of their income on kerosene than on gasoline, diesel, or liquid propane (Cooke et al. 2016).

Crucially, environmental taxation is more likely to be progressive in developing countries than in developed countries. Several factors that determine the distributional effects of environmental taxes (see box 1.3) are tilted toward progressivity in developing countries. For example, poorer households in poorer countries tend to spend a lower portion of income on polluting goods than poorer households in wealthy countries. India, for example, has low levels of car ownership and access to electricity among the poor. As a result, fuel and coal taxes are likely to have progressive effects (Parry, Mylonas, and Vernon 2017). Combined with expenditure policies on expanding energy access or social spending in an ETR, the reform would be even more progressive. A meta-analysis of 21 country studies found that taxes on motor fuels were progressive in 10 of the 12 developing countries studied (figure 1.18), and most regressive in the United States on which most of the existing distributional literature on ETR focused.

Because the burden of environmental taxes tends to be more evenly shared across the population in developing countries, targeted compensation may still be needed to protect the incomes of the poorest. Although the burden of taxation may be progressive, without appropriate expenditure policies it can still entail net income losses for the poorest. As a result, poverty could still rise. Without supplementary policies to compensate low-income households, environmental taxes can negatively affect a government's equity objectives.

Fortunately, governments need only a small portion of revenue to compensate low-income groups. In Europe and the United States, less than 12 percent of the tax revenues would be sufficient to compensate the poorest 20 percent for the distributional impacts of a broad-based carbon tax (Vivid Economics 2012; Dinan 2015).[23] In developing countries, where environmental taxes are more likely to be progressive, revenues required for compensation would likely be even less, and can be funneled through a variety of methods (see "Compensating low-income households," below).

Overall, then, concerns about distributional equity and poverty are not strong justifications for maintaining low environmental taxes. Even in instances where the poorest lose out in relative terms, only a small portion of environmental revenues is needed to compensate and protect lower-income groups. For low-income countries, the availability and capability of compensatory mechanisms (for example, through the tax system) need to be carefully evaluated before undertaking ETR. However, environmental taxes are less likely to be regressive in these countries (given factors described above), and so compensation schemes are also less likely to be needed in low-income contexts.

In absolute terms, failing to tax environmental externalities is regressive. With fossil fuel subsidies, for example, a clear majority of the benefits (in the form of consuming subsidized fuel) accrue to the wealthiest members of society. Using a sample of 20 developing countries, researchers found that, on average, the top 25 percent of households capture six times more in subsidies than the bottom 25 percent (Arze del Granado, Coady, and Gillingham 2012).

FIGURE 1.18

Fuel taxes tend to be progressive in developing countries (select countries)

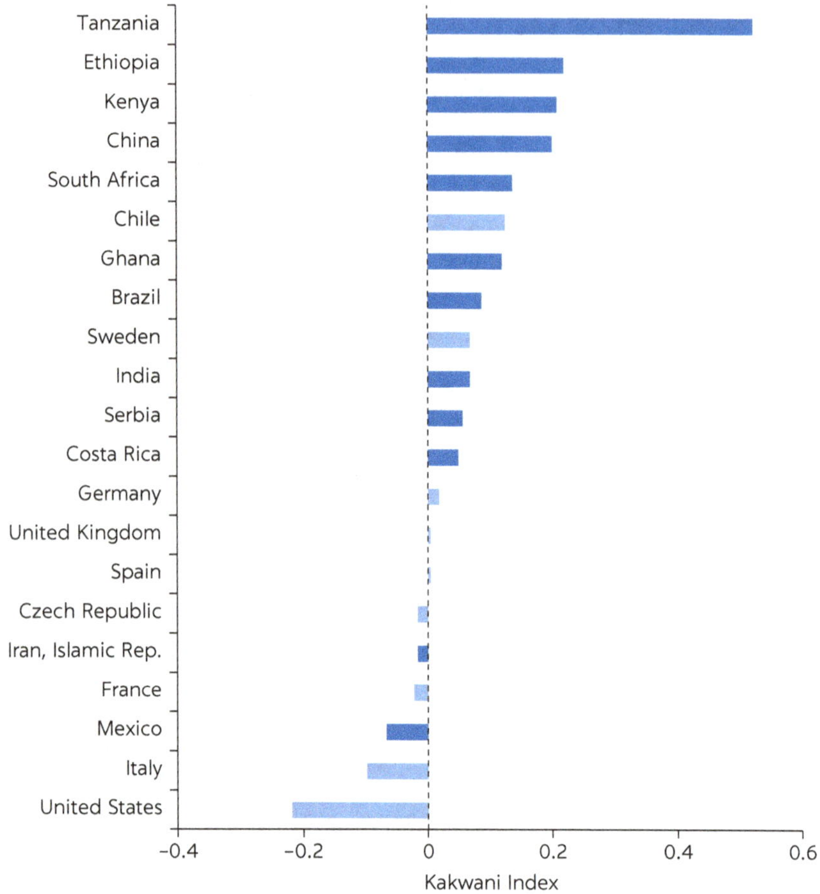

Source: Sterner et al. 2012.

Note: Figure shows the estimated progressivity of direct and indirect effects of motor fuel taxes in 21 countries: 12 developing (dark blue bars) and 9 developed (light blue bars). The Kakwani Index equals zero for a tax that does not change the prior income distribution of the country, is positive for progressive changes, and negative for regressive changes. Of the 12 developing countries studied, only 2 showed regressive effects (Mexico and the Islamic Republic of Iran).

In Indonesia, the top 30 percent of households capture 70 percent of the benefits of fossil fuel subsidies (Dartanto 2013); and, in Ghana, the top 5 percent capture 78 percent of the benefits (Cooke et al. 2016). Likewise, most of the benefits from failing to tax environmental externalities (of consuming polluting products that have externalized costs not reflected in prices) are reaped by the wealthiest. Further, a large portion of the welfare costs of environmental externalities—including increased mortality and morbidity and depletion of common pool resources—falls on the poor.

International competitiveness

Chapter 2 analyzes the effect of ETR on firm productivity and international competitiveness. The key message is that, under special conditions, an increase in energy prices, such as that under an ETR, can have positive effects on firm productivity and therefore may positively affect competitiveness. In addition, any residual negative effect can be managed. Where the government has identified industries it would like to protect, ETR can be adjusted to accommodate this objective (albeit subject to trade-offs with other objectives such as revenue-raising). Some ways of managing competitiveness effects are more desirable than others (see chapter 2).

HOW SUITABLE IS ETR FOR DEVELOPING COUNTRIES?

Having examined the effects of ETR on economic, environmental, and other government objectives, policy makers must also consider the suitability of such reforms for developing countries. This entails consideration of political economy factors—specifically, the likely political and administrative feasibility of ETR needs to be evaluated and contrasted with other environmental policies. An environmental policy that might be cost-effective for achieving an environmental objective may still be infeasible because of political economy considerations. If, for example, a large share of the burden falls on emitting firms, they may be more powerful politically than nonemitters. Or the burden could disproportionately affect low-income groups, whom governments should seek to protect. Both effects impact the political support that ETR is likely to face among firms and households (see "Building political support," below).

Alternatively, an instrument may be cost-effective and politically feasible, but administratively too challenging. ETSs, such as the European Union's ETS or the United States' Regional Greenhouse Gas Initiative, could theoretically result in the same level of emissions abatement as an emissions tax, assuming the price trajectories are the same. However, an ETS can entail additional complexity in design and implementation, and may therefore be more difficult to implement in contexts with limited administrative capability.

Table 1.2 offers an approximation of comparative economic, political, and administrative attributes of environmental policies for developing countries. In general, ETR is more cost-effective than regulations, while being easier to administer than ETSs. As noted earlier, ETR can have some negative effects on distributional equity and low-income households in certain circumstances, but these effects can be neutralized using a small portion of the revenues raised. In addition, although the burden with ETR tends to fall more on high-emitting firms compared with ETSs (which tend to allocate permits at least in part through free-allocation) and regulations, efficient protections for affected firms can be designed in the form of output-based rebates or by applying ETR through consumption-based excise taxes (see chapter 2).

The discussion above does not fully capture the numerous complexities in design and implementation that affect feasibility of alternative control instruments. Notably, governments may be effective at building broad political support among firms and households for ETR, irrespective of relative burden shares (see "Building political support," below). However, in terms of economic cost-effectiveness and political and administrative feasibility, ETR appears to be well suited to developing countries.

TABLE 1.2 **Attributes of alternative environmental control instruments**

	ECONOMIC COST-EFFECTIVENESS			POLITICAL FEASIBILITY		ADMINISTRATIVE FEASIBILITY
	FIRM AND INDUSTRY LEVEL[a]	ECONOMY-WIDE, STATIC[b]	ECONOMY-WIDE, DYNAMIC[c]	FIRM SUPPORT: LOW BURDEN ON EMITTERS	HOUSEHOLD SUPPORT: LOW BURDEN ON POORER HOUSEHOLDS	EASE OF ADMINISTRATION
Environmental tax reform (ETR):						
ETR	✓	✓	✓	×	✓	✓
Emissions trading systems (ETSs):						
Auctioned permits	✓	✓	✓	×	✓	×
Freely-allocated permits	✓	✓	✓	✓	×	×
Direct regulation:						
Technology mandates	×	×	✓/×*	✓	✓	✓/×*
Performance standards	×	×	✓/×*	✓	✓	✓/×*

Sources: World Bank approximations; Goulder and Parry 2008.
Note: Table shows attributes of different environmental control instruments across three dimensions: cost-effectiveness (at firm/industry level, as well as static and dynamic across the entire economy), political feasibility (burden on emitters and equity), and administrative feasibility. Checkmarks indicate a given instrument has an advantage along the dimension in question. It does not mean other instruments have no impact on that dimension. Estimations assume that emissions taxes and ETSs with auctioned permits are revenue-neutral—that is, funds raised are recycled through a mix of reductions in more distortionary taxes and targeted compensation schemes to low-income households. * indicates that results depend on design.
a. Firm-level cost-effectiveness entails promoting the lowest-cost abatement choice across firms: input choice, end-of-pipe treatment, and output reduction. Industry-level cost-effectiveness entails promoting the equalization of marginal emissions reductions costs among heterogeneous firms.
b. Economy-wide static cost-effectiveness entails the minimization of general equilibrium costs (deadweight losses)—that is, by reducing more distortionary taxes.
c. Economy-wide dynamic cost-effectiveness entails incentivizing firms to invest in research, development, adoption, and diffusion of pollution-control technologies.

HOW CAN DEVELOPING COUNTRIES BEST IMPLEMENT ETR?

Although this chapter has identified several uncertainties around the general effects of ETR on a variety of governmental objectives, there is consensus over two decades of double dividend theory, ex ante simulations, and ex post empirical studies that design and implementation are crucial determinants of ETR's desirability and success. Positive overall effects on economic activity (output, employment, and innovation) and direct measures of well-being (for example, human health) are all possible with effective design and implementation of ETR. Likewise, negative effects on economic activity and welfare due to ineffective design and implementation are also possible.

This section addresses key issues in design and implementation of ETR, including drawing on lessons from experience, use of revenues, scope of taxation, and the need for supplementary policies. It also suggests potential "off-the-shelf" ETR designs for different types of countries.

Norms from experience

In designing and implementing ETRs, developing countries should first seek to apply the lessons learned by others—for example, experience with specific ETRs such as fuel taxes and explicit carbon taxation in Mexico, South Africa, and Turkey, and reforms with similar effects, such as energy price reform in Bolivia, Ghana, the Islamic Republic of Iran, Jordan, Malaysia, Morocco, and Nigeria (for details refer to appendix A).

By applying the following norms, countries can increase their chances of success with ETR:

- Policy makers should work to ensure that ETRs are *fair*, *aligned* with other objectives, *stable* and predictable, *transparent* in design and implementation, and focused on *market efficiency and cost-effectiveness*, and that the ETRs lead to *substantive reductions* in emissions (environmental effectiveness) and other harmful activities (these are the World Bank and OECD's "FASTER Principles" for carbon pricing; see box A.2 in appendix A).
- Reform strategies need to commence with a *well-sequenced comprehensive review* of the existing tax system to ensure policies are integrated with existing *monetary and fiscal* policies, are supplemented with *communications* strategies that raise public support, include specific *protections* for the most vulnerable, and are *implemented gradually* (these are the International Monetary Fund's "Rules of Thumb" for energy price reform; see box A.3 in appendix A).

ETR design process

The World Bank's (2017) *Carbon Tax Guide* offers detailed guidance on designing and implementing carbon taxes (see figure 1.19). This guidance is also applicable

FIGURE 1.19
Stages of design for ETR

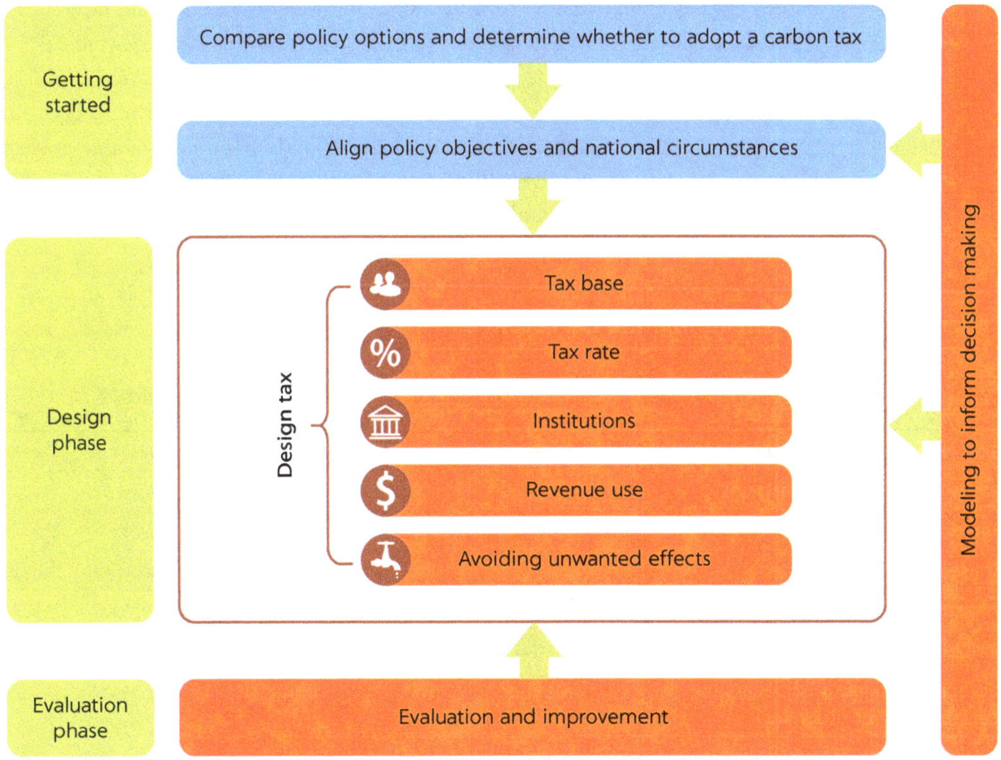

Source: World Bank 2017.
Note: Figure shows stages of defining the ETR from preimplementation (getting started and initial design) to post-implementation (evaluation and improvement) phases. This applies to carbon taxes and other environmental taxes.

to other ETRs beyond those that incorporate carbon taxation. The stages of design include the following:

- *Deciding* whether to adopt an ETR
- *Defining* objectives and national circumstances
- *Determining* the tax base, tax rate, and use of revenues
- *Ensuring* effective oversight and compliance
- *Evaluating* outcomes and improving the ETR design

ETR should be focused on achieving specific objectives, tailored to national circumstances, informed by modeling, and improved over time through evaluation. Specific design issues—notably revenue use, tax base and rates, and avoiding unwanted effects, including on competitiveness, poverty, and other side effects, through supplementary policies, as well as building political support—are discussed in the following sections.

Revenue use

One of the most important design decisions for ETR is what to do with environmental revenues. Revenues can be recycled (through reductions in other taxes) or used for expanding government expenditures (raising domestic resources mobilized for investments). Revenue use both determines likely effects on economic activity (especially output and employment) and affects the political support ETR is likely to receive from firms and households.

Table 1.3 outlines likely attributes of alternative allocation of environmental revenues. It shows how likely effects on economic efficiency, political support among firms and households, and ease of implementation by administrative bodies vary. No single use of revenues dominates economically and politically: there are trade-offs across economic, political, and administrative variables. For example, recycling revenues fully through reductions in labor taxes or capital taxes is regarded in the theoretical literature as being most efficient. This type of recycling minimizes economic costs at worst or yields a double dividend at best. However, households are more likely to prefer reduction in labor taxes whereas firms may prefer reduced capital taxes.

TABLE 1.3 **Attributes of alternative uses of environmental tax revenues**

TYPE OF USE	RECYCLING OR EXPENDITURE METHOD	ECONOMIC EFFICIENCY	POLITICAL SUPPORT: INDUSTRY	POLITICAL SUPPORT: HOUSEHOLDS	EASE OF IMPLEMENTATION
Revenue-neutral recycling	Labor taxes (wage and social security contributions)	High	Low	High	High
	Capital taxes (profits and capital gains)	High	High	Low	High
	Lump sum transfers to households	Low	Low	High	Medium
	Output-based rebates to industry	Low	High	Low	Medium
Revenue-raising expenditures	Public infrastructure investments (energy, transport)	Medium	Medium	Medium	Medium
	Basic services (education, health, sanitation)	Medium	Low	High	Medium
	Social protection programs (social assistance, insurance, labor market programs)	Medium	Low	High	Medium
	National debt reduction (for heavily indebted country)	High	Medium	Low	High

Note: Table shows approximate relative attributes of different revenue-neutral recycling (reducing other taxes) and revenue-raising methods (raising overall tax-to-GDP ratios to spend on specific expenditures). Many complexities are not shown by the table—for example, import-competing firms may have different preferences across revenues than exporting or nontrading firms. As such, this is a rough approximation.

Mixed use of revenues is also possible and potentially desirable. Policy makers may deem that, in order to increase the environmental effectiveness of the policy, a portion of revenues should be set aside for complementary policies such as increasing public expenditure on green energy infrastructure and relevant research and development. Alternatively, policy makers may feel the need to recycle at least part of the revenues to maintain support among firms and households. By earmarking part of the revenues for recycling through reduced capital taxes, governments can at least partially compensate polluting firms while nonpolluting firms become net beneficiaries. This practice would come at some cost to market efficiency. At minimum, part of the revenues should be used for compensating any low-income households if they lose out from the reform.

Revenue use should therefore be tailored to a country's context and objectives. For example, countries with high levels of DRM should consider recycling revenue mostly through reductions in labor or capital taxes. By contrast, countries with low levels of DRM may find a mixture of revenue use, such as reducing the wage bill while moderately increasing the proportion of public spending in GDP, to be a pragmatic, welfare-enhancing form of ETR.

Tax base and rate

Other important design decisions are the environmental tax base and rates of taxation. For the tax base, policy makers should generally seek to cover as large a proportion of the environmental externality/externalities as possible but to minimize the number of entities that pay the tax. In this way, they ensure that environmental effectiveness is maximized at the lowest economic cost.[24] For example, for the external costs of climate change, taxes should cover as much of a jurisdiction's GHG emissions as possible. With fewer entities subject to the tax, compliance costs are minimized and the policy is more manageable, which is especially important where administrative capacities are low.

When taxing fuels, developing countries should consider taxing upstream rather than downstream. By taxing fuels as they enter the economy (through import or extraction), governments can effectively dissipate price effects down the supply chain and throughout the economy, maximizing the scope of emissions covered. In addition, upstream fuel taxes tend to entail taxing fewer entities (importing or extracting firms) compared to downstream emissions taxes (such as taxes on the pollution released from individual entities burning the fuel), which minimizes the administrative burden, both for firms and for government bureaucracy. In addition, upstream taxes can be an effective way of shifting the burden of taxation from the formal to the informal sector, which is especially desirable economically in developing countries. Many countries already have upstream fuel pricing systems, so ETR in these countries can be undertaken without a need for new administrative systems. ETR is therefore in reach even for countries where existing political impasses allow for only marginal adjustments to tax systems.

For rates of taxation, broadly, governments have two options: starting with low tax rates with commitment to gradualist increases to the socially desirable level, potentially buttressed by a commitment to specific future tax hikes, or a one-shot increase in tax rates to the social optimum.

A gradualist policy of lower initial tax rates may appear more politically desirable, but it has downsides and risks. Implementing low environmental taxes with a commitment to raise them over time may increase political support and allow for learning over time. However, there are two notable risks. First is the reduction in the positive effects of reform on economic activity and welfare co-benefits. Fewer available revenues mean fewer opportunities to improve the efficiency of the tax system through reducing other taxes, and fewer opportunities to invest in public infrastructure and expanded social services. The direct welfare co-benefits such as health improvements will also be lower. Second, low rates can become locked in politically, and then eroded over time by inflation, as has tended to be the case in OECD countries (OECD 2010a). Raising the rate later may then become harder.

Commitment device strategies could be used to support gradualism, but these are not failure-proof either. The government could commit to a pathway of future taxes, with subsequent hikes approved in subsequent legislative cycles. This strategy has been adopted by British Columbia (Canada), France, and Switzerland (Carattini et al. 2017), and more recently South Africa. However, future increases could trigger political opposition that could arise at each cycle. In 1991, the United Kingdom committed to raise its fuel taxes by a set percentage per year but abandoned the policy in 2000 (Seely 2011).

By contrast, immediately setting environmental taxes at the socially optimal level is the most economically desirable strategy, but higher initial public opposition may necessitate more proactive engagement. Taxes at the social optimum maximize the incentive effect of price signals toward undesirable activities, while maximizing the revenues available for improving the efficiency of the tax system or investing in public services. However, higher taxes may face more opposition (initially) than a gradualist strategy, particularly from those most affected by the reform. This approach therefore calls for more proactive engagement with the public and affected firms.[25]

Overall, environmental taxes should cover as much of the environmental externality as possible, be paid by as few entities as possible, and be set at their full external cost. Whether the last criterion is done immediately or gradually is an important decision that should weigh a country's economic, environmental, fiscal, and political economy factors.

Supplementary policies

This chapter has argued that tweaks in environmental taxation, such as fuel taxes, should be combined with changes in expenditure policies, such as reductions in labor taxes or increases in infrastructure investment. Because environmental taxation interacts with other policies, however, it may have undesirable impacts on other government objectives, such as poverty, equity, and competitiveness. Therefore, supplementary policies may be required to ensure reforms are environmentally effective while managing any undesirable effects on other government objectives. Notably, supplementary policies may be needed to manage interactions with other environmental policies, compensate low-income households, protect internationally competing firms, and manage any other undesirable consequences.

Managing environmental policy interactions

The environmental effectiveness of environmental taxation will be affected by the existence of other policies (complementary, overlapping, and countervailing). There is a strong consensus among economists of the cost-effectiveness of market-based instruments such as environmental taxation for controlling pollution (Reason 2 in the earlier section titled "Why ETR?"). However, taxation may not be a sufficient policy intervention to achieve a socially optimal outcome. The effectiveness and efficiency of environmental taxation can be constrained or enhanced by its interactions with other preexisting complementary, overlapping, or countervailing policies (box 1.4). These interactions need to be considered because they will influence the effectiveness of taxation in achieving its environmental objective.

When such interactions occur, supplementary policies may be needed to enhance the environmental effectiveness of ETR. The existence of other market failures beyond the external costs of emissions may limit the effectiveness of environmental taxes. For example, firms unable to internalize positive learning-by-doing knowledge spillovers will underinvest in low-carbon technology, creating a barrier to deeper decarbonization. Although environmental taxes can by themselves promote investments in innovation, they may need to be supplemented by complementary environmental policies (box 1.4). In this example of "double market failure" (pollution oversupply and innovation undersupply), taxation may be complemented by more targeted measures such as investment rebates that encourage the development or diffusion of energy efficiency innovations (OECD 2010b; Baranzini et al. 2017). In addition, governments can make complementary adjustments in public spending, such as increased investments in energy infrastructure (Siegmeier et al. 2015).

BOX 1.4

Environmental taxation's interactions with other environmental policies

Environmental taxation will tend to interact with other policies, and these interactions can reduce or amplify environmental effects. For example, for carbon taxation, the World Bank, Ecofys, and Vivid Economics (2016) identify three axes of interaction—complementarities, overlaps, and countervailing effects.

- *Complementary policies* are combined with environmental taxation in such a way as to increase the effectiveness of achieving emissions abatement.
- *Overlapping policies* operate in parallel to carbon pricing. Although often motivated by objectives other than climate mitigation, overlapping policies—such as subsidies for renewable energy and vehicle fuel efficiency standards—can trigger the same incentive effect as carbon pricing, and so contribute to emissions reduction. However, because of this overlap, they may also affect and create tension with the carbon-pricing signal. There may be an additional rationale for these overlapping policies, and policy makers need to consider adjustments to ensure policy alignment.
- *Countervailing policies* conflict with environmental taxes by negatively affecting the behavioral incentives faced by investors and consumers. For example, fossil fuel subsidies can still exist and undermine the price signal an environmental tax might offer. Often, these policies are unsuccessful or inefficient in achieving their stated objectives, for example, lowering the cost of energy for less affluent households. There are ways to achieve these objectives without distorting the intended price signal, such as through public investment in energy infrastructure. In addition, environmental taxes do not have to wait for the phasing out of countervailing policies like fossil fuel subsidies. Instead, taxes can be used as part of a package of gradual reforms of fossil fuel subsidies, for example by using revenues to help address political economy barriers to subsidy removal.

An important example for developing countries is the case of state-owned energy markets. The existence of a monopolistic, state-owned, vertically integrated utility may impede the effectiveness of ETR. In this case, price signals, and therefore incentive effects of an environmental tax, may be blunted. As a result, ETR may need to be complemented by energy market liberalization policies. The introduction of competition in energy generation and distribution would enable households and firms, alongside energy producers, to better respond to price signals (World Bank, Ecofys, and Vivid Economics 2016b). In this way energy market reform can be an important complement to ETR.

Compensating low-income households

The effects of environmental taxation on equity across households and generations will vary across countries and tax types (see "Distributional equity and poverty," above). For many developing countries the distributional effects of environmental taxes will be progressive. If these taxes result in net gains for the poor, there is no need for compensation. However, if they result instead in (absolute) losses for lower-income groups, this could threaten poverty objectives. Supplementary policies may therefore be required to ensure lower-income groups are compensated and poverty rates do not rise.

Compensation measures can reduce the negative impact of the tax on low-income households while maintaining the price signal (OECD 2006), and can be funneled to the poor using a variety of methods. Countries with large numbers of workers registered formally can use *direct per capita lump sum transfers*. Where administratively possible, these transfers can more than compensate low-income groups. For policy makers significantly weighting distributional objectives, ETR can be designed in this way to be highly progressive. In the United States, a number of studies have found revenue-neutral ETR—in the form of carbon taxes that recycle three-quarters of revenues through per capita lump sum payments—to be highly progressive (Metcalf and Hassett 2012; Klenert et al. 2016; Horowitz et al. 2017). Further, sharing the tax burden between households and firms (that is, when the assumption of complete pass-through is dropped to include changes in factor prices for capital and labor) increases that progressivity.

In addition, where income tax coverage is high, recycling revenues through *reduced labor taxes* is likely to be progressive, especially where the reduced taxes target low earners. Raising income tax thresholds or personal allowances could take many taxpayers out of the system, thereby disproportionately benefitting low-income groups while lowering administration and compliance costs.[26] However, if the poor do not pay income taxes anyway because of, for example, low levels of formality, then income tax recycling could theoretically be regressive if it raises the incomes of middle-income earners.

Recycling with lump sum transfers or reduced labor taxes may not be possible or effective in contexts with low levels of tax registration (for example, economies with high levels of informality or low income tax registration among households). However, *targeted cash transfers*—which have become increasingly popular among developing countries—can be used or expanded to achieve the same objective (Sdralevich et al. 2014; Cooke et al. 2016; Cockburn, Robichaud, and Tiberti 2017). As always, however, issues of undercoverage (missing certain poor households) and leakage (including households that are not poor) need to be managed with cash transfers.

Alternatively, revenues could be earmarked for *minimum basic incomes*. Experience with the Islamic Republic of Iran's fossil fuel subsidy reform is illustrative. In 2010–12, the country replaced its fuel subsidies with a minimum basic income, using 50 percent of the saved revenue (Guillaume, Zytek, and Reza Farzin 2011). This program was enough to reduce inequality dramatically—from a Gini coefficient of 0.42 to a coefficient of 0.34 (Salehi-Isfahani 2011).

Buffering the social impact of ETR with other subsidization strategies, such as food subsidies, is not generally desirable because of cost-ineffectiveness. Even food subsidies, which may be more easily targeted at the poor, "are generally not better targeted than uniform cash handout to the entire population" (Sdralevich et al. 2014). Both "food and fuel subsidies have been shown to be regressive and ineffective in terms of protecting the poorest" (Monchuk 2013), and so neither is a viable strategy.

Last, recycling through *capital taxes* is likely to be regressive. Because the benefits of reducing corporate income taxes are greater for richer households than for poorer ones, such a form of ETR would be regressive, even though it may raise economic growth (Metcalf 2007). In this case, compensatory policies may need to be even greater.

Protections for internationally competing firms

Although competitiveness effects of ETR are not necessarily negative in general, policy makers may seek to protect exporting and import-competing firms, in part to maximize political support among industry for reform. There are several ways to protect firms, but these are not equally effective. See chapter 2 for more detailed discussion of competitiveness.

Managing other undesirable effects

Countries should also design supplementary policies to address other likely undesirable effects of the reform. For example, a country with a large shadow economy and porous borders may find that raising fuel taxes significantly above those of neighboring countries results in increases in illegal fuel imports. These imports would reduce the economic and political desirability of the policy, but they may not be significant enough to alter the decision of whether to implement taxes (see the discussion of Turkey in appendix A). In another example, increasing the price of one polluting energy source like kerosene can result in suboptimal shifts to even worse energy sources like charcoal (box 1.5). Effects such as these need to be managed with appropriate, targeted supplementary policies.

Building political support

Building political support is crucial for ensuring effective and sustained ETR. Without the support of firms and households, ETR is likely to face significant obstacles at the implementation stage, and may not last long enough to have the desired economic, environmental, or fiscal impacts. Public support for ETR, however, tends to be low. Behavioral economics offers potential insights into why. Behavioral factors that can affect political support for ETR include concentrated losses, rational ignorance, discounting, beliefs about ETR, lack of trust in the government, risk aversion, perceived coercion of ETR, distributional concerns, and stigmatization of poverty (described more in appendix A).

BOX 1.5

Managing shifts to untaxed informal fuel substitutes

A complication exists for taxing cooking fuels in rural areas of developing countries. Increases in prices for "dirty" fuels like natural gas could increase demand for even "dirtier" fuels like fuelwood or waste incineration. In this scenario, effects on health can be worse for the population in these areas than in the "no tax" scenario. This problem occurs with the taxation of cooking fuels such as butane, kerosene, and coal in rural areas.

This inefficient substitution from taxed but dirty to untaxed and dirtier fuels can, however, be managed. The use of untaxed, informal fuels is closely associated to people's lack of access to formal sector fuels; therefore, a best practice is to supplement policies that increase fuel prices with policies that raise access to energy (PMR and ICAP 2016). Raising energy access can involve using a share of the expected revenues from the ETR to expand energy access to poorer households. In rural areas with concentrated informal consumption of firewood or charcoal, off-grid decentralized energy systems such as photovoltaic panels and solar water heaters may be provided through subsidies, and may be more desirable than expanding the grid. For example, China successfully improved access of remote rural households to modern energy while reducing the consumption of informal, substitute fuels. The World Bank has also supported gas-fired cooking stoves, in addition to renewable energy systems. A recent World Bank program in the Democratic Republic of Congo delivered cooking stoves that require only a quarter of the fuel used in standard stoves, making the poor more resilient to fuel price shocks in general.

There are strong development co-benefits to providing the poor with these more efficient technologies. Half of global deaths from air pollution arise from smoke inside houses. This number can be significantly reduced through expanded access to clean energy. Supplementary policies that increase access can help safeguard the welfare of the poor by providing them the means to move away from low-quality substitute energy to better-quality energy.

To overcome these barriers, policy makers can implement behavioral economics–informed strategies to build and maintain political support for ETR. They include the following:

- *Antedating of benefits:* Traditionally, the costs of ETRs accrue before most of the benefits. Paying compensation to households before, instead of after, the environmental tax is introduced can overcome several biases (such as discounting, lack of trust in the government, and risk aversion). The Islamic Republic of Iran, for example, formally locked compensation payments into personal bank accounts that were unfrozen on the day of energy price increase (box 1.6). As a result, the reforms were perceived as more credible and personally valuable.
- *Informational campaigns:* Informational campaigns are a primary means of communicating to the public the benefits of ETR. By setting clear expectations for citizens about the expected effects of reform, informational campaigns can reduce opposition that stems from risk aversion. Governments should communicate the net effects of reform, including revenue use. Campaigns should highlight local co-benefits and distributional consequences, and seek public endorsement from a variety of experts and leaders. Messages should be simple, framed within preexisting narrative and norms that prevail in the country, delivered in advance of reform, and diffused through traditional media (television, newspapers, and radio) and nontraditional media (texting and social media) to reach broad swathes of the public.

BOX 1.6

Antedating of benefits: The 2010 Iranian strategy

In 2010, the Islamic Republic of Iran embarked on a significant energy price reform. In one day, the government increased the consumer price of diesel by about 2,000 percent (Guillaume, Zytek, and Reza Farzin 2011). At the same time, the government provided significant compensation to households. At least 50 percent of the revenues were earmarked for household compensation, initially in the form of bimonthly cash transfers. In addition, 30 percent of the revenues were earmarked to support firms during the transition phase toward less energy-intensive production, and the remaining 20 percent were retained in the public sector.

Uniquely, the reform used antedated benefits: cash transfers were visible on bank accounts before and then released to citizens on the day of the price increase. Iranians were allocated frozen personal bank accounts in their name, which were visible via a website and publicized in the media in advance of the reform. Having already paid, or appeared to have paid, compensation into citizens' accounts, the government sent a stronger signal of its commitment to compensation. In addition, while the lock was in place, the government communicated that, if it had to abandon the fuel price increase because of opposition, it would not unlock the accounts. Because the compensation in these locked accounts amounted to very significant sums for most Iranians, the cash transfers and the locking mechanism provided a strong incentive for the population to support the reform's implementation (Guillaume, Zytek, and Reza Farzin 2011).

Public support for this reform was also raised by a large-scale informational campaign. Different types of media and a diverse set of communicators (politicians, business people, clerics, and researchers) were employed to reach different sections of society. The authorities also instituted phone hotlines to answer citizens' questions.

- *Broad consultation*: Consultation goes beyond informational campaigns, allowing stakeholders to directly influence policy. This engagement endows the reform with public legitimacy, while also allowing policy makers to communicate clearly its objectives (OECD 2006). Consultations should be as broad and transparent as possible to maximize the perceived legitimacy of the reform and to minimize risks that they become beholden to vested interests. They should also include input from a diverse set of experts.
- *Labeling ETR as subsidy reduction*: Taxes may be perceived as more coercive than the removal of subsidies. As a result, the public may be more supportive of policies that eliminate or reduce subsidies than of those that introduce or raise taxes. Environmental taxes can be framed as a form of subsidy removal. For example, some economists argue that failure of the government to implement policies that internalize environmental externalities is equivalent to the provision of an implicit subsidy (Stiglitz 2006; Coady et al. 2017). In this view, if polluters do not have to pay for the costs they inflict on others, government inaction implicitly subsidizes polluters. Relabeling environmental taxes as the removal of these implicit subsidies may increase support for ETR.
- *Smart spending*: Using revenues to decrease taxes that are more salient can help increase support and address rational ignorance and risk aversion issues. For example, using revenues to prevent tax increases (such as through deficit reduction) is less salient than reducing income taxes. Tax reductions could also be targeted toward those most likely to oppose reform (subject to any adverse effects, for example, on income distribution), or toward reducing taxes that are themselves unpopular. Using revenues to compensate poor

households can also address citizens' aversion toward regressive reforms. Last, a share of the revenues could be used to increase energy access for underserved households, such as through grid or mini-grid investment or provision of photovoltaic panels, solar water heaters, or efficient lighting and cooking stoves. Such investments can reduce public fears about the effects of energy price increases on poor members of society.

- *Timing of reforms*: ETRs tend to have more support during periods of low energy prices. In countries where energy consumption follows predictable cycles (such as with the seasons), ETRs should be initiated when energy use is the lowest. More generally, the current low global fuel prices make now a particularly favorable time to implement ETRs.

Overall, governments should seek to proactively disseminate information about the numerous benefits of ETR. This strategy includes linking taxes explicitly with expenditure policies (for example, reduced labor taxes, increased social spending, public investment, and targeted compensation) while highlighting the numerous local health and environmental benefits of reform. When presented this way, reforms are more likely to be effective and durable.

FINDINGS AND POLICY RECOMMENDATIONS

This chapter summarizes and builds upon the emerging body of knowledge and experience of ETR in developing countries. In presenting the following findings, it seeks to inform current discussions, debates, and designs of ETR, especially among country economists in development institutions and finance ministries in developing countries.

- *ETR can be desirable for all countries.* Environmental taxes can be raised and allocated to meet multiple objectives simultaneously. These objectives include environmental, economic, fiscal, energy, and social objectives, as reflected in the Paris Agreement NDCs and the SDGs. Environmental taxes should therefore be a part of all modern fiscal systems.
- *For developing countries, ETR is especially desirable for two reasons. First, ETR is more likely to have positive effects on economic activity.* In terms of climate change mitigation, effective implementation of ETR could render the costs of mitigation negative. Many factors have been identified that make ETR more likely to *increase economic activity while cutting emissions* (the double dividend), and many of these factors are more prevalent among developing countries:
  - *Large shadow economies*: For countries with large informal sectors, ETR can help raise economic activity. If revenues are used to reduce formal sector taxes (labor or capital), the informal sector's relative share of the economy can be reduced, enhancing output, growth, and employment.
  - *Inefficient tax systems*: ETR can reduce the economic costs of the tax system, which is especially desirable for countries with relatively inefficient tax systems. For example, ETR can help reduce distortions, broaden tax bases, and incentivize productive activities like entrepreneurship by taxing natural resource rents.
  - *Low levels of domestic taxation*: ETR can be used to raise domestic resources to fund important public goods, such as health, education, social spending, and infrastructure.

- *Second, the welfare gains from ETR (co-benefits) tend to be larger in developing countries.* By internalizing external costs of pollution, ETR can have substantial direct effects on human well-being. These effects include cleaner air, improved health, and reduced congestion. Such co-benefits can be substantial, in some cases significantly dwarfing the benefits of reduced climate risks. These co-benefits also tend to be much higher in developing countries, and may justify the use of ETR even before climate change is considered.
- *In addition, ETR can support distributional objectives, while neutralizing and compensating for negative effects on poverty.* In developing countries, a greater proportion of the burden of environmental taxes falls on the wealthy than in developed countries. Further, while some compensation may be needed to avoid losses in purchasing power among the poorest, this typically requires earmarking only a small portion of environmental revenues raised.
- *By contrast, failing to tax environmental externalities means maintaining a regressive fiscal policy.* A larger portion of the benefits of failing to tax environmental externalities, such as overconsumption of underpriced fuel, accrues to the rich. By contrast, the welfare costs of environmental externalities, such as ill health due to local air pollution, falls disproportionately on the poor. By addressing these inequities in benefits and costs, ETR can support both shared prosperity and poverty alleviation objectives.
- *ETR can be designed to protect competitiveness of domestic industries.* Policy makers may be concerned about the negative effects on the international competitiveness of exporting and import-competing sectors. However, industry protections can be designed that align economic and environmental incentives while protecting competitiveness. Chapter 2 describes these protections in detail.
- *ETR can also be simple in design and easy to implement.* Design and implementation are crucial for ETR effectiveness, and ETRs vary in type and complexity. Some ETRs are especially simple to design and administer, and are well suited to contexts where administrative capacity is limited. For example, upstream fuel taxes can reap many of the rewards of a more complex reform package. As a result, ETR can be administratively feasible in virtually all developing country contexts.
- *Despite the strong potential for ETR, there is a large gap between current and desirable levels of environmental taxation.* Current environmental tax levels are below the social optimum in general, and are insufficient to cost-effectively meet the countries' targets under the Paris Agreement. This gap is especially high in developing countries.

Accordingly, for all countries, this chapter recommends the following:

- *Finance ministries should aim to achieve efficient pricing by internalizing environmental externalities.* Internalizing external costs into prices is an important prerequisite for the efficient functioning of markets. Environmental externalities appear especially costly in terms of human welfare. Fiscal policy can be the principal lever through which these costs are internalized. By implementing ETR, all countries can reap substantial direct benefits in welfare, and many can also likely raise welfare indirectly through increased economic activity.

- *Finance ministries should seek to "get energy prices right," working closely with energy ministries.* Energy will continue to be an important contributor to global output. But, as the broad swathe of economic opinion now recognizes, fossil fuel subsidies (negative taxes) are economically undesirable for numerous reasons. Equivalently, positive taxes on energy are desirable for the same reasons. Failing to tax environmental externalities sufficiently is an ineffectual strategy for redistribution or energy access objectives. That said, taxes are not the only instruments that can be used to achieve efficient pricing, nor are price signals always effective at achieving environmental and other objectives. However, in most cases, environmental taxes will be central to getting energy prices right.

For developing countries, this chapter makes the following recommendations:

- *Finance ministries should seek to implement ETR as soon as possible.* In developing countries, price gaps and welfare opportunities of ETR are greatest. In addition, although environmental policies are the purview of environment ministries, finance ministries need to deeply understand and proactively implement ETR. Given the crucial role of price incentives throughout the economy, and the substantial potential for co-benefits, environmental taxation can have an important role within all modern fiscal strategies for achieving development.
- *There is no "one-size-fits-all" ETR, so developing countries should match designs to their diverse economic, political, and administrative contexts.* Concerns about the potential effect of environmental taxes on output, equity, and competitiveness are prevalent. However, this chapter argues that these concerns can be addressed. For example, although ETR may improve competitiveness and productivity of affected firms, protections can be designed using output-based rebates.
- *Taxing "upstream" may be especially desirable and feasible for developing countries.* Taxing at the point of extraction or import of fossil fuels—as opposed to the point of combustion—can disseminate the effect on prices throughout the economy. This broad scope of coverage increases economic efficiency of the reform while minimizing the administrative burden and raising revenue from the informal sector.
- *In implementing ETR, developing countries should learn from the experience of others, especially on the need to ensure that reforms are fair and transparent.* Developing countries that have reduced or eliminated fossil fuel subsidies, and the smaller number that have implemented carbon taxes, offer valuable lessons. Specifically, policy makers must ensure that taxes are fair, aligned with other objectives, stable and predictable, transparent in design and implementation, and focused on economic efficiency and cost-effectiveness, and that the taxes lead to substantive reductions in emissions and other harmful activities. In addition, reform strategies need to commence with a well-sequenced comprehensive review of the existing tax system and related fiscal policies, supplemented with communications strategies that raise public support, include specific protections for the most vulnerable, and are implemented gradually.

Finally, for donors, this chapter recommends the following:

- *The toolkit used to appraise ETRs needs to be brought up to date.* The tools used for analyzing ETRs are, at present, insufficient. Existing models often miss key contextual considerations that recent academic literature has identified as being important to estimating economic effects. These considerations include effects that are particularly important to developing countries, such as interactions with the informal sector. In addition, existing models may not capture substantial direct welfare benefits, crucial to fully appraising environmental taxation. These tools need to be upgraded to reflect new best practices.

- *CGE models should be calibrated carefully to developing country contexts, but also caveated clearly where they exclude co-benefits.* CGE models, which are widely used to appraise tax changes, should include the important effects of informality on output estimates, and seek to take into account other considerations where they are especially relevant for developing countries. By their nature, CGE models still miss important co-benefits such as those on health, efficiency, congestion effects, and dynamic effects on growth. Such limitations should be made clear to policy makers, and alternative tools such as endogenous growth models should be further developed to the extent feasible. And new tools are needed for estimating countries' optimal environmental tax rates generally, and cost-effective carbon price pathways for achieving NDCs specifically.
- *Gaps in the literature on ETR need to be narrowed or closed.* Although consensus exists in the literature and across development institutions on the need for increased environmental taxation, key controversies need to be addressed. The gulf between definitions and estimates of fossil fuel subsidies, external costs, corrective taxes, and implicit carbon prices is large; and conceptual ambiguity can dilute the clarity of policy advice. By narrowing or closing this gap, and with the World Bank potentially leading the charge to generate and disseminate a shared understanding of these concepts across multilateral institutions, much-needed policy advice can be made more credible, consistent, and valuable.
- *The existing empirical evidence base needs bolstering.* A plethora of ex ante studies model the potential effects of ETR on economic metrics, including growth, employment, innovation, and competitiveness. But comparatively few empirical ex post studies exist, even among developed countries. Given that some developed countries have implemented ETRs for many years, this lack is disappointing. That said, existing empirical evidence does not support concerns that ETR will negatively impact growth, employment, innovation, or competitiveness.
- *Last, support to World Bank client countries on environmental taxation should be ramped up.* The world entered a new phase of development with the signing of the Paris Agreement and the SDGs. Previous instruments that were widespread under the Kyoto Protocol, such as ETSs and offsetting mechanisms, are arguably less relevant in this new era. As developing countries seek to meet their NDCs while developing sustainably, environmental taxation has become more important compared to, for example, carbon markets. But the gap in experience with environmental taxation is wider in developing countries. Accordingly, the World Bank needs to embody the new reality while ramping up ETR support. Furthermore, given the pervasive uncertainty about how carbon markets will function in a post-Paris world, expanding tailored support for ETR may be both prudent and timely.

NOTES

1. According to the Environmental Defense Fund, potentially disastrous "tipping points" include dieback of the Amazon rainforest, disappearance of boreal (coniferous) forests, and a weakening of the "marine carbon pump" (sea carbon sequestration by plankton). More immediate "worrisome threats" include the disappearance of artic summer sea ice, melting of the Greenland and West Antarctic ice sheets, and collapse of the coral reefs (Ivanovich 2017).
2. Unusually, upper-middle-income countries fare worse compared to poorer countries on reducing inequality (SDG10) and responsible consumption and production (SDG12). However, all non-high-income countries have similar median scores for sustainable cities and communities (SDG11), climate action (SDG13), life on water and land (SDG14 and 15), institutions for justice and peace, and partnerships for global goals (SDG17). This is not to imply that no progress is required on these scores, merely that they are not significantly dissimilar across income groups.
3. Environmental taxation has elsewhere been called environmentally related taxation, green levies, green taxation, ecotaxes, environmental levies, and ecological taxation. There are some differences between these terms (see note 6 below, for example), but they broadly refer to the same thing: compulsory payments to the government levied on environmental tax bases (such as energy, emissions, and natural resources).
4. A charge or fee is a *requited* payment to the government, meaning the payer gets something in return. A tax or duty is a compulsory, *unrequited* payment for the damage caused to others. For example, a fee on road users could theoretically vary based on mileage (road charge/fee) or on damage to roads and other road users (road tax/duty). In practice, although the intention of the charge or tax may vary, the effect is often the same. This distinction has important legal and administrative implications. Taxes are defined in budget law and administered by finance ministries. Charges or fees are often introduced by special laws, are administered by line ministries, and can be integrated into the budget directly or in annexes. This chapter uses these terms interchangeably, however.
5. For a complete list of environmentally related taxes in the OECD and select non-OECD countries, refer to the OECD's Database on Policy Instruments for the Environment at https://pinedatabase.oecd.org/.
6. A number of studies allude instead to "environmental fiscal reform." This concept has been contrasted with ETR in some places, for example as an extension of ETR to "include the reduction of environmentally harmful subsidies, so as to free up scarce financial resources for more efficient use" (Anderson, Speck, and Gee 2013). This definition is not universal, however. ETR-like policies have also been called "ecological tax reform," "green fiscal reform," and "green tax reform." Despite some differences in places, broadly, these terms refer to the same thing.
7. Costs could also, theoretically, be addressed through decentralized bargaining rather than by taxation (Coase 1960). By allocating property rights, such as the right to clean air, agents (polluters and victims) can engage in "Coasian bargaining": negotiating financial transfers and reaching the same efficient equilibrium. This is the operating logic of quantity instruments like emissions trading schemes. However, allocation of property rights and coordination can be notoriously costly. Coase himself argued that the theorem was restricted to cases where transactions costs are small (Coase 1960). As a result, under certain conditions, price instruments such as Pigouvian taxes are preferable. For discussion of the pros and cons of various instruments of environmental control refer to appendix A.
8. This is the basic argument for why the equalization of costs from a uniform tax is economically efficient. Some authors, however, argue that it may be more desirable to induce stronger effort (for example, from a nonuniform carbon tax) in sectors where abatement is more costly if, for example, future abatement opportunities are also higher (see Vogt-Schilb, Meunier, and Hallegatte 2018).
9. Note, however, that certain regulations can also exhibit dynamic efficiency in certain circumstances: for example best available technology (BAT) mandates, such as those under the European Union's Industrial Emissions Directive, may have similar effects on the timing of investments in energy-saving technologies (van Soest 2005).
10. *Pre-tax subsidies* are the financial costs of subsidies to the government. *Post-tax subsidies* include this financial support plus broader costs to society from overconsumption of fossil fuel–based energy.

11. For example, the International Energy Agency restricts the definition of fossil fuel subsidies to the pre-tax version, estimated at US$493 billion in 2013 (see IEA 2016).
12. *Energy price reform* or *fossil fuel subsidy reform* variably refers to eliminating the pre-tax subsidies and forgone VAT, or the entire post-tax subsidy. *Carbon pricing* can mean policies that internalize the global warming externality, all externalities (a Pigouvian tax), or the total post-tax subsidy.
13. Note that the total estimate includes costs from global warming (22 percent of the total), air pollution (46 percent), broader vehicle externalities (13 percent), supply costs (11 percent), and the gap with other consumer taxes (8 percent). It excludes losses from underinvestment in energy efficiency measures and increased vulnerability to global energy prices because these are difficult to estimate.
14. Sweden's carbon tax has the highest overall carbon price (roughly US\$135/tCO_2), but it covers roughly 42 percent of emissions. The effective price for all emissions is therefore roughly US\$57/tCO_2. However, it remains questionable whether this is cost-effective because environmental taxes tend to be more efficient the larger their coverage.
15. As noted in this chapter, climate change is certainly not the only external cost from energy consumption. In some instances, the value of reduced climate risk can be dwarfed by health and other direct welfare benefits of environmental taxes. Accordingly, if effective carbon taxes are estimated and compared to cost-effective taxes needed to achieve the Paris Agreement, this approach may understate desirable tax rates. For example, OECD notes that, although fuel tax rates in some developed countries are close to the external costs of carbon, considering nonclimate external costs means that "transport fuel taxes are still too low from an environmental point of view" (OECD 2018b). Arguably, the value of nonclimate externalities should be subtracted from effective tax rates (to give effective tax rates on energy not explained by nonclimate externalities, for example), which could then be compared to what is needed to achieve the Paris Agreement. This topic is contentious, however, with no consensus in the literature.
16. Found measures of welfare (Social Progress Index) were heavily correlated (R-squared of 0.961) with measures of national development (National Development Index) across 128 countries in 2016. The Social Progress Index includes measures of basic human needs (nutrition and basic medical care, water and sanitation, shelter, and personal safety), foundations of well-being (access to basic education, information, and protection of the natural environment), and opportunity (personal rights and freedoms such as access to higher education). The National Development Index includes equal shares of GDP per capita, POLITY index of autocracy/democracy, and World Governance Indicators of Government Effectiveness (Pritchett 2016).
17. However, one general caveat from the perspective of environmental effectiveness is that many of the externalities related to fuel consumption are location specific. As a result, uniform corrective tax rates may be neither efficient nor effective in achieving desired environmental effects. For example, health effects of pollution depend on preexisting local concentration of polluting substances, which justifies nonuniform tax rates: Chile applied higher pollution taxes in areas where local ambient quality standards were exceeded. In addition, environmental taxation may be less effective at reducing specific externalities like road accidents than other policies. In such instances, complementary policies such as those as discussed in appendix A may be desirable.
18. As the OECD (2010b) study notes, "there is significant noise from cross-country variation, underlying product price movements, and the interaction of many other environmental and economic policy instruments. These interactions can make it difficult to draw out clear conclusions about the specific impacts of environmentally related taxes on innovation."
19. However, note that informal agents are nonetheless taxed indirectly: the price of inputs purchased from the formal market includes elements of taxation (for example, sales taxes, excises, and withholding taxes).
20. Note, however, that taxes may not significantly alter if transportation alternatives (for example, public transport) are not available. In these cases, there may be a stronger justification for using revenues from environmental taxes for investment in public transportation.
21. Using instrumental variables to control for potential endogeneity.
22. This finding is robust to omitted variable bias as long as any potential confounders are not correlated with both fuel prices and instruments in the study (for example, road safety policies are unaffected by global oil prices). Refer to the study for more detail (Burke and Nishitateno 2015).

23. Vivid Economics (2012) finds that compensating the poorest 20 percent of households would require at least 6 percent of environmental revenues in Hungary, 7 percent in Spain, and 8 percent in Poland. Dinan (2015) finds that compensating the poorest 20 percent in the United States would cost 12 percent of revenues, and compensating the second-poorest 20 percent of households would require 27 percent of revenues.
24. As the scope of emissions rises, so does the opportunity for reducing overall costs from a given level of emissions abatement. This is because costs of abatement are distributed heterogeneously across agents, so the more agents are captured the larger the prospect is for abatement to take place at the least-cost location. See "Minimizing the costs of environmental policy."
25. Note also that the optimal level itself can change over time as more information becomes available, for example on the risks of climate change or the health costs of local air pollution. It may therefore be impossible to fix taxes at "the" optimal level. However, optimal levels can still be estimated using available information.
26. Note, however, for countries with high levels of worker registration, lowering income taxes can in some circumstances be regressive (Metcalf 1999). If the poorest citizens need to consume a certain minimum (subsistence) level of pollution-intensive goods to maintain their welfare in carbon-intensive economies, increases in costs could be greater than reductions in income taxes (Grainger and Kolstad 2010; Klenert and Mattauch 2016). However, this situation is less likely in developing countries (Sterner 2012).

REFERENCES

Acemoglu, Daron, Philippe Aghion, Leonardo Bursztyn, and David Hemous. 2012. "The Environment and Directed Technical Change." *American Economic Review* 102 (1):131–66. https://doi.org/10.1257/aer.102.1.131.

Acemoglu, Daron, Simon Johnson, and James Robinson. 2000. "The Colonial Origins of Comparative Development: An Empirical Investigation." *The American Economic Review* 91 (5): 1369–1401. https://doi.org/10.2139/ssrn.244582.

Aghion, Philippe, Antoine Dechezleprêtre, David Hemous, Ralf Martin, and John van Reenen. 2016. " Carbon Taxes, Path Dependency and Directed Technical Change: Evidence from the Auto Industry." *Journal of Political Economy* 124 (1):1–51. http://ideas.repec.org/p/fem/femwpa/2012.99.html.

Anderson, Mikael Skou, Stefan Speck, and David Gee. 2013. "Environmental Fiscal Reform: Illustrative Potential in Portugal." EEA Staff Position Note SPN13/01, European Environment Agency, Copenhagen, April.

Anger, Niels, Christoph Böhringer, and Andreas Löschel. 2010. "Paying the Piper and Calling the Tune?. A Meta-Regression Analysis of the Double-Dividend Hypothesis." *Ecological Economics* 69 (7): 1495–1502. https://doi.org/10.1016/j.ecolecon.2010.02.003.

Arrow, Kenneth. 1951. "An Extension of the Basic Theorems of Classical Welfare Economics." In *Second Berkeley Symposium on Mathematical Statistics and Probability*, edited by J Neyman, 507–32. Berkeley: University of California Press.

Arze del Granado, Francisco, David Coady, and Robert Gillingham. 2012. "The Unequal Benefits of Fuel Subsidies: A Review of Evidence for Developing Countries." *World Development* 40 (11): 2234–48. https://doi.org/10.1016/j.worlddev.2012.05.005.

Baranzini, Andrea, Jeroen van den Bergh, Stefano Carattini, Richard Howarth, Emilio Padilla, and Jordi Roca. 2017. "Carbon Pricing in Climate Policy: Seven Reasons, Complementary Instruments, and Political Economy Considerations." *Wiley Interdisciplinary Reviews: Climate Change* 8 (4):1–17. https://doi.org/10.1002/wcc.462.

Bassi, Samuela, and Chris Duffy. 2016. "UK Climate Change Policy: How Does It Affect Competitiveness?" Policy Brief, Grantham Research Institute on Climate Change and the Environment and the Centre for Climate Change Economics and Policy, May.

Bathiany, Sebastian, Vasilis Dakos, Marten Scheffer, and Timothy M Lenton. 2018. "Climate Models Predict Increasing Temperature Variability in Poor Countries." *Science Advances* 4 (5): EAAR5809.

Beck, Marisa, Nicholas Rivers, Randall Wigle, and Hidemichi Yonezawa. 2015. "Carbon Tax and Revenue Recycling: Impacts on Households in British Columbia." *Resource and Energy Economics* 41 (August): 40–69. https://doi.org/10.1016/j.reseneeco.2015.04.005.

Bento, Antonio, and Mark Jacobsen. 2007. "Ricardian Rents, Environmental Policy and the 'Double-Dividend' Hypothesis." *Journal of Environmental Economics and Management* 53 (1):17–31. https://doi.org/10.1016/j.jeem.2006.03.006.

Bento, Antonio, Mark Jacobsen, and Antung Liu. 2017. "Environmental Policy in the Presence of an Informal Sector." *The World Bank Economic Review* 9 (Suppl. 1): S126–34. https://doi.org/10.1093/wber/lhv026.

Bettis, Oliver, Simon Dietz, and Nick Silver. 2017. "The Risk of Climate Ruin." *Climatic Change* 140 (2): 109–18. https://doi.org/10.1007/s10584-016-1846-3.

Blincoe, L., A. Seay, E. Zaloshnja, T. Miller, E. Romano, S. Luchter, and R. Spicer. 2002. "The Economic Impact of Motor Vehicle Crashes, 2000 NHTSA Technical Report." National Highway Traffic Safety Administration, Washington, DC. http://citeseerx.ist.psu.edu/viewdoc/download?doi=10.1.1.131.9418&rep=rep1&type=pdf.

Böhringer, Christoph, Mirjam Kosch, Florian Landis, and Sebastian Rausch. 2017. "Efficient and Equitable Policy Design: Taxing Energy Use or Promoting Energy Savings?" https://www.ethz.ch/content/dam/ethz/special-interest/mtec/cer-eth/economics-energy-economics-dam/documents/people/srausch/paper_efficient_equitable_policydesign_Switzerland_March2018.pdf.

Bosquet, Benoît. 2000. "Environmental Tax Reform: Does It Work? A Survey of the Empirical Evidence." *Ecological Economics* 34 (1): 19–32. https://doi.org/10.1016/S0921-8009(00)00173-7.

Bovari, Emmamuel, Gaël Giraud, and Florent McIsaac. 2018. "Coping with Collapse: A Stock-Flow Consistent Monetary Microdynamics of Global Warming." *Ecological Economics* 147 (May): 383–98.

Burke, Marshall, Solomon Hsiang, and Edward Miguel. 2015. "Global Non-Linear Effect of Temperature on Economic Production." *Nature* 527 (12): 235–39. https://doi.org/10.1038/nature15725.

Burke, Paul J., and Shuhei Nishitateno. 2015. "Gasoline Prices and Road Fatalities: International Evidence." *Economic Inquiry* 53 (3): 1437–50. https://doi.org/10.1111/ecin.12171.

Carattini, Stefano, Andrea Baranzini, Philippe Thalmann, Frédéric Varone, and Frank Vöhringer. 2017. "Green Taxes in a Post-Paris World: Are Millions of Nays Inevitable?" *Environmental and Resource Economics* 68 (1): 97–128. https://doi.org/10.1007/s10640-017-0133-8.

Carbone, Jared, Richard Morgenstern, Roberton Williams III, and Dallas Burtraw. 2013. "Deficit Reduction and Carbon Taxes: Budgetary, Economic, and Distributional Impacts." Considering a Carbon Tax: A Publication Series from RFF's Center for Climate and Electricity Policy. Resources for the Future: Washington, DC. http://www.rff.org/files/sharepoint/WorkImages/Download/RFF-Rpt-Carbone.etal.CarbonTaxes.pdf.

———. 2014. "Getting to an Efficient Carbon Tax." http://www.rff.org/files/sharepoint/WorkImages/Download/RFF-Resources-185_Feature-Carbone.etal.pdf.

Carson, Richard, Mark Jacobsen, and Antung Liu. 2014. "Comparing the Cost of a Carbon Tax in China and the United States." American Economic Association. https://www.aeaweb.org/conference/2015/retrieve.php?pdfid=634&usg=%5CnAFQjCNGhW1bl9fFYsDXU3ujw-Wfyv7BW3A&sig2=DeUCH.

Coady, David, Ian Parry, Louis Sears, and Baoping Shang. 2017. "How Large Are Global Fossil Fuel Subsidies?" *World Development* 91 (March): 11–27. https://doi.org/http://dx.doi.org/10.1016/j.worlddev.2016.10.004.

Coase, Ronald. 1960. "The Problem of Social Cost." *The Journal of Law and Economics* 3 (1): 1–44.

Cockburn, John, Véronique Robichaud, and Luca Tiberti. 2017. "Energy Subsidy Reform and Poverty in Arab Countries: A Comparative CGE-Microsimulation Analysis of Egypt and Jordan." *Review of Income and Wealth* 67 (April): 1–25. https://doi.org/10.1111/roiw.12309.

Cooke, Edgar, Sarah Hague, Luca Tiberti, John Cockburn, and Abdel El Lahga. 2016. "Estimating the Impact on Poverty of Ghana's Fuel Subsidy Reform and a Mitigating Response." *Journal of Development Effectiveness* 8 (1):105–28. https://doi.org/10.1080/19439342.2015.1064148.

CPLC (Carbon Pricing Leadership Coalition). 2017. "Report of the High-Level Commission on Carbon Prices." Washington, DC, May 29.

Dartanto, Teguh. 2013. "Reducing Fuel Subsidies and the Implication on Fiscal Balance and Poverty in Indonesia: A Simulation Analysis." *Energy Policy* 58 (July): 117–34. https://doi.org/10.1016/j.enpol.2013.02.040.

Dinan, Terry. 2015. "Offsetting a Carbon Tax's Burden on Low-Income Households." In *Implementing a US Carbon Tax,* edited by Ian Parry, Adele Morris, and Roberton Williams III. Abingdon: Routledge.

Dissou, Yazid, and Muhammad Shahid Siddiqui. 2014. "Can Carbon Taxes Be Progressive?" *Energy Economics* 42 (March): 88–100. https://doi.org/10.1016/j.eneco.2013.11.010.

Edenhofer, O., B. Knopf, C. Bak, and A. Bhattacharya. 2017. "Aligning Climate Policy with Finance Ministers' G20 Agenda." *Nature Climate Change* 7 (7): 463–65. https://doi.org/10.1038/nclimate3331.

EDGAR (Emissions Database for Global Atmospheric Research). 2014. "Global Emissions EDGAR v4.2 (November 2011)." Emissions Database for Global Amospheric Reseach. https://doi.org/10.2904/EDGARv4.2.

Ekins, Paul, and Stefan Speck, eds. 2011. *Environmental Tax Reform (ETR): A Policy for Green Growth.* Oxford Scholarship Online. https://doi.org/10.1093/acprof:oso/9780199584505.001.0001.

Elgie, Stewart, and Jessica McClay. 2013. "BC's Carbon Tax Shift: Results—An Environmental (and Economic) Success Story." July. https://institute.smartprosperity.ca/sites/default/files/bcs-carbon-tax-shift-after-5-years-results.pdf.

Eskeland, Gunnar, and Shantayanan Devarajan. 1996. *Taxing Bad by Taxing Goods: Pollution Control with Presumptive Charges.* Directions in Development. World Bank: Washington, DC.

Freire-González, Jaume. 2017. "Environmental Taxation and the Double Dividend Hypothesis in CGE Modelling Literature: A Critical Review." *Journal of Policy Modeling* 40 (1): 194–223. https://doi.org/10.1016/j.jpolmod.2017.11.002.

Fullerton, Don. 2001. "A Framework to Compare Environmental Policies." *Southern Economic Journal* 68 (2): 224–48. https://doi.org/10.3386/w8420.

Fullerton, Don, and Gilbert Gravelle. 1998. "The Irrelevance of the Double Dividend." *Proceedings. Annual Conference on Taxation and Minutes of the Annual Meeting of the National Tax Association* 91: 75–80. http://www.jstor.org/stable/41954582.

Gaspar, Vitor, Laura Jaramillo, and Philippe Wingender. 2016a. "Political Institutions, State Building, and Tax Capacity : Crossing the Tipping Point." *IMF Working Papers* 16 (233).

———. 2016b. "Tax Capacity and Growth: Is There a Tipping Point?" *IMF Working Papers* 16 (234). https://doi.org/10.5089/9781475558173.001.

Grainger, C., and C. Kolstad. 2010. "Who Pays a Price on Carbon?" *Environmental and Resource Economics 46* (3): 359–76. https://doi.org/10.1007/s10640-010-9345-x.

Guillaume, Dominique, Roman Zytek, and Mohammad Reza Farzin. 2011. "Iran: The Chronicles of the Subsidy Reform." *IMF Working Papers* 2011 (167): 28. https://doi.org/10.5089/9781462303212.001.

Hammond, Peter. 1998. "The Efficiency Theorems and Market Failure." In *Elements of General Equilibrium Analysis,* edited by Alan Kirman. Malden, MA: Basil Blackwell. https://web.stanford.edu/~hammond/effMktFail.pdf.

Hansson, Erik, Kristoffer Mattisson, Jonas Björk, Per-Olof Östergren, and Kristina Jakobsson. 2011. "Relationship between Commuting and Health Outcomes in a Cross-Sectional Population Survey in Southern Sweden." *BMC Public Health* 11 (1): 834. https://doi.org/10.1186/1471-2458-11-834.

HCSS (The Hague Centre for Strategic Studies). 2014. "Climate Change Vulnerability Monitor." The Hague: The Hague Centre for Strategic Studies. http://projects.hcss.nl/monitor/70/.

Heady, C., J. Markandya, W. Blyth, J. Collingwood, and P. Taylor. 2000. "Study on the Relationship between Environmental/Energy Taxation and Employment Creation." Revised Final Report Prepared for the European Commission. http://ec.europa.eu/environment/enveco/taxation/pdf/entaxemp.pdf.

HERE and Swiss Re. 2015. "The Future of Motor Insurance: How Car Connectivity and ADAS Are Impacting the Market." Swiss Re, Zurich.

Hoehner, Christine M, Carolyn E Barlow, Peg Allen, and Mario Schootman. 2012. "Commuting Distance, Cardiorespiratory Fitness, and Metabolic Risk." *American Journal of Preventive Medicine* 42 (6): 571–78. https://doi.org/10.1016/j.amepre.2012.02.020.

Horowitz, John, Julie-Anne Cronin, Hannah Hawkins, Laura Konda, and Alex Yuskavage. 2017. "Methodology for Analyzing a Carbon Tax." Office of Tax Analysis Working Paper 115, Department of the Treasury: Washington, DC.

Huntington, Hillard, James Barrios, and Vipin Arora. 2017. "Review of Key International Demand Elasticities for Major Industrializing Economies." Working Paper EMF SR 12, Energy Modeling Forum, Stanford, CA.

IEA (International Energy Agency). 2016. "Fossil Fuel Subsidy Reform in Mexico and Indonesia." Partner Country Series, International Energy Agency, Paris. https://www.iea.org/publications/freepublications/publication/PartnerCountrySeriesFossil_Fuel_Subsidy_Reform_Mexico_Indonesia_2016_WEB.pdf.

IEEP (Institute for European Environmental Policy). 2013. "Evaluation of Environmental Tax Reforms: International Experiences." IEEP, Brussels.

IMF (International Monetary Fund). 2017. *Fiscal Monitor, April 2017: Achieving More with Less.* Washington, DC.

IPCC (Intergovernmental Panel on Climate Change). 2014. *Climate Change 2014: Synthesis Report. Contribution of Working Groups I, II and III to the Fifth Assessment Report of the Intergovernmental Panel on Climate Change*. Cambridge: Cambridge University Press. http://www.ipcc.ch/pdf/assessment-report/ar5/syr/AR5_SYR_FINAL_SPM.pdf.

Ivanovich, Casey. 2017. "Everything You Need to Know about Climate Tipping Points." Climate 411 (blog), Environmental Defense Fund, November 1. http://blogs.edf.org/climate411/2017/11/01/everything-you-need-to-know-about-climate-tipping-points/.

Jiang, Zhujun, Xiaoling Ouyang, and Guangxiao Huang. 2015. "The Distributional Impacts of Removing Energy Subsidies in China." *China Economic Review* 33 (April): 111–22. https://doi.org/10.1016/j.chieco.2015.01.012.

Klenert, David, and Linus Mattauch. (2016). "How To Make a Carbon Tax Reform Progressive: The Role of Subsistence Consumption." *Economics Letters* 138 (January): 100–103. https://doi.org/10.1016/j.econlet.2015.11.019

Klenert, David, Gregor Schwerhoff, Ottmar Edenhofer, and Linus Mattauch. 2016. "Environmental Taxation, Inequality and Engel's Law: The Double Dividend of Redistribution." *Environmental and Resource Economics*, 1–20. https://doi.org/10.1007/s10640-016-0070-y.

Koźluk, Tomasz, and Christina Timiliotis. 2016. "Do Environmental Policies Affect Global Value Chains? A New Perspective on the Pollution Haven Hypothesis." OECD Economics Department Working Papers 1282, OECD Publishing, Paris.

Lange, Oskar. 1942. "The Foundations of Welfare Economics." *Econometrica* 10 (3/4): 215–28.

La Porta, Rafael, and Andrei Shleifer. 2014. "Informality and Development." *Journal of Economic Perspectives* 28 (3): 109–26. https://doi.org/10.1257/jep.28.3.109.

Lerner, Abba. 1934. "The Concept of Monopoly and the Measurement of Monopoly Power." *Review of Economic Studies* 1 (3): 157–75.

Lindahl, Erik. 1958. "Just Taxation—A Positive Solution." In *Classics in the Theory of Public Finance*, edited by R. A. Musgrave and A. T. Peacock, 168–76. London: Palgrave Macmillan. https://doi.org/10.1007/978-1-349-23426-4_11.

Liu, Antung. 2013. "Tax Evasion and Optimal Environmental Taxes." *Journal of Environmental Economics and Management* 66 (3): 656–70. https://doi.org/10.1016/j.jeem.2013.06.004.

Liu, Antung, and Hiroaki Yamagami. 2017. "Environmental Policy in the Presence of Induced Technological Change." *Environmental and Resource Economics*, 1–21. https://doi.org/10.1007/s10640-017-0150-7.

Markandya, Anil. 2012. "Environmental Taxation: What Have We Learnt in the Last 30 Years?" In *Environmental Taxes and Fiscal Reform*, edited by Laura Castellucci and Anil Markandya. Basingstoke: Macmillan. https://doi.org/10.1057/9780230392403.

Markandya, Anil, Mikel González-Eguino, and Marta Escapa. 2012. "Environmental Fiscal Reform and Unemployment in Spain." In *Carbon Pricing, Growth and the Environment*, edited by Lawrence Kreiser, Ana Sterling, Pedro Herrera, Janet Milne, and Hope Ashiabor, 3–15. Edward Elgar Publishing.

Markandya, Anil, Mikel González-Eguino, and Marta Escapa. 2013. "From Shadow to Green: Linking Environmental Fiscal Reforms and the Informal Economy." *Energy Economics* 40 (Supplement 1, December): S108–18. https://doi.org/10.1016/j.eneco.2013.09.014.

Marsiliani, Laura, and Thomas Renström. 2000. "Imperfect Competition, Labour Market Distortions, and the Double Dividend Hypothesis. Theory and Evidence from Italian Data." FEEM Working Paper 11.00, Fondazione Eni Enrico Mattei, Milan. https://papers.ssrn.com/sol3/papers.cfm?abstract_id=229157.

Martin, Matthew, and Jo Walker. 2015. "Financing the Sustainable Development Goals. Lessons from Government Spending on the MDGs." Government Spending Watch 2015 Report. https://www.oxfam.org/sites/www.oxfam.org/files/file_attachments/rr-financing-sustainable-development-goals-110615-en.pdf.

Martin, Ralf, Laure B. De Preux, and Ulrich J. Wagner. 2009. "The Impacts of the Climate Change Levy on Business: Evidence from Microdata Centre for Climate Change Economics and Policy the Environment." Centre for Climate Change Economics and Policy Working Paper No. 7 and Grantham Research Institute on Climate Change and the Environment No. 6.

Metcalf, G. 1999. "A Distributional Analysis of Green Tax Reforms." *National Tax Journal* 52 (4): 655–81.

——. 2007. "Corporate Tax Reform: Paying the Bills with a Carbon Tax." *Public Finance Review* 35 (3): 440–59.

Metcalf, Gilbert, and Kevin Hassett. 2012. "Distributional Impacts in a Comprehensive Climate Policy Package." In *The Design and Implementation of US Climate Policy*, edited by Don Fullerton and Catherine Wolfram. Chicago: University of Chicago Press.

Mirhosseini, Seyyedeh, Naman Mahmoudi, and Seyyedeh Valokolaie. 2017. "Investigating the Relationship between Green Tax Reforms and Shadow Economy Using a CGE Model—A Case Study in Iran." *Iranian Economic Review* 21 (1): 153–67.

Mirrlees, James, ed. 2011. *Tax by Design: The Mirrlees Review*. Oxford: Oxford University Press.

Monchuk, Victoria. 2013. "Reducing Poverty and Investing in People: The New Role of Safety Nets in Africa - Experiences from 22 Countries." World Bank, Washington, DC. https://doi.org/10.1596/978-1-4648-0094-8.

Murray, Brian, and Nicholas Rivers. 2015. "British Columbia's Revenue-Neutral Carbon Tax: A Review of the Latest 'Grand Experiment' in Environmental Policy." *Energy Policy* 86 (November): 674–83. https://doi.org/10.1016/J.ENPOL.2015.08.011.

Musgrave, Richard. 1959. *Theory of Public Finance: A Study in Public Economy*. McGraw-Hill.

National Audit Office. 2007. "The Climate Change Levy and Climate Change Agreements." London, August.

Nemet, G. F., T. Holloway, and P. Meier. 2010. "Implications of Incorporating Air-Quality Co-Benefits into Climate Change Policymaking." *Environmental Research Letters* 5 (1). https://doi.org/10.1088/1748-9326/5/1/014007.

OECD (Organisation for Economic Co-operation and Development). 2006. *The Political Economy of Environmentally Related Taxes. The Political Economy of Environmentally Related Taxes*. Vol. 53. Paris: OECD Publishing.

——. 2010a. *Choosing a Broad Base–Low Rate Approach to Taxation*. OECD Tax Policy Studies 19. Paris: OECD Publishing.

——. 2010b. "Growth-Oriented Tax Policy Reform Recommendations." In *Tax Policy Reform and Economic Growth*. Paris: OECD Publishing.

——. 2010c. *Taxation, Innovation and the Environment*. Paris: OECD Publishing. https://doi.org/10.1787/9789264087637-en.

——. 2013. "The Swedish Tax on Nitrogen Oxide Emissions." *OECD Environment Policy Papers* 2, OECD Publishing, Paris. https://doi.org/10.1787/5k3tpspfqgzt-en.

——. 2017. "Environmental Fiscal Reform: Progress, Prospects, and Pitfalls." OECD Report for the G7 Environment Ministers, OECD Publishing, Paris.

——. 2018a. "OECD Glossary of Statistical Terms." https://stats.oecd.org/glossary/.

——. 2018b. *Taxing Energy Use: Companion to the Taxing Energy Use Database*. Paris: OECD Publishing. https://one.oecd.org/document/23201804/en/pdf.

Orlov, Anton, Harald Grethe, and Scott McDonald. 2013. "Carbon Taxation in Russia: Prospects for a Double Dividend and Improved Energy Efficiency." *Energy Economics* 37 (May): 128–40. https://doi.org/10.1016/J.ENECO.2013.01.008.

Oueslati, Walid. 2013. "Short and Long-Term Effects of Environmental Tax Reform." FEEM Working Paper 09.2013, Fondazione Eni Enrico Mattei, Milan. http://www.econstor.eu/handle/10419/72997.

Parry, Ian, Victor Mylonas, and Nate Vernon. 2017. *Reforming Energy Policy in India: Assessing the Options*. Washington, DC: International Monetary Fund. https://doi.org/10.5089/9781475595734.001.

Parry, Ian, Chandara Veung, and Dirk Heine. 2015. "How Much Carbon Pricing Is in Countries' Own Interests? The Critical Role of Co-Benefits." *Climate Change Economics* 6 (4). http://www.worldscientific.com/doi/abs/10.1142/S2010007815500190.

Patuelli, Roberto, Peter Nijkamp, and Eric Pels. 2005. "Environmental Tax Reform and the Double Dividend: A Meta-Analytical Performance Assessment." *Ecological Economics* 55 (4): 564–83. http://www.sciencedirect.com/science/article/pii/S092180090500008X.

Pereira, Alfredo, and Rui Pereira. 2016. "On the Optimal Use of Revenues from a CO2 Tax and the Importance of Labor Market Conditions." MPRA Paper 77630, Munich Personal RePEc Archive, December.

Pereira, Alfredo, Rui Pereira, and Pedro Rodrigues. 2016. "A New Carbon Tax in Portugal: A Missed Opportunity to Achieve the Triple Dividend?" *Energy Policy* 93 (June): 110–18. https://doi.org/10.1016/j.enpol.2016.03.002.

Piggott, John, and John Whalley. 2001. "VAT Base Broadening, Self Supply, and the Informal Sector." *American Economic Review* 91 (4): 1084–94.

Pigou, Arthur. 1932. *The Economics of Welfare*. London: Macmillan.

PMR (Partnership for Market Readiness) and ICAP (International Carbon Action Partnership). 2016. "Emissions Trading in Practice: A Handbook on Design and Implementation." Washington, DC, World Bank.

Pritchett, Lant. 2016. "Turns Out, Development Does Bring Development." *Center for Global Development* (blog), September 21. https://www.cgdev.org/blog/turns-out-development-does-bring-development.

Rausch, Sebastian, Gilbert E. Metcalf, and John M. Reilly. 2011. "Distributional Impacts of Carbon Pricing: A General Equilibrium Approach with Micro-Data for Households." *Energy Economics* 33 (S1): S20–33. https://doi.org/10.1016/j.eneco.2011.07.023.

Rigaud, Kantra Kumari, Alex de Sherbinin, Bryan Jones, Jonas Bergmann, Vivane Clement, Kayly Ober, Jacob Schewe, Susan Adamo, Brent McCusker, Silke Heuser, and Amelia Migley. 2018. "Groundswell: Preparing for Internal Climate Migration." World Bank, Washington, DC.

Salehi-Isfahani, Djavad. 2011. "Iran: Subsidy Reform amid Regional Turmoil." Brookings, Washington, DC, March 3.

Santos, Georgina, Hannah Behrendt, Laura Maconi, Tara Shirvani, and Alexander Teytelboym. 2010. "Part I: Externalities and Economic Policies in Road Transport." *Research in Transportation Economics* 28 (1): 2–45. https://doi.org/10.1016/j.retrec.2009.11.002.

Sdralevich, Carlo, Randa Sab, Younes Zouhar, and Giorgia Albertin. 2014. *Subsidy Reform in the Middle East and North Africa: Recent Progress and Challenges Ahead*. Washington, DC: International Monetary Fund.

SDSN (Sustainable Development Solutions Network). 2017. "SDG Index and Dashboards Report 2017." https://doi.org/10.1016/S0140-6736(09)61513-0.

Seely, Antony. 2011. "Taxation of Road Fuels: The Road Fuel Escalator (1993–2000)." House of Commons Briefing Paper, London.

Siegmeier, Jan, Linus Mattauch, Max Franks, David Klenert, Anselm Schultes, and Ottmar Edenhofer. 2015. "A Public Finance Perspective on Climate Policy: Six Interactions That May Enhance Welfare." FEEM Working Paper No. 031.2015, Fondazione Eni Enrico Mattei, Milan. https://doi.org/10.2139/ssrn.2596604.

Siegmeier, Jan, Linus Mattauch, Max Franks, David Klenert, Anselm Schultes, and Edenhofer. 2017. "The Fiscal Benefits of Stringent Climate Change Mitigation: An Overview." *Climate Policy* 18 (3): 1469–3062. https://doi.org/10.1080/14693062.2017.1400943.

Smith, Adam. 1776. *The Wealth of Nations: An Inquiry into the Nature and Causes of the Wealth of Nations [1776]*. Reproduced. Project Gutenberg.

Stern, Nicholas. 2016. "Current Climate Models Are Grossly Misleading." *Nature* 530 (751): 407–8.

Sterner, Thomas. 2012. "Distributional Effects of Taxing Transport Fuel." *Energy Policy* 41 (February): 75–83. https://doi.org/10.1016/j.enpol.2010.03.012.

Stiglitz, Joseph. 2006. "A New Agenda for Global Warming." *The Economists' Voice* 3 (7): 1–4.

Stolper, Samuel. 2016. "Who Bears the Burden of Energy Taxes? The Critical Role of Pass-Through." Working Paper, Cambridge, MA. https://scholar.harvard.edu/sstolper/publications/who-bears-burden-energy-taxes-critical-role-pass-through.

Taylor, Lance. 2016. "CGE Applications in Development Economics." *Journal of Policy Modeling* 38 (3): 495–514. https://doi.org/10.1016/j.jpolmod.2016.02.010.

Tullock, Gordon, Gordon Brady, and Arthur Seldon. 2002. *Government Failure: A Primer in Public Choice*. Washington, DC: Cato Institute.

UNDESA (United Nations Department of Economic and Social Affairs). 2017. "World Population Prospects: The 2017 Revision." https://www.un.org/development/desa/publications/world-population-prospects-the-2017-revision.html.

UNEP (United Nations Environment Programme). 2015. "Fiscal Policies and the SDGs." Green Economy Policy Brief, UN, Geneva. http://www.greenfiscalpolicy.org/wp-content/uploads/2016/05/Fiscal-Policies-and-the-SDGs-Briefing-note.pdf.

USGCRP (U.S. Global Change Research Program). 2017. *Climate Science Special Report: Fourth National Climate Assessment, Volume I*. Washington, DC: USGCRP.

van Soest, Daan P. 2005. "The Impact of Environmental Policy Instruments on the Timing of Adoption of Energy-Saving Technologies." *Resource and Energy Economics* 27 (3): 235–47. https://doi.org/10.1016/J.RESENEECO.2004.11.002.

Vivid Economics. 2012. "Carbon Taxation and Fiscal Consolidation: The Potential of Carbon Pricing to Reduce Europe's Fiscal Deficits." Brussels.

Vogt-Schilb, Adrien, Guy Meunier, and Stéphane Hallegatte. 2018. "When Starting with the Most Expensive Option Makes Sense: Optimal Timing, Cost and Sectoral Allocation of Abatement Investment." *Journal of Environmental Economics and Management* 88 (March): 210–33. https://doi.org/10.1016/J.JEEM.2017.12.001.

Weisbrod, Glen, Don Vary, and George Treyz. 2003. "Measuring Economic Costs of Urban Traffic Congestion to Business." *Transportation Research Record: Journal of the Transportation Research Board* 1839 (January): 98–106. https://doi.org/10.3141/1839-10.

Weitzman, Martin. 2011. "Fat-Tailed Uncertainty in the Economics of Catastrophic Climate Change." *Review of Environmental Economics and Policy* 5 (2): 275–92. https://doi.org/10.1093/reep/rer006.

West, Jason, Steven Smith, Raquel Silva, Vaishali Naik, Yuqiang Zhang, Zachariah Adelman, Meridith Fry, Susan Anenberg, Larry Horowitz, and Jean-Francois Lamarque. 2013. "Co-Benefits of Mitigating Global Greenhouse Gas Emissions for Future Air Quality and Human Health." *Nature Climate Change* 3 (10): 885–89. https://doi.org/10.1038/nclimate2009.

WHO (World Health Organization). 2015. "Global Status Report on Road Safety." Geneva. https://doi.org/http://www.who.int/violence_injury_prevention/road_safety_status/2015/en/.

World Bank. 2005. *Environmental Fiscal Reform: What Should Be Done and How to Achieve It.* Washington, DC: World Bank.

———. 2016. "Domestic Resource Mobilization." Washington, DC, March 29. http://www.worldbank.org/en/topic/governance/brief/domestic-resource-mobilization.

———. 2017. Carbon Tax Guide: A Handbook for Policy Makers. Washington, DC: World Bank Group.

———. 2018. "Countries Must Strengthen Tax Systems to Meet SDGs." 2018. http://www.worldbank.org/en/news/press-release/2018/02/12/countries-called-to-strengthen-tax-systems-to-meet-sdgs.

World Bank Group. 2017. *The High Toll of Traffic Injuries: The Macro-Economic And Welfare Benefits of Reducing Road Traffic Injuries in Low & Middle-Income Countries.* Washington, DC: World Bank. https://openknowledge.worldbank.org/bitstream/handle/10986/29129/HighTollofTrafficInjuries.pdf?sequence=5&isAllowed=y.

World Bank and Ecofys. 2018. "State and Trends of Carbon Pricing." World Bank, Washington, DC.

World Bank, Ecofys, and Vivid Economics. 2016. "State and Trends of Carbon Pricing." World Bank, Washington, DC. https://doi.org/10.1596/978-1-4648-0268-3.

World Bank and OECD (Organisation for Economic Co-operation and Development). 2015. "The FASTER Principles for Successful Carbon Pricing : An Approach Based on Initial Experience." World Bank, Washington, DC. http://documents.worldbank.org/curated/en/2015/09/25060584/faster-principles-successful-carbon-pricing-approach-based-initial-experience.

WRI (World Resources Institute). 2017. "CAIT Climate Data Explorer." Washington, DC. http://cait.wri.org.

2 Staying Competitive: Productivity Effects of Environmental Taxes

ANTOINE COSTE, MASSIMILIANO CALI, NICOLA CANTORE, AND DIRK HEINE[1]

INTRODUCTION

As discussed in chapter 1, developing countries are increasingly interested in environmental taxation as an instrument to mitigate climate change. Although countries such as China, Colombia, Malaysia, Turkey, and Vietnam have collected pollution charges and levies or taxed gasoline for some time, environmental taxation has historically been more prevalent in high-income countries.[2] More recently, however, carbon-pricing initiatives (taxes or emission trading schemes [ETSs]) have been introduced in several middle-income countries, such as China, Colombia, Mexico, and South Africa (World Bank 2017b).[3] Moreover, over 100 countries have mentioned some form of carbon pricing in their Nationally Determined Contributions (NDCs) under the Paris Agreement (World Bank 2016a). Likewise, a growing number of developing countries have started to reduce fossil fuel subsidies, with similar impacts on firms as the introduction of fuel taxes.

Despite their interest in addressing climate issues, finance ministries have expressed some concern about the impact of environmental taxation and environmental tax reform (ETR) on competitiveness. The fear that an additional tax burden would disadvantage domestic industries, especially energy-intensive and trade-exposed (EITE) firms, relative to foreign competitors has been voiced by both public and private stakeholders in countries that have considered carbon or other environmental taxes. Partly because of these concerns, carbon taxes adopted so far in emerging economies have been modest in terms of their coverage and tax levels. In addition, they have often included generous exemptions to affected industrial sectors (see appendix B). Are fears of adverse competitiveness effects, and the resulting dilution of ETRs justified? Although a large academic and policy literature has dealt with these issues for advanced economies, the available evidence in developing contexts remains scarce.

This chapter seeks to help fill the knowledge gap on the potential competitiveness impacts of environmental taxes in developing countries. Building on the discussions of competitiveness in recent World Bank publications on carbon pricing (World Bank 2015, 2017), it provides (i) new empirical evidence for different emerging economies, using energy price changes as a proxy for the effects of environmental taxes, and (ii) an updated presentation of policy options to minimize the costs and maximize the benefits of such reforms for vulnerable industries. The chapter is structured as follows. The next section gives some background on environmental taxation and competitiveness, provides a conceptual framework to understand the different channels through which environmental taxes can affect firms, and reviews the literature. The third section offers new empirical evidence on the influence of rising energy prices on firm performance in developing countries. The fourth section presents different policy options and complementary interventions to mitigate potential negative impacts of environmental taxes on vulnerable firms and industries, focusing on tax-reducing measures, support measures, and trade-related measures. The last section concludes and provides recommendations.

HOW CAN ENVIRONMENTAL TAXES AFFECT COMPETITIVENESS, AND WHAT DOES THE EVIDENCE TELL US?

Background

Competitiveness has been a central element of debates around environmental taxes. Along with some concerns for social impacts, which are addressed in chapter 1, fears that taxes will undermine the international competitiveness of domestic firms by increasing energy and input prices have been the main cause of political resistance in countries that have introduced or considered introducing environmental taxes. In contrast, proponents of environmental taxes argue that these taxes are a crucial tool in the transition toward a greener growth model and that they can foster efficiency, productivity, and innovation. In recent years, intense debates on this issue have led to the delaying or shelving of carbon tax proposals both in high-income countries, such as France and the United States, and in developing ones, such as South Africa. In the case of South Africa, a carbon tax has been considered since 2010, but its implementation was repeatedly postponed between 2013 and 2017 primarily because of industry resistance, despite planned exemptions for EITE sectors.[4]

What is competitiveness, and why could it be harmed by a tax? For a firm, *competitiveness* can be defined as the ability to provide customers with goods or services that are cheaper, of a better quality, or otherwise more attractive than those of its competitors in a given market. On the one hand, from a static point of view, environmental taxes adopted unilaterally may undermine competitiveness if foreign competitors do not face equivalent cost increases.[5] The cost competitiveness of domestic firms could be hampered by higher energy prices, especially in EITE sectors. This result would make it harder for the firms to enter or stay in foreign markets or to maintain their domestic market share in the face of cheaper imports, and could reduce their profit margins. This reduced competitiveness could also push some of those industries to relocate to countries with no or lower environmental taxes. From an environmental effectiveness point of view, both static and dynamic effects could result in unintended "leakages" of pollution and greenhouse gas (GHG) emissions in competing jurisdictions.

On the other hand, competitiveness impacts could be moderate (or even positive). Energy represents a relatively minor share of production costs in most industries (but not all). In such cases even substantial taxes on energy would generally amount to a small proportion of sales or profits. Depending on their circumstances, firms (even energy-intensive ones) may be able to deal with such cost increases in various ways, as discussed in the next subsection. Additionally, cost is only one of several dimensions on which firms compete (Porter 1980), although it is an essential one for commodity producers. Moreover, the implications of an environmental tax are not the same if one considers the level of a firm, sector, or country; and competitiveness losses for some firms or sectors may not preclude overall gains at the national level if others benefit from the tax.[6] Finally, governments are not devoid of policy options to avoid competitiveness losses (see the section titled "What policies can minimize adverse competitiveness impacts?" for discussion of the main options). The case is therefore not clear-cut, and determining the impact of an environmental tax on an industry requires a good understanding from a conceptual perspective.

Conceptual framework

Several transmission channels and mediating factors will shape a new environmental tax's eventual impact(s) on any given firm. This chapter proposes a conceptual framework (summarized in figure 2.1) to facilitate the assessment of competitiveness impacts.[7] In addition to (i) tax-induced cost pressures, important factors include (ii) the sector and firm characteristics that determine exposure, (iii) the different response measures that a firm can adopt depending partly

FIGURE 2.1

Channels of impact and mediating factors

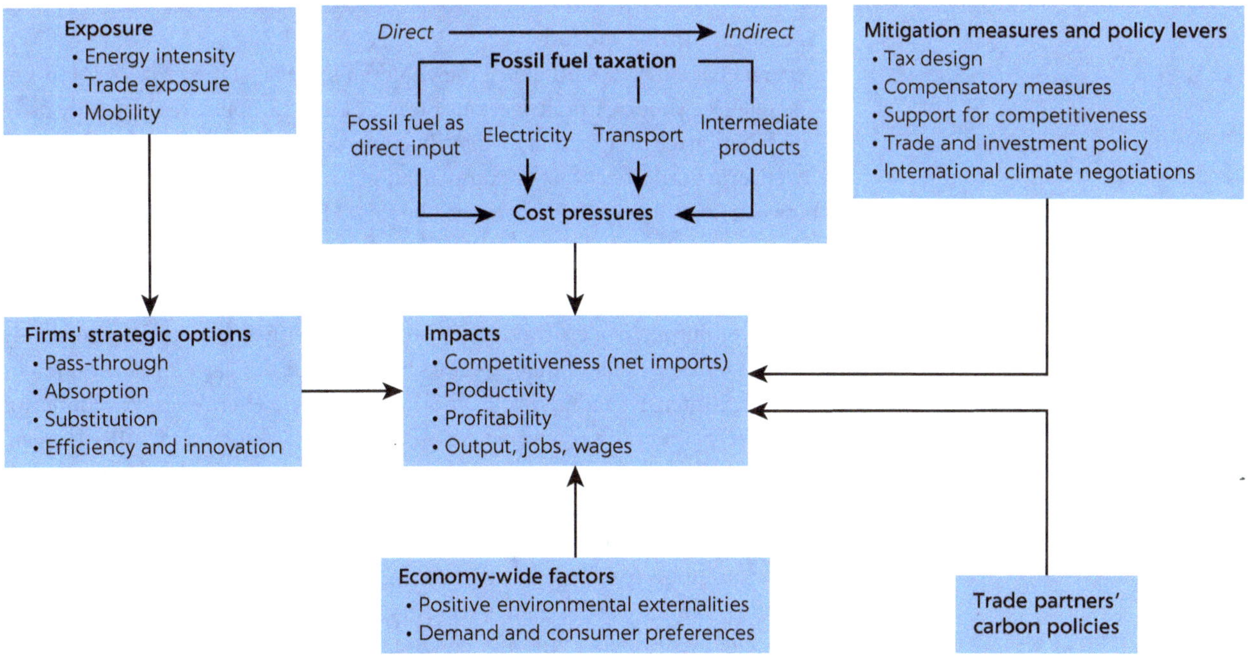

on those characteristics ("strategic options" in the figure), (iv) the mitigation policies and accompanying measures that can accompany the tax, and (v) several other economy-wide factors. For each, the discussion covers both static effects that will kick in relatively rapidly after the tax is implemented and dynamic effects that could materialize over the longer run.

Cost pressures from taxation

At the level of firms and sectors, a tax on fuels will affect cost structures through different direct and indirect channels:

- **Fossil fuel use:** A tax will directly increase the price of fossil fuels used in production processes as an energy source (for example, coal, oil, and natural gas).
- **Electricity consumption:** A tax can also increase the price for firms of grid electricity generated from fossil fuels.[8] This effect may also be felt rapidly, although its magnitude will depend on the way electricity prices are set and regulated.
- **Supply chains:** More *indirectly*, a tax can also have a ripple effect up and down supply chains (backward and forward links), via the price of domestically produced, nonenergy goods (such as steel) and services (such as transport). Such impacts are likely to take more time to materialize than direct ones, and, as discussed later, their magnitude largely depends on the extent to which producers of these goods and services pass on the added cost to their customers.

In the longer run, environmental taxes help accelerate the growth of competitive greener energy sources (such as renewables and lower-carbon gas-powered generation), transport and logistics services, and intermediate products. Added to the incentives for firms to reduce their use of fossil fuels and improve their energy efficiency (see the discussion of efficiency in "Firms' strategic options," below), this growth can be expected to gradually reduce the cost pressures from environmental taxes.

Sector and firm exposure

Several characteristics influence the vulnerability of specific firms or sectors to energy price shocks. Countries considering fuel or carbon taxes generally use a combination of these factors to identify vulnerable sectors and establish eligibility criteria for derogations or compensation.[9] Importantly, wide heterogeneity between firms in any given sector can be found for each of these factors.

- **Energy intensity**, defined as the ratio of a firm's energy input costs to the value of its output or of its production costs, or as the energy quantity used per unit of output, is a crucial factor. Although energy accounts for a relatively low share of costs in many sectors,[10] this is not the case for several major energy-intensive industries, such as iron and steel, where energy accounts for 20–40 percent of production costs (World Steel Association 2018); cement; chemicals; pulp and paper; and glass production. Directly, changes in an environmental tax will mainly affect energy-intensive sectors using fossil fuels as a major energy source. For example, coal represents 61 percent of final energy consumption for iron and steelmaking, where it is used in blast furnaces, and 66 percent for the cement industry, which uses it to fuel kilns to produce clinker (World Bank 2016b). Likewise, the air, road, and maritime transport sectors use large quantities of kerosene, diesel, and heavy fuel oil, which account for significant shares of their operating expenses—for example, 17–36 percent for airlines (IATA 2018), 30–50 percent for trucking companies (ATRI 2017; Teravaninthorn and Raballand 2009), and 45–50 percent for shipping lines (Rodrigue 2017). Less directly, other sectors that rely heavily on electricity for production would be affected by tax-induced electricity price increases. For example, despite technological advances over the last decades, electricity still represents 20–40 percent of the cost of producing aluminum.[11]

- **Trade exposure**—that is, measures of exposure to international competition (for example, share of imports in domestic consumption and share of exports in domestic production)—is another key variable when considering competitiveness. Sectors integrated into competitive international markets where cost is a deciding factor, such as commodities, could lose market share if their production costs increase significantly. In contrast, producers of energy-intensive goods that are difficult to trade because of, for example, a low value-to-weight ratio (like cement), or are protected by trade barriers, are less likely to lose market share.
- **Energy intensity of inputs:** Firms and sectors relying heavily on domestic equipment, intermediate products (such as steel), and services (such as transport) directly affected by tax-induced energy price shocks may see their production costs increase (conversely, firms relying mostly on imported energy-intensive inputs may be more insulated from the effects of the tax). For example, ex ante computable general equilibrium (CGE) simulations for Vietnam suggested that cost increases in the fuel-dependent fisheries sector due to a new fuel tax could cause the fish-processing sectors to contract by 2.8–11.6 percent (Willenbockel 2011). Data on the type and origin of material expenditures from enterprise surveys and on the energy embodied in common industrial materials can be used to assess sectors and firms' vulnerability to this risk (Rentschler, Kornejew, and Bazilian 2017).
- **Mobility:** Some industries and firms may be bound to a production location or may face prohibitive relocation costs, for example, because of substantial infrastructure investments and sunk costs or the need to remain near specific inputs (such as agricultural inputs).

Firms' strategic options

Firms affected by energy price shocks can adapt in different ways, influencing the tax's overall impacts on competitiveness and productivity. Some of these strategies can be adopted in the short term and do not require investments. Others require more time and resources over a longer time horizon, and therefore critically depend on the predictability of future tax rates.

- **Pass-through:** Firms facing higher production costs may be able to maintain their margin by increasing their output prices when the tax is introduced. However, the capacity to do so without excessively undermining their sales and market shares will depend on exposure to foreign and domestic competition, and on the price elasticity of demand. A high pass-through capacity thus implies that an environmental tax presents limited risks to competitiveness, although it may negatively affect consumer welfare via higher prices. Price controls in regulated markets can also be an obstacle to pass-through. In practice, pass-through rates vary greatly across industries, even for the extreme cases of perfect competition or monopoly, and must be estimated on a case-by-case basis (Arlinghaus 2015). Estimating pass-through rates in different industries after past energy price shocks can give policy makers an indication of the likelihood that a new environmental tax will result in competitiveness losses, but also of the tax's potential to trigger energy efficiency or fuel substitution on its own (Rentschler 2017).

- **Absorption:** If pass-through is constrained, firms may also be able to absorb part or all of the tax's impact by reducing their profit margins, provided these margins are sufficiently high compared to the cost increases faced. Absorption can be an important coping strategy for affected firms because it can be done rapidly, but it can also have negative consequences in the longer term if it forces firms to compress wages or delay productive investments (Rentschler 2017). Industries with low profit margins are likely to put up strong resistance to the introduction of new taxes, even with low rates.
- **Substitution:** Firms may adapt their energy mix or modify the inputs they use to reduce their consumption of fuels or inputs that have become relatively more expensive because of the tax. Firms may also be able to use imported inputs instead of domestically produced ones, although the environmental impact of the tax would be undermined if these are produced using equally polluting production methods in countries without equivalent environmental taxes. Such substitution notably requires sufficiently flexible production technologies and a reliable supply of alternative energy sources (for example, access to the grid or distributed energy) or inputs (Rentschler 2017). Depending on the nature of the new energy source used, substitution can contribute to the environmental impact of the tax positively (for example, cleaner or renewable energy) or negatively (for example, burning of trash or waste tires). Moreover, this strategy is likely to take more time than the ones previously discussed and could require some investments to adapt production methods. Additionally, some firms faced with higher energy prices may also be able to switch or focus on the production of less energy-intensive goods, as shown by Abeberese (2017) in the case of India.
- **Efficiency:** Reducing the quantity of energy and material needed to produce a unit of output is an important way for firms to reduce their vulnerability to a tax on fuels because doing so is consistent with the environmental objective of the tax and generates productivity gains. Research has shown the long-term constancy in energy expenditure relative to gross domestic product (GDP) across countries and time, meaning that firms in countries with rising energy prices tend to adapt by improving their energy efficiency (Bashmakov 2007; Grubb et al. 2017). Because energy efficiency is associated with higher productivity in high-income (Martin et al. 2012) and developing countries alike (Cantore, Calì, and te Velde 2016), this strategy could also have a direct positive effect on competitiveness. Nonetheless, several factors may hinder cost-effective investments in energy efficiency, such as biases and bounded rationality of managers (for example, present and status quo bias, endowment effect[12]) (Nielsen 2012) and artificially low energy prices (Clements et al. 2013). The quality of a firm's management is also relevant here: an increasing body of research suggests that management quality plays a determinant role in firm performance and innovation capacity, including in developing countries (Cirera and Maloney 2017). This effect can be substantial, even in advanced

economies: in a sample of 300 manufacturing firms in the United Kingdom, Bloom et al. (2010) find that better management quality is associated with lower energy intensity. The potential for efficiency gains depends on the initial level of efficiency and degree of "slack" in firm operations. Various adjustments to production technologies and processes may deliver such efficiency gains in different sectors, although larger gains generally require larger investments and more time. However, energy and resource efficiency audits in developing countries suggest that firms in energy-intensive sectors, including small and medium enterprises (SMEs), can often achieve significant gains with low or even no investment cost and short payback periods (see, for example, IFC, NPO, and CPI 2016; World Bank 2014).

- **Innovation:** In the longer term, firms can introduce more fundamental changes to their production methods or products to improve their energy efficiency, lower their pollution discharges, and reduce their exposure to an environmental tax on fuels. Such green innovation tends to find broader applications than traditional innovation in fossil fuel sectors (World Bank 2015), potentially generating stronger productivity and competitiveness gains for several sectors. However, public policy is often needed to overcome several market failures and behavioral obstacles.[13] Innovation can occur through firms' own research and development efforts, cooperative arrangements (such as licensing of foreign technology, joint ventures), or other research institutions. This is an important source of dynamic efficiency from environmental taxes (Barde and Godard 2012) and is linked to the "Porter hypothesis," according to which well-designed environmental policy, particularly market-based instruments such as taxes, can foster innovation and productivity gains over time that at least partially offset the cost of compliance and mitigate competitiveness losses (Porter 1991; Porter and van der Linde 1995).[14] This hypothesis continues to be studied, but a comprehensive review of the empirical literature by Ambec et al. (2013) concludes that the available evidence generally supports it. Well-known examples consistent with this finding include the case of Sweden's nitrogen oxides (NO_x) tax, which has been shown to accelerate the introduction of greener technologies (Bonilla et al. 2015). Conversely, low energy prices can have long-term negative consequences on innovation (Aghion et al. 2016). However, as pointed out in World Bank (2015), the empirical evidence has largely been based on advanced industrialized countries. The situation may differ in less advanced countries, where, on the one hand, the potential for catch-up innovation is higher but, on the other, firms generally face higher obstacles to innovation in terms of awareness of available technologies, technical capacity and skill level, and availability of affordable financing for innovation. Moreover, some evidence for Organisation for Economic Co-operation and Development (OECD) countries suggests that the productivity impact of more stringent environmental policies, although positive at the national level, is limited to the most productive firms and industries, whereas the least productive firms may be negatively impacted (Albrizio et al. 2014), thus contributing to the selection of efficient firms by the market.
- **Other:** Firms may adopt a variety of other strategies to adapt to tax-induced energy price shocks, such as temporarily delaying costly investments (although this would undermine productivity and competitiveness if maintained in the long run), closing production sites, or relocating abroad.

Mitigation measures and policy levers

Various types of policies can affect the impact of environmental taxes on competitiveness. Governments can adopt measures specifically to reduce the exposure of vulnerable industries and firms to the tax, using revenue from the tax to reduce other distortive taxes on businesses, or provide firms with different forms of support (these policies are discussed later in the chapter). Additionally, several other relevant types of policies can be used in conjunction with environmental taxes. Trade and investment policies can facilitate access to foreign technologies, goods, and services that help make domestic industries greener, and could in theory be used to address an import surge for vulnerable industries in line with the World Trade Organization (WTO) Safeguards Agreement. In some contexts, sector-specific regulatory reforms and liberalization (such as power sector reform) can reduce other obstacles to productivity growth and strengthen concerned firms' capacity to cope with environmental taxes.

Economy-wide factors

Several broader supply- and demand-side factors influence the overall impact of environmental taxes on industries. On the supply side, this impact includes the extent to which environmental taxes may improve productivity via better environmental health (box 2.1).[15]

BOX 2.1

Environmental health, resource efficiency, and productivity

The benefits from reducing emissions, pollution, and resource use are a central element justifying the introduction of environmental taxes. However, these benefits are rarely factored in analyses of their impacts on competitiveness, whereas the costs of worsening pollution remain largely invisible.

These benefits matter from social and environmental points of view, but they also have a clear economic dimension. Recent research suggests that pollution is responsible for 9 million premature deaths in the world each year (16 percent of total deaths), 92 percent of which occur in low- and middle-income countries (Landrigan et al. 2017). Pollution has a strong impact on current and future labor productivity, as well as on labor force participation, by causing diseases and affecting cognitive abilities. Studies have estimated that reducing air and water pollution in various contexts increased the hours worked and productivity of local workers by 3–6 percent. Overall, the annual cost to GDP due to productivity loses caused by pollution-related diseases has been estimated at 2 percent in low- and middle-income countries.

The public health impacts of pollution are costly for national budgets and health care spending, especially in rapidly industrializing developing economies, and may require collecting higher taxes, including from businesses. More directly, the increasing incidence of smog in countries such as China, India, and Pakistan in recent years has caused major disruptions for industries, power generation, and transport. Research suggests that factoring in the inverse relationship between pollution and labor productivity and supply significantly increases the measurement of environmental taxes' positive impacts on firm profitability and welfare (Williams 2002; Pang 2018).

Beyond pollution, investments in more energy-efficient technologies can also have labor productivity co-benefits, as shown in India with the adoption of energy-efficient LED lighting in factories (Adhvaryu, Kala, and Nyshadham 2017). Additionally, benefits for firms can come from the preservation of the quantity and quality of natural resources. For example, it is estimated that the adoption of resource-efficient and cleaner technologies in the Bangladeshi textile and leather industries could reduce long-term investments and operational expenditures needed to ensure a continued supply of water by up to US$9 billion by 2030 (WRG 2015).

Part of environmental taxes' impacts can come from reduced domestic and foreign demand for energy and for carbon-heavy goods and services. Faced with higher prices because of the tax, or because of evolving technologies and preferences, downstream firms and consumers may either reduce their total consumption of these goods (material efficiency) or substitute with similar foreign products (Aldy 2016). For example, a modeling exercise for the South African carbon tax predicted that the increased prices of energy-intensive goods (such as iron and steel) and services (such as transport) would reduce the demand for these goods in downstream sectors relative to a no-tax scenario, although all would still grow in absolute terms even with a tax (PMR 2016). Although this would affect the sales of domestic firms, it would represent a competitiveness challenge only if foreign goods are not equally affected by lower demand (for example, less carbon-heavy production technologies).

Several other economy-wide factors may play a positive or negative role in determining the overall competitiveness impacts of environmental taxes. A positive example would be if the taxes benefit the formal, export-oriented sector by reducing competition from the informal sector (Bento, Jacobsen, and Liu 2017) or if they lead the domestic financial sector to reassess the long-term profitability of carbon-heavy industries and to reduce their credit for these industries. The impacts of a tax on firms are also likely to vary depending on energy price levels before its introduction, especially if energy prices were particularly high or particularly low compared to competitors. Other factors, such as the evolution of international energy prices or taxes' impacts on consumers' disposable income, are important when considering the overall impacts on firms but should not have effects on competitiveness.

Trade partners' environmental taxation policies are also directly relevant. Competitiveness concerns for developing countries may be minimized to the extent that their main trade partners, including large economies such as China, the European Union (EU), and the United States have or will introduce equivalent or higher environmental taxes. Conversely, the export competitiveness of developing countries without environmental taxes could be threatened if their trade partners adopt such taxes and combine them with border tax adjustments (BTAs) on their imports. For example, Alton (2014) finds that the welfare losses resulting from a unilateral imposition of carbon taxes and BTAs by South Africa's partners would equal or exceed those from a domestic tax, and the South African carbon tax proposal was notably designed to preemptively avoid this risk (PMR 2016). Likewise, Bao et al. (2013) find that the imposition of BTAs by the United States and the EU would negatively affect China's GDP. For this reason, some have suggested that countries exporting carbon-heavy products, such as China, could benefit from a self-imposed carbon tax on their exports, as a transitional measure before the adoption of fully fledged domestic carbon pricing scheme (Li, Wang, and Zhang 2012; Helm, Hepburn, and Ruta 2012). Although trade partner's policies are outside the control of domestic policy makers, international sectoral agreements between governments or companies for sensitive industries, such as steel, have been discussed to determine common emissions reduction pathways while addressing competitiveness concerns (Bodansky 2007; Colombier and Guerin 2008; Wooders 2010).

Overall impacts on competitiveness

Given the different factors at play, predicting the overall impacts of a specific environmental tax on firms' productivity and competitiveness is not straightforward. These consequences will vary from country to country and, within each national context, are likely to differ between and within sectors. At the firm and sector levels, a tax could have overall positive or negative impacts on competitiveness, as measured by the evolution of net imports. This in turn could result in higher or lower output, employment, and wages. Carbon leakage is closely linked to negative competitiveness impacts, although it refers more to the environmental effectiveness of a tax than to its economic effects (see notably PMR 2015; World Bank 2015). For taxes on fuels, a key element determining the direction of overall impacts for a particular firm is its capacity to adjust to energy price shocks.

At the national level and in a more dynamic perspective, environmental taxes foster energy efficiency, a shift toward renewable energy, green innovation, and a gradual reallocation from carbon-intensive to greener sectors. These outcomes all contribute to long-term national competitiveness, as defined in the previous section. By forcing firms with different marginal abatement costs to internalize pollution, environmental taxes give a competitive edge to firms that can abate more efficiently and thus improve allocative efficiency. In this regard, changing sectors' relative competitive position and rewarding efficiency and cleanliness are expected effects of taxing fossil fuels (World Bank 2015). In addition to limiting GHG emissions and raising revenue, promoting low carbon development and addressing local environmental issues have often been central objectives of jurisdictions that introduce carbon taxes (World Bank 2017a).

Literature review on overall impacts

A rich literature on the nexus between environmental taxes, energy prices, and trade has found limited evidence of negative competitiveness impacts. Research specifically dealing with the competitiveness impacts of environmental taxes increased in the 1990s, as these taxes gained prominence in the United States and in Europe (Goulder 1992; Ekins and Speck 1999). Building on the older research on the impacts of environmental regulation, the extensive literature on taxes developed since the 1990s has been the object of several reviews, summarized in table 2.1. Overall, both ex ante modeling studies and ex post evaluations generally find that environmental taxes, and more broadly environmental regulation, have not had significant adverse effects on competitiveness. Negative impacts, if any, tend to be concentrated in a few EITE sectors, to be relatively small, and to be more a short-term issue than a durable concern.

Moreover, little empirical evidence of significant carbon leakage has been found in tradable sectors. A long list of factors, such as sunk costs in infrastructure, transport costs, the availability of skilled labor, the quality of the investment climate, governance and political stability, exchange rate fluctuations, and an industry's overall "footlooseness" may influence investors' location decisions more than the differential in energy or carbon taxation (Jeppesen, List, and Folmer 2002; Ederington, Levinson, and Minier 2005; PMR 2015).[16]

The potential impacts of environmental taxes on firms are not all linked to competitiveness. In a simulation of the competitiveness impacts of a carbon tax at US$15 per ton on manufacturing industry in the United States, Aldy and Pizer (2014, 2015) find that energy-intensive sectors could see their output decrease by 3–5 percent, and could reduce employment by 0.4–2.2 percent. However, the competitiveness impact, measured by the change in net imports (reflecting both the evolution of exports and competition from foreign firms), would not exceed

TABLE 2.1 **Reviews of the literature on the economic impacts of environmental regulation and taxes**

STUDY	LITERATURE	OVERALL	EITE SECTORS
Dechezleprêtre and Sato (2017)	Ex post econometric studies of impacts on competitiveness of environmental regulation asymmetries, within and across countries	• **Trade and investment:** Small effect on trade flows, but no clear evidence for FDI location decisions. Very low trade impact of energy price differences. Effect of regulatory asymmetries overwhelmed by other trade and investment determinants. • **Employment:** Undetermined direction of long-run aggregate impact, but likely small magnitude. • **Productivity:** Direction of impact varies across sectors and type of pollutant regulated. • **Innovation:** Strong evidence of induced innovation in cleaner technologies and knowledge spillovers, but not more than compensating compliance costs for regulated firms	• **Trade:** Some evidence of limited increase in imports due to tighter environmental regulation or higher energy prices • **Employment:** Within-country evidence of small losses in the short run (no cross-country evidence available, but effect likely smaller) • **Productivity:** Some evidence of short-term losses and longer-term gains
Carbone and Rivers (2017)	Meta-analysis of 54 CGE modeling studies on competitiveness impact of unilateral carbon pricing	Compared to prepolicy baseline, 20% emission abatement effort in carbon pricing country(ies) estimated to result in: • **Employment:** No impact (by model construction) • **Welfare:** Small loss of ≈0.5% of GDP (models considered ignore environmental benefits of GHG mitigation and do not consider offsetting carbon tax by lowering other distorting taxes) • **Carbon leakage:** ≈10–30%	Impacts for EITE sectors under the same abatement scenario: • **Output:** ≈5% decrease • **Exports:** ≈7% decrease, large variance across models • **Imports:** No discernible relationship across models • **Employment:** ≈5% decrease, but few studies
Aldy (2016)	CGE and econometric studies of unilateral carbon pricing in the United States	• 80% of U.S. manufacturing sector would not experience statistically or economically significant impact on employment or production under US\$15/tCO_2 price.	• **Output:** Unilateral US\$10–40/tCO_2 price in the United States would result in ≈1–2.5% decrease in output in EITE sectors; dwarfed by annual variations in EITE output • **Trade:** Only small fraction of lost output compensated by increased imports (<1% output) • **Employment:** 0.4/2.2% loss under US\$15 carbon price
Arlinghaus (2015)	Ex post econometric studies of carbon pricing's impacts on various indicators of competitiveness, with focus on Europe	• **Emissions and energy efficiency:** Positive impacts • **TFP, output, employment:** No economically meaningful effects of studied carbon prices at current levels and as designed. Some evidence that exemptions/reduced rates not necessarily needed to protect competitiveness • **Trade:** No clear causal impact of EU ETS	• **Output, employment, trade:** No evidence of significant impact • **Productivity:** High variance of impact, even among sectors with similar energy and technology use • **Cost pass-through:** Some evidence of very high rate in iron, steel, chemicals
Speck et al. (2011)	CGE and macro-econometric studies on impacts of ETR in EU	• **GDP:** Small impact predicted, negative or positive depending on treatment of induced innovation and revenue recycling • **Employment:** Small gain generally predicted if carbon tax offset with other tax reductions (esp. social security contributions)	• Possibly larger impacts

Note: CGE = computable general equilibrium; EITE = energy-intensive and trade-exposed; ETR = environmental tax reform; ETS = emissions trading system; EU = European Union; FDI = foreign direct investment; GDP = gross domestic product; GHG = greenhouse gas; tCO_2 = tonnes of carbon dioxide; TFP = total factor productivity.

0.8 percent for the most energy-intensive industry. In fact, output would mostly decrease because consumers would reduce their demand for these products and substitute others for them. Moreover, these changes in production and net imports are both dwarfed by annual variations experienced historically in these sectors, suggesting that energy prices are not the strongest determinant of trade even in EITE sectors.

The literature has largely focused on European and North American cases; fewer studies exist of environmental taxes in developing countries. As pointed out earlier, the applicability of results for high-income economies to low- and middle-income ones is not evident because the latter often differ substantially in several relevant dimensions, such as energy efficiency, carbon intensity, and innovation capacity of industries.[17] The studies available for developing countries generally do not provide an in-depth analysis of the competitiveness dimension or focus on a specific country case. Several broad studies analyzed the application of environmental taxation in developing contexts and reviewed the experience in Asia, Latin America, Eastern and Central Europe, and Africa, but without considering competitiveness issues (Eskeland and Jimenez 1992; Huber, Ruitenbeek, and da Motta 1998; Bluffstone 2003; Spratt 2013). Cottrell et al. (2016) include some discussion of competitiveness as part of their broad review of environmental taxes in developing countries, although this is not a focus of their report.

At the country level, modeling studies were conducted for a handful of developing countries. The results of general equilibrium studies have generally suggested that adopting carbon taxes would result in small economic costs, concentrated in some sectors, which could be partially or even more than compensated with adequate revenue-recycling strategies (table 2.2). Although informative, these models estimate the possible impacts of environmental taxes on the basis of assumptions on, rather than observation of firms' responses. The models do so because only a few low- and middle-income countries have adopted environmental taxes to date, and those that have, have set low rates. This has largely prevented ex post analyses of the impacts of such taxes on firm performances and competitiveness in developing contexts.

TABLE 2.2 **CGE studies of environmental taxes in developing countries**

COUNTRY	MAIN RESULTS ON COMPETITIVENESS
China (Liang, Fan, and Wei 2007)	Output and competitiveness of EITE sectors negatively affected by a carbon tax in the absence of exemptions or targeted revenue recycling.
Mexico (Landa-Rivera et al. 2016)	Application of a carbon tax would reduce GDP and exports in the long run. However, recycling carbon revenue by lowering other taxes for households and firms significantly reduces emissions, while increasing GDP compared to the baseline scenario without a carbon tax (even if no other country adopts a carbon tax).
South Africa (PMR 2016)	Tax proposal would significantly reduce GHG emissions without hampering economic growth. Although a few EITE sectors' output and exports would grow more slowly than without the tax, the opposite would be true for several other important sectors, resulting in total exports being 3.5 percent higher in 2035 compared to the baseline. Results significantly influenced by the revenue-recycling strategy selected and the extent to which it benefits a broad or narrow range of sectors.
Vietnam (Willenbockel 2011)	No detailed analysis of trade competitiveness, but at the higher end of the proposed tax rate band, the refined liquid fuel tax could lower CO_2 emissions at little overall economic costs. It could, however, reduce output and employment in some fuel-intensive sectors, such as fisheries and linked downstream sectors, but this impact could easily be offset with output-based subsidies.

Note: CGE = computable general equilibrium; CO_2 = carbon dioxide; EITE = energy-intensive and trade-exposed; GDP = gross domestic product; GHG = greenhouse gas.

ESTIMATING THE IMPACT OF ENERGY PRICE INCREASES ON FIRMS IN DEVELOPING COUNTRIES

Energy price variations can be used as a proxy to study the impact of environmental taxes. In the absence of long-lasting experiences with carbon taxes in developing countries, the easiest way to evaluate their potential impact is to estimate the relationship between energy prices and performance across firms, and then use this elasticity to simulate the possible effect of an ETR.[18]

Two recent studies estimate this relationship between energy prices and firm performance in developing countries, focusing on electricity alone. Abeberese (2017) uses a large panel of Indian manufacturing firms and finds that exogenous increases in electricity prices reduce firms' productivity growth (but not levels) and induce a switch to less electricity-intensive production. The study—like others in high-income contexts reviewed above—focuses on the impact of electricity prices on performance, while disregarding the impact of prices for other energy sources. Rentschler and Kornejew (2017) examine the effects of energy price changes on micro and small Indonesian manufacturing firms, finding small but significant negative effects of energy price increases on profitability. That finding is despite firms adjusting their energy mix and increasing their output prices in response to energy input price increases. However, the analysis uses a cross-section of firms and is thus unable to control for potentially important time-invariant firm-specific confounding factors. In addition, the study does not include other, more relevant measures of competitiveness, including productivity, exports, and sales.

This section substantially expands this incipient empirical work by providing novel evidence on impacts of energy price fluctuations on firm performance in developing countries. It summarizes the results from three complementary background studies carried out to shed more light on the firm-level impacts of energy price changes on firms' competitiveness (studies available upon request). In addition, it distinguishes between the effects of price changes for different energy sources.

The first study assesses these impacts for a panel of firms across a sample of middle- and upper-middle-income countries. It uses World Bank Enterprise Survey (WBES) data for countries with repeated surveys to examine how firms' performance varies in response to changes in energy taxes and prices. The advantage of this approach is twofold. First, it can provide evidence for a substantial number of developing countries, enhancing the results' external validity. Second, it allows exploiting the variation of energy taxes and prices across countries and over time to identify relevant firm responses. However, the wider country coverage comes at a cost in terms of precision. The WBES data do not identify firms' energy mix, which prevents one from observing to what extent firms adjust to price changes by modifying their energy mix or reducing the energy intensity of their output. In addition, the data on policies and prices necessarily eschew details about exemptions, variation in taxes across users of different size, and so on, thus making the policy data less precise.

The second and third studies use panels of (predominantly) medium and large manufacturing firms in Indonesia and Mexico. These studies provide a more precise test of the effects of energy taxes—proxied by energy prices—on firms' competitiveness and allow for specific tests of the impact of environmental fiscal reforms on firm performance. Indonesia and Mexico are particularly interesting case studies because recent policy decisions have increased energy prices in both countries. Indonesia scrapped part of its large fuel subsidy starting at the end of 2014, and Mexico gradually liberalized energy prices and introduced a carbon tax in 2015. Before these reforms, both countries had some of the lowest fuel prices in the world, whereas electricity prices were in the middle of the pack of the countries for which data are available (figure 2.2). Those low prices contributed to keeping Mexican, and even more so Indonesian, firms dependent on fuels as an energy source. Fuels accounted on average for about 60 percent of total energy expenditures among Indonesian manufacturers in 2014. The different relative subsidization of energy sources highlights the importance of distinguishing between them when considering the impact of energy prices on performance. This distinction is also in line with the greater focus of carbon taxes on fuels than on electricity, given the higher carbon dioxide (CO_2) emissions associated with the former.

FIGURE 2.2
Energy prices across countries, 2012

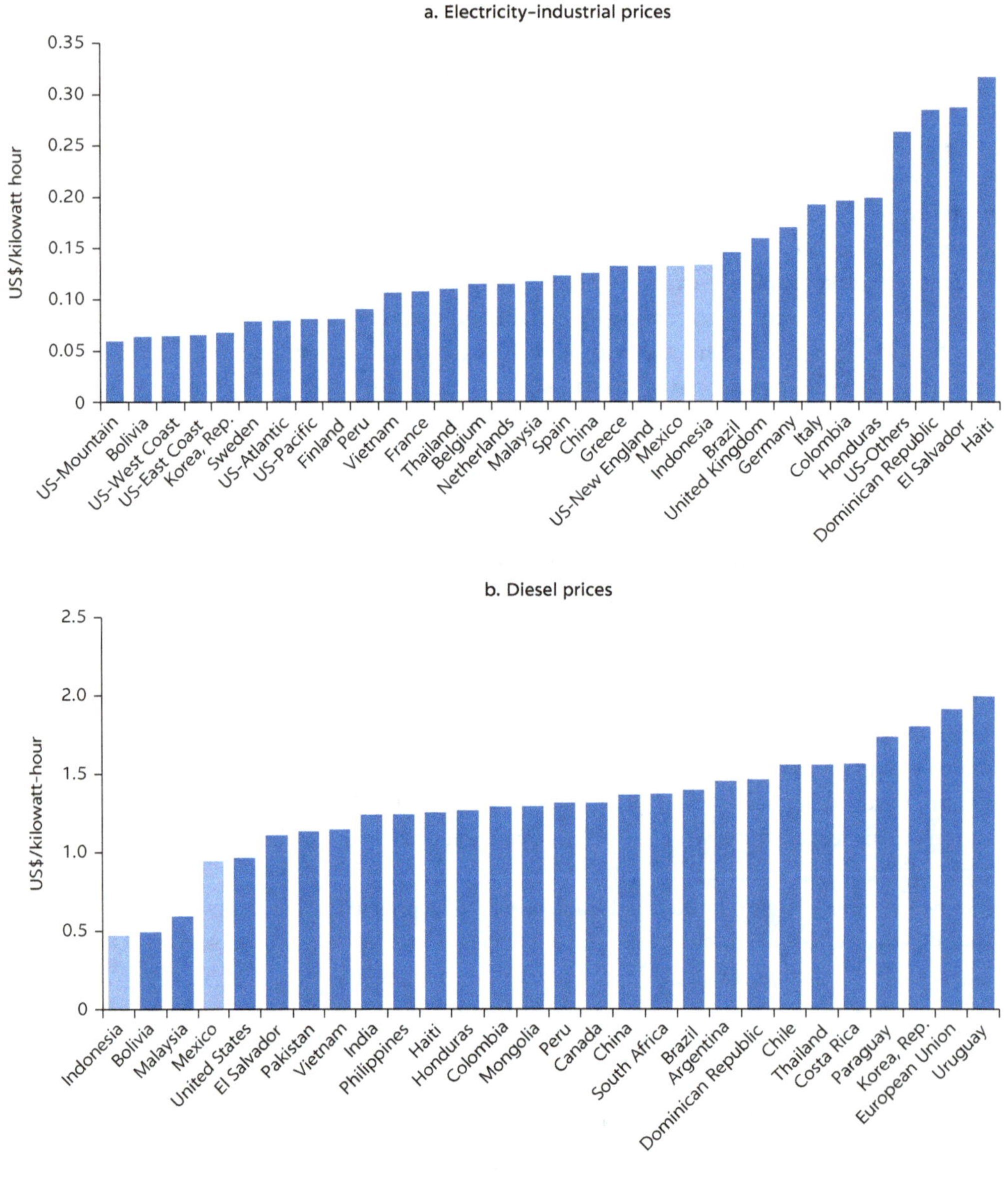

Source: Beylis and Cunha 2017.

Multicountry panel analysis

A simple panel data econometric model is used to assess the relationship between changes in energy prices and in firm performances for a group of countries with available WBES data.[19] The model for this analysis regresses a set of firm performance measures on national or sector-country-specific energy prices, firms' energy intensity, and the interaction between energy prices and energy intensity, as well as firm, sector, and year fixed effects. Furthermore, average sector-country energy intensity is used as an instrumental variable (IV) for firm-level energy intensity to address the potential endogeneity of firms' energy intensity and performance. Matching energy price data from Sato et al. (2015) with WBES panel data results in a dataset with 11 upper-middle-income and high-income countries if national-level prices are used, but only 8 countries when using sector-level data.[20]

The results suggest that an increase in energy prices generally has a positive impact on different measures of firm performance. Table 2.3 presents the results from the basic model specification with firm fixed effects and without instrumenting the energy variables. The effects are tested over different measures of firm performance/competitiveness as dependent variable (logs of total employment, log of sales per employee, log of labor productivity, profits over sales, and share of exports in sales). The results show that higher energy prices might be associated with better economic performance. This outcome seems consistent with the strong version of the Porter hypothesis, that is, the idea that an improvement in production efficiency prompted by higher energy prices more than compensates the increase in production costs due to environmental regulation. This result is particularly strong for productivity indicators (with 1 percent statistical significance) and profitability as well.

The positive effect of energy prices on performance is weaker in more energy-intensive firms, but remains positive even for the most energy-intensive firms. The last five lines of table 2.3 report the values for different percentiles of the energy intensity distribution, helping to quantify the effect of the EP–EI interaction term. Except for labor productivity, for which the effect of energy

TABLE 2.3 **Energy prices and firms' performance across countries (fixed effect estimation)**

	(1)	(2)	(3)	(4)	(5)
	LOG (TOT EMP)	LOG (SALES/EMP)	LOG (VA/EMP)	RETURN ON SALES	EXPORT SHARE
Log EP	0.213	1.410***	2.114***	0.268**	0.0669
	(0.234)	(0.450)	(0.728)	(0.123)	(0.0688)
Log EP x log EI	−0.560	−7.709**	−26.62***	−0.487	−0.0325
	(1.077)	(3.102)	(5.642)	(0.567)	(0.469)
N	4101	3405	1962	3037	3995
Effect at 10th percentile of EI	0.211	1.381	1.982	0.266	0.0668
Effect at 25th percentile of EI	0.208	1.333	1.834	0.263	0.0665
Effect at 50th percentile of EI	0.199	1.215	1.475	0.255	0.0660
Effect at 75th percentile of EI	0.184	1.015	0.831	0.243	0.0652
Effect at 90th percentile of EI	0.157	0.648	−0.301	0.220	0.0636

Note: Fixed effect estimator. Robust standard errors in parenthesis. EI = energy intensity; EP = energy prices; TOT EMP = total employment; SALES/EMP = sales per employee; N = number of firms; VA = value added. * p<0.1, ** p<0.05, *** p<0.01. Additional controls: country-specific linear trends, year-specific size class dummies, year-specific dummy for foreign-owned firms.

prices becomes negative at the 90th percentiles of energy intensity, the effect of energy price increases on other performance variables is still positive or not significant even above the 90th percentile.

There is no evidence that these results may be explained by a substitution between energy and labor inputs, higher output prices, or research and development (R&D) investments. Employment and exports are unaffected by energy price changes. Hence, increases in production efficiency due to energy price changes may occur through other channels than labor cost savings. It could also be the case that higher energy prices may stimulate firm's performance through higher output prices, a hypothesis that cannot be tested with the WBES data. However, the fact that exports and employment do not decline in response to energy price changes suggests that price increases may not be a key average response of firms. Additional analysis also suggests that the share of production workers increases with energy prices, and that energy price changes seem to have no effect on firms' R&D investments. This result may be consistent with the fact that firms in developing countries tend to be far from the technological frontier and hence may adopt, rather than invent, energy-saving technologies in response to energy price increases.

The results are robust to various checks, including instrumenting energy intensity and using country-sector instead of national energy prices. Given the possible endogeneity of firm-level energy intensity, table 2.4 presents the results instrumenting the interaction between energy prices and firm-level energy intensity with the interaction between energy prices and the average sector-country energy intensity. The results are very similar to those of table 2.3, except for the effect on labor productivity, which is now estimated less precisely. The results also hold when using country-sector energy prices instead of country-level prices as the main regressor, despite reducing the sample size and number of countries (see table B.3). Finally, the results are largely robust to clustering standard errors by country-year, in line with the unit of variation of energy prices.

TABLE 2.4 **Energy prices and firms' performance across countries (IV estimation)**

	(1)	(2)	(3)	(4)	(5)
	LOG (TOT EMP)	LOG (SALES/EMP)	LOG (VA/EMP)	RETURN ON SALES	EXPORT SHARE
Log EP	0.160	2.102***	0.983	0.488***	0.109
	(0.341)	(0.681)	(1.042)	(0.183)	(0.0947)
Log EP x log EI	0.481	−20.01**	−8.184	−4.003*	−0.862
	(4.045)	(8.712)	(12.80)	(2.196)	(1.444)
F test of excluded instruments	43.29	40.53	19.79	65.37	42.33
N	4101	3405	1962	3037	3995
Effect at 10th percentile of EI	0.162	2.026	0.942	0.470	0.106
Effect at 25th percentile of EI	0.165	1.902	0.897	0.445	0.101
Effect at 50th percentile of EI	0.172	1.595	0.787	0.384	0.0876
Effect at 75th percentile of EI	0.185	1.077	0.589	0.286	0.0641
Effect at 90th percentile of EI	0.208	0.125	0.241	0.0966	0.0230

Note: IV-Fixed effect estimator. Robust standard errors in parenthesis. EI = energy intensity; EP = energy prices; IV = instrumental variable; TOT EMP = total employment; SALES/EMP = sales per employee; N = number of firms; VA = value added. * $p<0.1$, ** $p<0.05$, *** $p<0.01$. Additional controls: country-specific linear trends, year-specific size class dummies, year-specific dummy for foreign owned firms.

The analysis does not find much heterogeneity in the effects of energy prices on performance across firm size, business constraints, and workforce composition. The analysis suggests that domestic firms are the main drivers of the declining effect of energy prices on labor productivity as energy intensity increases. Conversely, energy price increases appear to be more associated with increases in employment in large firms than in the others, whereas no significant difference is apparent with respect to performance measures. Similarly, firms exposed to different business environments, proxied by the time spent by managers dealing with government regulations and the number of visits by tax officials, do not seem to react differently to energy price changes.

The effects of energy price changes are particularly large for the poorer half of countries in the sample. Table 2.5 excludes from the analysis countries that have crossed the high-income threshold during or before the period of analysis—the Czech Republic, Poland, the Slovak Republic, and Slovenia. The elasticity of performance with respect to energy price is even larger for the remaining set of middle-income countries, in contrast with the idea that emerging economies could be the major losers of increases in energy prices because they are more in need of cheap sources of energy to industrialize.

TABLE 2.5 **Energy prices and firms' performance across countries, upper-middle-income sample**

	(1)	(2)	(3)	(4)	(5)
	LOG (TOT EMP)	LOG (SALES/EMP)	LOG (VA/EMP)	RETURN ON SALES	EXPORT SHARE
Log (EP)	−0.348	1.920**	16.11***	1.114***	0.278*
	(0.662)	(0.960)	(4.904)	(0.391)	(0.150)
Log (EP) × log (EI)	−0.678	−14.51***	−30.49***	−1.070	−0.327
	(1.107)	(5.389)	(7.178)	(0.845)	(0.843)
N	2807	2286	1700	2041	2699
Effect at 10th percentile of EI	−0.351	1.862	15.97	1.108	0.277
Effect at 25th percentile of EI	−0.355	1.775	15.80	1.102	0.275
Effect at 50th percentile of EI	−0.365	1.570	15.41	1.087	0.270
Effect at 75th percentile of EI	−0.383	1.194	14.74	1.060	0.261
Effect at 90th percentile of EI	−0.419	0.500	13.50	1.014	0.244

Note: Fixed effect estimator. Robust standard errors in parenthesis. EI = energy intensity; EP = energy prices; TOT EMP = total employment; SALES/EMP = sales per employee; N = number of firms; VA = value added. * $p<0.1$, ** $p<0.05$, *** $p<0.01$. Additional controls: country-specific linear trends, year-specific size class dummies, year-specific dummy for foreign owned firms.

Indonesia

The multicountry panel data analysis is complemented with a thorough examination of the effects of energy prices on the performance of manufacturing firms in Indonesia and Mexico. Indonesia is an ideal case study because it has a long-standing policy of subsidized energy prices, including for industrial users, resulting in some of the lowest energy prices internationally. Although the subsidy was largely phased out in the public budget at the end of 2014, energy prices continue to be implicitly subsidized by the state-owned monopolists of electricity production/distribution and of fuels distribution, generating concerns for their economic sustainability. The effects of exogenous energy price variations on firm performance were examined using a large panel of

Indonesian manufacturing plants (with at least 20 employees) between 1990 and 2015. To address possible endogeneity, plant-level energy prices were instrumented with province-level price deviation from national average due to geographical locations in the Indonesian archipelagos. Although state-owned monopolists set energy prices nationally, price deviations occur. This is because different distribution costs lead to different prices for users across the archipelago (Rentschler and Kornejew 2017). Electricity and fossil energy sources were considered separately and each source weighted by its initial share in each plant's total energy expenditure.

The results—which are robust to a variety of checks—suggest opposite effects of electricity versus fuel price changes on performance. Table 2.6 reports the regression results obtained with simple ordinary least squares, as well as IV specifications. On the basis of the IV results, which should avoid the endogeneity bias, for a typical plant a 10 percent increase in the price of electricity decreases revenue total factor productivity (RTFP) by 0.5 percent. In contrast, a 10 percent increase in fossil fuel prices *increases* RTFP by 1.4 percent. Similarly, additional results suggest that electricity and fuel prices have respectively a negative and positive effect, although a quantitatively small one, on profit margins as well as on labor productivity.

The key channel through which fuel price increases raise firms' performance appears to be a switch to more efficient capital equipment. In particular, the data show that plants replace inefficient fuel-powered machinery, the use of which has been incentivized by highly subsidized fossil fuel prices, with more efficient electricity-powered capital. Table 2.7 shows that an increase in fuel prices results in increased machinery turnover (columns 1 and 2), larger electricity consumption per unit of capital (columns 3 and 4), greater energy efficiency (column 5), and higher capital productivity. As for incumbents, new plants entering the market in periods of high fossil fuel prices are shown to be more energy-efficient but consuming more electricity per unit of capital, which results in higher capital productivity.

TABLE 2.6 **Indonesia: Energy prices and RTFP**

	(1)	(2)	(3)	(4)	(5)	(6)	(7)
	OLS	OLS	OLS	IV	IV	IV	IV
Electricity price	0.127***	0.139***		-0.054***	-0.038**		
	(0.004)	(0.004)		(0.019)	(0.018)		
Fuel price	0.114***		0.137***	0.139***		0.099***	
	(0.006)		(0.006)	(0.032)		(0.040)	
Fuel/electricity price							0.066***
							(0.018)
Observations	257,980	266,508	265,161	257,980	263,639	265,161	257,980
No. of plants	30,706	34,690	32,021	30,706	31,821	32,021	30,706
Plants FE	Yes	Yes	Yes	Yes	Yes	Yes	Yes
Sector-year FE	Yes	Yes	Yes	Yes	Yes	Yes	Yes
Region trends	Yes	Yes	Yes	Yes	Yes	Yes	Yes

Note: Robust standard errors in parenthesis. FE = fixed effects; IV = instrumental variable; OLS = ordinary least squares; RTFP = revenue total factor productivity. * p<0.1, ** p<0.05, *** p<0.01. Dependent variable is (log of) RTFP.

TABLE 2.7 **Indonesia: Energy prices and technological upgrading**

	(1)	(2)	(3)	(4)	(5)
	PURCHASE	**SALE**	**QELEC/K**	**QFOSSIL/K**	**QENERGY/K**
Electricity price	-0.368***	-0.002	-1.058***	-0.111***	-0.429***
	(0.067)	(0.032)	(0.036)	(0.039)	(0.034)
Fuel price	0.203*	0.219***	0.203***	-0.407***	-0.234***
	(0.114)	(0.054)	(0.070)	(0.080)	(0.067)
Observations	303,192	306,186	222,411	233,735	255,552
Number of plants	32,023	32,057	29,287	29,331	30,644
Plant FE	Yes	Yes	Yes	Yes	Yes
Sector-year FE	Yes	Yes	Yes	Yes	Yes
Region trends	Yes	Yes	Yes	Yes	Yes

Note: Robust standard errors in parenthesis. FE = fixed effects; qElec/K = quantity of electricity over capital stock; qEnergy/K = quantity of energy over capital stock; qFossil/K = quantity of fuel over capital stock. * p<0.1, ** p<0.05, *** p<0.01. Regressions are estimated using 2-stage least squares.

Fossil fuel prices have a negative impact on the aggregate capital stock, consistent with the scrapping of older capital vintages and with lower employment. The latter effect might result from newer vintages of capital being less labor intensive, an intuition supported by the data, which show that higher fuel prices are associated with a shift toward more capital-intensive production technology.

The effects of fuel prices on performance vary across firm types, as well as levels of energy dependence. Consistent with the technological upgrading hypothesis, we find that increases in fuel prices boost productivity less in plants with foreign direct investment and in large plants. Such plants are more likely to be close to the technological frontier and to operate the latest capital vintage. Like in the cross-country analysis, more-energy-dependent firms benefit less from fuel price increases because the increase in costs of production becomes harder to compensate for such firms.

There is no indication that the positive impact on productivity reflects increases in output prices rather than in technical efficiency. In theory, higher RTFP could reflect higher markups by firms passing the higher energy costs they face on to consumers.[21] However, various pieces of evidence are more consistent with the technical efficiency than the output price mechanism. First, fuel price increases raise plants' purchase and scrapping of machinery. Second, plants become more energy efficient and use more electricity in response to fuel price increase, consistent with changes in the technical efficiency of production. Third, the opposite effects of electricity compared to fuel prices on performance are not consistent with the output prices channel, which should apply irrespective of the sources of energy price increase. This asymmetry is rather consistent with the idea that electricity-powered machines tend to be closer to the efficiency frontier than fuel-powered machines and that the price increase therefore reduces the firms' performance. Fourth, performance is less affected by fuel price increases in larger, foreign-owned and exporting firms, consistent with the idea that these firms operate closer to the technological frontier than small, domestic, and non-exporting firms, and as a result have less room to adopt new machinery. This result is again less consistent with the output price increase hypothesis because larger firms typically have a higher market power than small firms.

Mexico

The last analysis carried out used a large panel of manufacturing firms for the 2009–15 period to investigate the effects of energy price changes on performance in Mexico. Mexico's relevance stems not only from its status as a developing country but also from the institutional background of its energy sector. Mexico's energy sector has undergone a major reform since 2014, transitioning from a heavily regulated system, including both price controls and subsidies, to a sector with liberalized prices moving with the market. Besides gradual price liberalization, this reform included opening energy sector activities, the transformation of state-owned companies, and the strengthening and independence of regulatory bodies. Additionally, Mexico introduced a carbon tax in 2014 with the objective of mitigating environmental impacts from fossil fuel consumption, but the tax was limited in terms of its scope.

Composite firm-level energy prices were computed, using as weight the consumption of each type of energy input (electricity and fuels), to assess the relationship between energy prices and various measures of firm performance.[22] In order to deal with the endogeneity of energy prices, the estimated firm-level price indices were instrumented with three alternative sets of variables: (i) average energy price index of the sector-tariff-state triplet which the firm belongs to; (ii) average energy price index of the tariff-state pair, excluding the firm's own sector; (iii) average energy price index of the sector-tariff pair, excluding the firm's own state.[23]

Consistent with previous analyses presented, the results for Mexico suggest that higher energy prices have a positive effect on labor productivity and total factor productivity (TFP), across industries. A 1 percent energy price increase leads to a 0.3 percent increase in labor productivity (measured as value added per worker) and an increase in TFP (table 2.8). In general, less energy-intensive firms tend to have a better performance. Additionally, increases in TFP due to price increases are even larger for more energy-intensive firms. Energy efficiency also increases when energy prices go up, which is likely to be a key driver of these results.

TABLE 2.8 **Mexico: Energy prices and performance across manufacturers**

	(1)	(2)	(3)	(4)	(5)
	LOG (VA/WORKER)	LOG (NET PROFITS)	LOG (TFP INDEX)	LOG (ENERGY EFFICIENCY)	LOG (WORKERS)
Log (EP)	0.315***	0.0390	0.112**	0.484***	−0.169**
	(0.0926)	(0.0736)	(0.0354)	(0.101)	(0.0551)
Log (EI)	−0.400***	−0.210**	−0.0674	−1.112***	0.0728
	(0.0952)	(0.0741)	(0.0350)	(0.101)	(0.0551)
Log (EP) x log (EI)	0.0100	0.00269	0.0425***	0.0580	−0.0155
	(0.0282)	(0.0320)	(0.0123)	(0.0310)	(0.0202)
Firm fixed effects	Yes	Yes	Yes	Yes	Yes
Year effects	Yes	Yes	Yes	Yes	Yes
Observations	39,141	39,965	36,189	39,165	40,354
F-statistic	122.4	120.9	110.6	122.7	122.8
Weak identification F-test	40.62	41.66	38.54	40.71	42.26

Note: The total factor productivity (TFP) index is calculated as a Törnqvist index following the methodology from Aw, Chen, and Roberts 2001. Energy efficiency is measured as value added/firm energy consumption. The instrument for prices is the average price within the same sector and state. For energy intensity, the instrument is the average index within sector and state. For the interaction, the interaction of the two previous instruments is used. The results are robust to assuming that the energy intensity is exogenous. EI = energy intensity; EP = energy prices; TFP = total factor productivity; VA = value added.
* $p<0.1$; ** $p<0.05$; *** $p<0.01$.

TABLE 2.9 **Mexico: Energy prices and performance across manufacturers (electricity vs. fuels)**

	(1)	(2)	(3)	(4)	(5)
	LOG (VA/WORKERS)	LOG (NET PROFITS)	LOG (TFP INDEX)	LOG (ENERGY EFFICIENCY)	LOG (WORKERS)
Log (EP)	−0.847***	−2.324***	−0.555***	−0.0688	−1.930***
	(0.144)	(0.113)	(0.0435)	(0.123)	(0.0733)
Log (EI)	0.700***	−0.0137	0.242***	0.628***	0.179
	(0.204)	(0.144)	(0.0546)	(0.159)	(0.0932)
Log (EP) x log (EI)	−0.154***	−0.0411	−0.0572***	−0.195***	−0.0558**
	(0.0366)	(0.0274)	(0.0105)	(0.0301)	(0.0177)
Log (fuel price)	−0.000745	0.0360***	0.0154***	−0.0120	0.0162*
	(0.0147)	(0.0105)	(0.00405)	(0.0114)	(0.00682)
Log (fuel intensity)	−7.967**	−3.485	−1.239	−20.67***	0.187
	(2.556)	(1.889)	(0.717)	(2.030)	(1.221)
Log (fuel price) x	1.384**	0.396	0.0387	1.011**	−0.145
log (fuel intensity)	(0.509)	(0.362)	(0.140)	(0.391)	(0.234)
Firm fixed effects	Yes	Yes	Yes	Yes	Yes
Year effects	Yes	Yes	Yes	Yes	Yes
Observations	38,565	39,385	35,672	38,584	39,772
F-statistic	149.3	662.2	579.5	638.4	667.3
Weak identification F-test	28.12	112.6	98.49	108.6	113.5

Note: The total factor productivity (TFP) index is calculated as a Törnqvist index following the methodology from Aw, Chen, and Roberts 2001. Energy efficiency is measured as value added/firm energy consumption. The instrument for prices is the average price within the same sector and state. For energy intensity, the instrument is the average index within sector and state. For the interaction between energy prices and firm-level energy intensity, the interaction of the two previous instruments is used. The results are robust to assuming that the energy intensity is exogenous. EI = energy intensity; EP = energy prices; TFP = total factor productivity; VA = value added. * p<0.1; ** p<0.05; *** p<0.01.

Like for Indonesia, decomposing energy prices into the main energy sources reveals heterogeneous effects between electricity and fuels. To allow for the varying effects of each input price on performance, we construct separate prices for electricity and other fuels, considering the specific price-setting mechanisms for each. The results indicate that electricity price increases affect performance negatively, especially for firms in more electricity-intensive sectors (table 2.9). In fact, being highly electricity intensive amplifies the adverse effect of prices on performance, as shown by the negative interaction term between electricity price and energy intensity. Conversely, an increase in other fuel prices tend to have positive effects over profits, TFP, and firm size, with these effects on firm performance being amplified by energy intensity.

Time to revisit the trade-off between energy prices and competitiveness?

Taken together, these new sets of firm-level results strongly support a reevaluation of the conventional wisdom that environmental taxes necessarily harm competitiveness by increasing energy costs. The wide spectrum of data, contexts, and methods employed in the analyses can give confidence in the validity of the main result—that fuel price increases do not seem to harm firms' performance and may even improve it. In addition, the combination of results from two large emerging economies and 11 mainly upper-middle-income countries also supports the external validity of these results.

The role of fuels and their often-subsidized price, along with low management quality in developing countries, emerge as the key elements behind the positive impact of fuel prices on performance. First, to the extent that subsidized fuel prices, such as in Indonesia and Mexico, incentivize firms to hold inefficient fuel-powered capital equipment, those firms could be caught in a perverse low-level equilibrium with low productivity and high energy inefficiency. In developing countries this equilibrium is maintained also because management quality tends to be lower (Cirera and Maloney 2017), and management quality is positively correlated with energy efficiency (Bloom et al. 2010; Martin et al. 2012). Second, poorly managed firms are unlikely to change technology on their own, even if doing so would yield net positive returns, because they lack information on their true managerial quality and the potential for improvement (Cirera and Maloney 2017; Bloom et al., 2012). Hence, an external incentive—such as an input price increase—could help incentivize investment in information and eventually in new capital adoption. This adoption enables firms to improve productivity, and it could offset the adverse effects of energy price increases, particularly in developing countries where firms are typically further away from the efficiency frontier.[24] This finding is consistent with the strong version of the Porter hypothesis (Porter 1980; Porter and van der Linde 1995).

This combination of low energy prices—particularly for fuel—and distance to the efficiency frontier bodes well for the external validity of the results. As suggested by Grubb et al. (2017), a nonlinear convex relation seems to exist between energy prices and energy intensity across countries (figure 2.3). In economies with low energy prices, price increases result in large reductions in energy intensity. To the extent that changes in energy intensity are achieved via technological changes, this may explain why energy price increases in emerging countries, such as those analyzed in the cross-country analysis with WBES data, positively impact firm-level productivity. That is not the case for Western European countries and other high-income countries, which are at a point on the curve where energy intensity does not respond much to energy price increases. As a result, the Porter hypothesis may more likely hold at lower initial levels of environmental regulation and development.

Although surprising, these results are in fact consistent with various empirical findings. First, many empirical studies in high-income countries find that increased stringency of environmental regulation, such as pollution control and air quality regulation, has a positive association with firms' performance because these regulations stimulate within-firm innovation (Berman and Bui 2001; Hamamoto 2006); this chapter estimates similar effects in response to energy price changes. Second, the positive relation between energy efficiency and firms' productivity is well documented in the literature (Worrell et al. 2003; Martin, De Preux, and Wagner 2014; Cantore, Calì, and te Velde 2016), although the evidence presented in this chapter is the first to use the price of fuel as the trigger. Third, recent studies find that the positive impact on performance does not apply to electricity prices is a common finding of recent studies (Marin and Vona 2017; Abeberese 2017). This finding is consistent with the fact that electricity-powered machines tend to be closer to the efficiency frontier than fuel-powered ones, hence the static negative effects of price increases on performance dominate, at least in the short run. Finally, the results from the literature on the—generally negative—firm-level impact of oil price shocks (for example, Lee and Ni

FIGURE 2.3

The nonlinear energy price–energy intensity relation across countries

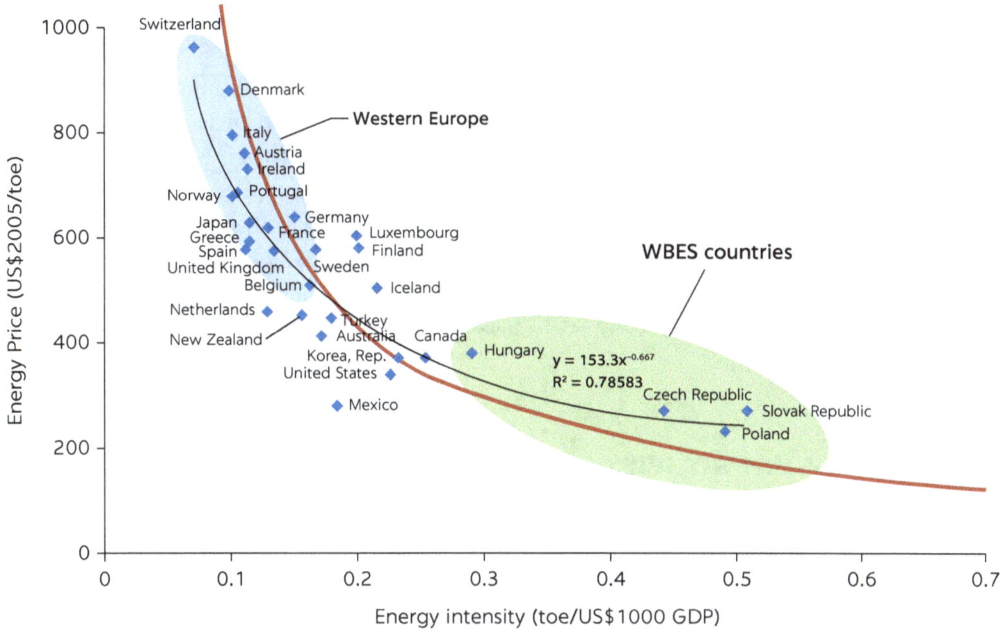

Source: Grubb et al. 2017.
Note: GDP = gross domestic product; toe = ton of oil equivalent; WBES = World Bank Enterprise Survey.

2002; Narayan and Sharma 2011) do not necessarily contradict those in this chapter. That literature tests for the impact of the oil shocks mainly through the demand rather than the supply channel—that is, oil price increases reduce overall demand via general equilibrium effects. In addition, the literature focuses on high-income countries and typically uses stock prices as the measure of performance (so focusing only on listed firms). The oil price shock in that literature is a large transitory shock due to international conditions, which is different from the type of policy-driven price fluctuations captured in this study.

It is more difficult—and beyond the scope of this report—to explain why firms do not adopt such technologies even in the absence of energy price increases, although some hypotheses can be drawn. As discussed above, various factors, such as bounded rationality and poor management, can lead firms to ignore cost-effective investments in energy efficiency. Earlier evidence shows that firms do not exploit available profitable opportunities in energy-saving technologies (DeCanio and Watkins 1998). DeCanio (1993) discusses how information frictions and limited attention could also lead firm managers to give low priority to improving energy efficiency because energy costs usually represent a small fraction of overall expenses.[25] When market distortions have greater importance, the Porter hypothesis seems more likely to hold; therefore, the frictions that might be responsible for suboptimal investment decisions in advanced economies might be even more relevant in a developing country such as Indonesia. For example, managers in developing countries might be less sensitive to energy savings opportunities than in advanced economies, which might lead to suboptimal investment decisions. Lower competitive pressure might also reduce incentives to adopt the most productive technologies and practices.

Although more analysis is needed to confirm and refine these results, they provide reason to be cautiously optimistic about the impact of ETR in developing countries. Studies that cover more developing countries, including low-income ones, reflect contexts with higher initial energy prices and focus on small firms could all improve our understanding of energy prices' impacts on firms. No strong adverse impacts were found for energy-intensive firms, but studies focusing on EITE sectors could shine more light on their specific reactions. Additionally, partial equilibrium studies could be completed with general equilibrium studies. Finally, results from quantitative analysis would benefit from more qualitative information to confirm firms' adaptation strategies, including investments in more efficient equipment. Overall however, the results presented here suggest that competitiveness risks in developing countries, if any, should be moderate.

WHAT POLICIES CAN MINIMIZE ADVERSE COMPETITIVENESS IMPACTS?

The finding that increasing energy prices can improve firm performance in developing countries does not necessarily preclude the need for transitional support to enable the most vulnerable firms to adapt and to minimize risks for competitiveness. As shown in the previous section, efficiency gains may depend on innovation and investments in new technologies, and are thus likely to take some time to materialize. Moreover, the most energy-intensive firms may find it harder to fully offset the effect of higher energy prices on production costs, and even small cost increases may undermine competitiveness in industries highly exposed to trade. In many cases, some support or relief measures to mitigate potential or actual adverse impacts on industrial competitiveness and pollution/emission leakage may thus be needed in EITE sectors, at least temporarily, including to ensure the political acceptability of a new tax.[26]

Several tools are available for governments to reduce competitiveness and leakage risks arising from an environmental tax.[27] Policies and interventions for this purpose include measures targeting production, trade, or consumption that (i) directly reduce vulnerable industries' tax burden (for example, ETR, exemptions, refunds), (ii) support firms to cope with the additional tax burden (for example, output-based rebates, support for resource efficiency), or (iii) reduce the tax asymmetry with international competitors (for example, BTA and consumption-based taxation) (figure 2.4; see also table 2.10).[28] Because potential losses depend on the specific circumstances of local industries, the type of tax considered, and other domestic factors, the decision to use such measures should be based on context-specific evidence from rigorous analysis. Although no instrument is clearly superior in all cases, tax exemptions are generally deemed the least efficient way to preserve competitiveness (Carbone and Rivers 2017), but they are the most commonly implemented measure.

Each type of measure has advantages and drawbacks, and some can jeopardize the tax's effectiveness and limit the scope for efficiency gains in industries if inappropriately used. As discussed in this section, the different policy options differ notably in terms of technical and administrative complexity, implications for tax revenue and budget outlays, and impact on price signals from the tax and incentives for firms (figure 2.4). Aldy (2016) reviews potential risks inherent to different "competitiveness policies," distinguishing

FIGURE 2.4

Policy options to address competitiveness and leakage risks

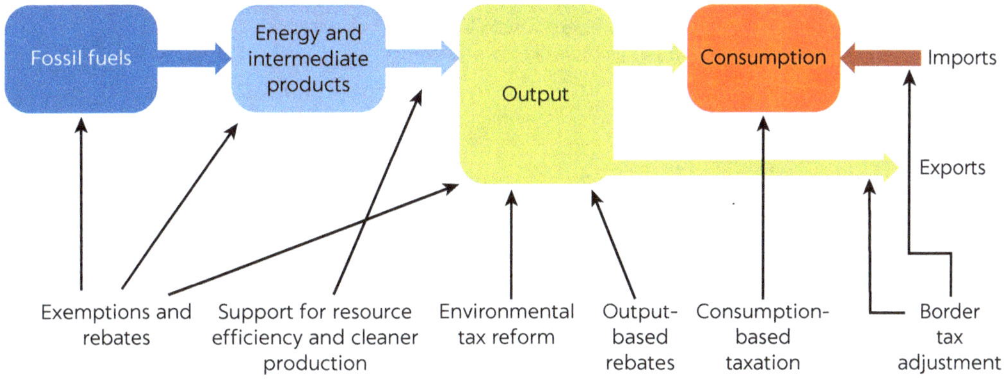

TABLE 2.10 **Summary of competitiveness policy options**

CATEGORY	MEASURE	ADVANTAGES	DRAWBACKS
Tax-reducing measures	**Reducing broad-based taxes on production (environmental tax reform)**	Reduce distortions from the tax system, for example, by reducing corporate income taxes or electricity taxes	Tax revenue reduced by using environmental tax to finance reductions in other taxes
		Potential "double dividend" (creating net gains to output/welfare/employment)	Benefitting the economy rather than individual sectors with industry-specific competitiveness problems
	Exemptions	Target and effectively protect vulnerable industries (at least in the short term)	Undermine tax price signals and environmental effectiveness
	Reduced rates	Relatively simple to implement (but only for downstream tax)	Difficult to determine appropriate level and extent ex ante
	Tax payments refund	Popular with industry groups; easy to communicate	Risk of rent-seeking and challenge from/extension to nonexempted industries
			Increase abatement costs for other sectors
			Costliest option in terms of tax revenue
			Risk of long-term competitiveness loss
	Offsets	Incentivize emission reductions in uncovered sectors	Undermine price signals for the taxed industry
		Incentivize private investment in emission reductions	Administratively complex to ensure environmental effectiveness
			Reduced tax revenues
			Effectiveness at improving competitiveness depends on offset prices
Support measures	**Output-based rebates**	Retain tax price signals and abatement incentives for producers	High cost to public budget (although less than exemptions)
		Strong leakage protection	Reduce incentives for producers to adopt cleaner inputs and for consumers to shift to cleaner products relative to BTA and CBT (but better than for exemptions)
		Divides industry opposition: Up to half of industry enjoys net gain (if sufficient revenue used to finance rebates)	
	Support for resource efficiency and cleaner production	Retain price signal and additional abatement incentives	Scope for gains varies depending on country, sector, firm type, etc.
		Promote green innovation	May not provide immediate or full relief to industries
		Popular with industry groups	Depending on scheme, widely varying cost and can be difficult to scale up at industry level
		Possibility to leverage commercial finance	
		Flexible in design	

(continued)

TABLE 2.10, *continued*

CATEGORY	MEASURE	ADVANTAGES	DRAWBACKS
Trade-related measures	**Border tax adjustment (BTA)**	Effectively prevent competitiveness losses and leakage while maintaining tax price signal Prevent free-riding by non-taxing jurisdictions Do not put pressure on public budgets	Administratively challenging Uncertainty regarding WTO compatibility (though well-designed measures could likely be defended) Risk retaliations by partners and damaging trade/climate negotiations Limited experience to date
	Consumption-based taxation (CBT)	Effectively address competitiveness and leakage risks Extend pricing to extraterritorial emissions Lower legal/political risks than border trade adjustment	Limited experience to date with application to climate (although standard for taxation of other "bads" like tobacco and alcohol) Administratively complex for design options with best environmental effectiveness
	International cooperation	Retain price signal and protect against leakage Leverages domestic tax to encourage equivalent effort in partner jurisdictions No administrative cost or legal risk	Not controlled by domestic policy makers only Difficult to negotiate across many countries and in sectors with many competitors Only regional examples to date, no global ones.

Source: Adapted from World Bank 2017a.

those related to (i) redistribution (for example, fiscal transfers in favor of supported sectors at the expense of others; opportunity costs for alternative uses of tax revenue, such as lowering other taxes or supporting green innovation), (ii) the economic efficiency of pricing carbon (for example, lowering effective tax rates for polluting sectors, resulting in higher emissions or increased total abatement costs; increased administrative complexity creating opportunities for circumventing rules and rent seeking), and (iii) international relations on trade and climate policy (for example, legal and political risks of BTAs). In addition to these risks, excessive relief or support measures may also prevent benefitting industries from reaping the kind of efficiency gains emphasized in the previous section.

For these reasons, policy makers should approach competitiveness policies carefully to ensure the costs do not exceed the benefits. As more countries adopt such policies along with environmental taxes, there is a need for more research into the policies' efficiency and compatibility with the objectives of environmental taxes (Dechezleprêtre and Sato 2017), especially in low- and middle-income contexts. As a general principle, however, policy makers should ensure that measures that can undermine the tax's environmental effectiveness and that entail fiscal costs are not made more generous than necessary, target the most vulnerable industries, and decrease over time.

Tax-reducing measures

Environmental tax packages adopted to date have generally included various design features aiming at eliminating or reducing the additional tax burden for specific sectors.[29] One option is to use revenues from environmental taxes for reductions in other taxes, whereas another is exemptions.

If vulnerable sectors face sector-specific taxes, a simple solution to maintaining their competitiveness is to scale back these taxes while introducing the environmental tax. For example, if the power generation sector of a country currently pays electricity taxes, those can be reduced or eliminated in parallel with the increase of environmental taxation on generation fuels. In this case, environmental incentives can improve for electricity generators without affecting their tax burden.[30] The general principle here is to replace existing environmental taxes with better-targeted ones, while leaving the overall tax burden unchanged.

In many cases, reducing broad-based taxes on production factors is the most efficient use of environmental tax revenue for the economy overall.[31] Recycling revenues from an environmental tax to reduce broad-based taxes, like corporate income or labor taxes can increase the country's competitiveness. However, the benefits of these tax reductions are spread across the economy and would not be targeted at EITE sectors. These sectors that bear a greater proportion of the environmental tax would still face a net tax burden, whereas low-emitting sectors would see a net improvement in their fiscal burdens. There may then remain a need to address competitiveness problems in EITE sectors.

Exemptions and refunds

Exemptions and refunds are costly but popular ways to protect vulnerable sectors. In the case of a downstream tax on direct fuel consumption/emissions, firms and sectors deemed vulnerable can be exempted fully or in part can benefit from a lower rate. Such provisions can also be applied to particular energy products used by certain industries, or to certain regions with fewer mitigation options. In the case of an upstream tax, firms in downstream sectors can receive partial or full refunds for the amount paid indirectly through the purchase of taxed products (such as electricity), although this requires reliable data on firms' indirect tax payment and raises administrative costs. Alternatively, a threshold of fuel consumption/emissions can be set below which liable entities do not have to pay the tax. A ceiling can also be defined to limit the maximum tax burden for companies. Such rules would, however, severely impact marginal mitigation incentives and be complex administratively, in combination with upstream taxes. Exemptions or reduced rates can be permanent or temporary and may be gradually increased to the standard rate. Finally, for carbon taxes, offset allowances can be set to enable liable entities to reduce their tax payments by investing in GHG-mitigating activities outside the scope of the tax.[32] Examples of tax-reducing measures in developing countries include (i) the cap for the carbon tax at 3 percent of the fuel sales price in Mexico; (ii) the tax-free thresholds of at least 60 percent and up to 95 percent considered for different industries in the draft South African carbon tax, depending on various factors including trade exposure and emission performance; and (iii) the use of offsets in the Colombian carbon tax.[33]

Although widespread, exemptions are the least efficient way to address competitiveness concerns. In theory, exemptions can be effective in protecting EITE sectors, at least initially, because they directly reduce or eliminate the additional burden from an environmental tax. Exemptions are relatively simple to implement for downstream environmental taxes, although there are additional administration costs, such as for collecting and verifying claims in the case of tax refunds. Conversely, exemptions and lower rates reduce the internalization of external costs that justifies environmental taxes from an economic point of view. This undermines the environmental effectiveness of taxes by weakening the incentives for polluting firms to invest in cleaner technologies and the price signals intended to favor a shift to cleaner sectors.[34] Exemptions also reduce economic efficiency by increasing economy-wide abatement costs for a given level of emissions or pollution reduction (Ekins and Speck 1999). Negative knock-on effects on other industries can also occur: revenue losses from exemptions mean that less revenue is available to reduce broad-based taxes (see previous subsection). Moreover, targeting the firms and sectors most at risk, and setting the level of tax-reducing measures to address this risk, is likely to be difficult and to lead to lobbying by interest groups during the legislative process. In a review of ex post studies comparing firms benefitting from preferential treatment to firms paying the full rate, Arlinghaus (2015) finds no evidence that tax-reducing measures played a role in maintaining the competitive position of the former. Finally, short-term relief from tax-reducing measures can undermine long-term competitiveness because, if other countries push their industries to become more efficient and innovate through more stringent taxes or regulation, exempted domestic industries fall behind compared to their foreign competitors.

When using exemptions, policy makers should attempt to minimize their environmental and economic costs. Exemptions must be targeted, be time-bound, be reviewed regularly, and combine short-term relief for industries and long-term incentives for them to adapt by adopting cleaner and more efficient technologies (Cottrell et al. 2016). A credible schedule to reduce exemptions and refunds over time may be negotiated and announced when the tax is introduced. This schedule can be replaced by more targeted support measures outside the tax for vulnerable sectors.

Support measures

Measures can be adopted to reduce the overall financial burden for vulnerable industries, while preserving the price signals that determine a tax's environmental effectiveness. Two examples discussed in this section are output-based rebating (OBR) and targeted support for resource efficiency and cleaner production (RECP).[35] Such measures do not reduce the amount of carbon tax paid by firms for a given level of pollution but provide them with a separate form of support that incentivizes the adoption of cleaner technologies and practices. Well-designed support measures can therefore avoid the loss of environmental effectiveness typical of tax-reducing measures. These support measures entail some fiscal costs, but they are likely to be less costly than exemptions and more cost-effective in the long-run to the extent that they incentivize innovation and investment in cleaner technologies that can boost productivity and competitiveness.

Output based rebating (OBR)

OBR can be an efficient way to protect industries against competitiveness losses, while preserving the effectiveness of an environmental tax.[36] The simplest design is to return the total tax revenue paid by a vulnerable sector to each producer in proportion to its share of domestic output, which provides incentives for producers to abate and thus reduce their tax obligations. For example, a country could protect its steel sector from the competitiveness impacts of an upstream coal tax by using the revenue obtained from the sector's overall contribution to this tax to fund subsidies granted per ton of steel produced by each steel mill. Each steel mill would thus have incentives to produce steel with as little coal as possible (and thus to reduce emission) and to produce as much steel as possible in the country. Schemes of this sort can use data already recorded in many countries on production volumes of emissions-intensive products, such as cement, glass, and steel. It has been argued that OBR is particularly appropriate in developing countries where regulators' capacity to face resistance from politically powerful polluting industries may be more limited and the need to incentivize the adoption of cleaner technologies more urgent (Sterner and Isaksson 2006).

The empirical evidence confirms that OBR can be effective. A classic example is the OBR system accompanying the tax on NO_x emissions adopted by Sweden in the early 1990s. Under this scheme, electricity power stations pay a tax on NO_x emissions, and the tax revenue is used to finance subsidies per kilowatt-hour of electricity they produce. Studies of this scheme have found that, despite implementation challenges, it successfully reduced resistance to the tax and efficiently fostered abatement from industries, both through innovation by first-movers and diffusion of technology to other firms (Sterner and Isaksson 2006; Sterner and Turnheim 2009; Braathen 2012; Bonilla et al. 2015). Modeling studies also suggest that OBR can substantially reduce adverse impacts from unilateral carbon pricing for EITE industries.[37]

Despite its advantages, OBR also has drawbacks from economic and environmental perspectives. OBR schemes entail significant costs that are likely to grow larger in the long run (Fischer 2001). However, this cost increase is smaller than with exemptions because firms retain incentives to mitigate and innovate that gradually reduce the need for assistance. OBR should thus be revised periodically as technologies evolve with a view to phase it out; however, there is a risk that it becomes difficult to remove once granted. Weaknesses of OBR, notably relative to the BTA and CBT discussed in the next section, include the following:

- For some products and in some contexts, an environmental tax may not result in a significant substitution in favor of untaxed foreign products, but rather in a shift of demand toward greener substitutes.[38] In such cases, granting OBR to the industry in question limits this demand-side abatement by making producers pay for, and potentially pass on, only the cost of emissions above the benchmark. As a result, OBR is more efficient when there are large variations in pollution intensity across firms and opportunities to improve efficiency and make production processes cleaner. Conversely, it is less efficient when the tax is mostly expected to induce a demand shift in favor of cleaner alternative products and new low-carbon/pollution technologies.
- Another related issue is that OBR schemes limit incentives for producers to reduce pollution/emission intensity to their own production processes. They do not incentivize the reduction of indirect emissions caused

by the consumption of polluting or carbon-heavy inputs, such as clinker for cement production, because the input prices for downstream users do not increase despite the environmental tax (Quirion 2009, Branger and Sato 2017).

Different forms of OBR may be more or less challenging to implement. Basic OBR requires only (i) accurate data (often available) on firms' output levels by product in physical units, such as the tons of a steel type produced by a steel mill, and (ii) at least an approximation of the protected industry's total environmental tax burden,[39] which can be calculated with available emissions factors and assumptions on cost pass-through (for upstream environmental taxes). However, data availability can be an issue for more advanced types of OBR. For example, if OBR rebates are scaled by sector-level pollution/emission intensity benchmarks, various measurement issues apply as well as risks of manipulation (Sterner and Isaksson 2006; Fischer and Fox 2012). This information will likely be particularly difficult to obtain in data-scarce developing contexts, which might then prefer basic OBR. In each case, however, OBR schemes must be designed in a way that ensures that the implicit production subsidies do not violate international trade agreements, such as the WTO's Subsidies and Countervailing Measures Agreement (for example, no contingency on export performance or use of domestic inputs, based on objective criteria) (World Bank 2017a). Ensuring compliance is possible, but requires careful design.

ALthough OBR is more environmentally effective than exemptions, policy makers should carefully trade off the costs with the opportunity to instead lower other taxes. As discussed previously, revenues from carbon taxes can be used to reduce other, more distortive, taxes and yield a double dividend. As a general principle, governments should therefore favor broad-based tax reforms over OBR, and grant the latter only revenues needed to protect competitiveness. Moreover, the appeal of broad-based tax cuts is likely to increase over time, as sectors protected by OBR become greener and more trade partners introduce carbon-pricing measures.

Support for resource efficiency and cleaner production (RECP)

Besides direct financial compensation, governments can accompany adjustment in vulnerable industries by actively supporting firms' efforts to adopt greener technologies and practices. As previously argued, there is evidence of significant and profitable investment opportunities in RECP for energy-intensive firms in developing countries. Recent research shows that, even in more advanced countries, a wide range of technological options exist to reduce energy and process GHG emissions in heavy industries, such as cement, steel, and chemicals (IEA 2017). By promoting substitution in favor of cleaner inputs, resource efficiency, and green innovation,[40] such support can preserve the price signals from an environmental tax and generate additional abatement incentives for firms to reduce their production costs and tax obligation. Conversely, these interventions are unlikely to provide immediate relief to EITE industries following the introduction of a tax, and may not fully offset the additional tax burden or be deemed a fair compensation. Additionally, some measures can entail substantial budget outlays, which can be partly financed with environmental tax revenue.

The scope for gains through investments in RECP will be higher in some cases than in others. It may be higher, for example, in countries where artificially low energy prices have encouraged its inefficient use, and for SMEs, which tend to be less efficient and have lower technical and financial capacity. One difficulty faced in developing countries where polluting industries are mostly made up of SMEs and with a large informal sector is to scale up successful interventions from pilot cases and mainstream RECP in entire industries. Moreover, despite the many examples of successful RECP programs, there is still a lack of comprehensive evaluation of the environmental and economic benefits from such programs.

RECP can be supported through a variety of means depending on the issue at hand, type of industries and firms targeted, and resources available. Interventions can be broadly categorized as follows:

- **Information dissemination:** As pointed out earlier, several informational and behavioral constraints may prevent firm managers from carrying out profitable investments in energy and resource efficiency. This may justify interventions to nudge industries and raise awareness about how such investment can reduce adverse impacts from the environmental tax and bolster competitiveness (Nielsen 2012). Efforts can notably aim at drawing firms' attention to current inefficiencies and the magnitude of potential savings through RECP investments; facilitating the regular monitoring of resource use and efficiency in industries; disseminating information about best-available technologies (for example, through industry associations, study tours abroad); subsidizing firm-level RECP audits[41] and fostering the emergence of specialized service providers; and facilitating decision making by introducing standards and labeling schemes for efficient industrial equipment.
- **Technical assistance:** Even if they are convinced that profitable RECP investment opportunities exist, firms may lack the technical capacity to efficiently install and use new cleaner technology. Support can, for example, be provided through training, through programs to pilot and demonstrate new technologies, or by helping individual firms prepare feasibility studies and bankable investment projects. Many developing countries on all continents have established national cleaner production centers to provide such services.[42]
- **Financial incentives:** Countries frequently subsidize R&D and investment in cleaner technologies in several ways (grants, low-interest loans, tax credits) to accelerate the uptake of such technologies and innovation. For example, in the United States, various state-level tax credits reduce the upfront cost for businesses of investments in air, water, or soil pollution control facilities and equipment (Potter, Stewart, and Kessler 2017). Likewise, South Africa provides an allowance for businesses to implement energy efficiency savings through waste heat recovery and co-generation.[43] Côte d'Ivoire and Morocco provide tax expenditures for solar energy equipment. Governments also broadly use R&D subsidies to foster green innovation in industries, with trade-offs between public and private R&D and between support to general-purpose and industry-specific technologies (OECD 2011; World Bank 2012). Experience suggests that subsidies carefully designed to ensure cost-effectiveness can be effective when used complementarily with other key policy instruments (Rodrik 2014; Veugelers 2016). Among developing countries, the promotion of frontier innovation through R&D grants may be desirable only for countries with sufficient existing technological

capabilities, whereas the promotion of catch-up innovation, technology diffusion, and local absorptive capacity for new technologies should be priorities for others (Dutz and Sharma 2012).

- **RECP finance:** Given the limits to public subsidies, scaling up the adoption of RECP in polluting industries requires leveraging commercial finance. There are many examples of government initiatives and donor-funded projects aiming at promoting the commercial financing of RECP through credit lines and guarantees. For example, in 2016 the Bangladesh Bank launched a US$200 million Green Transformation Fund for participating financial institutions to provide low-rate long-term financing for the purchase of more efficient and cleaner machinery and equipment in the export-oriented textile and leather sector. Likewise, in Vietnam the World Bank supports the Energy Efficiency for Industrial Enterprises project, which includes a US$100 million line of credit to support investment by industrial firms in energy-saving technologies and a component to build banks' capacity to finance such projects.[44] In Brazil, the US$25 million Energy Efficiency Guarantee Mechanism has been implemented since 2009 with support from the Inter-American Development Bank to assist companies in securing commercial bank financing for investments in energy efficiency, by covering performance risk of energy efficiency projects and credit risk of the borrowers.[45]
- **Broader and complementary approaches:** In addition to firm-level support, several less targeted public policies and investments can help resource-intensive and polluting sectors become greener and more efficient. For example, the Republic of Korea has actively promoted eco-industrial parks and industrial symbiosis as ways to reduce the environmental footprint of industrial clusters, with positive results (GGGI 2017; see also UNIDO, World Bank Group, and GIZ 2017). Investing in energy infrastructure and supporting the deployment of renewable energies can also reduce industries' reliance on carbon-heavy energy sources. As noted earlier, trade and investment policies can be used to facilitate access to foreign technologies, goods, and services that help make domestic industries greener. Regulatory reforms and liberalization in key sectors, such as power, can reduce other obstacles to industrial productivity growth. Governments can also adopt green procurement standards to increase the demand for cleaner industrial products (IEA 2017). California recently adopted a law to set maximum acceptable global warming potential for eligible materials, such as steel and glass.[46] Finally, governments can support programs to increase the supply of RECP-relevant skills, such as the Energy Efficiency and Demand Side Management Hub established by the South Africa National Energy Development Institute at the University of Pretoria, which trains specialized master and doctoral students.[47]

Trade-related measures

Border Tax Adjustments (BTAs)

BTAs could in theory be a very effective way to offset the adverse competitiveness impacts of an environmental tax and to prevent leakage.[48] BTAs can be implemented for imports to protect the domestic market share of national producers, for exports to protect their market share abroad, or for both. In the first case, selected imported goods would be subject at the border to a tax equivalent to the difference between the domestic environmental tax and any similar tax applied in their origin country. For exports, domestic producers would be allowed to claim a tax rebate for the exported part of their production. From a conceptual perspective, BTAs can effectively reduce any competitive disadvantage due to a unilateral environmental tax without muting its price signals and, in the case of import BTAs, at no cost to the public budget compared to exemptions and rebates. If implemented by countries representing a substantial share of global markets, BTAs could also push countries that do not apply environmental taxes to introduce one and, in the case of carbon taxes, could thus reduce the risk that any country "free rides" on others' climate mitigation efforts.[49] Modeling studies have confirmed that BTAs would be capable of addressing competitiveness risks[50] and would generally be more effective than alternative policy options (see Fischer and Fox 2012; Böhringer, Carbone and Rutherford 2012; Böhringer, Fischer and Rosendahl 2014). Alton (2014) also found that BTAs on imports and exports would be effective in the case of South Africa.

Although BTAs have been much debated and analyzed, several obstacles explain why they have so far not been implemented in a significant way by any country, high-income or developing.[51] These obstacles include potentially high administrative costs, uncertainty regarding compliance with international trade law, and the risk of political backlash:

- **Administrative:** Implementing BTAs involves several practical difficulties that could lead to complex, inaccurate, and politically tainted procedures (Friis-Jensen 2009; Kortum and Weisbach 2017). The complexity may be more challenging still for developing countries with limited administrative capacity. The implementation of an import BTA in a country notably requires a method to estimate the pollution/emissions embodied in foreign goods and services subject to it. In the absence of access to verified data on foreign producers' production processes, countries could use different benchmarks (such as sector averages, best available technologies), but each has disadvantages. Additionally, assessing trade partners' environmental policies to determine whether they are comparable to the domestic environmental tax is a complex endeavor. All these difficulties are multiplied for manufactured products with more complex supply chains spanning several countries. Combined with the risk that foreign firms will evade BTAs by using transshipping strategies through exempted countries (Aldy 2016), complex supply chains would make it difficult to apply BTAs beyond commodities or basic products with simpler supply chains.
- **Legal:** Because they provide tax rebates to exports or apply a tax on imports, BTAs have been the object of extensive analysis and discussion regarding their compatibility with WTO requirements.[52] In the case of export BTAs, this discussion concerns WTO rules restricting the use of subsidies. In the case of import BTAs, it mainly concerns two key clauses of the General Agreement on Tariffs and Trade (GATT): the Most-Favored Nation principle, which prohibits discrimination between foreign products from different countries, and the National Treatment principle, which prohibits discrimination between foreign and domestic products. Any BTA would thus have to be consistent with these two principles. Alternatively, a BTA with the sole purpose of reducing carbon leakage could aim to qualify for an exception under GATT Article XX, but this necessitates passing several additional tests (Mehling et al. 2017). In all cases, preventing a competitiveness loss would theoretically not be an eligible motivation to override trade law obligations (Cosbey et al. 2012; Trachtman 2017).

- **Political:** Even with WTO-consistent BTAs, the concern has been raised that the use by one country of trade taxes to implement domestic environmental or climate policy could be suspected of being disguised protectionism (Holmes, Reilly, and Rollo 2011), expose this country to retaliation by affected trade partners, and undermine future multilateral trade and climate negotiations (Houser et al. 2008).[53] Some emerging countries, such as China and India, have vocally opposed BTAs (Aldy 2016), although Mexico mentioned them as a prospective instrument in its NDC under the Paris Agreement (Mehling et al. 2017). It has also been argued that the use of BTAs in high-income countries could unfairly shift the burden of emission reductions to developing countries (Condon and Ignaciuk 2013), if the BTAs do not consider the United Nations Framework Convention on Climate Change's (UNFCCC) principle of "common but differentiated responsibilities and respective capabilities" (CBDR-RC) (Cosbey et al. 2012). To address this issue, some authors have suggested that import BTAs should exclude all exports from developing countries with low emissions per capita (Mehling et al. 2017; Odell 2018). Such exemptions/reductions could, however, distort trade, and the benefit may not stay with developing countries if the incidence is shared with trade partners. A way of avoiding these problems while incorporating CBDR-RC into BTAs in developed countries would be to use some of the tax revenue to support mitigation action in developing countries, for example through the Green Climate Fund (Grubb 2011).

Countries considering introducing BTAs should carefully consider these complexities and ensure that benefits outweigh costs. It remains an open question whether BTAs will become a standard instrument for policy makers, including those in developing countries, to address competitiveness aspects of environmental taxes. In all cases, any BTA should be designed to minimize administrative complexity, legal uncertainty, and political risks, taking into account the characteristics of the industries to be covered.[54] Cosbey et al. (2012) provide detailed and practical guidance on how to design BTAs that would (i) effectively prevent leakage, (ii) be consistent with international trade/investment law and climate agreements, (iii) entail a reasonable administrative burden and (iv) be implemented transparently and in accordance with other good governance principles.[55] This chapter concludes that, for administrative, legal, and political reasons, BTAs should be applied only for imports, cover only taxed EITE sectors, and provide only temporary transition support with clear phase-out provisions. Mehling et al. (2017) also propose a design for a temporary import BTA on EITE commodities, considering BTA scope and coverage, methodology to assess carbon content, adjustment level, revenue use, expiration clause, and establishment process. Regarding the methodology to calculate carbon embedded in production, they notably argue that legal durability, ease of implementation, and environmental performance can best be balanced by using regional or global sectoral benchmarks for emission factors, combined with a transparent process allowing individual producers to document actual emissions and improved performances.

Policy makers should approach the issue of WTO compatibility particularly carefully. Design features that may maximize the chance of BTAs passing legal muster in the case of a carbon tax are suggested in Hillman (2013), Mehling et al. (2017), and Trachtman (2017). Trachtman's detailed analysis argues that chances of WTO compliance would be highest with a BTA in connection with a product-based tax, rate for which is established for specific categories of products but does not vary with the carbon intensity of their production. He also finds that export BTAs would reduce the likelihood that a parallel import BTA would qualify for exceptions established in WTO law, and suggests WTO-compliant subsidies to vulnerable industries as a viable alternative. Finally, he argues that a consumption-based carbon tax could provide many of the benefits of a production-based tax combined with an import BTA in terms of competitiveness, with a good possibility of being eligible for an exception under WTO law. This option is discussed next.

Consumption-based taxation

Consumption-based taxation (CBT) would not be levied on producers but on domestic consumers, like a consumption-based excise tax. In this way, CBT would resemble most countries' current use of excise taxes on products such as alcohol and tobacco. Countries tax these products when they are consumed in their territory, irrespective of whether the products were imported or produced domestically, but exempt them if they are produced for export. Taxing carbon or pollution through such a consumption-based excise tax could by itself achieve the functions of a tax on producers, coupled with import and export BTAs.

In its administratively simplest form, the tax rate could be set per product on the basis of sector-specific benchmarks (such as best practice). The same tax rate would then apply for imported and domestically produced goods, even if the actual emissions intensity varies by origin. In addition to keeping administrative costs low,[56] holding the tax rate stable in this manner may increase chances of compliance with GATT Article III.2 (*National Treatment on Internal Taxation and Regulation*). However, the price signal would be disjointed from the emissions released to produce a specific product, therefore weakening abatement incentives.

The environmental incentives of CBT could be further improved by combining it with incentives for producers using cleaner technologies. For example, a steel mill proving that it uses a low-carbon electric arch, rather than a high-carbon blast furnace, could be granted a tax credit or subsidy (Fullerton and Wolverton 2003; Trachtman 2017). Producers would thus be rewarded for producing at lower emissions than those assumed in setting the excise tax. This incentive would be provided to both domestic and foreign manufacturers of eligible products that are consumed in the implementing country. These payments are effectively rebates for a tax that should not have been collected on low-carbon products in the first place—so they do not represent net revenue losses relative to a first-best BTA that was able to tax each product perfectly according to its emissions. The burden of proof would be on producers to reduce administration costs and information constraints for overseas productions. Governments can hold down administration costs by funneling these applications for rewards through third-party certification companies (Heine, Faure, and Lan 2017).

Like for BTAs, administrative feasibility may require limiting CBT to EITE industries. It is essential for CBT that a unit of the product be clearly identified and that average emissions can be estimated. These criteria are feasible for primary EITE products, such as tons of steel, but not for complex products, such as computers. Subject to this caveat, CBT would involve manageable administration costs and allow countries to directly apply their experience with taxing other traded "bads," such as tobacco and alcohol.

The political economy of CBT, especially compared with that of BTAs, merits further exploration. Where proposed, BTAs have tended to be politically popular with influential constituencies, such as affected industries and labor unions. The extent to which CBT would get the same support is an open question, especially if CBT involves rebating tax payments to foreign producers using cleaner technologies. Additionally, CBT may not be as effective as BTAs at incentivizing the adoption of more ambitious environmental policies by affected trade partners.

International cooperation

Coordinating environmental policies with trade partners would be the ideal way to address the concerns of vulnerable domestic industries. In the case of taxes, minimizing rate differentials would reduce the underlying cause for competitiveness losses and leakage, and thus reduce the need for targeted support for these industries. It would also largely avoid the administrative, legal, and political risks of previously discussed policy options. In addition to taxes, different market-based or regulatory environmental policies could be coordinated between competing countries, if they have similar stringency levels for key sectors. Reciprocal agreements on pollution/emission pricing levels—in the form of a binding treaty or a less formal political agreement, multilateral or regional, and covering a sufficiently large portion of trade in EITE commodities between major competitors—have been presented as a potential complement (World Bank 2017a). As previously noted, international sectoral agreements between governments or companies to determine common emissions reduction pathways in sensitive industries have also been considered, as a complement to economy-wide mitigation commitments (Bodansky 2007; Colombier and Guerin 2008; Wooders 2010).

Negotiating the alignment of environmental taxes is not easily done in practice. In the case of climate change, the commitment made by 190 countries under the Paris Agreement to implement mitigation measures through periodically revised NDCs is a welcome step, although the varying levels of ambition and difficulty in comparing different types of measures remain challenging. Sectoral agreements, which were largely discussed in the run-up to the 2009 UNFCCC summit in Copenhagen, have lost momentum since then, except in international maritime and air transport. Since then, the heads of state of France, the Netherlands, and the United Kingdom, as well as leading economists, have called for a "carbon price floor" (Cramton et al. 2017; Farid et al. 2016), but no action has materialized so far. Unlike the other policy options discussed in previous sections, by definition, coordination does not depend on any single country's efforts and is thus unlikely to provide relief to that country's industries within the desired time frame.

Consistency with the UNFCCC's common but differentiated responsibilities and respective capabilities principle may require differentiated approaches or compensatory measures. One option is to allow a tiered approach of carbon prices, where developed countries commit to a higher environmental tax (or ETS) level than developing countries. Such a differentiation would lose some of the gains of the agreement in terms of providing a level playing field for green competitiveness, but it could nevertheless go some way toward reducing those concerns. A second option is to complement the agreement on a carbon price floor with a system to share some of the tax revenues to finance mitigation action in developing countries, for example through the Green Climate Fund.

Transition assistance in affected industries

Support to minimize the social impacts of downsizing in carbon-intensive industries is likely to be a needed complement to competitiveness policies. As previously noted, reducing reliance on polluting/emission-intensive industries and promoting low-carbon development pathways are integral objectives of environmental taxes. In the longer run, achieving these objectives likely implies output and employment losses in firms and industries unable to adapt. Although temporary support to address the risk of competitiveness losses due to unilateral environmental tax is important, if only to ensure the political acceptability of ambitious environmental taxes, this support is not sufficient to accompany the necessary transitions in the long run. Additionally, this issue is broader than competitiveness and leakage: a large part of output and employment losses could come from lower demand for polluting and carbon-heavy products.

Several traditional policies can help affected industries and minimize the social costs of low-carbon transitions. In this regard, useful parallels can be drawn with policies used in the past by different countries to mitigate the negative impacts on industries, regions, and workers disproportionately affected by firm exits due to various industrial and trade policies (Fay et al. 2015; Vogt-Schilb and Hallegatte 2017). Implementing ambitious environmental taxes may be easier if policies are in place that can support firms and workers in downsizing industries, such as horizontal social protection schemes (such as unemployment insurance) or targeted support for affected firms (such as financial assistance) and displaced workers (such as social assistance, retraining and assistance/incentives for employment in expanding sectors). The evidence suggests that such policies can effectively help mitigate most of the losses and have generally modest costs (Porto 2012). However, the relative weakness of social protection and education systems in many developing countries and the poor global track record in compensating losers from globalization (Obstfeld 2016; Rodrik 2017) suggest the need for active efforts to ensure the provision of effective support. In low-income countries, this support will likely require international assistance in the form of resource transfers and institutional strengthening (World Bank 2015).

CONCLUSION

Going forward, concerns over competitiveness and carbon/pollution leakage will remain a major element of national-level debates on environmental taxation. Real or perceived risks of lower production, job losses, and leakage due to unilateral environmental taxes are likely to continue fueling opposition from industry and undermining public support for such measures. Although overall impacts may be limited, the economic costs could be significant in some EITE sectors, at least in the short run. They could also increase in the future if countries introduce the more ambitious environmental taxes likely to be needed to achieve the emission reduction targets they committed to in international climate negotiations. Over time, competitiveness concerns should become less relevant as more countries accounting for a large share of global trade in EITE products adopt comparable taxes. Until this happens, providing satisfactory responses to these risks will remain a political as much as an economic imperative for policy makers willing to mitigate GHGs or reduce pollution through environmental taxes. Managing the political economy of environmental policy, including by avoiding concentrated losses and smoothing the transition for those who stand to be most affected, is critical to promote low-carbon economic development (Fay et al. 2015).

It is essential for policy makers in countries that consider introducing new environmental taxes to have a clear understanding of (i) how the competitiveness of different sectors could be affected in the short, medium, and long term and (ii) which policy options can efficiently mitigate potential adverse effects. Although much has been written on these issues for high-income economies, this chapter fills a knowledge gap for developing countries.[57] It does so by analyzing the impact of energy price variations on firm performance in different developing contexts, and by reviewing the most recent knowledge on relevant policy options.

The impact of environmental taxes on competitiveness will vary across countries, and this chapter suggests that impact is likely to be more positive where firms are farther from the global efficiency frontier. A broad range of factors interact to determine the direction and magnitude of the impact an environmental tax may have on a country, its industries, and its firms. Competitiveness losses in some sectors do not preclude overall gains at the national level. Likewise, short-term adjustment costs may lead to dynamic efficiency gains in the longer run. As far as environmental fuel taxes are concerned, the empirical evidence on several developing countries presented in this chapter suggests that the fuel cost increases may not harm firm performance—and may even strengthen it. The cases of Indonesia and Mexico show that policies that keep fuel prices artificially low make firms excessively dependent on fuels, as opposed to cleaner energy sources, and disincentivize investments in energy efficiency. The evidence strongly suggests that reversing such policies can lead to efficiency gains that more than compensate for increased energy costs, more so when firms are distant from the efficiency frontier (importantly, this result holds even for energy-intensive firms, although they tend to benefit less than the others). At the very least, there is no sign that higher energy prices necessarily undermine productivity in middle-income countries. However, this does not preclude adjustment costs in the short term and competitive pressures for EITE sectors faced with high environmental taxes.

Different policy instruments can mitigate competitiveness risks, but policy makers should understand their trade-offs and avoid measures that would undermine the very objectives of environmental taxation or prevent reaping efficiency gains. Exemptions, despite their frequent use, are the least efficient way to preserve competitiveness and may be counterproductive in the longer run. In contrast, ETR, OBR, support for resource efficiency, BTAs, and CBT all have potential to bring relief to EITE industries, while retaining price signals and encouraging green innovation. These instruments can be used separately or in parallel, but their cost-effectiveness will depend on their design modalities and the way they are implemented in practice. Generally, support measures should target EITE sectors, be time-bound and reviewed regularly, and combine short-term relief for industries and long-term incentives to adopt cleaner and more efficient technologies.

According to the analysis in this chapter, policy makers in countries considering environmental taxation should consider the following principles:

- **Use environmental taxes to achieve both environmental and economic objectives.** As discussed earlier in the chapter, environmental taxes (or reduction of environmentally harmful subsidies) have broad economic benefits while reducing environmental externalities. The evidence on middle-income countries also suggests that they can foster firm-level efficiency gains by encouraging more efficient energy use and investment in more modern equipment. As argued by Vogt-Schilb and Hallegatte (2017), environmental/climate policy is more likely to be successful if it is grounded in other economic and social development goals. In this light, environmental taxes could be seen as a way to promote industrial energy efficiency and innovation, and as a source of revenue to help industries transition to greener processes and products.
- **Consider providing support only if there is clear evidence that some sectors will not be able to adapt to the tax before losing competitiveness.** A rigorous country-specific empirical assessment should provide evidence about the industries and firms that could be positively or negatively affected. Concerns to consider include (i) the expected impacts in the short, medium, and long term; (ii) the extent to which vulnerable sectors stand to lose because of competitiveness issues or because of lower demand for taxed products; (iii) the scope for efficiency gains in vulnerable industries; and (iv) the weight of these industries in domestic output, exports, and employment.[58]
- **Target support or relief measures and avoid making them more generous than needed.** Using an in-depth review of policy options, policy makers should identify which instrument, or combination of instruments, is likely to be the most cost-effective to address expected adverse competitiveness impacts. Besides administrative or legal considerations, a key factor in the decision should be the capacity of competitiveness policies to preserve incentives for protected sectors to grow cleaner and more efficient over time. Competitiveness policies should target vulnerable EITE sectors, provide relief or support proportionally to the expected impacts, and decrease over time as domestic industries adapt and trade partners adopt equivalent environmental policies.
- **Design taxes in a way that increases political acceptability.** Even without mitigation measures, experience shows that good tax design can increase the chances that an environmental tax be broadly accepted, even by industries. Effective design includes setting explicit objectives for the tax and a clear place in the government's strategy; inclusive stakeholder consultations; a gradual, predictable, and credible implementation, allowing firms to adapt their investment plans; a clear communication of expected benefits (including to build public support and coalition from industries standing to benefit disproportionately) compared to potentially more costly alternatives; and so on.[59]
- **Coordinate taxes and complementary policies.** Setting carbon taxes high enough to meet the targets of the Paris Agreement could have major impacts on energy-intensive industries, especially in developing countries farther from the

efficiency frontier. In all cases, industry resistance to carbon tax initiatives so far, which have generally involved low effective taxation rates, suggests that this would be politically difficult and could only be done gradually over time. Given the urgency to mitigate climate change and environmental degradation, this implies that environmental taxes should be thought of as a complement to other policy instruments to reduce emission/pollution (for example, performance standards, support for R&D, "feebates," labeling). Of course, policy makers must also understand that such instruments will have different impacts on the productivity and competitiveness of domestic producers.

NOTES

1. The empirical analysis was led by Massimiliano Calì and Nicola Cantore (UNIDO) on the basis of three background papers prepared jointly with Massimiliano Mazzanti, Giovanni Marin, and Francesco Nicolli (cross-country analysis); Taufik Hidayat and Giorgio Presidente (Indonesia); and Leonardo Iacovone, Mariana De La Paz Pereira Lopez, and Julio Valle Pereña (Mexico).
2. As some authors have argued, previous initiatives in developing countries have tended to be insufficient to strongly affect firm behavior and deter pollution, have not targeted industries (for example, gasoline taxation primarily affecting motorists), and were designed for revenue generation more than environmental protection (Parry, Norregaard, and Heine 2012).
3. ETSs are outside the scope of this study, but the competitiveness issues and policy options discussed here are largely relevant for this alternative form of carbon pricing.
4. See Nakhooda (2014) for a presentation of the carbon tax proposal in South Africa and of debates around its consequences for export competitiveness and jobs in energy-intensive industries. A second carbon tax bill was passed in December 2017 with implementation planned to begin in 2019.
5. This concern over environmental taxes echoes long-standing and broader debates about the competitiveness dimension of business taxes (see, for exampel, Knoll 2012). In this regard, Summers (1988) challenged the conventional view that lowering taxes on domestic firms necessarily improves their trade competitiveness, if it attracts internationally mobile capital and leads to an appreciation of the real exchange rate.
6. The relevance of the concept of competitiveness at the national level has been contested (Krugman 1994), and countries do not "compete" in the way firms do. Nonetheless, national competitiveness can still be a useful concept to analyze a country's overall ability to thrive in global markets (Porter 1990). For example, the World Economic Forum defines it as the "the set of institutions, policies, and factors that determine the level of productivity of a country," which in turn "sets the level of prosperity that can be reached by an economy." For a detailed discussion on the use of the concept of competitiveness when analyzing the economic impacts of unilateral climate policies, see Carbone and Rivers (2017).
7. Rentschler, Kornejew, and Bazilian (2017) provide a similar framework to assess the potential impacts of fossil fuel subsidy reforms on firms, and cite additional references on the different channels highlighted.
8. According to the International Energy Agency, in 2015 about 68.5 percent of world electricity production was from fossil fuel–generating plants (coal, gas, oil), compared to 16 percent from hydroelectricity and 10.6 percent from nuclear.
9. In practice, energy intensity and trade exposure have been the most commonly used criteria, partly because they are easier to assess.
10. In the United States, the average energy intensity of manufacturing was 2 percent in 2007. About 90 percent of the value of all manufacturing shipments was produced by sectors with an energy intensity under 5 percent (U.S. EPA 2009).
11. Information on aluminum production comes from the website of The Aluminum Association, http://www.aluminum.org/industries/production/primary-production.
12. In behavioral economics, the endowment effect refers to agents' tendency to ascribe more value to things they already own than to similar things they do not own, which can lead them to stick with certain assets even though better options may be available.

13. The combination of knowledge and environmental externalities, path dependency due to the current dominance of carbon-intensive technologies in various sectors, and high upfront capital requirements and risk level compared to traditional sectors drives a wedge between private and social returns to investment in green technologies and generates a financing gap. All this prevents markets alone from ensuring sufficient creation and use of clean technologies (see, for example, Popp, Newell and Jaffe 2010; Dutz and Sharma 2012 for detailed discussions of market and behavioral failures in green innovation). The public sector's role in establishing a conducive environment for green innovation has been widely recognized, and researchers have generally argued for a combination of instruments to address simultaneously the market failures related to environmental externalities (for example, environmental tax and regulations) and knowledge externalities (for example, research and development subsidies) (Acemoglu et al. 2012; Bosetti et al. 2011). Specifically, on the interaction between environmental taxes and innovation, see OECD (2010).
14. A stronger version of the Porter hypothesis holds that the innovation induced by environmental policy more than offsets compliance costs and boosts competitiveness (for a discussion, see Ambec et al. 2013).
15. Chapter 1 discusses such channels in more detail.
16. As noted by Aldy (2016), transport costs could become an even more important factor in the future if progress continues on international negotiations to curb GHG emissions in shipping and aviation.
17. The potential impact in developing relative to high-income countries is ambiguous ex ante. On the one hand, firms in developing countries could be relatively more vulnerable to tax-induced energy price shocks if they are more reliant on polluting technologies and less able to adapt. On the other hand, being further from the technology frontier may mean that they have more scope for efficiency gains to compensate for higher energy prices.
18. In practice, changes in energy prices can reflect market variations, including fluctuations in the international fossil fuel prices, or policy changes, including taxation and changes in state-sanctioned tariffs and prices. The elasticity to a price change due to a fuel tax or to a change in mandated prices typically exceeds that from market-induced fuel price changes because the former is more salient than the latter (Rivers and Schaufele 2015), sends a clear price signal as opposed to noise from fluctuation, and is more likely to be interpreted as a stable long-term change. For this reason, elasticities estimated on the basis of market fluctuations are likely to underestimate firms' potential reaction when faced with tax-induced price increases.
19. See appendix B for more details on the methodology and data.
20. Included countries with national-level data are Brazil, the Czech Republic, Hungary, Kazakhstan, Mexico, Poland, Romania, the Russian Federation, the Slovak Republic, Slovenia, and Turkey.
21. In Indonesia, Rentschler and Kornejew (2017) find some weak evidence of pass-through of energy prices on sale prices but not fuel prices. Changes in fuel prices do not translate to changes in sales prices (contrary to changes in energy prices, which are reflected in changes in sales prices).
22. Although firms tend to face similar prices, monthly variations of prices and firm output allow for the construction of firm-specific prices.
23. Different tariffs apply only to electricity.
24. In developing countries, firms have more room to adopt existing technology in response to energy price increases rather than undergoing the more costly process of moving the technological frontier as is often the case in high-income countries (Cirera and Maloney 2017).
25. Incomplete information has also been used in other contexts to explain, for example, why firms in developing countries do not adopt more efficient management practices despite large actual net returns from adoption (Bloom et al. 2013).
26. See Vogt-Schilb and Hallegatte (2017) for a discussion on the political economy of domestic climate policy and an overview of normative debates about government compensation for industries standing to lose out from such policies.
27. This section draws on and complements the review in World Bank (2017a) of policy options to mitigate leakage and distributional risks from carbon taxes.
28. Another aspect concerning ETSs not discussed here is the allocation method of emission allowances. Options include free allocation to certain industries based on historical emissions (grandfathering) or output, as opposed to allocation through auction. For a detailed discussion in the European case, see Grubb and Neuhoff (2006).

29. See Ekins and Speck (2012) for a detailed presentation and analysis of tax-reducing measures adopted by European policy makers to address competitiveness concerns from energy and environmental taxes.
30. Fuel taxes better capture the emissions than electricity taxes, which apply to renewable energies as well.
31. See chapter 1 for a discussion of development co-benefits of ETR.
32. See section 8.2.3 in World Bank (2017a) on the use of offsets.
33. See appendix A.
34. Exemptions can also be used strategically to strengthen the incentives built into the tax. For example, Mexico has initially zero-rated emissions from gas-powered electricity generation, aiming to further increase the incentive for shifting from coal to gas. However, this eliminates the incentive to switch from gas to renewables (World Bank 2017a).
35. Compensation through reductions in other taxes paid on labor or capital (that is, revenue-neutral ETR) is not discussed here because it may not be the preferred approach in many developing countries with low tax take. The efficiency and fairness aspects of this type of reform are reviewed in World Bank 2017a (section 8.2.1.2).
36. Output-based allocation (OBA) of emission allowances has been used as an equivalent measure in ETSs (see, for example Fischer and Fox 2004; Quirion 2009). A related measure is the use of tax revenue to capitalize a fund that can indirectly benefit taxed polluting firms, for example by subsidizing research and investments in abatement technologies.
37. For example, Adkins et al. (2012) use both partial and general equilibrium frameworks to study the impacts of unilateral carbon pricing with OBR on U.S. EITE industries over different time frames. They find that OBR would keep output losses about 0.5 percent and virtually eliminate any increase in net imports due to the tax over time. Using a CGE model, Fischer and Fox (2010) find that in some circumstances (presence of distorting labor taxes, absence of comparable emission pricing scheme abroad, and incomplete coverage of pricing scheme), OBA of emission allowances for EITE industries can yield higher welfare and lower emission leakage than full auctioning with revenue recycling through lowering of distortive taxes. Hagem et al. (2015) compare OBR with an alternative rebating scheme based on firms' expenditures on abatement equipment.
38. As discussed in "Conceptual framework," the available evidence suggests that such demand effect can account for a large share of output losses in EITE sectors due to an environmental tax.
39. If the government's estimate is perfect and the entire revenue collected from the industry is rebated, the average firm can be completely shielded from a net tax incidence. If the estimate is instead too low, the average firm faces some net tax incidence, but still receives a significant protection. The point of OBR is to provide sufficient protection to ensure competitiveness, but this does not necessarily require no-net incidence. Accordingly, a slight underestimation of the industry's tax burden is no major concern for practical policy purposes. Overestimation of the tax burden is more serious as it entails a transfer from other industries to the protected one. Again, this risk is no reason to reject OBR in favor of exemptions where those indirect transfers (of abatement costs for achieving economy-wide mitigation targets) are higher. For practical policy, governments should therefore strive to form good estimates of the vulnerable industries tax burdens, but small mistakes are no major concern.
40. See section 2.1.c in IEA (2017) on firms' strategic options.
41. For example, Japan subsidizes energy audits for firms with an annual energy use exceeding 1,500 kiloliters in crude oil equivalent and publishes aggregate data (showing that potential energy savings average 8 percent across sectors) to help convince other firms (IEA 2015).
42. UNIDO and UNEP have established a Global Network for RECP (RECPnet) that gathers data on 69 members in 63 countries, collects technical knowledge on RECP, maintains a roster of experts, and organizes international events. For more information, see http://www.recpnet.org.
43. For more information, visit the South African National Energy Development Institute website at http://www.sanedi.org.za/12L.html.
44. For more information on this project, visit its web page at http://projects.worldbank.org/P151086?lang=en.
45. For more information on this mechanism, visit its web page at https://www.iadb.org/en/project/BR-L1111.

46. For more information, see the Buy Clean California website at http://buycleancalifornia.org.
47. For more information, visit the University of Pretoria website at http://www.up.ac.za/national-hub-for-postgraduate-programme-in-energy-efficiency-and-demand-side-management-eedsm-hub.
48. For a critique of the economic rationale for using BTAs, see Kortum and Weisbach 2017.
49. More recently, "climate clubs"—an agreement between a group of countries to introduce harmonized emission reduction efforts and collectively sanction nonparticipants through a low and uniform tariff on all their exports to club countries (assuming international trade law would be modified to authorize this)—have been suggested as another potential mechanism, although designed more to solve free riding than to address leakage or competitiveness concerns (Nordhaus 2015).
50. Analyses have mostly considered BTAs in the context of carbon pricing (tax or ETS), generally referring to border carbon adjustment (BCA), and mostly from the perspective of OECD economies. See Condon and Ignaciuk (2013) for a literature review. See also Branger and Quirion (2014) for a meta-analysis of 25 empirical studies, which finds carbon leakage rates of –5 percent to 15 percent (mean 6 percent) with BTAs compared to 5–25 percent (mean 14 percent) without policy. Böhringer, Balisteri, and Rutherford (2012) summarize results from different models and also find that BTAs would be effective. Looking at the case of the United States, McKibbin et al. (2017) find that BTAs' impact on real exchange rates could result in lower net exports.
51. BTAs have been applied to imported electricity in California's ETS, and there is some experience in applying analogous instruments to excise taxes, such as those on tobacco and fuel (World Bank 2017a). See Mehling et al. (2017) for a detailed review of past BTA proposals in the EU and United States.
52. For general presentations of these debates, see WTO and UNEP (2009), Fischer and Fox (2012), and Condon and Ignaciuk (2013).
53. On the contrary, some have argued that the absence of a carbon price in nonregulated markets is the implicit subsidy that ought to be seen as a welfare-reducing distortion, and that BTA could in fact help advance international climate negotiations (Stiglitz 2006; Helm, Hepburn, and Ruta 2012). More recently, Mehling et al. (2017) argue that the Paris Agreement, by setting the international climate architecture for the period beyond 2020, has made less relevant fears that debates about BTAs could disrupt sensitive negotiations.
54. See Cook (2011) for an analysis of BTA as it may apply to the cement industry.
55. Elements reviewed include the scope of applicability (for example, exemptions, goods/sectors covered), level and type of adjustment (for example, method to assess carbon content, pricing), use of revenue, sunset provisions, and so on).
56. Administration costs may also be lowered by making the producer/importer a withholding agent (Trachtman 2017).
57. Because of data availability constraints, the empirical research has focused on middle-income countries. Further work could explore the same issues in low-income contexts.
58. For example, in the United States, an assessment found that four EITE sectors that could be significantly affected by a domestic carbon price accounted for 12 percent of manufacturing output and 6 percent of manufacturing employment (0.5 percent of nonfarm employment), but for half of manufacturing GHG emissions (U.S. EPA 2009).
59. See also the FASTER principles for carbon pricing adopted by the World Bank and OECD (2015): **F**airness, **A**lignment of Policies and Objectives, **S**tability and Predictability, **T**ransparency **E**fficiency and Cost-Effectiveness, and **R**eliability and Environmental Integrity.

REFERENCES

Abeberese, Ama Baafra. 2017. "Electricity Costs and Firm Performance: Evidence from India." *Review of Economics and Statistics*, 99 (5): 839–52.

Acemoglu, Daron, Philippe Aghion, Leonardo Bursztyn, and David Hémous. 2012. "The Environment and Directed Technical Change." *American Economic Review* 102 (1): 131–66.

Adhvaryu, Achyuta, Namrata Kala, and Anant Nyshadham. "The Light and the Heat: Productivity Co-benefits of Energy-Saving Technology." CEEPR Working Paper 2017-019, MIT Center for Energy and Environmental Policy Research, Cambridge, MA.

Adkins, Liwayway, Richard Garbaccio, Mun Ho, Eric Moore, and Richard Morgenstern. 2012. "Carbon Pricing with Output-Based Subsidies: Impact on U.S. Industries over Multiple Time Frames." RFF Discussion Paper 12-27, Resources for the Future, Washington, DC.

Aghion, Philippe, Antoine Dechezleprêtre, David Hemous, Ralf Martin, and John van Reenn. 2016. "Carbon Taxes, Path Dependency and Directed Technical Change: Evidence from the Auto Industry." *Journal of Political Economy* 124 (1): 1–51.

Albrizio, Silvia, Tomasz Kozluk, and Vera Zipperer. 2014. "Empirical Evidence on the Effects of Environmental Policy Stringency on Productivity Growth." OECD Economics Department Working Papers No. 1179, Organisation for Economic Co-operation and Development, Paris.

Aldy, Joseph E. 2016. "Frameworks for Evaluating Policy Approaches to Address the Competitiveness Concerns of Mitigating Greenhouse Gas Emissions." RFF Discussion Paper 16-06, Resources for the Future, Washington, DC.

Aldy, Joseph E., and William A. Pizer. 2014. "The Employment and Competitiveness Impacts of Power-Sector Regulations." In *Does Regulation Kill Jobs?* edited by Cary Coglianese, Adam M. Finkel, and Christopher Carrigan, 70–88. Philadelphia: University of Pennsylvania Press.

——. 2015. "The Competitiveness Impacts of Climate Change Mitigation Policies." *Journal of the Association of Environmental and Resource Economists* 2 (4): 565–95.

Alton, Theresa, Channing Arndt, Rob Davies, Faaiqa Hartley, Konstantin Makrelov, James Thurlow, and Dumabi Ubogu 2014. "Introducing Carbon Taxes in South Africa." *Applied Energy* 116 (March): 344–54.

Ambec, Stefan, Mark A. Cohen, Stewart lgie, and Paul Lanoie. 2013. "The Porter Hypothesis at 20: Can Environmental Regulation Enhance Innovation and Competitiveness?" *Review of Environmental Economics and Policy* 7 (1): 2–22.

Arlinghaus, Johanna. 2015. "Impacts of Carbon Prices on Indicators of Competitiveness: A Review of Empirical Findings." OECD Environment Working Papers No. 87, Organisation for Economic Co-operation and Development, Paris.

ATRI (American Transportation Research Institute). 2017. "An Analysis of the Operational Costs of Trucking: 2017 Update." ATRI, Arlington, VA, October. http://atri-online.org/wp-content/uploads/2017/10/ATRI-Operational-Costs-of-Trucking-2017-10-2017.pdf.

Aw, B. A., X. Chen, and M. Roberts. 2001. "Firm-Level Evidence on Productivity Differentials and Turnover in Taiwanese Manufacturing." *Journal of Development Economics* 66 (1): 51–86.

Bao, Qin, Ling Tang, ZhongXiang Zhang, and Shouyang Wang. 2013. "Impacts of Border Carbon Adjustments on China's Sectoral Emissions: Simulations with a Dynamic Computable General Equilibrium Model." *China Economic Review*, 24 (March): 77–94.

Barde, Jean-Philippe, and Olivier Godard. 2012. "Economic Principles of Environmental Fiscal Reform." In *Handbook of Research on Environmental Taxation*, edited by Janet E. Milne and Mikael Skou Andersen, 33–58. Northampton: Edward Elgar.

Bashmakov, Igor. 2007. "Three Laws of Energy Transitions." *Energy Policy* 35 (7): 3583–94.

Bento, Antonio, Mark Jacobsen, and Antung Liu. 2017. "Environmental Policy in the Presence of an Informal Sector." *The World Bank Economic Review* 9 (Suppl. 1): S126–34. https://doi.org/10.1093/wber/lhv026.

Berman, Eli, and Linda T. Bui. 2001. "Environmental Regulation and Productivity: Evidence from Oil Refineries." *Review of Economics and Statistics* 83 (3): 498–510.

Beylis, Guillermo, and Barbara Cunha. 2017. *Energy Pricing Policies for Inclusive Growth in Latin America and the Caribbean.* Washington, DC: World Bank Group.

Bloom, Nicholas, Christos Genakos, Ralf Martin, and Rafaella Sadun. 2010. "Modern Management: Good for the Environment or Just Hot Air?" *The Economic Journal* 120 (544): 551–72.

Bloom, Nicholas, Christos Genakos, Raffaella Sadun, and John Van Reenen. 2012. "Management Practices across Firms and Countries." *Academy of Management Perspectives* 26 (1): 12–33.

Bloom, Nicholas, Benn Eifert, Aprajit Mahajan, David McKenzie, and John Roberts. 2013. "Does Management Matter? Evidence from India." *The Quarterly Journal of Economics* 128 (1): 1–51.

Bluffstone, Randall A. 2003. "Environmental Taxes in Developing and Transition Economies." *Public Finance and Management* 3(1): 143–75.

Bodansky, Daniel. 2007. "International Sectoral Agreements in a Post-2012 Climate Framework." Pew Center on Global Climate Change Working Paper. https://ssrn.com/abstract=1028187.

Böhringer, Christoph, Edward Balisteri, and Thomas Rutherford. 2012. "The Role of Border Carbon Adjustment in Unilateral Climate Policy: Overview of an Energy Modeling Forum Study (EMF 29)." *Energy Economics* 34 (S2): S97–S110.

Böhringer, Christoph, Jared Carbone, and Thomas Rutherford. 2012. "Unilateral Climate Policy Design: Efficiency and Equity Implications of Alternative Instruments to Reduce Carbon Leakage." *Energy Economics* 34 (S2): S208–S217.

Böhringer, Christoph, Carolyn Fischer, and Knut Einar Rosendahl. 2014. "Cost-effective Unilateral Climate Policy Design: Size Matters." *Journal of Environmental Economics and Management* 67 (3): 318–39.

Bonilla, Jorge, Jessica Coria, Kristina Mohlin, and Thomas Sterner. 2015. "Refunded Emission Payments and Diffusion of NOx Abatement Technologies in Sweden." *Ecological Economics* 116 (August): 132–45.

Bosetti, Valentina, Carlo Carraro, Romain Duval, and Massimo Tavoni. 2011. "What Should We Expect from Innovation? A Model-Based Assessment of the Environmental and Mitigation Cost Implications of Climate-Related R&D." *Energy Economics* 33 (6): 1313–20.

Braathen, Nils Axel. 2012. "Lessons in Environmental Policy Reform: The Swedish Tax on NOx Emissions." Report ENV/EPOC/WPIEEP(2011)20/FINAL. Paris: Organisation for Economic Co-operation and Development.

Branger, Frédéric, and Misato Sato. 2017. Solving the Clinker Dilemma with Hybrid Output-based Allocation. *Climatic Change*, 140(3–4): 483–501.

Branger Frédéric and Philippe Quirion. 2014. "Would Border Carbon Adjustments Prevent Carbon Leakage and Heavy Industry Competitiveness Losses? Insights from a Meta-analysis of Recent Economic Studies." *Ecological Economics* 99 (March): 29–39.

Cantore, Nicola, Massimiliano Calì, and Dirk Willem te Velde. 2016. "Does Energy Efficiency Improve Technological Change and Economic Growth in Developing Countries?" *Energy Policy* 92 (May): 279–85.

Carbone Jared C., and Nicholas Rivers. 2017. "The Impacts of Unilateral Climate Policy on Competitiveness: Evidence from Computable General Equilibrium Models." *Review of Environmental Economics and Policy* 11 (1): 24–42.

Cirera, Xavier, and William F. Maloney. 2017. *The Innovation Paradox: Developing-Country Capabilities and the Unrealized Promise of Technological Catch-Up*. Washington, DC: World Bank Group.

Clements, Benedict, David Coady, Stefania Fabrizio, Sanjeev Gupta, Trevor Alleyne, and Carlo Sdralevich. 2013. *Energy Subsidy Reform: Lessons and Implications*. Washington, DC: International Monetary Fund.

Colombier, Michel, and Emmanuel Guerin. 2008. "Sectoral Agreements." Breaking the Climate Deadlock Briefing Paper, The Climate Group, London. https://www.theclimategroup.org/sites/default/files/archive/files/Sectoral-Agreements.pdf.

Condon, Madison, and Ada Ignaciuk. 2013. "Border Carbon Adjustment and International Trade: A Literature Review." OECD Trade and Environment Working Papers, 2013/06, Organisation for Economic Co-operation and Development, Paris.

Cook, Gregory. 2011. "Use of Border Adjustment Measures: A Cement Sector Perspective." Climate Strategies Working Paper, Climate Strategies, London. http://climatestrategies.org/publication/use-of-border-adjustment-measures-a-cement-sector-perspective.

Cosbey, Aaron, Susanne Droege, Carolyn Fischer, Julia Reinaud, John Stephenson, Lutz Weischer, and Peter Wooders. 2012. "A Guide for the Concerned: Guidance on the Elaboration and Implementation of Border Carbon Adjustment." ENTWINED Policy Report 03, ENTWINED, Stockholm. http://www.iisd.org/pdf/2012/bca_guidance.pdf.

Cottrell, Jacqueline, Kai Schlegelmich, Matthias Runkel, and Alexander Mahler. 2016. "Environmental Tax Reform in Developing, Emerging and Transition Economies." Study No. 93, Deutsches Institut für Entwicklungspolitik, Bonn.

Cramton, Peter, David J. C. MacKay, Axel Ockenfels, and Steven Stoft, eds. 2017. *Global Carbon Pricing: The Path to Climate Cooperation*. Cambridge, MA: The MIT Press.

DeCanio, Stephen. 1993. "Barriers within Firms to Energy-Efficient Investments." *Energy Policy* 21 (9): 906–14.

DeCanio, Stephen, and William Watkins. 1998. "Investment in Energy Efficiency: Do the Characteristics of Firms Matter?" *Review of Economics and Statistics* 80 (1): 95–107.

Dechezleprêtre, Antoine, and Misato Sato. 2017. "The Impacts of Environmental Regulations on Competitiveness." *Review of Environmental Economics and Policy* 11 (2): 183–206.

Dutz, Mark A., and Siddarth Sharma. 2012. "Green Growth, Technology and Innovation." Policy Research Working Paper 5932, World Bank, Washington, DC.

Ederington, Josh, Arik Levinson, and Jenny Minier. 2005. "Footloose and Pollution-Free." *The Review of* Economics *and Statistics* 87 (1): 92–99.

Ekins, Paul, and Stefan Speck. 1999. "Competitiveness and Exemptions From Environmental Taxes in Europe." *Environmental and Resource Economics* 13 (4): 369–96.

——. 2012. "Impacts on Competitiveness: What Do We Know from Modeling?" In *Handbook of Research on Environmental Taxation*, edited by Janet E. Milne and Mikael Skou Andersen, 377–96. Northampton: Edward Elgar.

Eskeland, Gunnar S., and Emmanuel Jimenez. 1992. "Policy Instruments for Pollution Control in Developing Countries." *The World Bank Research Observer* 7 (2): 145–69.

Farid, Mai, Michael Keen, Michael Papaioannou, Ian Parry, Catherine Pattillo, Anna Ter-Martirosyan, and other IMF staff, 2016. *After Paris: Fiscal, Macroeconomic, and Financial Implications of Climate Change*. Staff Discussion Note 16-01. Washington, DC: International Monetary Fund.

Fay, Marianne, Stéphane Hallegatte, Adrien Vogt-Schilb, Julie Rozenberg, Ulf Narloch, and Tom Kerr. 2015. *Decarbonizing Development: Three Steps to a Zero-Carbon Future*. Washington, DC: World Bank Group.

Fischer, Carolyn. 2001. "Rebating Environmental Policy Revenues: Output-Based Allocations and Tradable Performance Standards." RFF Discussion Paper 01-22, Resources for the Future, Washington, DC.

Fischer, Carolyn, and Alan Fox. 2004. "Output-Based Allocations of Emissions Permits: Efficiency and Distributional Effects in a General Equilibrium Setting with Taxes and Trade. RFF Discussion Paper 04-37. Washington, DC: Resources for the Future.

——. 2010. On the Scope for Output-Based Rebating in Climate Policy When Revenue Recycling Isn't Enough (or Isn't Possible)." RFF Discussion Paper 10-69, Resources for the Future, Washington, DC.

——. 2012. "Comparing Policies to Combat Emissions Leakage: Border Carbon Adjustments versus Rebates." *Journal of Environmental Economics and Management* 64 (2): 199–216.

Friis-Jensen, Michael. 2009. "Leveling or Mining the Playing Field? Implementation Problems of Carbon-Motivated Border Adjustment Taxes." PREM Note 146, World Bank, Washington, DC.

Fullerton, Don, and Ann Wolverton. 2003. "The Two-Part Instrument in a Second-Best World." *Journal of Public Economics* 89 (9): 1961–75.

GGGI (Global Green Growth Institute). 2017. *Greening Industrial Parks—A Case Study on South Korea's Eco-Industrial Park Program*. Seoul: GGGI.

Goulder, Lawrence. 1992. "Carbon Tax Design and U.S. Industry Performance." In *Tax Policy and the Economy 6*, edited by James M. Poterba, 59–104. Cambridge: MIT Press.

Grubb, Michael. 2011. "International Climate Finance from Border Carbon Cost Leveling." *Climate Policy* 11 (3): 1050–57.

Grubb, Michael, Igor Bashmakov, Paul Drummond, Anna Myshak, Nick Hughes, Andrea Biancardi, Paolo Agnolucci, and Robert Lowe. 2017. "An Exploration of Energy Cost Constants, Affordability Limits and Adjustment Processes." Report to the Institute of New Economic Thinking, UCL Institute for Sustainable Resources, London.

Grubb, Michael, and Karsten Neuhoff. 2006. "Allocation and Competitiveness in the EU Emissions Trading Scheme: Policy Overview." *Climate Policy* 6 (1): 7–30.

Hagem, Cathrine, Michael Hoel, Bjart Holtsmark, and Thomas Sterner. 2015. "Refunding Emissions Payments." RFF Discussion Paper 15-05, Resources for the Future, Washington, DC.

Hamamoto, Mitsutsugu. 2006. "Environmental Regulation and the Productivity of Japanese Manufacturing Industries." *Resource and Energy Economics* 28 (4): 299–312.

Heine, Dirk, Michael G. Faure, and Chih-Ching Lan. 2017. "Augmenting Forest Sustainability Certificates with Fiscal Instruments." Rotterdam Institute of Law and Economics, Working Paper No. 2015/7, Rotterdam.

Helm, Dieter, Cameron Hepburn, and Giovanni Ruta. 2012. "Trade, Climate Change, and the Political Game Theory of Border Carbon Adjustments." *Oxford Review of Economic Policy* 28 (2): 368–94.

Hillman, Jennifer. 2013. "Changing Climate for Carbon Taxes: Who's Afraid of the WTO?" Climate & Energy Policy Paper Series, German Marshall Fund of the United States, Washington, DC.

Holmes, Peter, Tom Reilly, and Jim Rollo. 2011. "Border Carbon Adjustments and the Potential for Protectionism." *Climate Policy* 11 (2): 883–900.

Houser, Trevor, Rob Bradley, Britt Childs, Jacob Werksman, and Robert Heilmayr. 2008. *Leveling the Carbon Playing Field: International Competition and U.S. Climate Policy Design.* Washington, DC: Peterson Institute for International Economics and World Resources Institute.

Huber, Richard, Jack Ruitenbeek, and Ronaldo Serôa da Motta. 1998. "*Market-Based Instruments for Environmental Policymaking in Latin America and the Caribbean: Lessons from Eleven Countries.*" Washington, DC: World Bank Group.

IATA (International Air Transport Association). 2018. "Fact Sheet: Fuel." IATA, June. https://www.iata.org/pressroom/facts_figures/fact_sheets/Documents/fact-sheet-fuel.pdf.

IEA (International Energy Agency). 2015. "Accelerating Energy Efficiency in Small and Medium-Sized Enterprises: Powering SMEs to Catalyse Economic Growth." Policy Pathway Series Paper, Organisation for Economic Co-operation and Development and IEA, Paris.

———. 2017. "Renewable Energy for Industry—From Green Energy to Green Materials and Fuels." IEA Insights Paper, IEA, Paris.

IFC (International Finance Corporation), NPO (National Productivity Organization), and CPI (Cleaner Production Institute). 2016. *Sustaining Growth: Cleaner Production in Pakistan.* Washington, DC: World Bank.

Jeppesen, Tim, John A. List, and Henk Folmer. 2002. "Environmental Regulations and New Plant Location Decisions: Evidence from a Metra-Analysis." *Journal of Regional Science* 42 (1): 19–49.

Kortum, Samuel, and David Weisbach. 2017. "The Design of Border Adjustments for Carbon Prices." *National Tax Journal* 70 (2): 421–46.

Krugman, Paul. 1994. "Competitiveness: A Dangerous Obsession." *Foreign Affairs* 73 (2): 28–44.

Landa-Rivera, Gissela, Frédéric Reynès, Ivan Islas-Cortes, François-Xavier Bellocq, and Fabio Grazid. 2016. "Towards a Low Carbon Growth in Mexico: Is a Double Dividend Possible? A Dynamic General Equilibrium Assessment." *Energy Policy* 96 (September): 314–27.

Landrigan, Philip, et al. 2017. "The Lancet Commission on Pollution and Health." *The Lancet*, October 19. http://www.thelancet.com/commissions/pollution-and-health.

Lee, Kiseok, and Shawn Ni. 2002. "On the Dynamic Effects of Oil Price Shocks: A Study Using Industry Level Data." *Journal of Monetary Economics* 49 (4): 823–52.

Li, Ji Feng, Xin Wang, and Ya Xiong Zhang. 2012. "Is It in China's Interest to Implement an Export Carbon Tax?" *Energy Economics* 34 (6): 2072–80.

Liang, Qiao-Mei, Ying Fan, and Yi-Ming Wei. 2007. "Carbon Taxation Policy in China: How to Protect Energy- and Trade-Intensive Sectors?" *Journal of Policy Modeling* 29 (2): 311–33.

Marin, Giovanni, and Francesco Vona. 2017. "The Impact of Energy Prices on Employment and Environmental Performance: Evidence from French Manufacturing Establishments." Sciences Po OFCE Working Paper n°23, 2017-10-23, Observatoire francais des conjonctures économiques, Paris.

Martin, Ralf, Laure B. De Preux, and Ulrich J. Wagner. 2014. "The Impact of a Carbon Tax on Manufacturing: Evidence from Microdata." *Journal of Public Economics* 117 (September): 1–14.

Martin, Ralf, Mirabelle Mulus, Laure B. De Preux, and Ulrich J. Wagner. 2012. "Anatomy of a Paradox: Management Practices, Organizational Structure and Energy Efficiency." *Journal of Environmental Economics and Management* 63 (2): 208–23.

McKibbin, Warwick, Adele Morris, Peter Wilcoxen, and Weifeng Liu. 2017. "The Role of Border Carbon Adjustment in a U.S. Carbon Tax." Climate and Energy Economics Discussion Paper, Brookings, Washington, DC.

Mehling, Michael, Harro van Asselt, Kasturi Das, Susanne Droege, and Cleo Verkuijl. 2017. *Designing Border Carbon Adjustments for Enhanced Climate Action*. London: Climate Strategies.

Nakhooda, Smita. 2014. "Carbon Taxes in South Africa: The Political and Technical Challenges of Pricing Carbon." ODI Working Paper No. 399, Overseas Development Institute, London.

Narayan, P. K., and S. Sharma. 2011. "New Evidence on Oil Price and Firm Returns." *Journal of Banking and Finance* 35 (12): 3253–62.

Nielsen, Helle. 2012. "Bounded Rationality in An Imperfect World of Regulations: What If Individuals Are Not Optimizing." In *Handbook of Research on Environmental Taxation*, edited by Janet E. Milne and Mikael Skou Andersen, 439–55. Northampton: Edward Elgar.

Nordhaus, William. 2015. "Climate Clubs: Overcoming Free-riding in International Climate Policy." *American Economic Review* 105 (4): 1339–70.

Obstfeld, Maurice. 2016. "Get on Track with Trade." *Finance & Development* 53 (4): 12–16.

Odell, John. 2018. "Our Alarming Climate Crisis Demands Border Adjustments Now." ICTSD Climate and Energy Think Piece, International Center for Trade and Sustainable Development, Geneva.

OECD (Organisation for Economic Co-operation and Development). 2010. *Taxation, Innovation and the Environment*. Paris: OECD Publishing.

——. 2011. *Fostering Innovation for Green Growth*. Paris: OECD.

Pang, Yu. 2018. "Profitable Pollution Abatement? A Worker Productivity Perspective." *Resource and Energy Economics* 52 (May): 33–49.

Parry, Ian W.H., John Norregaard, and Dirk Heine. 2012. "Environmental Tax Reform: Principles from Theory and Practice." *Annual Review of Resource Economics* 4 (1): 101–12.

PMR (Partnership for Market Readiness). 2015. "Carbon Leakage: Theory, Evidence and Policy Design." PMR Technical Note 11, World Bank, Washington, DC.

——. 2016. "Modeling the Impact on South Africa's Economy of Introducing a Carbon Tax." PMR Country Paper, World Bank, Washington, DC.

Popp, David, Richard G. Newell, and Adam B. Jaffe. 2010. "Energy, the Environment, and Technological Change." Chapter 21 in Handbook of the Economics of Innovation, edited by Bronwyn H. Halland and Nathan Rosenberg, 873–938. Burlington: Academic Press.

Porter, Michael. 1980. *Competitive Strategy: Techniques for Analyzing Industries and Competitors*. New York: Free Press.

——. 1991. "America's Green Strategy." *Scientific American* 264 (4): 168.

Porter, Michael, and Claas van der Linde. 1995. "Toward a New Conception of the Environment-Competitiveness Relationship." *Journal of Economic Perspective* 9 (4): 97–118.

Porto, Guido. 2012. "The Cost of Adjustment to Green Growth Policies: Lessons from Trade Adjustment Costs." Policy Research Working Paper 6237, World Bank, Washington, DC.

Potter, Kevin, Darilyn Stewart, and Bruce Kessler. 2017. "Credits & Incentives Talk with Deloitte: Pollution Control Tax—State and Local Credits & Incentives." *Journal of Multistate Taxation and Incentives* 27 (4).

Rentschler, Jun, and Martin Kornejew. 2017. "Energy Price Variation and Competitiveness: Firm Level Evidence from Indonesia." *Energy Economics* 67 (September): 242–54.

Rentschler, Jun, Martin Kornejew, and Morgan Bazilian. 2017. "Fossil Fuel Subsidy Reforms and Their Impacts on Firms." *Energy Policy* 108 (September): 617–23.

Rivers, Nicholas, and Brandon Schaufele. 2015. "Salience of Carbon Taxes in the Gasoline Market." *Journal of Environmental Economics and Management* 74 (November): 23–36.

Rodrigue, Jean-Paul. 2017. *The Geography of Transport Systems*, Fourth Edition. New York: Routledge.

Rodrik, Dani. 2014. "Green Industrial Policy." *Oxford Review of Economic Policy* 30 (3): 469–91.

———. 2017. "Too Late to Compensate Free Trade's Losers." *Project Syndicate*, April 11. https://www.project-syndicate.org/commentary/free-trade-losers-compensation-too-late-by-dani-rodrik-2017-04.

Sato, Misato, Gregor Singer, Damien Dussaux, and Stefania Lovo. 2015. "International and Sectoral Variation in Energy Prices 1995-2011: How Does it Relate to Emissions Policy Stringency?" Working Paper No. 187, Grantham Research Institute on Climate Change and the Environment, London.

Speck, Stefan, Philip Summerton, Daniel Lee, and Kirsten Wiebe. 2011. "Environmental Taxes and ETRs in Europe: The Current Situation and a Review of the Modeling Literature." In *Environmental Tax Reform (ETR): A Policy for Green Growth*, edited by Paul Ekins and Stefan Speck, 99–130. Oxford: Oxford University Press.

Spratt, Stephen. 2013. "Environmental Taxation and Development: A Scoping Study." IDS Working Paper 433, Institute of Development Studies, Brighton.

Sterner, Thomas, and Bruno Turnheim. 2009. "Innovation and Diffusion of Environmental Technology: Industrial NOx Abatement in Sweden under Refunded Emission Payments." *Ecological Economics* 68 (12): 2996–3006.

Sterner, Thomas, and Lena Höglund Isaksson. 2006. "Refunded Emission Payments Theory, Distribution of Costs, and Swedish Experience of NO_x Abatement." *Ecological Economics* 57 (1): 93–106.

Stiglitz, Joseph. 2006. "A New Agenda for Global Warming." *The Economists' Voice* 3 (7): 1–4.

Summers, Lawrence H. 1988. "Tax Policy and International Competitiveness." In *International Aspects of Fiscal Policies*, edited by Jacob A. Frenkel, 349–86. University of Chicago Press / NBER.

Teravaninthorn, Supee, and Gaël Raballand. 2009. *Transport Prices and Costs in Africa: A Review of the International Corridors*. Washington, DC: World Bank Group.

Trachtman, Joel. 2017. "WTO Law Constraints on Border Tax Adjustment and Tax Credit Mechanisms to Reduce the Competitive Effects of Carbon Taxes." *National Tax Journal* 70 (2): 469–94.

UNIDO (United Nations Industrial Development Organization), World Bank Group, and GIZ (Deutsche Gesellschaft für Internationale Zusammenarbeit). 2017. "An International Framework for Eco-Industrial Parks." World Bank, Washington, DC.

U.S. EPA (Environmental Protection Agency). 2009. "The Effects of H.R. 2454 on International Competitiveness and Emission Leakage in Energy-Intensive Trade-Exposed Industries." An Interagency Report Responding to a Request from Senators Bayh, Specter, Stabenow, Mccaskill, and Brown, EPA, Washington, DC.

Veugelers, Reinhilde. 2016. "Empowering the Green Innovation Machine." *Intereconomics* 51 (4): 205–08.

Vogt-Schilb, Adrien, and Stéphane Hallegatte. 2017. "Climate Policies and Nationally Determined Contributions: Reconciling the Needed Ambition with the Political Economy." *WIREs Energy and Environment*, August 18. doi: 10.1002/wene.256.

Willenbockel, Dirk. 2011. "Environmental Tax Reform in Vietnam: An Ex Ante General Equilibrium Assessment." MPRA Paper No. 44411. http://mpra.ub.uni-muenchen.de/44411.

Williams, Roberton III. 2002. "Environmental Tax Interactions when Pollution Affects Health or Productivity." *Journal of Environmental Economics and Management* 44 (2): 261–70.

Wooders, Peter. 2010. International Sectoral Approaches and Agreements: Case Studies of the Steel Sector in China, India and Japan – Emerging Policy Recommendations." Working Paper, Climate Strategies, London. http://www.iisd.org/library/international-sectoral-approaches-and-agreements-case-studies-steel-sector-china-india-and.

World Bank. 2005. *Environmental Fiscal Reform: What Should Be Done and How to Achieve It.* Washington, DC: World Bank Group.

——. 2012. *Inclusive Green Growth: The Pathway to Sustainable Development.* Washington, DC: World Bank Group.

——. 2014. *The Bangladesh Responsible Sourcing Initiative: A New Model for Green Growth.* Washington, DC: World Bank.

——. 2015. *State and Trends of Carbon Pricing 2015.* Washington, DC: World Bank Group.

——. 2016a. *State and Trends of Carbon Pricing 2016.* Washington, DC: World Bank Group.

——. 2016b. *A Greener Path to Competitiveness: Policies for Climate Action in Industries and Products.* Washington, DC: World Bank Group.

——. 2017a. *Carbon Tax Guide: A Handbook for Policy Makers.* Washington, DC: World Bank Group.

——. 2017b. *State and Trends of Carbon Pricing 2017.* Washington, DC: World Bank Group.

World Bank and OECD (Organisation for Economic Co-operation and Development). 2015. "The FASTER Principles for Successful Carbon Pricing: An Approach Based on Initial Experience." World Bank, Washington, DC. http://documents.worldbank.org/curated/en/2015/09/25060584/faster-principles-successful-carbon-pricing-approach-based-initial-experience.

World Steel Association. 2018. "Fact Sheet: Energy Use in the Industry." WorldSteel, Brussels, February. https://www.worldsteel.org/en/dam/jcr:f07b864c-908e-4229-9f92-669f1c3abf4c/fact_energy_2018_.pdf.

Worrell, Ernst, John Laitner, Michael Ruth, and Hodayah Finman. 2003. "Productivity Benefits of Industrial Energy Efficiency Measures." *Energy* 28 (11): 1081–98.

WRG (Water Resources Group). 2015. "An Analysis of Industrial Water Use in Bangladesh with a Focus on the Textile and Leather Industries." 2030 Water Resource Group, Washington, DC. https://www.2030wrg.org/wp-content/uploads/2016/02/WRG-Bangladesh-Report.pdf.

WTO (World Trade Organization) and UNEP (United Nations Environment Programme). 2009. *Trade and Climate Change: A Report by the United Nations Environment Programme and the World Trade Organization.* Geneva: World Trade Organization.

3 Increasing Resilience: Fiscal Policy for Climate Adaptation

LORENZO FORNI, MICHELE CATALANO, AND EMILIA PEZZOLLA

INTRODUCTION

Climate change and climate-related natural disasters pose a growing threat to both developed and developing countries. However, developing countries are particularly vulnerable to climate change because they have fewer financial and institutional resources to counter its negative impact. The capacity of developing countries to adapt to a changing climate or to cope with extreme weather events, such as floods, hurricanes, or droughts, tends to be far more limited than that of their wealthier peers. Underdeveloped private insurance markets compound the risks of climate change, particularly the threat those risks pose to lower-income households.

In addition to their devastating cost in lives and property, climate change and natural disasters have important fiscal consequences. Gradual changes in temperature and rainfall can profoundly alter economic activities—especially in sectors that are highly sensitive to climatic conditions, such as agriculture, fishing, and tourism—with important implications for the level and composition of tax revenues. Meanwhile, natural disasters and weather-related shocks can exacerbate revenue volatility and slow potential gross domestic product (GDP) growth. Natural disasters can severely weaken a government's fiscal position because of the short-term costs of disaster relief, the longer-term costs of reconstruction, and the forgone-revenue impact of damaged capital and depressed economic activity. Several factors influence the fiscal consequences of natural disasters and climate change, including an economy's degree of exposure, the level of protection already in place, and the state's liability for the damages incurred. The cost of dealing with these impacts can be extremely high, particularly in small island nations and very poor countries, and can threaten their fiscal sustainability and the future of their development efforts.

Fiscal policy can play a key role in mitigating climate change and adapting to its effects, yet the international literature on the fiscal implications of climate change remains limited. This chapter aims to contribute to a better understanding of how fiscal policy can help countries adapt to the gradual long-term effects of climate change and cope with the severe short-term impact of climate-related natural disasters. It uses a simplified macroeconomic model of an open economy with overlapping generations (OLG) in which climate change is assumed to affect the depreciation rate of the capital stock. The model includes capital-adjustment costs and external borrowing constraints. For illustrative purposes, it differentiates between impacts of climate change that occur slowly, with costs mounting over time, (*gradual factors*) and effects that manifest as sudden, unpredictable disasters (*extreme events*).

In the baseline scenario, no attempt is made to adapt to climate change or address its negative impact on the capital stock. Against this baseline, the study evaluates the relative effectiveness of two different strategies: (i) preventive action, under which policy makers implement adaptation measures in anticipation of the effects of climate change, and (ii) remedial action, under which policy makers focus solely on responding to impacts that have already occurred. The analysis reveals that preventive action leads to higher GDP growth rates than either taking no action or waiting until remedial action is necessary. Preventive investments in climate change adaptation, funded by taxes or by reduced spending in other areas, can increase the resilience of the capital stock, keep public debt dynamics manageable, and maintain adequate fiscal space to cope with natural disasters while responsibly accessing international capital markets.

This chapter is organized into six sections. Following the introduction, the next two sections briefly discuss the literature on the macroeconomics of climate change and the role of fiscal policy in climate-change adaptation. The fourth section presents the proposed model, and the following sections—"Adapting to the gradual effects of climate change" and "Adapting to extreme events"—discuss its findings. The final sections discuss policy implications and conclude the analysis.

THE MACROECONOMICS OF CLIMATE CHANGE

The macroeconomic costs of climate change can be grouped into three categories: mitigation, adaptation, and residual costs. *Mitigation* includes all costs incurred by policies that slow the pace and limit the severity of climate change, particularly via reduced greenhouse gas emissions. *Adaptation* includes all costs incurred by efforts, both preventive and remedial, to reduce the social, environmental, and economic impact of climate change. *Residual costs* are effects of climate change that cannot be offset through mitigation or adaptation.

Most macroeconomic models focus on assessing mitigation costs and residual costs. For example, Stern (2007), Nordhaus (2007, 2008), Bonen et al. (2016), and others use integrated assessment models (IAMs) to quantify the damages caused by climate change and the cost of efforts to limit its extent. These models apply *damage functions* (Bonen, Semmler, and Klasen 2014) that approximate the relationship between global temperature changes and climate-related phenomena such as rising sea levels, more frequent cyclones, lost agricultural productivity, and degraded ecosystem services. Most IAMs treat climate-related damages as a polynomial function of global mean temperature and examine its impact on the stock of capital at either the regional or the global level.[1]

By contrast, the literature on the macroeconomic implications of climate change adaptation is relatively limited. Early IAMs either ignored adaptation or treated it as implicit in the damage function. More recent IAMs include a dynamic representation of both the costs and benefits of adaptation.

These models find that optimal climate policies involve both adaptation and mitigation.[2] Bonen et al. (2016) show that, when mitigation policy is subject to diminishing returns, it is optimal to combine mitigation with adaptation. However, because there is no level of mitigation and adaptation that can fully compensate for the costs of climate change, residual damage is always a factor.

Adaptation becomes less effective at higher temperatures. Burke, Hsiang, and Miguel (2015) argue that the impact of temperatures on productivity is not linear; rather, it is positive at low temperatures and peaks at an average temperature of 13 degrees Celsius, after which it becomes increasingly negative. They also find that wealthier and poorer countries are subject to similarly nonlinear effects and that there is no evidence that experience gained in high-temperature contexts can accurately inform the global response to climate change. Once countries exceed a given threshold temperature, the correlation between their economic performance and further temperature increases becomes more intensely negative. In other words, the warmer a country is now, the more serious the economic damage from further warming will be. Consequently, a rapid rise in global temperatures would weaken the effectiveness of adaptation measures, and no amount of wealth, technology, and experience would enable countries to substantially reduce the economic losses incurred.

Some researchers have attempted to embed the effects of climate change in multicountry general equilibrium models. For example, Kotlikoff, Polbin, and Zubarev (2016) apply an overlapping-generation model similar to the model used in this study. They find that a lack of intragenerational or intracountry coordination makes climate change mitigation more difficult. Moreover, the Paris Climate Accord may inadvertently intensify the so-called green paradox, in which the adoption of emissions targets creates incentives for countries to increase their greenhouse gas output before the corresponding restrictions become binding.

LEVERAGING FISCAL POLICY TO SUPPORT CLIMATE CHANGE ADAPTATION

Adaptation strategies strive to contain and manage the damaging effects of climate change. The Intergovernmental Panel on Climate Change (IPCC) defines adaptation as "the process of adjustment to the actual or expected climate and its effects. In human systems, adaptation seeks to moderate or avoid harm or exploit beneficial opportunities. In some natural systems, human intervention may facilitate adjustment to the expected climate and its effects" (IPCC 2001). Whereas mitigation focuses on reducing the severity of climate change by, among other things, reducing global carbon emissions, adaptation seeks to address the impact of a changing climate. Adaptation includes both preventive measures, such as investment in infrastructure designed to limit the damage caused by extreme weather events, and remedial measures, such as disaster relief and reconstruction. The overarching objective of adaptation is to protect and restore the capital damaged by climate change while accommodating further economic and demographic growth.

Estimates of the global need for adaptation investment are evolving, and researchers have identified infrastructure and coastal zones as the areas requiring the costliest interventions.[3] International assistance and private investment can reduce the cost of adaptation at the country level. Harris and Roach (2018) find that the adaptation cost estimates produced by the United Nations Environment Programme (UNEP) exceed the annual amount committed by developed nations in the 2015 Paris Climate Accord two to three times over, and that "there will be a significant finance gap, [which is] likely to grow substantially over the coming decades, unless significant progress is made to secure new, additional and innovative financing for adaptation."

Despite the considerable explicit costs, investing in adaptation is vital to limit the immense economic damage caused by climate change and extreme weather events. UNDP (2007) argues that failing to adapt to climate change would severely affect the development process, and climate-related disasters are already seriously affecting growth in small states (Cabezon et al. 2015). The public and private sectors both have important roles to play in adaptation strategies. The private sector is the primary source of investment in human and physical capital, whereas the public sector is vital to coordinate the actions of individual agents into a collective response (Mendelsohn 2012). Barrage (2015) studies the optimal policy mix between climate change mitigation and adaptation and argues for full public provision of adaptation policies and investments, even when those policies and investments are financed through distortionary taxes. In the short term, climate change adaptation competes with other development objectives for scarce fiscal and aid resources. Over the long term, however, climate change adaptation is consistent with, and in some cases integral to, the achievement of broader development goals.

Adaptation strategies require various forms of public sector intervention. Some strategies focus on public investments in infrastructure designed to increase social and economic resilience to climate change and extreme weather events. Others involve adopting policies that increase the prices of public assets (such as water resources) to promote conservation and sustainable management by aligning their individual value more closely with their social value. Regulations can be used to adjust patterns of human activity to reflect climate-related risks. For example, zoning regulations can bar construction in areas vulnerable to flooding. Finally, fiscal incentives can encourage private investment in adaptation. For a more detailed review of the various policy tools currently being used to promote climate change adaptation, see Mechler, Mochizuki, and Hochrainer (2016).

AN ANALYTICAL FRAMEWORK THAT INCORPORATES CLIMATE CHANGE IN MEDIUM-TERM FISCAL PLANNING

Macroeconomic modeling can shed light on the pivotal role of fiscal policy in supporting climate change adaptation. A general equilibrium model, described in detail in appendix C, can capture the impact of climate change by estimating its effect on the depreciation rate of physical capital. In this model, adaptation reflects the extent to which public policies reduce the negative influence of climate change on the capital depreciation rate.[4]

The model describes a small open economy that trades and exchanges capital with the rest of the world.[5] Households save and supply labor on the basis of market-determined factor prices (that is, wages and interest rates), which are taken as given (see box 3.1 for a description of the assumptions of the model). GDP growth rates are calculated via a production function that includes labor input, physical capital, and human capital. Total factor productivity

BOX 3.1

Main characteristics of the model

Below we report the main characteristics and assumptions of the overlapping generations (OLG) model, which is described in detail in appendix C:

- The model describes a small open economy: goods and capital markets are open with the rest of the world.
- The economy has three core sectors: households, firms, and the government.
- Individuals are divided into 101 age cohorts (0–100) and split into three education levels (primary, secondary, and tertiary).
- The production function is a Cobb-Douglas with three inputs (labor, physical capital, and human capital) and with a parameter for the total factor productivity (TFP).
- The human capital index is calculated on the basis of the assumed educational level of the workforce.
- The TFP is endogenous as a function of the capital-to-labor ratio and the human capital index.
- The model assumes that the evolution of climate change is known to all agents in advance (perfect foresight).
- Agents save and decide on labor supply on the basis of market prices.
- The country faces a borrowing constraint: it can borrow from abroad up to a certain exogenous credit limit as a function of GDP.
- The impact of climate change is modeled as an increase in the depreciation rate of physical capital.
- Climate events are of two types: (i) gradual climate factors, which have an economic impact that progressively intensifies over time (for example, sea level rise), and (ii) extreme events, which have a significant and immediate impact on physical capital (for example, tornadoes).
- We consider two main policies for the public intervention: (i) increase of public investments to reduce capital erosion (early or late adaptation) and (ii) introduction of taxes to increase the fiscal space and address the impact of extreme climate events.
- We consider different hypotheses for funding increase in deficit spending; increase in taxation on consumption, labor income, and capital; and reduction in education expenditure or social transfers.
- We also consider the intervention by donors in the case of extreme weather events to finance reconstruction.

depends on capital intensity (that is, capital per worker) and the stock of human capital. The latter is computed on the basis of the education level of the workforce and its growth rate over the simulation period, which reflects UN population projections. The model assumes that the domestic economy can borrow up to a given credit limit, which is set exogenously, and that it cannot build a negative net foreign asset position greater than 150 percent of its GDP. The interest rate applied to external borrowing is the same rate that prevails on the international market, and therefore increased borrowing entails no risk premium. The model assumes that the country satisfies the intertemporal budget constraint, and default is not allowed.

Climate change affects the depreciation rate of capital. We assume that climate change accelerates the depreciation of the capital stock via two types of effects: (i) gradual factors, which are manifestations of climate change that have a relatively slow but progressively intensifying economic impact, such as crop displacement and rising sea levels, and (ii) extreme events, which are climate-related phenomena (such as tornadoes and cyclones) that severely affect the stock of physical capital in a brief period of time.[6] The model considers only one type of capital, and the capital replaced in the wake of a natural disaster is assumed to be more climate resilient if the government has previously invested in adaptation. Moreover, reconstruction after an extreme event boosts growth by accelerating capital accumulation.

The baseline scenario assumes that current climate trends will continue over the projection period. Although in reality climate trends are subject to significant uncertainty, the baseline scenario assumes "perfect foresight." In other words, all agents know in advance the evolution of gradual factors and extreme events. Uncertainty regarding the pace and trajectory of these trends in the real world should, if anything, further reinforce our conclusions—because risk-averse agents will attempt to hedge against downside risk. Ex post, however, adaptation spending could result in overadaptation if, for example, global warming is milder than expected.

We assume that investment in capital goods is subject to adjustment costs that prevent capital from being instantly restored. Investment will not respond immediately to shocks that reduce the capital stock, and the cost of the adjustment will slow the restoration of capital and delay its economic benefits. Capital-adjustment costs are particularly relevant when extreme events suddenly reduce the capital stock because postdisaster reconstruction cannot begin immediately.

The government can mobilize resources to invest in climate change adaptation. We assume that government investment in adaptation can increase resilience by lowering the aggregate depreciation rate[7] of the capital stock. We also assume that this effect applies not only to new capital but also to the entire stock of capital. This assumption does not weaken the generalizability of the results because the alternative assumption that adaptation spending affects the resilience only of new capital would similarly reduce the impact of climate change on the overall capital depreciation rate. Because the model assumes perfect foresight, agents can accurately assess the capital-depreciation profile and anticipate the economic cost of rebuilding the capital stock after an extreme event. Households adjust to these anticipated costs by increasing private savings at the expense of consumption. However, per the model's parameters, internal private resources can fail to cover the full cost of reconstruction in cases of particularly extreme climate-related events.

ADAPTING TO THE GRADUAL EFFECTS OF CLIMATE CHANGE

This section assesses the relative effectiveness of preventive and remedial strategies in leveraging limited fiscal resources to adapt to climate change. In the model, both strategies slow the "normal" capital depreciation rate, and greater investment in adaptation leads to a faster diffusion of climate-resilient technology across the entire capital stock. The model also allows us to simulate the effects of these strategies on GDP and debt dynamics, under different financing strategies such as distortionary taxation, a reduction in other spending, or a deficit increase. A high public debt level could prevent the country from accessing international capital markets even in the face of an extreme event, and in this circumstance donor grants could alleviate financial constraints.

Under the baseline scenario, the depreciation rate of capital increases gradually from 3 percent in 2018 to 10 percent in 2100. We assume that deficit-financed public investment can be used to contain the deterioration of the capital stock.

This adaptation spending, therefore, causes an initial increase in the debt stock. As the capital depreciation rate falls relative to the baseline, output increases and the debt-to-GDP ratio stabilizes. To illustrate the nonlinear nature of the challenge posed by climate change and assess the impact of investment timing, we simulate both an early intervention and a late intervention.

Early—rather than late—interventions are effective in reducing the negative impact of gradual factors associated with climate change. We model the early intervention as an increase in adaptation spending of 1 percent of GDP per year starting in 2018, whereas in the late intervention the same increase begins in 2040. The early intervention keeps the depreciation rate below the baseline level throughout the period (figure 3.1, panel a), and GDP remains above both the baseline level and the level of the late-intervention scenario (figure 3.1, panel c). Early adaptation spending initially boosts the public debt-to-GDP ratio about 7 percent above the baseline, but the ratio eventually falls below the baseline as faster growth increases the denominator (figure 3.1, panel b). Under the early-intervention scenario, 1 percent of GDP in annual adaptation spending permanently reduces the capital depreciation rate by 4 percentage points. However, these results are highly sensitive to how the model is calibrated (see "Gradual impacts of climate change" in appendix C).

The evolution of the debt-to-GDP ratio also depends on the intensity of the climate shock, but early intervention is always superior to late intervention. Assuming that the intensity of climate change increases the depreciation rate of capital from 10 percent to 20 percent by 2100 (figure 3.2, panel a), even early adaptation spending cannot prevent a contraction in real GDP (figure 3.2, panel c), with deeply negative implications for fiscal sustainability (figure 3.2, panel b). However, intervening late does less to counter the decline in real GDP, and debt dynamics worsen even more dramatically. These simulations highlight the importance of early intervention regardless of the pace and severity of climate change.

Financing investment in adaptation through taxation or spending cuts is more efficient than deficit financing. Even if taxes are increased by the amount necessary to leave the budget balance unchanged, tax-financed

FIGURE 3.1

The effects of early and late investment in climate change adaptation on capital depreciation, debt dynamics, and economic output

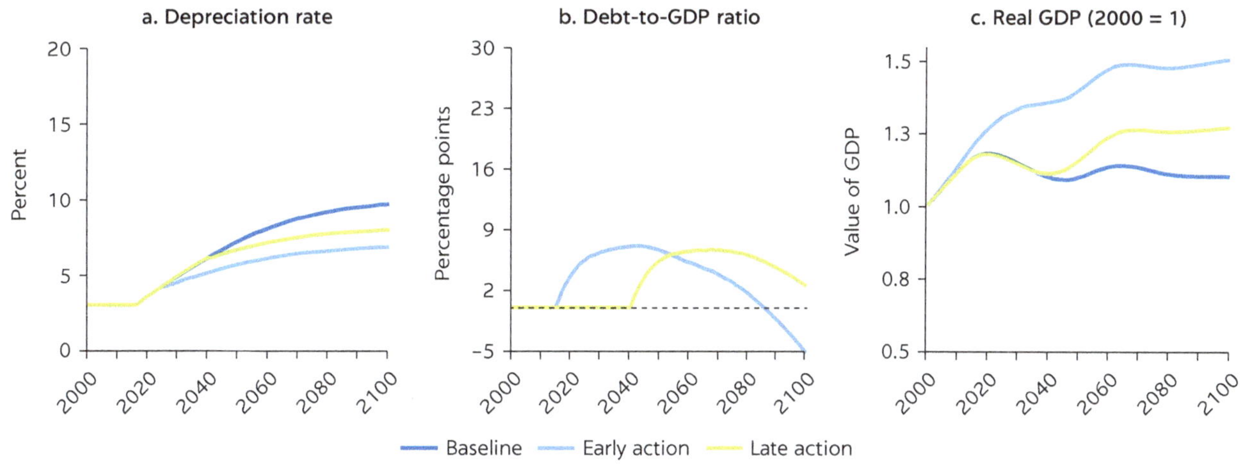

Note: Depreciation rate ceiling = 10%; GDP = gross domestic product.

FIGURE 3.2

The effects of early and late investment in climate change adaptation on capital depreciation, debt dynamics, and economic output

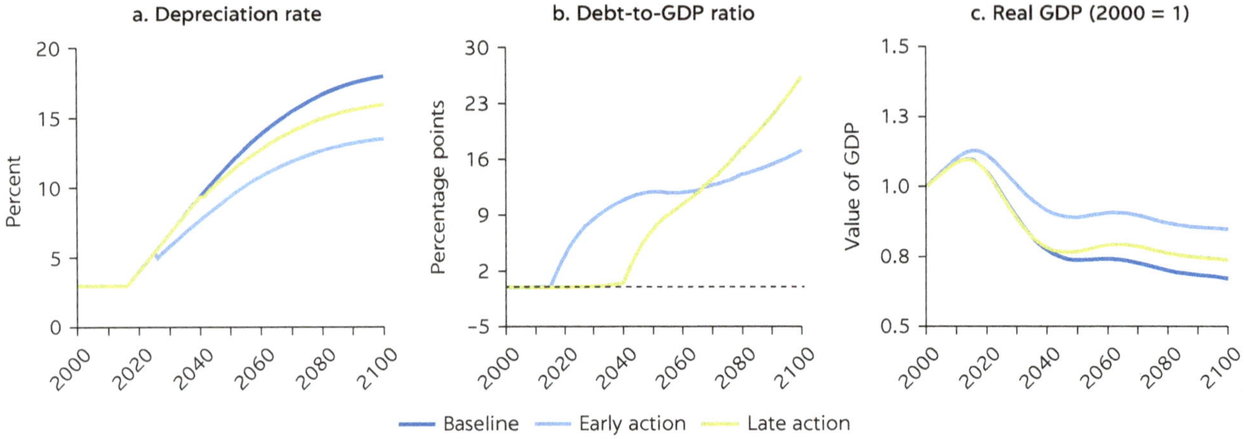

Note: Depreciation rate ceiling = 20%; GDP = gross domestic product.

adaptation spending is more sustainable than deficit financing despite its distortionary impact (table 3.1). This result holds even under the strong assumption that a rising debt-to-GDP ratio does not increase government borrowing costs. Deficit financing has a less positive effect on GDP because of the consumption-smoothing behavior of households, in the case of both gradual factors and extreme events. The increase in taxes (or the reduction in spending) to fund adaptation investment leaves households worse off. As a result, households increase their labor supply, boosting economic activity.

Financing adaptation spending through consumption taxes—which are less distortive than taxes on labor and capital—has less negative impacts on GDP. Although capital and labor taxes have similar long-term effects, capital taxes have a more positive short-term impact on GDP because the rigidity associated with capital-adjustment costs limits the extent to which higher capital taxes reduce investment. By contrast, cutting education spending negatively affects human capital, depressing productivity and pushing the GDP growth rate well below the baseline.

In addition, financing adaptation spending through capital taxes has positive implications for debt dynamics. Capital taxes are consistently associated with the lowest debt-to-GDP ratios across the entire projection period. Financing adaptation expenditures through consumption taxes, labor taxes, and reduced fiscal transfers would have comparable effects on debt dynamics. Each instrument would reduce household income, and households would compensate by boosting the labor supply. The main intuition behind this result is that the increase in taxes brings to the attention of economic agents the (otherwise difficult to perceive) existence of climate change. By increasing the depreciation of capital, climate change makes the economy—other things equal—poorer. Anticipating future losses, economic agents will therefore save, work and invest more, which will have a positive impact on GDP.

TABLE 3.1 **Alternative mechanisms for financing investment in adaptation to gradual climate shocks: Impact on economic output**

Real GDP (% deviation from the baseline projection)

FINANCING OF THE ADAPTATION SPENDING	2020	2030	2040	2050	2060	2070	2080	2090	2100
Deficit financing	4.8	15.6	21.4	24.8	28.0	28.9	30.6	32.9	34.1
Capital income taxes	17.6	27.1	34.4	39.1	43.4	46.6	50.2	53.6	55.3
Consumption taxes	11.5	24.4	33.4	39.1	44.7	48.6	52.5	56.1	57.9
Labor income taxes	11.0	23.3	31.9	37.5	42.8	46.5	50.2	53.7	55.4
Reduction in education spending	-11.7	-24.7	-33.9	-39.7	-45.3	-49.3	-53.2	-56.9	-58.7
Reduction in transfers	11.7	24.7	33.8	39.7	45.3	49.3	53.2	56.8	58.9

Note: GDP = gross domestic product.

TABLE 3.2 **Alternative mechanisms for financing investment in adaptation to gradual climate shocks: Impact on debt dynamics**

Debt-to-GDP ratio (percentage points deviation from the baseline projection)

FINANCING OF THE ADAPTATION SPENDING	2020	2030	2040	2050	2060	2070	2080	2090	2100
Deficit financing	3.2	5.7	6.2	5.7	4.3	2.9	1.0	-1.6	-4.9
Capital income taxes	-5.0	-6.5	-7.9	-8.7	-8.9	-9.8	-10.7	-11.2	-11.8
Consumption taxes	-1.6	-3.3	-4.6	-5.4	-5.7	-6.5	-7.2	-7.8	-8.2
Labor income taxes	-1.6	-3.1	-4.4	-5.1	-5.5	-6.2	-6.9	-7.4	-7.9
Reduction in education spending	1.6	3.3	4.6	5.4	5.7	6.5	7.2	7.8	8.3
Reduction in transfers	-1.5	-3.5	-4.5	-5.3	-5.7	-6.4	-7.2	-7.7	-8.2

Note: GDP = gross domestic product.

Funding adaptation through a reduction in education spending, hence on human capital, would increase the debt to GDP ratio all the way through 2100. Finally, deficit financing of adaptation is a poor strategy. The negative impact on debt is predominant and the debt to GDP ratio stabilizes and improves only far off into the future as GDP growth outpaces the growth of the debt stock (in our simulations after 2080, Table 3.2).

ADAPTING TO EXTREME EVENTS

In addition to the gradual factors described above, climate change increases the frequency and severity of extreme events such as hurricanes, floods, and droughts. We model extreme events as sudden and temporary spikes in the capital depreciation rate, which represent large-scale damage to the capital stock (figure 3.3). Under the baseline scenario, which assumes no adaptation spending, GDP falls substantially after an extreme event and then slowly recovers. This pattern reflects two key specifications of the model: (i) we have calibrated the cost of the extreme event so that the country hits the borrowing constraint, and (ii) we assume that adjustment costs slow the reconstruction of the capital stock.

FIGURE 3.3

The impact of extreme events on capital depreciation, debt dynamics, and economic output: Baseline scenario

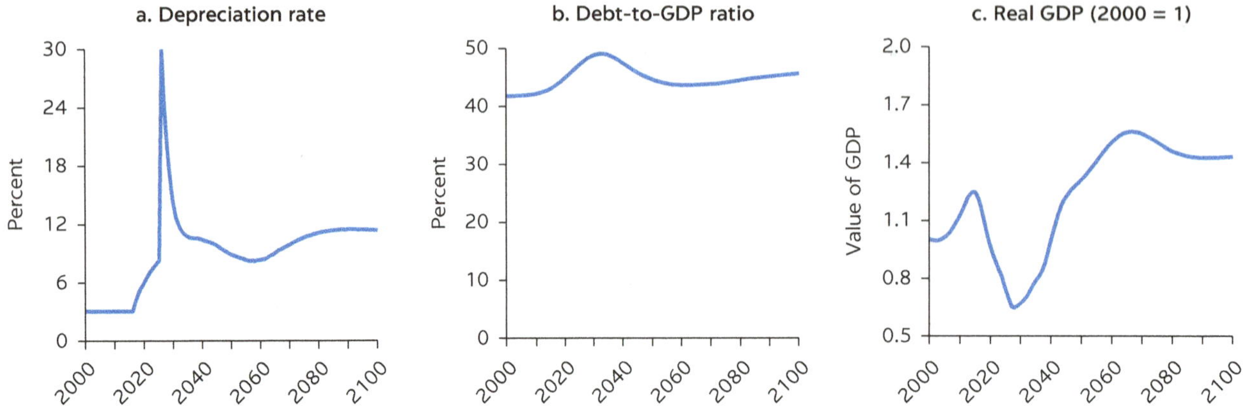

Note: GDP = gross domestic product.

Even if adaptation spending increases the resilience of the capital stock and boosts GDP growth over the long term, the financing necessary to rebuild the capital stock after an extreme event could exceed both a country's available domestic resources and its external borrowing capacity. To ease the borrowing constraint when an extreme event occurs, a country has many options: it could advance a reduction of the public debt-to-GDP ratio, establish a reserve fund in anticipation of extreme events, or rely on donor grants to partially finance the recovery process. The projections below assume the adoption of lump sum taxes to reduce the debt stock by 1 percent of GDP per year for 10 years prior to the extreme event and that donors provide grants equal to 1 percent of GDP per year for 10 years following the extreme event.

Relying on deficit financing, ex ante debt reduction/reserve funds, or donor grants leads to similar outcomes in terms of GDP growth, but very different outcomes in terms of debt dynamics. The GDP growth trajectory is similar under all three scenarios. Ex ante debt reduction or the accumulation of reserve funds has a more positive impact on the debt-to-GDP ratio than deficit financing because greater borrowing space enables the country to restore the capital stock more quickly after the extreme event (figure 3.4 and figure 3.5). Reliance on donor grants has little effect on debt dynamics relative to the baseline; because donor funding is provided only after an extreme event has occurred, GDP recovers more slowly than in cases where the government invested early in boosting the climate resilience of the capital stock (figure 3.6).

A strategy combining adaptation spending and ex ante debt reduction (figure 3.7) is likely to succeed in restoring GDP growth and debt sustainability. The additional availability of donor funding allows the country to restore its capital stock more rapidly and exit the recession with a higher level of GDP, but this difference is relatively modest (figure 3.8). The impact of donor grants is dwarfed by the much larger impact of early adaptation investment, which increases the resilience of the capital stock, and ex ante debt reduction, which allows the country to fully use international capital markets.

Financing investment through tax increases or expenditure cuts appears to be more effective than deficit financing. Every alternative financing scenario

FIGURE 3.4

Adaptation to extreme events: Deficit-financed early investment

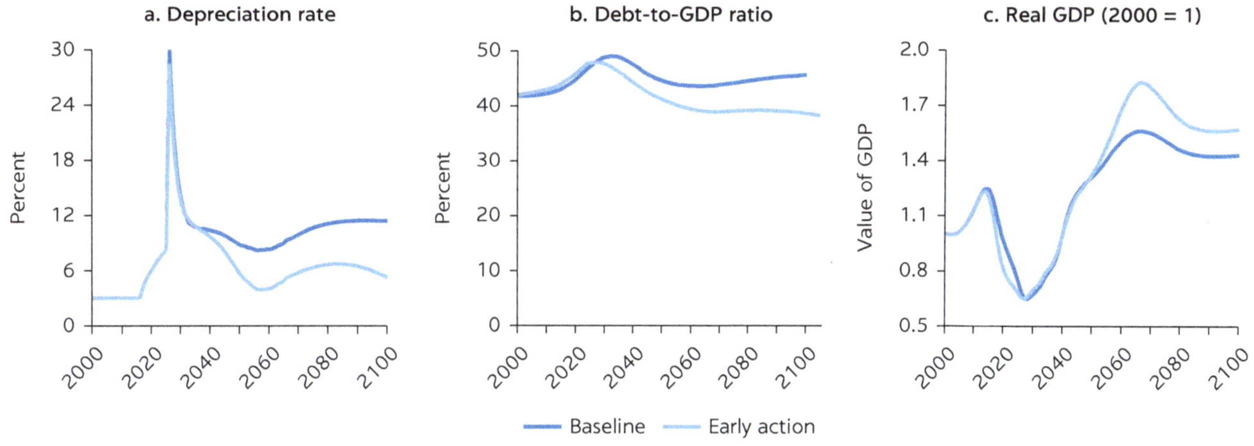

Note: GDP = gross domestic product.

FIGURE 3.5

Adaptation to extreme events: Ex ante debt reduction and reserve fund

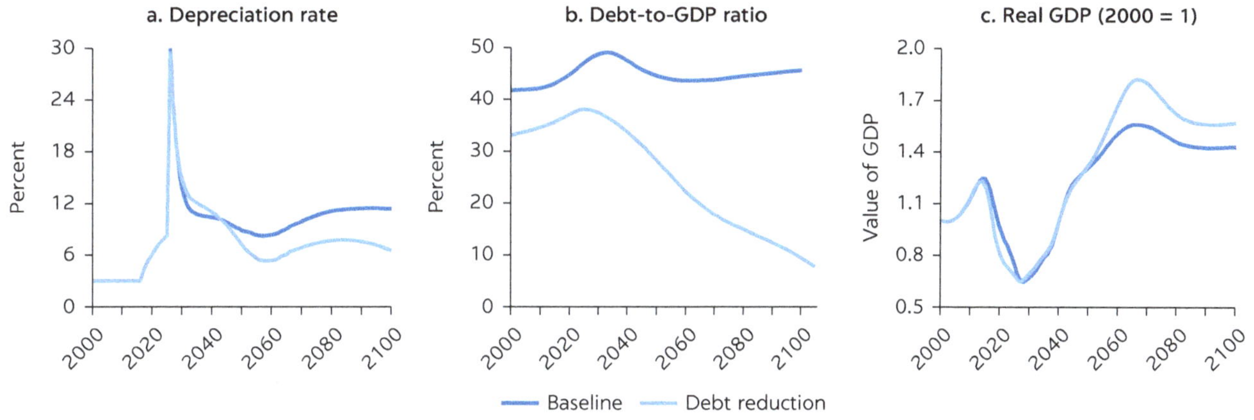

Note: GDP = gross domestic product.

FIGURE 3.6

Adaptation to extreme events: Donor grants

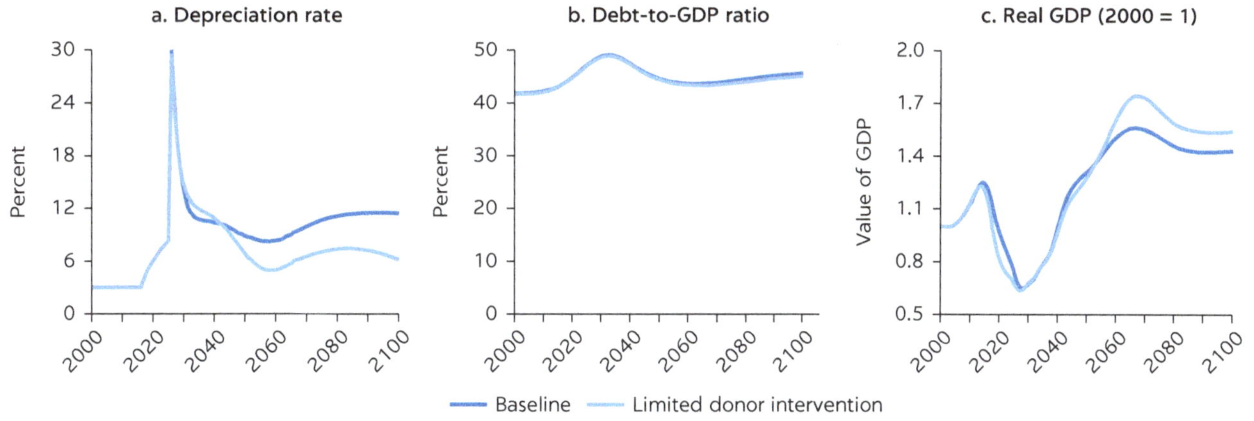

Note: GDP = gross domestic product.

FIGURE 3.7

Adaptation to extreme events: Early adaptation spending combined with ex ante debt reduction

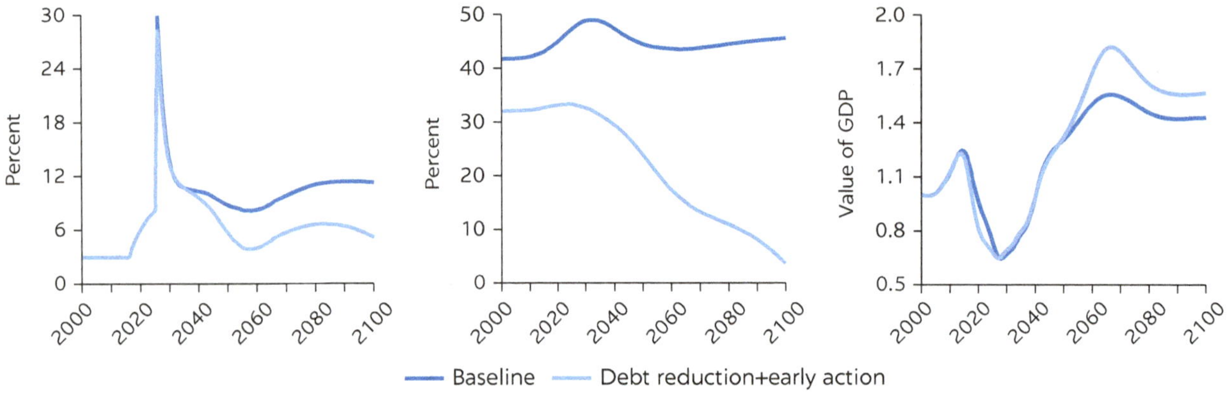

Note: GDP = gross domestic product.

FIGURE 3.8

Adaptation to extreme events: Early adaptation spending combined with ex ante debt reduction and donor grants

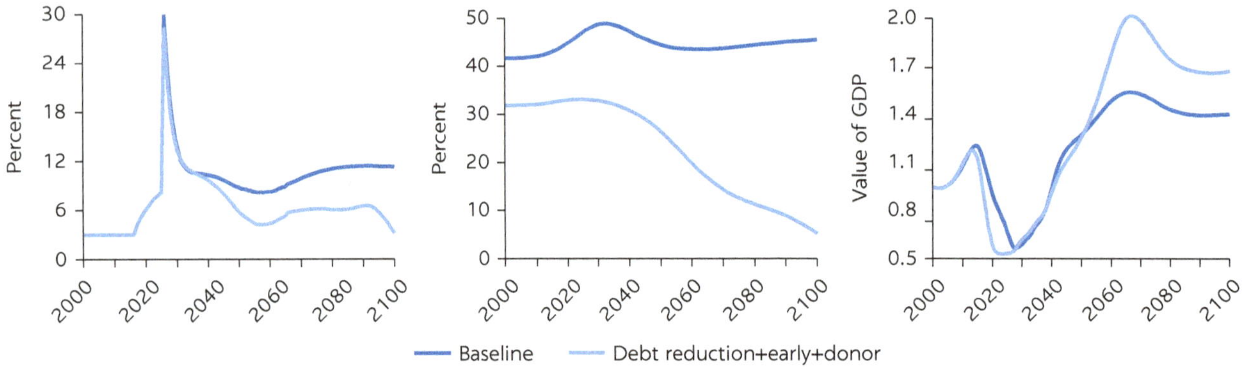

Note: GDP = gross domestic product.

results in a lower debt-to-GDP ratio and higher final GDP level—with the exception of cuts to education spending because those cuts have a negative effect on human capital formation (table 3.3 and table 3.4). Financing mechanisms other than deficit spending (or cuts to education spending) offer even greater advantages in the case of extreme events than they do in the case of gradual factors. Coping with extreme events requires a large amount of funding in a short amount of time, which causes the country to reach its borrowing limit in the capital market. Financing adaptation spending via taxes or spending cuts in other areas reduces the need for external borrowing and, per the model's calibration, enables the country to remain within its borrowing limit.

Moreover, external borrowing may be costlier than we have assumed, further underscoring the superiority of taxation or spending cuts over deficit financing. As noted above, our model includes no risk premium, and borrowing costs are independent of the debt level. This may be an oversimplification, however, because in the real world many countries have experienced sovereign defaults.

TABLE 3.3 **Alternative mechanisms for financing investment in adaptation to extreme events: Impact on economic output**

Real GDP (% deviation from the baseline projection)

FINANCING OF THE ADAPTATION SPENDING	2020	2030	2040	2050	2060	2070	2080	2090	2100
Deficit financing	-5.0	-9.0	5.0	19.0	42.0	52.0	39.0	32.0	29.0
Capital income taxes	-4.0	-9.0	3.0	16.0	42.0	73.0	90.0	98.0	77.0
Consumption taxes	-4.0	-10.0	-2.0	5.0	24.0	51.0	73.0	104.0	114.0
Labor income taxes	-6.0	7.0	19.0	21.0	36.0	49.0	40.0	64.0	73.0
Reduction in education spending	-3.2	-8.0	-1.6	-4.0	-19.2	-40.0	-57.6	-80.8	-87.2
Reduction in transfers	-6.0	4.0	24.0	35.0	42.0	56.0	42.0	85.0	77.0

Note: GDP = gross domestic product.

TABLE 3.4 **Alternative mechanisms for financing investment in adaptation to gradual climate factors: Impact on debt dynamics**

Debt-to-GDP ratio (percentage points deviation from the baseline projection)

FINANCING OF THE ADAPTATION SPENDING	2020	2030	2040	2050	2060	2070	2080	2090	2100
Deficit financing	6.9	5.9	0.2	-3.9	-8.4	-10.5	-8.9	-7.7	-7.2
Capital income taxes	7.9	4.6	-0.9	-5.0	-9.9	-14.6	-17.9	-19.4	-17.2
Consumption taxes	6.7	4.3	0.9	-1.9	-6.5	-11.8	-16.2	-20.2	-21.4
Labor income taxes	2.3	-2.9	-6.0	-6.9	-9.2	-11.8	-11.2	-15.6	-28.2
Reduction in education spending	6.0	3.9	0.8	1.7	5.9	10.6	14.4	17.8	18.8
Reduction in transfers	2.4	-2.0	-7.2	-9.9	-10.3	-12.8	-11.4	-18.3	-30.3

Note: GDP = gross domestic product.

In addition, the model includes just one homogeneous good that is traded depending on the savings–investment balance, which implies that there are no nominal exchange rate fluctuations and no possibility of exchange rate crises. Because of the absence of risk premiums and fluctuating exchange rates, external borrowing in our model is likely safer and less costly than it is in the real world.

The model's results highlight the importance of investing in climate change adaptation before an extreme event occurs. Although maintaining a low debt level or saving assets in a reserve fund would facilitate postdisaster reconstruction, these measures would do nothing to strengthen the resilience of the capital stock ex ante. However, if a country invests in adaptation prior to an extreme event, its capital stock becomes more resilient to the effects of climate change, and the depreciation rate after the event is lower than it would be otherwise. Capital-adjustment costs slow reconstruction, even given abundant fiscal resources, and the less reconstruction is necessary the faster the economy recovers.

Finally, it is important to stress that these are illustrative simulations and that the results strictly depend on the calibrated parameter values. Although realistic, the results reflect the model's underlying assumptions about how climate change affects the economy and how adaptation spending can counterbalance its effects. Thus, given the complexity of climate change and the model's degree of abstraction, these results should be interpreted with caution.

POLICY IMPLICATIONS

Countries around the world have made limited and uneven progress in incorporating climate-related issues into their macroeconomic policy frameworks. Adaptation policies—especially preventive spending actions—often face competing priorities, including social and economic development objectives, as well as the imperative of maintaining healthy fiscal and debt dynamics. Smaller and less-developed countries may assume that they lack the resources and capacity necessary to adapt to climate change, and they may instead choose to rely on donor assistance in the wake of extreme events. Donors in turn may reinforce this tendency by focusing on remedial action, such as disaster response and recovery, as opposed to preventive action. In addition, countries that embrace mitigation policies (such as the Paris Climate Accords) may be subject to moral hazard: policy makers may assume, incorrectly, that global mitigation efforts will effectively address the problem of climate change and become less inclined to invest in adaptation.

The available evidence indicates a clear bias in favor of remedial action over preventive action. Countries tend to stabilize budget revenues—for example, by mobilizing tax revenues—only after experiencing the effects of climate change, as opposed to saving revenues in advance (Gerling 2017). Governments may be especially likely to focus on remedial action if their fiscal policies are already procyclical. Although most governments make budgetary provisions for unforeseeable events—some even specifically designed to respond to natural disasters—the resources provided are often insufficient to cope with the exorbitant costs of climate change.[8]

Enhancing resilience to climate change requires a multifaceted strategy that includes both preventive and remedial action. Preventive action can support a higher long-term growth trajectory and greater macroeconomic stability by reducing the output and welfare losses associated with climate change. Preventive spending should be proportional to each country's capital stock; therefore, it should not be more onerous for smaller countries than it is for larger ones. Preventive actions include both investments in physical infrastructure and the creation of policy buffers designed to enhance resilience to shocks and ease borrowing constraints, including lower debt levels, stronger fiscal balances, and greater reserves.[9] To fully leverage the support of the international community, adaptation strategies should be designed and implemented in close collaboration with bilateral development partners and multilateral institutions.

A number of tools should be used to inform and manage adaptation-spending decisions. Cost-benefit assessment with multicriteria analysis, and decision tools such as Real Options Approach and other decision-making techniques that are designed to deal with uncertainty, should be used to select among the different types of adaptation spending. It would also be important to incorporate adaptation spending into fiscal planning. Public financial, budget, and expenditure management should be used to better inform spending decisions. To this regard, the use of climate change public expenditure reviews, climate reporting in budget appropriations, and tools for mainstreaming climate issues into national development planning are all practices that should be further developed (on these topics see World Bank Group 2014).

Expanding the use of risk-pooling mechanisms could strengthen fiscal resilience and accelerate postdisaster reconstruction. These mechanisms include private or sovereign insurance systems, multilateral safety nets, and regional catastrophe bonds. So far, participation in these mechanisms, and disbursements under them, has been limited. However, membership in multilateral organizations can also be viewed as a type of risk-pooling mechanism.

CONCLUSION

This chapter contributes to the nascent literature on fiscal policy and climate change adaptation. It uses a standard macroeconomic model to analyze the effectiveness of various revenue and expenditure strategies in addressing both the gradual factors associated with climate change and the impact of extreme climate-related events. The model's baseline scenario assumes that, if no action is taken to adapt to its impact, climate change will substantially reduce GDP, widen fiscal deficits, and increase debt stocks.

The chapter's key finding is that early, preventive action to address climate change is always superior to late, remedial action. Waiting to act simply means that larger and costlier adjustments will be needed in the future. Increasing spending on adaptation early, before gradual factors have eroded the capital stock and before extreme events have damaged it further, can increase fiscal and economic resilience, reducing the need for future spending.

Early action is necessary, but not sufficient, to manage extreme events associated with climate change. Small countries facing recurrent natural disasters may assume that investing in adaptation is futile because the scale and frequency of extreme events require much larger investments than they could realistically finance. These countries could combine public adaptation spending with public debt reduction (or the accumulation of savings in a reserve fund). Investing in adaptation increases the resilience of the capital stock whereas containing or reducing the debt burden improves financial sustainability and eases future borrowing constraints.

To date, both national policy makers and the international community have tended to focus on remedial action over preventive action. Because of fiscal constraints and competing priorities, countries tend to underinvest in climate change adaptation or build sufficient fiscal buffers to prepare for extreme events. No consensus has yet been reached regarding best practices for preventive action, and this uncertainty compounds incentives to delay investment in adaptation. Moral hazard and overreliance on international assistance further encourage remedial action over preventive action. However, as the social and economic impact of global warming continues to grow, further delay will likely necessitate much more extensive and costly interventions in the future, reducing long-run growth and destabilizing fiscal balances.

NOTES

1. For example, the Dynamic Integrated model of Climate and the Economy (DICE) aggregates all countries into a single economy (Nordhaus 2007, 2008). By contrast, the Regional Integrated model of Climate and the Economy (RICE) model divides the world into areas that trade with each other and can act cooperatively to cope with climate change (Nordhaus and Yang 1996; Nordhaus 2009). Both models are characterized by the presence of agents that optimize consumption over time and decide on investment in capital, education, and technology. Recent revisions of these models are provided in Nordhaus (2017). Other models focus on policies to increase the level of research and development (R&D) expenditure

and knowledge that allow for technological changes to improve energy efficiency. The return on investment in R&D is assessed to be four times higher than investment in physical capital, and this should therefore encourage technology to move toward a more environmentally friendly dynamic path (Bosetti, Carraro, and Galeotti 2006).

2. For a more complete literature review of these models, see Vivid Economics (2013).
3. Margulis and Narain (2010) provide a quantification of adaptation costs.
4. A possible extension would be to assume that climate change also affects the accumulation of human capital; however, to keep the exposition as simple as possible, we leave this extension for future analysis.
5. The model is multicounty, but it has been parametrized to focus on a single small open economy.
6. We model the impact of global warming as an autoregressive process that directly affects the capital depreciation rate (see "Government" in appendix C). This general formulation is intended to capture the fact that capital depreciation is a function of temperature increases.
7. We assume that public spending on adaptation permanently reduces the depreciation rate, implying a negative relationship between the stock of adaptive capital and the depreciation rate. This is consistent with Millner and Dietz (2015), who assume a negative relationship between the stock of adaptive capital and the damage function.
8. Guerson (2016) assesses the potential effectiveness of a reserve fund in the case of Dominica on the basis of several assumptions regarding the contribution rate to the fund (between 0.1 and 0.3 percent of GDP yearly). The simulations show that a 0.2 percent contribution enables the debt-to-GDP ratio to fall below a safe threshold of 60 percent, while also leaving adequate fiscal space to cope with the expected impact of climate-related events.
9. IMF (2016a) discusses the public finance and debt-management policies necessary to implement this type of preventive strategy. The International Monetary Fund–supported program for the Solomon Islands represents a practical application of the proposed framework (IMF 2016b). The World Bank's Comprehensive Debt and Development Framework (also called the "4-3-2 Initiative") proposed in 2012 for the Caribbean small states was a way of providing long-term solutions for growth and debt issues while addressing climate risks from frequent natural disasters in these countries. This translated into development plans in a number of Caribbean states thereafter.

REFERENCES

Barrage, Lint. 2015. "Climate Change Adaptation vs. Mitigation: A Fiscal Perspective." Working Paper, July 23. http://www.lintbarrage.com/wp-content/uploads/2016/12/Barrage_2015_UPDATED_Adaptation.pdf.

Bonen A., W. Semmler, and S. Klasen. 2014. "Economic Damages from Climate Change: A Review of Modeling Approaches." SCEPA Working Paper Series, Schwartz Center for Economic Policy Analysis (SCEPA), The New School.

Bonen A., P. Loungani, W. Semmler, and S. Koch (2016). "Investing to Mitigate and Adapt to Climate Change; A Framework Model." IMF Working Paper 16/164, International Monetary Fund, Washington, DC.

Bosetti, V., C. Carraro, and M. Galeotti. 2006. "The Dynamics of Carbon and Energy Intensity in a Model of Endogenous Technical Change." *Energy Journal, Endogenous Technological Changes and the Economics of Atmospheric Stabilization Special Issue.*

Burke M., S. M. Hsiang, and E. Miguel. 2015. "Global Non-linear Effect of Temperature on Economic Production." Nature 527 (November): 235–39.

Cabezon E., L. Hunter, P. Tumbarello, K. Washimi, and Y. Wu. 2015. "Enhancing Macroeconomic Resilience to Natural Disasters and Climate Change in the Small States of the Pacific." IMF Working Paper 15/125, International Monetary Fund, Washington, DC.

Gerling, Kerstin. 2017. "The Macro-Fiscal Aftermath of Weather-Related Disasters: Do Loss Dimensions Matter?" IMF Working Paper 17/235, International Monetary Fund, Washington, DC.

Guerson, Alejandro, Saji Thomas, Wayne Mitchell, and Ke Wang. 2016. "Dominica: Selected Issues." IMF Country Report No. 16/245, International Monetary Fund, Washington, DC.

Harris, J. M., and B. Roach. 2018. *Environmental and Natural Resource Economics: A Contemporary Approach*, Fourth Edition. New York: Routledge.

IMF (International Monetary Fund). 2016a. "Small States' Resilience to Natural Disasters and Climate Change—Role for the IMF." IMF Policy Paper, International Monetary Fund, Washington, DC.

IMF 2016b: Solomon Islands,: 2016 Article IV Consultation and Fifth and Sixth Reviews Under the Extended Credit Facility Arrangement-Press Release; Staff Report; and Statement by the Executive Director for Solomon Islands, March.

IPCC (Intergovernmental Panel on Climate Change). 2001. *Climate Change 2014: Synthesis Report. Fourth Volume of the Third Assessment Report of the Intergovernmental Panel on Climate Change*. Cambridge: Cambridge University Press.

Kotlikoff L. J., A. Polbin, and A. Zubarev. 2016. "Will the Paris Accord Accelerate Climate Change?" NBER Working Paper 22731, National Bureau of Economic Research, Cambridge, MA.

Margulis, Sergio, and Urvashi Narain. 2010. "The Costs to Developing Countries of Adapting to Climate Change: New Methods and Estimates—The Global Report of the Economics of Adaptation to Climate Change Study." Working Paper 55726, World Bank, Washington, DC.

Mechler, R., J. Mochizuki, and S. Hochrainer. 2016. "Disaster Risk Management and Fiscal Policy: Narratives, Tools, and Evidence Associated with Assessing Fiscal Risk and Building Resilience." Policy Research Working Paper 7635, World Bank, Washington, DC.

Mendelsohn, R. 2012. "The Economics of Adaptation to Climate Change in Developing Countries." *Climate Change Economics* 3 (2): 1250006 (21 pages).

Nordhaus, W. D. 2007. "The Challenge of Global Warming: Economic Models and Environmental Policy." Working Paper. http://www.econ.yale.edu/~nordhaus/homepage/OldWebFiles/DICEGAMS/dice_mss_072407_all.pdf.

——. 2008. *A Question of Balance: Weighting the Options on Global Warming Policies*. New Haven: Yale University Press.

——. 2009. "New Estimates of Efficient Approaches to the Control of Global Warming." Cowles Foundation Discussion Paper 1716, Yale University, August.

——. 2017. "Evolution of Modeling of the Economics of Global Warming: Changes in the DICE Model, 1992 - 2017." Cowles Foundation Discussion Paper No. 2084, Cowles Foundation Yale University.

Nordhaus, W. D., and Z. Yang. 1996. "A Regional Dynamic General-Equilibrium Model of Alternative Climate Change Strategies." *American Economic Review* 86 (4): 741–65.

Stern, N. 2007. *The Economics of Climate Change: The Stern Review*. Cambridge: Cambridge University Press.

UNDP (United Nations Development Programme). 2007. *Human Development Report 2007/08*. Basingstoke, U.K.: Palgrave McMillan.

Vivid Economics. 2013. "The Macroeconomics of Climate Change." Report prepared for Defra, May.

World Bank Group. 2017. *Climate Change Public Expenditure and Institutional Review Sourcebook*. Washington, DC: World Bank Group.

4 Managing the Fiscal Risks Associated with Natural Disasters

PHILIP SCHULER, LUIZ EDGARD OLIVEIRA[1], GIANLUCA MELE, AND MATIAS ANTONIO

INTRODUCTION

This chapter discusses the fiscal risks posed by climate-related natural disasters (hereafter, natural disasters) and their implications for fiscal and debt sustainability. First, it considers some specific fiscal risks that arise from climate change. Second, it presents a stochastic fiscal sustainability analysis model that the World Bank has developed for use by government officials. Finally, it applies the model to two middle-income island countries: Jamaica, a highly indebted country that has a history of low and volatile gross domestic product (GDP) growth, and the Dominican Republic, which has enjoyed relatively rapid economic growth and low debt. The chapter uses this model to construct probable paths of key fiscal variables—the budget balance, debt stock, and debt service costs—in the face of climate-related shocks of varying magnitudes and under alternative strategies for financing responses to climate shocks. The findings in the chapter support several policy recommendations for managing fiscal risks from climate change.

FISCAL RISKS FROM CLIMATE CHANGE

Fiscal risks are commonly defined as any substantial deviation in fiscal outturns from budget or other fiscal projections (Cebotari et al. 2006). The realization of fiscal risks often requires governments to make disruptive short-term adjustments to planned spending, revenue, or financing. These adjustments can undermine fiscal sustainability and the provision of public goods needed for the country's long-term economic growth. Shocks to interest rates or exchange rates, fluctuations in commodity prices, and changes in economic activity can directly and indirectly affect government revenue, spending, and financing. Judicial decisions can result in large, unplanned spending obligations. Economic activity—and therefore tax revenue from that activity—in agriculture and certain other industries is sensitive to weather. Governments face explicit and implicit contingent liabilities that can result in assuming costs or debts of state-owned enterprises, subnational governments, or private firms.

Climate change exposes governments to fiscal risks arising from the unexpected disruption of economic activity and damages to both public and private assets. Table 4.1 illustrates a range of likely fiscal risks from climate change, embedded in a standard taxonomy of fiscal factors. Disruption of

TABLE 4.1 **Fiscal risk factors and illustrative climate change channels**

RISK FACTOR	CONVENTIONAL EXAMPLES	CLIMATE CHANGE CHANNELS
Macroeconomic risks		
Economic growth (GDP or industry-level growth)	Tax revenue differs from planned level Payouts for unemployment insurance and other social protection schemes differ from planned level	Drought, excessive rainfall, storms, etc. disrupt agriculture, fishing, mining, tourism, transport, hydro-power, insurance, etc. Note that weather shocks in other countries can potentially boost demand for exports
Commodity prices	Changes in oil prices affect government procurement spending, customs duty collection, energy subsidies (for extractives exporters): government revenue differs from expected level Changes in global agricultural prices may affect domestic farm and food subsidy spending (depending on national policies)	Increased severity and likelihood of extreme weather events in large producers increase the volatility of world commodity prices
Interest rates	Debt service costs differ from expectations	..
Exchange rates	External debt service costs differ from expectations Government procurement spending on imports differs from expectations	..
Contingent liabilities		
State-owned enterprises (SOEs)	Sovereign loan guarantees are called Expectation that the government will cover SOE losses	Climate-sensitive SOEs suffer losses due to extreme weather events
Public-private partnerships (PPPs)	Contractual obligations (for example, service-level guarantees) Expectation that government will cover losses if the project fails	Infrastructure PPPs suffer damages or losses from extreme weather events
Natural disasters	Shocks to economic growth affect revenue and spending (see above) Unexpected spending on repair and reconstruction of government buildings and other public assets Unexpected relief and recovery spending; possible spending to cover private sector losses (including, for example, government-run fire, flooding, and crop insurance)	Increased severity and likelihood of extreme weather events (for example, tropical cyclones) increases the chances of natural disasters
Public health emergency	Increased health spending Reduced income tax revenue if health emergency affects employment and production	Changing climate and increased severity and likelihood of extreme weather events may affect the spread of vector-borne diseases, deaths from heat events, etc.
Judicial awards	Court judgments made against the government result in unexpected spending	Courts may determine that governments are liable for climate adaptation measures
Pension obligations	The number of retirees differs from expectations	..
Other fiscal risks		
Wage settlements	Higher-than-anticipated public service wage settlements	..
Government policy changes	Changes in (nonfiscal) government policies cause actual revenue and spending to differ from expectations	..

Note: .. = Negligible.

economic activity resulting from the effects of climate change reduces tax and other revenue that the government receives. Depending on a country's policy framework, social transfer payments may increase, if these payments are targeted at households that experience a loss in income because of a climate change–induced shock. Or the government may need to increase spending on price subsidies, for example, to keep agriculture supply shocks from raising food prices paid by consumers. A fiscal risk analysis by the U.S. Office of Management and Budget and Council of Economic Advisors, for example, identifies increased crop insurance payouts, increased spending on wildfire suppression, and increased public health spending due to extreme heat events as important causes of unplanned spending (OMB 2016).

Climate change is expected to increase the frequency and intensity of weather-related shocks. If climate change continues unabated and countries do not adapt, there is a significant long-run risk of disastrous consequences (Weitzman 2009, 2011): scientifically, there is "very high confidence in the potential for state shifts" (USGCRP 2017) in which the climate system passes tipping points, unleashing feedback mechanisms of escalating damages. For example, some scientists believe that we are at the tipping point for the melting of the Greenland ice sheet, an event that could raise sea levels by up to 20 feet, threatening the existence of some of the largest cities in the world, including New York City and Mumbai. In this state of the world, no preventive measure may be sufficient to contain the damages of the expected weather-related shock. It is therefore imperative to avoid this situation in the first place, through sustained mitigation and adaptation measures in all countries of the world (see, for example, Ackerman 2017).

Governments can also face large contingent liabilities. Climate change increases the likelihood of increased government spending to repair or replace publicly owned assets damaged by rising sea levels, tropical cyclones, and wildfires. Depending on a country's social and political context and government capacity, the public may expect the government to finance private costs of replacing or repairing assets damaged by effects of climate change. The analysis of data on contingent liabilities by Bova et al. (2016) covers 80 advanced and emerging market economies and finds that natural disasters (including those unrelated to climate change) are one of the most prevalent sources of contingent liabilities (see table 4.2). One should note, however, that these are not the largest source of contingent liabilities that governments face.

TABLE 4.2 **Fiscal costs of contingent liabilities**

TYPE OF CONTINGENT LIABILITY	TOTAL NUMBER	NUMBER WITH IDENTIFIED FISCAL COSTS	AVERAGE FISCAL COST (% OF GDP)	MAXIMUM FISCAL COST (% OF GDP)
Financial sector	91	82	9.7	56.8
Legal	9	9	7.9	15.3
Subnational government	13	9	3.7	12.0
State-owned enterprises	32	31	3.0	15.1
Natural disaster(s)	65	29	1.6	6.0
Private nonfinancial sector	7	6	1.7	4.5
Public-private partnerships	8	5	1.2	2.0
Other	5	3	1.4	2.5
Total	230	174	6.1	56.8

Source: Bova et al. 2016.

Governments can reduce fiscal risks from climate change by investing in adaptation. Making government-owned structures and other public assets more resilient to the effects of climate change reduces the government's direct exposure to possible future financial losses (Bonen et al. 2016). Public investments, fiscal incentives, and regulatory measures that increase the resilience of private assets and economic activity to climate change indirectly reduce fiscal risks. The central result of chapter 3 is that making early public investments in adaptation generates higher GDP growth than waiting until after the effects of climate change materialize.

Governments have a range of options for managing risks from climate change. The optimal response to frequent events that cause minor disruptions to economic activity is different from the response to major events that are likely to occur only once in a century. Table 4.3 presents a taxonomy of how governments are managing climate change risks, including through risk reduction, risk financing, and residual risk management.

Reallocation of spending is a government's first line of response to high-frequency, low-severity events, for example, weather events that cause localized, moderate damages and losses (in chapter 3 we called these events the "gradual factors" of climate change) (figure 4.1). A government can stay within its planned expenditure ceilings and adhere to fiscal balance targets by shifting resources within the approved budget. Such reallocation can be challenging, however, if a government's budget is dominated by statutory and other mandatory expenditures (such as debt service, wages, pensions, and the like). In the presence of these rigidities, governments often find themselves forced to cut social spending or postpone capital investment projects. These cuts can exacerbate crises because social safety nets are critical for allowing those hit by disasters to rebound after climate shocks, as well as for overcoming the

TABLE 4.3 **Approaches for managing climate change risks**

Risk reduction	Reduce vulnerability	Diversify economy into climate-resilient production and livelihoods
		Mainstream climate change into public investment management systems
	Reduce exposure to hazards	Improve buildings codes, land-use planning, and zoning
		Strengthen natural buffers (reefs, beaches, forests, etc.)
		Improve ecosystem management
Risk financing	Risk retention	Contingency and reserve funds
		Ex ante contingent credit
		Ex post borrowing
	Risk transfer and pooling	Insure public assets
		Multicountry sovereign disaster insurance
		Catastrophe bonds
Residual risk management	Postdisaster response	Livelihood support
		Budget reallocation
		Humanitarian relief

Sources: Adapted from World Bank 2014 and Mechler, Mochizuki, and Hochrainer-Stigler 2016.

FIGURE 4.1

Illustrative allocation of risks from natural disasters

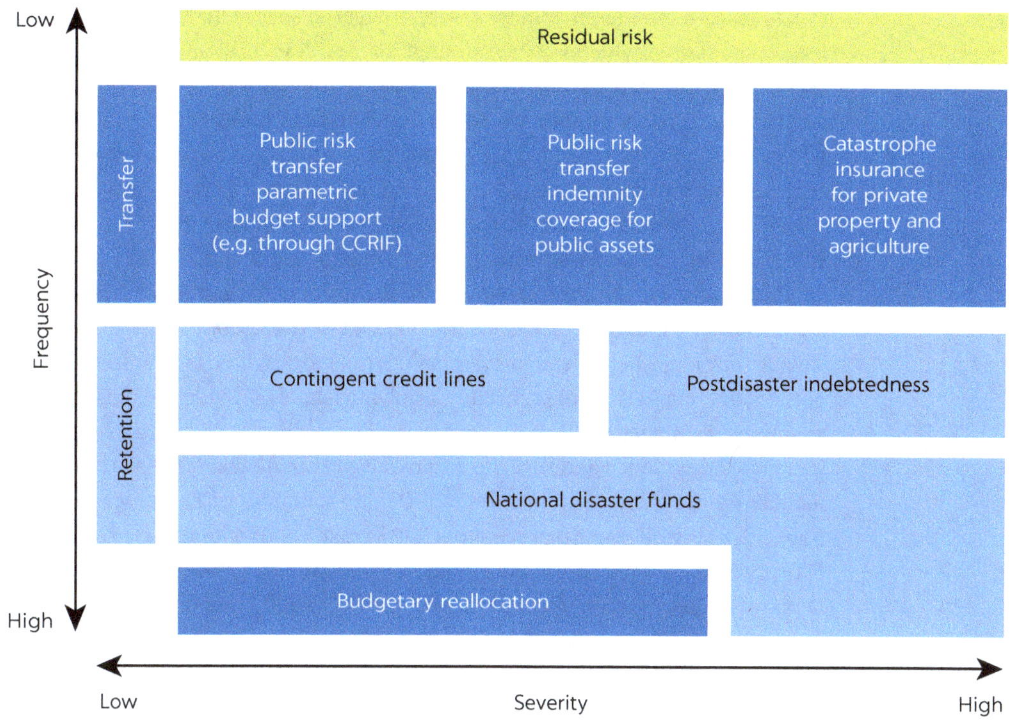

Note: CCRIF is the Caribbean Catastrophic Risk Insurance Fund.

inability of the poor to adapt toward future shocks (World Bank 2016). However, earmarking revenue to predetermined spending needs and the extensive use of tax exemptions and incentives also reduce a government's flexibility. As will be seen below, fiscal rigidity is a major challenge faced by the Dominican Republic. Even if postdisaster budget reallocation does not face these constraints, research suggests that it tends to be ad hoc and ineffective (see, for example, Mahul and Gurenko 2006).

If unplanned revenue shortfalls or spending needs become larger, it may no longer be possible to respond through budgetary reallocation. A government will need to find other sources of financing. "Rainy day funds" and other reserves accumulated through fiscal savings allow governments to meet fiscal targets when unplanned spending needs and revenue shortfalls become larger. A robust fiscal responsibility framework allows governments to generate these savings by discouraging overspending during economic upturns.[2] In addition to enabling a government to attain planned spending targets, ex ante contingency financing allows a government to respond more quickly to the unplanned demands. This readiness can be especially important in accelerating the implementation of reconstruction projects after a natural disaster because these activities have the potential to boost GDP growth. For example, research into the effects of Mexico's Fund for Natural Disasters (*Fondo de Desastres Naturales*, FONDEN)—a large, multihazard disaster contingency fund—estimates that municipalities with access to FONDEN grew by 2–4 percent more than those without FONDEN financing in the year following a natural disaster (de Janvry, del Valle, and Sadoulet 2016).

Increased borrowing is an alternative. The high opportunity cost of maintaining large reserve funds makes these tools less than optimal for responding to events that are infrequent or more severe. Increased borrowing also presents challenges, the first of which involves timing. It takes time to arrange new financing, especially project financing, which can delay government spending on relief, recovery, and reconstruction. In addition, credit conditions may be unfavorable when financing is most needed. Governments can address this timing challenge to some extent by arranging in advance contingent lines of credit, such as those offered by the World Bank and other international financial institutions, that provide financing when a prespecified natural catastrophe occurs.[3]

Many of the countries most exposed to the effects of climate change, however, are also highly indebted. The second challenge is therefore that increased borrowing may place debt on an unsustainable trajectory, which is a central concern of the modeling in this chapter. The Caribbean islands provide the most notable examples. Damages and losses from tropical cyclones (which are expected to increase in frequency and severity as a result of climate change) have been estimated at more than two multiples of GDP (for example, in Dominica in 2017). Public debt is well over 60 percent of GDP in many countries and currently over 100 percent in Barbados and Jamaica. The modeling of Jamaica and the Dominican Republic below explores debt sustainability and possible responses in more detail.

As natural disasters become more severe, governments should seek to transfer some fiscal risks to markets and spread risks across countries through insurance and other financial instruments. A well-developed market for insurance and other risk transfer mechanisms can dampen the impact of disasters on producers' and households' income, which can, in turn, attenuate the likely shocks to tax revenue and government spending on relief. National governments in the Caribbean, Central America, and the Pacific Islands have access to international insurance facilities that pay out when prespecified natural events occur (for example, winds, rainfall, or earthquakes of a given magnitude in given locations). Some governments have begun to experiment with catastrophe bonds—a financial instrument with a long history of use by insurance and reinsurance companies—to shift fiscal risks to markets.[4]

THE FISCAL SUSTAINABILITY MODEL

This chapter embeds the analysis of climate change into standard methods of fiscal risk analysis using a simple, spreadsheet-based tool developed by the World Bank.[5] The model assesses the sustainability of a country's fiscal policies under a baseline scenario based on the schedule of disbursement and amortization of the government's contracted debt, a schedule of future borrowing based on the government's debt strategy, and the government's medium-term macroeconomic and fiscal framework. The user constructs alternative scenarios and stress tests to assess, for example, the effects of exogenous shocks (including natural disasters) and realization of contingent liabilities (such as public–private partnerships and subnational guaranteed debt obligations), among others. Following best practice in fiscal risk analysis (IMF 2016), this chapter uses probabilistic forecasting methods to assess how policies or shocks affect fiscal outcomes in an uncertain environment. The model derives variances of key macroeconomic variables from the country's historical data. It then runs Monte Carlo simulations to generate short- to medium-term future projections, including fan charts for key fiscal and macroeconomic variables, under baseline and alternative scenarios.[6]

In the simulations presented below, the fiscal sustainability analysis (FSA) exercise includes a macroeconomic outlook (that is, baseline scenario) that assumes no major weather-related disasters over the next eight years and a few alternative scenarios illustrating varying potential damages to the capital stock of the economy if there were major weather-related disasters. The methodology involves stochastic simulations suitable to address macroeconomic uncertainties and fiscal risks, thus improving upon the traditional debt-only deterministic scenario analysis approach. New insights can then be obtained to inform the formulation of fiscal and debt policies.

The analysis of fiscal risks aims at quantifying the range and likelihood of possible fiscal outcomes that may result from natural disasters. As a first step, this analysis moves from the simulation of stochastic shocks to key macroeconomic variables. Next, all public finance variables of interest (budget balance, public debt stock, gross financing needs, and the like) are projected. Finally, a probability distribution for each variable is constructed (that is, the range of values and the associated probabilities of occurrence for each variable are plotted). This enables one to assess the source of (and the exposure to) fiscal risks. We construct alternative scenarios for Jamaica and the Dominican Republic on the basis of hypotheses about damages from natural disasters and about methods of financing the government's response to these disasters. We introduce stochastic shocks to three macroeconomic variables: economic growth (proxied by the real GDP growth), competitiveness (proxied by the real exchange rate), and revenue mobilization (proxied by the total government revenue). The model runs up to 3,000 Monte Carlo simulations with probabilistically generated shocks to the same three variables. Thus, each simulation gives rise to alternative macroeconomic projections that naturally depart from the baseline path. Their assessment is facilitated using fan charts, which depict the range of possible outcomes and their associated probabilities. These probabilities are essential for policy makers to quantitatively assess the likelihood that planned fiscal targets will or will not be achieved.

APPLICATION TO JAMAICA

Country context

Jamaica is a highly indebted country with a history of slow and volatile economic growth. For the past 30 years, real per capita GDP increased at an average of just 1 percent per annum, making Jamaica one of the slowest-growing developing countries. Natural disasters and adverse external shocks, coupled with insufficient fiscal discipline and the materialization of contingent fiscal liabilities, have resulted in persistent fiscal deficits that have kept public debt above 100 percent of GDP since the early 2000s. Jamaica's large debt burden has depressed investor sentiment and crowded out private sector investment needed for job creation and economic growth. High debt service obligations have limited the government's fiscal space for spending on poverty reduction and public goods.

Forecasting assumptions

The forecasting horizon runs from Jamaica's fiscal year (FY) 2017/18 through FY2021/22.[7] We produce a baseline forecast and two contrasting alternative scenarios, which are designed to illustrate the role played by contingent financing for disasters and risk transfer instruments.

Baseline scenario

The baseline scenario is that the government follows current policies aimed at reducing public debt and that the economy remains stable over the medium term.[8] Real GDP is projected to grow by 2.5 percent in FY2018/19, supported by a rebound from adverse weather in 2017, the reopening of the Alpart alumina refinery (which should support growth of more than 20 percent in mining and quarrying), and favorable external conditions, including continued strong tourism demand. GDP growth is expected to accelerate to about 2.9 percent by 2020. The momentum in global economic activity translates to a supportive demand from Jamaica's trading partners and will help boost growth over the medium term. Inflation is projected to remain in the Bank of Jamaica's target band of 4–6 percent.

We assume that the government remains committed to a target of reducing public debt to 60 percent of GDP by FY2025/26, as required by Jamaica's fiscal responsibility legislation. This target implies continuing to maintain a primary fiscal surplus of 7.0 percent of GDP. The tightening cycle in global capital markets will place upward pressure on interest rates, raising borrowing costs on new debt and offsetting some of the reduction in interest payments resulting from steady debt reduction. We assume no liability management operations during the forecast period, although one should note that the government has conducted several large operations since 2015. These have reduced the total debt stock, extended bond maturities, and smoothed future repayment obligations.

Figure 4.2 plots the historical data for four key macroeconomic variables—annual growth in real GDP, the primary fiscal balance as a share of GDP, the public debt-to-GDP ratio, and public debt service payments relative to government revenue—along with fans showing the probability distributions of future realization of these variables.

Fan charts for the baseline show wide dispersions of GDP growth and the primary fiscal balance, reflecting the volatility of these variables in the historical data. For example, although the government forecasts growth of 2.5–2.9 percent over the medium term, panel a shows about a 1–5 percent probability of a recession in any one of these years, based on the variance of macroeconomic variables in the past. Panel b incorporates the government's commitment to maintaining a primary fiscal surplus of 7.0 percent of GDP. The model assumes that meeting this target becomes less certain over time. Nevertheless, the probability that the government keeps the primary surplus from falling below 6 percent of GDP—which would be a significant accomplishment for most countries—remains quite high.

Debt continues its downward trajectory in the baseline, reflecting the tight fiscal stance and modest GDP growth. Panel c shows a 50 percent probability that debt will fall within a band of 80–90 percent of GDP. There is even a small possibility that maintaining a tight fiscal stance could enable the government to reach its debt target of 60 percent of GDP several years earlier than required, although there is an equal likelihood that debt could climb back to 120 percent of GDP by the end of FY2020/21.

FIGURE 4.2

Jamaica: Baseline scenario

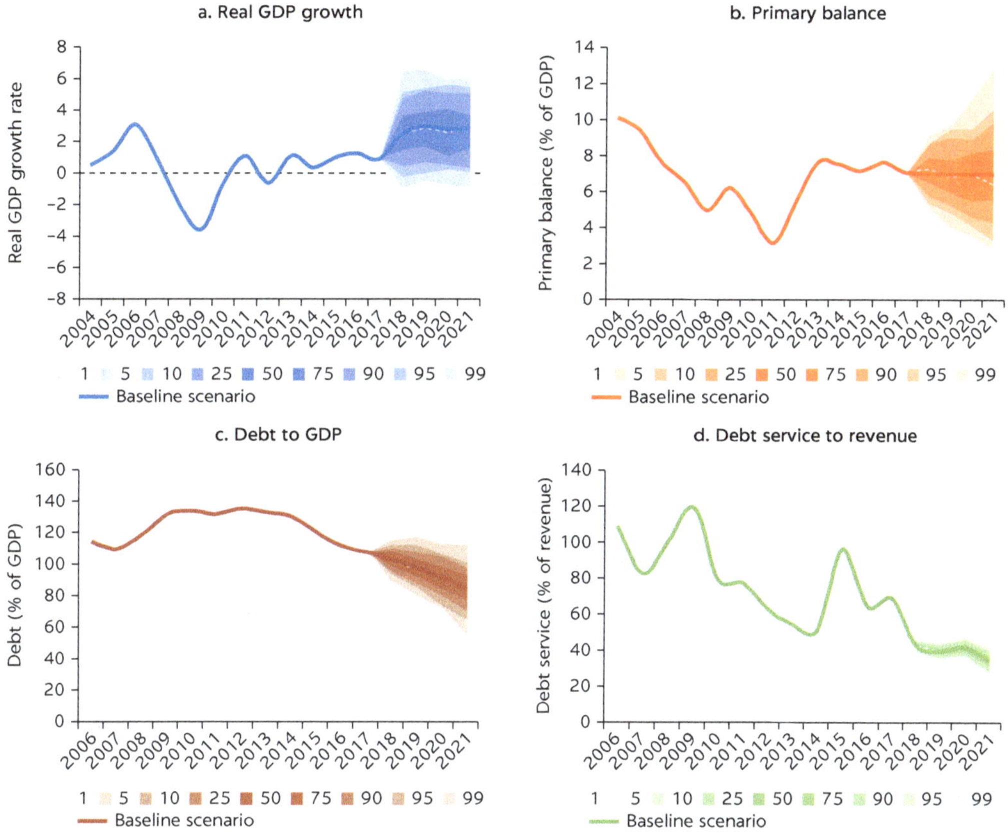

The ratio of debt service to government revenue declines slowly and within a relatively focused range of probabilities. This decline results from modeling assumptions and the structure of Jamaican public debt. The model assumes that a government will repay all debt according to the schedules set when the debt was contracted. Because most of the Jamaican public debt is in fixed interest rate instruments, shocks to interest rates affect only the interest payments on new debt. Exchange rate and revenue volatility are the main factors influencing the probability distribution. Liability management operations that the government has undertaken resulted in considerable variation in past debt service, as shown in panel d. Debt service payments spiked in 2015 when the government took advantage of favorable conditions to repay its PetroCaribe debt (at a discount), which it financed with a large Eurobond issue. The government also undertook operations in global capital markets in 2016 and 2017, swapping high-coupon bonds issued in the past for longer-dated and cheaper bonds. For the sake of simplicity, the baseline scenario assumes no such operations during the forecast period.

Alternative scenario 1: Major natural disaster

The first scenario models the impact on fiscal sustainability of a natural disaster with a historical probability of occurring once in 100 years in Jamaica.[9] This seems an appropriate event to use for the short to medium term, given that climate change is expected to increase the severity and frequency of tropical cyclones in the Caribbean, although perhaps not at levels that quickly exceed previous records.[10] On impact, GDP growth is hit with a –4.5 percentage point shock in this scenario, as flooding and infrastructural damages contract output (see figure 4.3, panel a). Reconstruction activities help to push GDP growth back to its baseline trajectory by the end of the forecast period.

The primary fiscal balance falls because of both lower revenue and higher spending (see figure 4.3, panel b). Lower firm and household income reduce government revenue from both direct and indirect taxation (for example, value added tax receipts). Additionally, an estimated J$1.7 billion in increased expenditures materialize over the forecasted four years because of reconstruction efforts.[11] We assume that expenditures during the forecast period follow an inverted-V shape. This assumption is based on the general pattern of postdisaster government spending where initially governments spend on relief activities, the level of spending then rises when reconstruction projects commence,

FIGURE 4.3
Jamaica: Alternative scenario 1

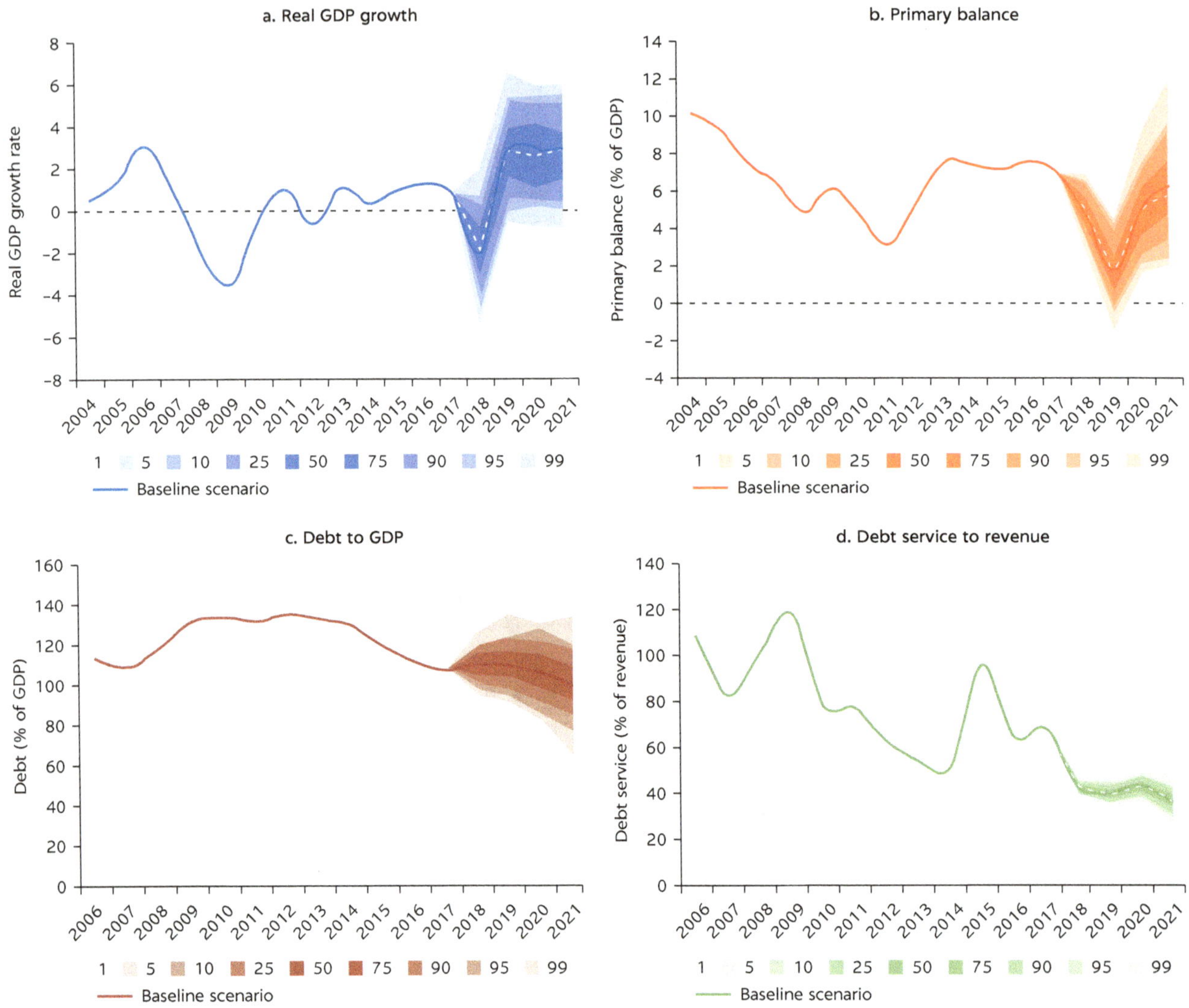

and then this spending tapers off over time (Ghesquiere and Mahul 2010). We assume that the government works to quickly resume running large primary fiscal surpluses that are needed to bring down debt in line with the target set in Jamaica's fiscal responsibility laws.

The increased fiscal burden is financed entirely through new commercial borrowing in this scenario. The additional borrowing reverses the downward trajectory of the debt-to-GDP ratio and increases debt service costs relative to government revenue (see figure 4.3, panels c and d).

Alternative scenario 2: Major natural disaster with contingent financing

The second alternative scenario is constructed to highlight the role of contingent financing. This scenario assumes that the same natural disaster event of historically major proportions occurs in Jamaica, but that the use of various financing instruments that can be arranged in advance and deployed quickly enables the government to respond more quickly with recovery and reconstruction, and with less use of new commercial borrowing. This causes a different expenditure pattern than the previous scenario, with most expenditure occurring upon impact.

The amount of financing procured prior to the disaster totals US$544 million. We assume that this is sourced from the Caribbean Development Bank, U.S. Agency for International Development grants, payouts from the Caribbean Catastrophic Risk Insurance Fund, use of financing available under the ongoing International Monetary Fund Stand-by Arrangement program (which the government presently treats as precautionary), and a catastrophe bond. Apart from the catastrophe bond—which has never been issued by the Jamaican government—these sources of financing are either currently available or have been used in the past. We assume in this scenario that the government has already entered into a transaction like the World Bank's catastrophe bond for the Pacific Alliance countries which provides access to US$50 million and pays a 3 percent annual premium (that is, US$1.5 million annually).[12]

The striking difference in the results from this scenario is that the debt-to-GDP ratio continues to move along a downward trajectory, despite the major shock to GDP and increased fiscal burden (see figure 4.4).

Comparison across scenarios

Despite temporarily suffering from considerable GDP impacts caused by natural disasters, medium-term growth would remain robust. Natural disaster shocks would immediately be followed by increased construction activity, boosting growth in the year immediately after the event. If stochastic shocks to real GDP growth from natural disasters are not significantly larger in the future than major events of the past, the Jamaican economy is resilient over the medium term, with negative growth occurring only in the very left tail of the distribution (that is, mostly in the first through 10th percentile range). Under these assumptions, increasing the preparedness of financing mitigates the shock slightly, but not in a meaningful way.

Primary fiscal balances would suffer a clear deterioration across scenarios because of the disruption in revenue mobilization caused by the shock to

FIGURE 4.4

Jamaica: Alternative scenario 2

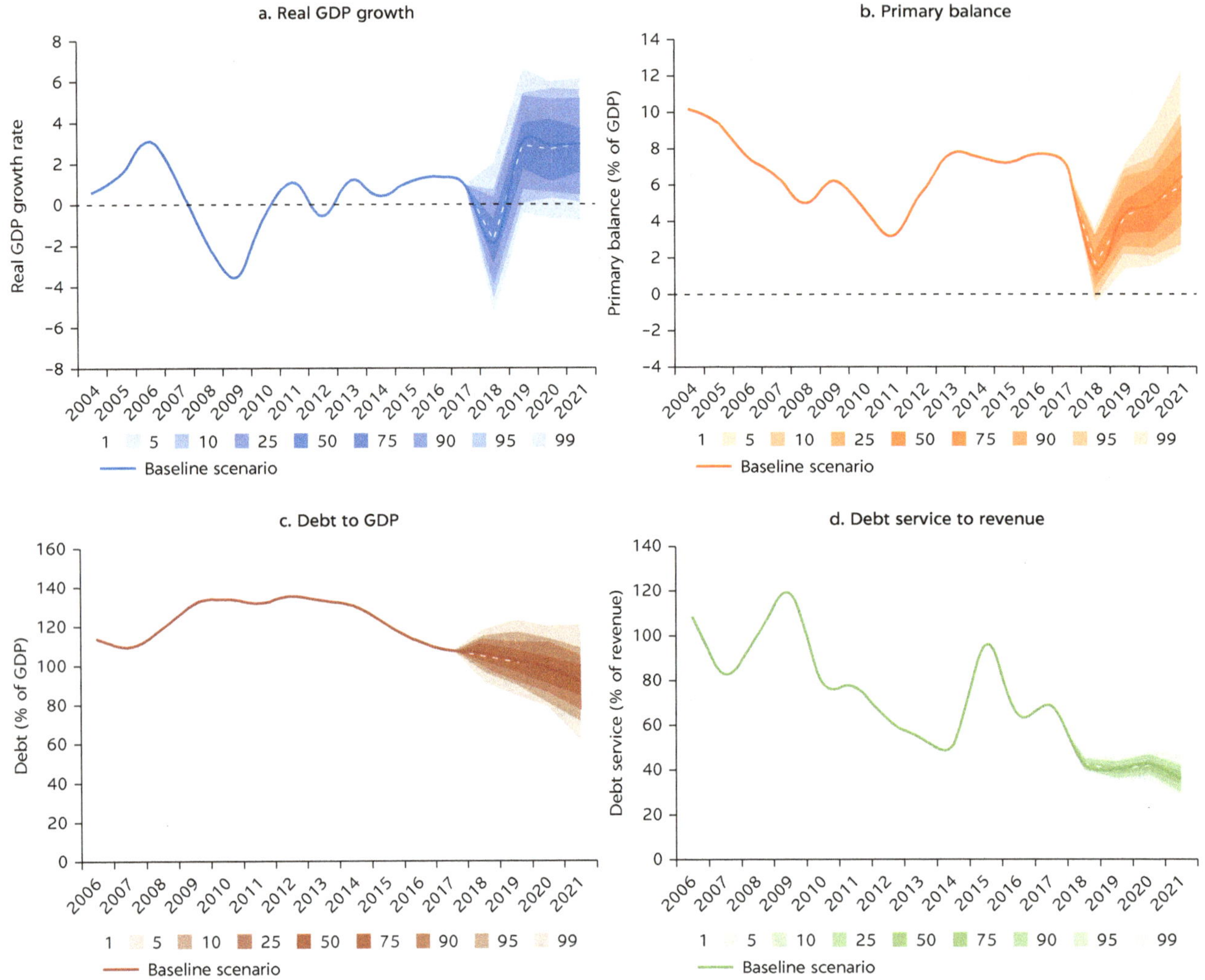

FIGURE 4.5

Jamaica: Fiscal balances across scenarios

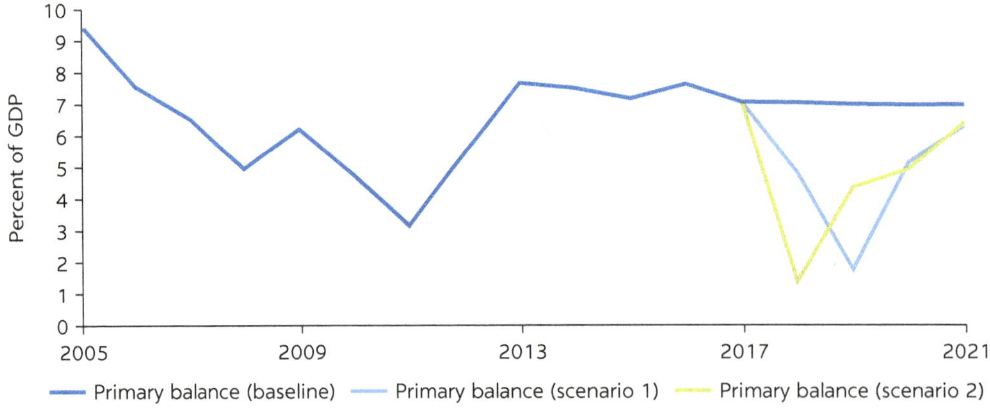

FIGURE 4.6
Jamaica: Debt trajectory across scenarios

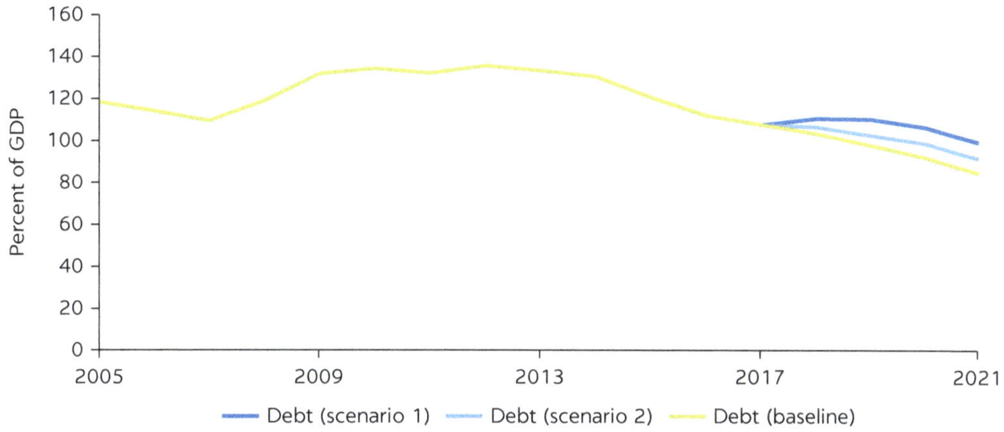

output and the increase in expenditure required to respond to the shock (figure 4.5). Under the baseline scenario, the primary fiscal balance is expected to remain at 7 percent of GDP, as required by Jamaica's fiscal responsibility laws. A natural disaster causes a severe deterioration of the fiscal position. Procuring financing prior to the event causes the primary balance to suffer more on impact because of the government's ability to frontload expenditures. However, this frontloading causes a speedier recovery of the primary balance back at about 7 percent of GDP.

Worsening fiscal primary balances would lead to an increase in debt accumulation but would not derail Jamaica's deleveraging path (figure 4.6). Given the maintenance of the very high 7 percent of GDP primary balance, the public debt is expected to be on a decreasing trend going well below 100 percent by FY2021/22. Upon impact of a major natural disaster, debt levels increase in the short run as expenditures become financed using newly issued debt. If Jamaica were to have procured disaster-relief financing, the increased debt burden would be substantially mitigated, and the decreasing debt trend would be more robust. Only in the tail events above the 10th percentile does the path of debt change into an increasing path. Therefore, Jamaica's fiscal stance is resilient to natural disasters of the proportions observed in the past, and insurance-type financing would go a long way in aiding the country to maintain its deleveraging path.

Conclusions

The application of the FSA tool to Jamaica finds that the increased likelihood of an extreme weather event resulting from global climate change puts pressure on the sustainability of fiscal policy. The shocks to GDP, revenue, and spending would push the fiscal balance well off its target. In the absence of contingent financing, the trajectory of debt to GDP would reverse, albeit temporarily if the government is able to resume running large primary fiscal surpluses. The policy message that this analysis supports is that governments—especially highly indebted governments—should seek to arrange contingent financing, in addition to constructing a robust fiscal responsibility framework.

APPLICATION TO THE DOMINICAN REPUBLIC

Country context

The Dominican Republic has been one of the top economic performers in Latin America and the Caribbean, despite some growth deceleration in 2017. GDP grew by 4.6 percent in 2017, declining from an average annual rate of 7.1 percent in 2014–16. Recovering oil prices have put upward pressure on inflation, while sizeable foreign direct investment inflows and various sources of foreign exchange are ample to finance the current account deficit. External borrowing, tourism activities, and remittances have pushed foreign exchange reserves to record levels.

Despite strong macroeconomic performance, however, the Dominican economy is marked by limited fiscal space that is deeply rooted in inadequate revenue collection. Tax mobilization is low, with tax revenues at about 13.6 percent of GDP in 2016–17. Revenue collection capacity is further hampered by high levels of informality (half of the country's total employment) and existing tax exemptions (6.4 percent of GDP in 2017).

Recent public expenditure dynamics, coupled with social spending reforms, have heightened the rigidity of fiscal space. Total budgetary expenditure has been contained to roughly 17.4 percent of GDP since 2014. The composition of government expenditure has shifted in favor of current expenditure (from 12.0 to 14.2 percent of GDP between 2011 and 2016). This shift has been mainly driven by an increasing wage bill, increasing interest payments, and sizeable current transfers, especially toward an inefficient electricity sector.

Although public debt has historically been low by Caribbean standards, the Dominican Republic's fiscal policies are placing debt on an upward trajectory. The stock of consolidated public debt, including both external and domestic, is estimated at 51 percent at end-2017. The government has built a sound economic and financial reputation, which has permitted the country to diversify its financing resources and diminish the relative weight of direct bilateral debt in its portfolio. Debt sustainability indicators depict a manageable fiscal position over the medium term, with most debt profile vulnerability indicators below the upper early warning benchmarks.

Exposure to fiscal risks from climate change effects

Among the various sources of fiscal risks, natural disasters are expected to pose the most significant challenge to the Dominican Republic's macro and fiscal stability. The Dominican Republic is highly exposed to a wide range of hydrometeorological hazards (such as hurricanes, tropical storms, flooding, and drought), ranking 21st out of 171 countries in the United Nations' World Risk Index. The country's high vulnerability to adverse weather events is exacerbated by a lack of climate change adaptation—apparent in its unplanned urban growth, land degradation, weak enforcement of building codes and zoning regulations, and gaps in social safety nets. The contingent fiscal liabilities arising from a natural disaster can impose a major toll on fiscal accounts because of the destruction of fixed capital. Estimated damages from earthquakes and tropical cyclones are high, ranging between 0.5 and 2.8 percent equivalent of GDP.[13] Major hurricanes such as Hurricane Georges in 1998 resulted in economic losses equivalent to 14 percent of GDP, and, as recently as November 2016, heavy rainfall events caused losses of about 1 percent of GDP (World Bank 2017a).

Baseline scenario

Under the baseline scenario, the Dominican economy is projected to be stable over the medium term.[14] Growth is expected to remain above 4.5 percent until 2019 but to slow in the long run as GDP converges to its potential level, mainly because of a normalization of investment levels. Construction, services, manufacturing, and the small but rapidly expanding mining sector are expected to make the largest contributions to growth. Rising global oil prices are projected to push inflation to within the government's target band of 3–5 percent in 2018. Increasing prices for oil and nonoil imports are also expected to keep the current account deficit at about 2.5 percent of GDP, despite a solid service-export surplus created by the tourism industry. Remittances, foreign direct investment inflows, and foreign exchange reserves are expected to continue comfortably financing the current account deficit.

Alternative scenario 1: Moderate natural disaster

The first alternative scenario aims to model the impacts of a "moderate" natural disaster event.[15] This model is computed on the basis of information on the economic impact of past events, since 1999. More specifically, the analysis considers the changes in the GDP growth rate before and after the natural disaster. The approach consists in comparing the projections right before the materialization of the disaster with the actual figures registered right after the occurrence of the event. Thus, the damage caused by a "moderate" natural disaster is estimated as the average of the reported damages for each of these historical events, measured in U.S. dollars.[16] Although a major weakness of this approach is that it excludes exogenous factors that may potentially add noise to the GDP data, the large number of natural events considered permits one to mitigate this limitation and determine a reasonably contained and consistent range of outcomes. In fact, the natural disasters considered by this analysis are many, and they include cyclones, hurricanes, storms, and floods that occurred between 1998 and 2016. For statistical reasons, outliers were excluded from the computation.

Results show that a "moderate" natural disaster event in the Dominican Republic can still produce significant damage. The average impact of such a moderate natural disaster event is estimated as a downward revision of 1.8 percentage points in the real GDP growth rate for the relevant year. The average damage to the economy, in nominal terms, corresponds to US$305.5 million. This scenario assumes that a natural event of this magnitude takes place virtually in 2017.[17]

Alternative scenario 2: Major natural disaster of historical proportion

The second alternative scenario aims to model the impacts of a large natural disaster event (that is, an event that historically was the worst case observed so far). Estimates for the second scenario are calculated adopting the same methodological approach as in the first scenario, except that the most extreme recorded case is used instead of a historical average. The impact of a large natural disaster event in the Dominican Republic is estimated to result in a reduction of 4.7 percentage points in real GDP growth rate for the relevant year. The average damage to the economy, in nominal terms, is assessed as US$1,981.5 million, which corresponds to the estimated damage of Hurricane Georges, which hit the island of Hispaniola in 1998. Other assumptions are kept unchanged from the first alternative scenario, except for the extension of the reconstruction period to four years in this case, to account for the increased magnitude of the event.

Comparison across scenarios

The model predicts that GDP growth would remain strong over the medium term. Major hurricanes are typically followed by increased construction activity, which boosts growth in the year immediately after the event. Stochastic shocks to real GDP growth show that the Dominican economy is resilient over the medium term, with negative growth rates being predicted only in the left tail end of the distribution (that is, mostly in the 1st through 10th percentile range). Even in the historically high-impact scenario, the probability of the Dominican economy falling into a recession is only apparent within the high-probability band (50th–75th percentile) for 2017, which is the year of the virtual natural disaster shock under the historically most extreme scenario.

Fiscal balances would suffer a clear deterioration across scenarios. Figure 4.7 shows that under the baseline scenario the primary fiscal balance is expected to hover around zero over the medium and long term, and transition into small surpluses beyond 2026. The introduction of natural disaster shocks in 2017 not only causes a downward shift in the projections but also results in a worsened trend in the primary fiscal balance over the long term, thus producing long-lasting effects on the stabilization of fiscal accounts.

Worsening fiscal balances would trigger a significant acceleration in debt accumulation. Figure 4.8 shows that, although public debt is expected to build up at a moderate rate under the baseline scenario (reaching nearly 40 percent of GDP by 2024), the impact of increasingly severe natural disaster shocks would

FIGURE 4.7
Dominican Republic: Primary fiscal balance across scenarios

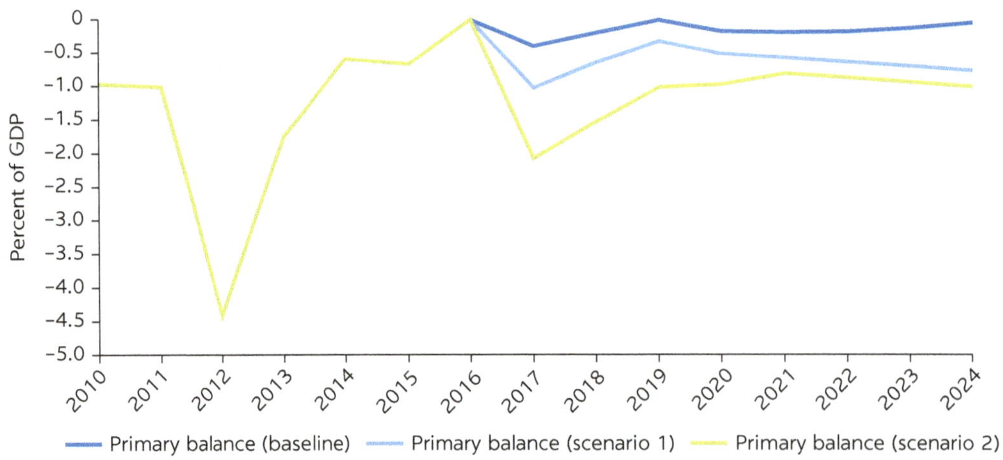

FIGURE 4.8
Dominican Republic: Debt accumulation across scenarios

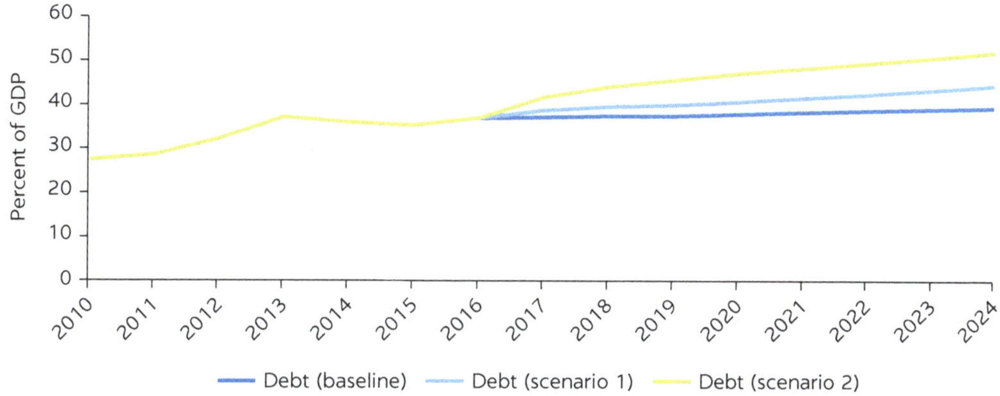

FIGURE 4.9
Dominican Republic: Debt service across scenarios

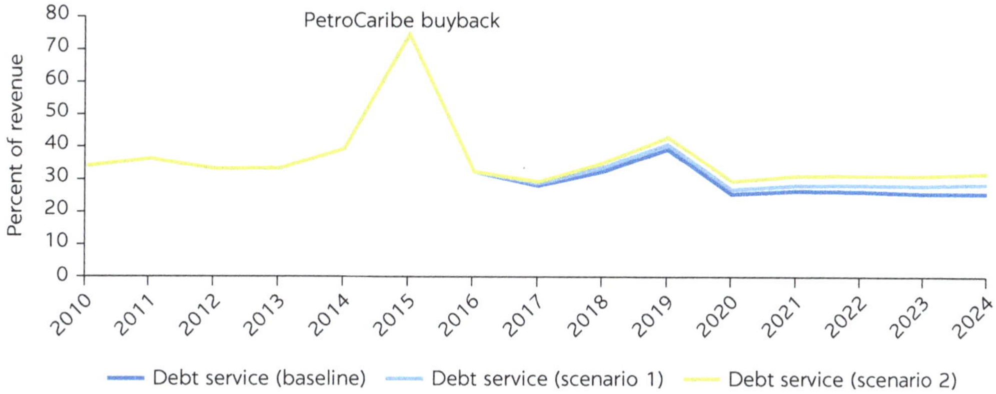

see public debt accumulate, by 2024, to 44 percent of GDP under the first alternative scenario and 52 percent of GDP under the second alternative scenario. These estimates may seem to be manageable at first glance, but it is important to note that they exclude central bank liabilities, which currently account for about 15 percent of GDP and are not expected to fall under 14 percent of GDP by 2024. In other words, public debt, including central bank liabilities, could climb sharply to 58–66 percent of GDP within a period of only six to seven years because of the materialization of a disastrous natural event. The stochastic analysis provides additional information and shows that, under the most extreme scenario (excluding central bank–related liabilities), by 2024 public debt stocks could reach up to 70 percent of GDP within the 75th percentile of confidence.[18]

Increasing debt levels would result in higher debt service payments (figure 4.9), exerting even more pressure on an already inelastic fiscal space. Under the baseline scenario, debt service is expected to stabilize at about 25 percent of fiscal revenues over the long run. This measure increases to 29 and 32 percent of fiscal revenue under the first and second alternative scenarios, respectively. It is important to note that the model assumes constant interest rates into the future, so these estimates should be interpreted as lower bounds, given that interest rates would be expected to rise as the stock of public debt rises.

Also note that large domestic bond issues are scheduled to mature in 2019 and 2026, and the need to roll over these debts is likely to further exert upward pressures on public debt accumulation and debt-servicing payments.

Conclusions

The application of the FSA tool to the Dominican Republic shows that the country is significantly vulnerable to fiscal risks brought about by potential natural disasters. Although current projections suggest that output growth over the medium run is unlikely to be derailed unless shocks are much larger than in the past, the fiscal situation appears much more vulnerable. A moderate natural disaster shock could be sufficient to cause increases in debt service of about 0.5 percent of GDP over the projection period. This is a significant amount of resources, roughly equivalent to the cost of increasing health coverage to all Dominicans living under US$4 PPP (purchasing power parity) per day. In contrast, the fiscal impact of a shock of historically extreme proportions is about 1 percent of GDP, or nearly the amount needed to fill both the health and education coverage gaps for Dominicans living under the US$4 PPP/day threshold.

CONCLUSIONS AND POLICY RECOMMENDATIONS

This chapter's application of the FSA tool suggests several measures that governments should take to manage fiscal risks from climate change events. As a first step, governments need to invest to reduce their exposure and vulnerability to natural disasters associated with climate change, as discussed in chapter 3 of this report. Adaptation should include initiatives to diversify the economy out of climate-sensitive activities, mainstreaming climate change into public investment management systems, improving zoning and building codes, strengthening natural buffers to climate change, and building effective social safety nets (World Bank 2016).

Governments should incorporate and quantify climate change risks into the fiscal risks statements that accompany the budget presentation.[19] This would start with conducting a hazard and vulnerability analysis to develop probability distributions of damages and losses from different types of climate-related shocks. Simulations from the FSA tool (or a similar tool) can then be used to quantify the fiscal effects of a natural disaster with different probabilities. Governments should also incorporate forward-looking assessments of future climate shocks (such as from IPCC 2014) into their scenario analysis.

Establishing a robust fiscal responsibility framework is a second measure that governments should consider when seeking to minimize fiscal risks from natural disasters and climate shocks. Credible fiscal rules would help governments to avoid procyclical policies that would magnify these shocks and to constrain the growth of the wage bill and other spending components that are rigid in the short run (for example, when the government needs to reallocate spending after a disaster). The modeling in this chapter suggests that Jamaica's fiscal responsibility framework would be instrumental in helping the country keep debt to a downward trajectory in the face of a major shock. Credible fiscal rules would also provide the discipline that governments need to gradually build fiscal buffers, such as a contingency savings fund. One challenge for the fiscal authority is to decide on the size of this savings fund, identify the trade-offs in maintaining it, and assess how it can be increased (through additional revenues or spending cuts) if the current buffer falls short.

This chapter highlights the value of arranging ex ante disaster financing in addition to building up reserve funds. Contingent lines of credit offered by international financial institutions and market-based instruments, such as catastrophe bonds, enable governments to quickly mount relief, recovery, and reconstruction efforts needed for the economy to rebound from natural disasters. In the case of highly indebted countries, these financial instruments may also have a secondary effect of giving capital markets confidence that a natural disaster will not push a government into debt distress, which in turn could reduce borrowing costs. Moreover, governments need to seek ways of transferring risks to markets and pool risks across countries. They are less likely to be called upon to cover private losses from natural disasters if firms and households are covered by affordable insurance policies. Governments that self-insure public buildings and infrastructures may want to consider pursuing market-based insurance for public assets. Multicountry catastrophe insurance schemes, such as the Caribbean Catastrophe Risk Insurance Facility (CCRIF) in the Caribbean, have played a role in spreading risks across countries, although the CCRIF and other regional schemes suffer from the problem that members largely face the same risks. Finding ways to broaden risk pools is critical.

Finally, the application of the FSA tool offers some lessons for incorporating climate change into analytical tools used to design macroeconomic and fiscal policies. The FSA tool is useful for assessing risks from climate events that have transitory effects, for example, where production is temporarily disrupted but resumes when the event ends and after a period of recovery and reconstruction. Built into the modeling is an assumption that GDP converges over time to its long-run potential, which in turn is based on the country's endowments of land, labor, and capital, and on the productivity of using these factors of production. Climate change is expected to affect these underlying endowments, and therefore potential GDP. In some countries, for example, climate change may permanently destroy or degrade natural assets, or it is likely to induce substantial cross-border labor migration. Chapters 1–3 argue that governments need to undertake policy reforms and investments to prevent or adapt to these effects. This chapter suggests that analysts also need to incorporate risks of changes to long-run potential GDP into their macroeconomic models and medium-term projections.

NOTES

1. *Disclaimer: The views expressed are those of the author and do not necessarily reflect the views of the Federal Reserve Bank of San Francisco or the Federal Reserve System.*
2. It is all the more important for countries that are the most exposed to effects of climate change to put in place mechanisms that promote countercyclical fiscal policies.
3. For example, the Cat-DDO is a World Bank development policy financing instrument that allows a government to defer use of the financing until a catastrophic event occurs.
4. Catastrophe bonds are issued by special-purpose vehicles established by a firm or government. Buyers receive a coupon payment (as would owners of conventional bonds). If the specified catastrophe occurs, bondholders lose their principal, which the special-purpose vehicle pays instead to the beneficiary government or firm.
5. The tool is based on the model described in Bandiera et al. 2007.
6. Fan charts summarize risks to debt dynamics (or other variables) by representing the frequency distribution of a large sample of debt paths generated by means of stochastic

simulations. Different colors delineate deciles in the distributions of debt ratios, with the darker/lighter zones reflecting the various confidence intervals around the median projection.

7. The Jamaican government's fiscal year runs from March through April.
8. The government presents its medium-term macroeconomic and fiscal forecast in its semi-annual Fiscal Policy Paper (see Ministry of Finance and the Public Service 2018).
9. The distribution of event probabilities for Jamaica is produced in World Bank 2017b.
10. The widely agreed reference that countries should use for judging to what extent the historical data on disasters in their region predict expected future ones is IPCC 2014.
11. This amount is derived from postdisaster analyses conducted by Planning Institute of Jamaica. These data were incorporated into simulations in World Bank 2017b.
12. In this transaction, the World Bank established a special-purpose vehicle and has issued a catastrophe bond that will benefit the four Pacific Alliance members in the event of an earthquake of specified magnitude. The four Pacific Alliance countries pay an annual "insurance" premium. This structure allows the four countries to benefit from the catastrophe bond without having to set up an offshore special-purpose vehicle.
13. This projection is based on the authors' calculations as well as on data from the Caribbean Catastrophe Risk Insurance Facility's Multi-hazard Parallel Risk Evaluation System (MPRES) platform.
14. Historical data for 1990–2016 are drawn from official national statistics. Medium-term projections (2017–19) are estimated using the World Bank's macro-structural model, MFMod. Finally, long-term projections (2020–24) are based on a mix of historical growth rates and shares of GDP. Additional assumptions for the long term include that growth stabilizes at 4 percent per annum, and that exchange rates depreciate at their historical average of about 3 percent annually. A detailed breakdown of projected debt service for both existing and planned debt as of September 2016 was obtained from the *Ministerio de Hacienda*. Detailed information on MFMod (that is, MFM Macro-Fiscal Model) can be found in Burns 2015.
15. For simplicity, we do not report the fans charts showing the probability distributions of future realization of economic variables but just report the results of the scenarios.
16. Data for these calculations were obtained from a model managed by the Disaster Risk Management team at the World Bank covering the Dominican Republic.
17. Other important assumptions are that (i) the impact of lower GDP growth in government revenues is accounted for entirely by lower value added tax receipts; (ii) the impact of lower GDP growth in government expenditure is accounted for entirely by higher capital expenditure (that is, reconstruction efforts); (iii) additional financing needs are entirely covered by new borrowing, the sources of which are expected to have the same characteristics as the current financing sources; and (iv) the reconstruction efforts, and hence capital expenditures and necessary additional borrowing, would take place over a three-year period following the natural disaster event.
18. For space reasons, fan charts showing probability distributions are not shown.
19. Systematic disclosure and analysis of fiscal risks is one of the core principles of the International Monetary Fund's Fiscal Transparency Code. The 2014 update of the Fiscal Transparency Code is presented at http://blog-pfm.imf.org/files/ft-code.pdf. Fiscal transparency includes disclosing the revenue from environmental taxes in budget documents, as well as the spending on mitigation and adaptation (e.g. tax expenditures and fiscal incentives designed to encourage diversification out of climate-sensitive activities). Some preconditions to more effective monitoring of expenditures on climate change mitigation and adaptions include adding a climate dimension to the chart of accounts, so that spending can by tracked systematically, and mainstreaming climate into the identification, appraisal, selection, and monitoring systems in the public investment program.

REFERENCES

Ackerman, Franck. 2017. *Worst-Case Economics*. London: Anthem Press.

Bandiera, Luca, Nina Budina, Michel Klijn, and Sweder van Wijnbergen. 2007. "The 'How to' of Fiscal Sustainability: A Technical Manual for Using the Fiscal Sustainability Tool." Policy Research Working Paper 4170, World Bank, Washington, DC.

Bova, Elva, Marta Ruiz-Arranz, Frederik Toscani, and H. Elif Ture. 2016. "The Fiscal Costs of Contingent Liabilities: A New Dataset." IMF Working Paper 16/14. International Monetary Fund. Washington, DC.

Bonen, Anthony, Prakash Loungani, Willi Semmler, and Sebastian Koch. 2016. "Investing to Mitigate and Adapt to Climate Change; A Framework Model." IMF Working Paper 16/164, International Monetary Fund, Washington, DC.

Burns, Andrew. 2015. "The Economics of the Macro-Fiscal Model." Working Paper, Macroeconomics and Fiscal Management Department, World Bank, Washington, DC.

Cebotari, Aliona, Jeffrey M. Davis, Lusine Lusinyan, Amine Mati, Paolo Mauro, Murray Petrie, and Ricardo Velloso. 2008. "Fiscal Risks: Sources, Disclosure, and Management," International Monetary Fund, Fiscal Affairs Department, Washington, DC.

de Janvry, Alain, Alejandro del Valle, and Elisabeth Sadoulet. 2016. "Insuring Growth: The Impact of Disaster Funds on Economic Reconstruction in Mexico." Policy Research Working Paper 7714, World Bank, Washington, DC.

Ghesquiere, Francis, and Olivier Mahul. 2010. "Financial Protection of the State Against Natural Disasters." Policy Research Working Paper 5429, World Bank, Washington, DC.

IMF (International Monetary Fund). 2016. "Analyzing and Managing Fiscal Risks—Best Practices." International Monetary Fund, Washington, D.C.

IPCC (Intergovernmental Panel on Climate Change). 2014. *Climate Change 2014: Synthesis Report. Contribution of Working Groups I, II and III to the Fifth Assessment Report of the Intergovernmental Panel on Climate Change*. Cambridge: Cambridge University Press. http://www.ipcc.ch/pdf/assessment-report/ar5/syr/AR5_SYR_FINAL_SPM.pdf.

Mahul, Olivier, and Eugene Gurenko. 2006 "The Macro Financing of Natural Hazards in Developing Countries." Policy Research Working Paper 4075, World Bank, Washington, DC.

Mechler, Reinhard, Junko Mochizuki, and Stefan Hochrainer-Stigler. 2016. "Disaster Risk Management and Fiscal Policy," Policy Research Working Paper 7635, World Bank, Washington, DC.

Ministry of Finance and the Public Service. 2018. "Fiscal Policy Paper FY2018/19." Government of Jamaica, Kingston.

OMB (U.S. Office of Management and Budget). 2016. "Climate Change: The Fiscal Risks Facing the Federal Government." Executive Office of the President of the United States, Washington, DC.

USGCRP (U.S. Government Interagency Global Change Research Program). 2017. "Climate Science Special Report." Fourth National Climate Assessment, Volume 1, USGCRP, Washington, DC.

Weitzman, Martin. 2009. "On Modeling and Interpreting the Economics of Catastrophic Climate Change." *Review of Economics and Statistics* 91 (1): 1–19.

———. 2011. "On Modeling and Interpreting the Economics of Catastrophic Climate Change." *Review of Environmental Economics and Policy* 5 (2): 275–92.

World Bank. 2014. "Climate Change Public Expenditure and Institutional Review Sourcebook."

———. 2016. "Fiscal Policy and Redistribution in the Dominican Republic." Report No. 105723, World Bank, Washington, DC.

———. 2017. "Disaster Risk Management Development Policy Loan with a Catastrophe Deferred Drawdown Option to the Dominican Republic." Program Document, World Bank, Washington, DC.

———. 2018. "Advancing Disaser Risk Financing in Jamaica." World Bank, Washington, DC.

Appendix A
Benefits beyond Climate: Environmental Tax Reform

This appendix discusses various important issues from chapter 1 in more detail. First, it elucidates situations where environmental tax reform (ETR) may not be the appropriate policy for environmental control. Second, it describes the various factors (channels) raised in chapter 1 that may affect estimates of ETR's impact on well-being and economic activity aggregates. Third, it quantifies the effects of these channels on the basis of the literature, with an indication of possible effects for developing countries. Fourth, it describes developing country experiences with ETR and ETR-like reforms that inform the lessons from experience in chapter 1. Finally, it describes various issues raised from the behavioral economics literature that may present obstacles to raising political support for ETR.

ENVIRONMENTAL EFFECTIVENESS OF ETR

As discussed in chapter 1, ETR is widely regarded as a cost-effective instrument for achieving environmental objectives, such as abatement of greenhouse gas (GHG) emissions. However, ETR is not the only set of policies for achieving environmental objectives. Regulations such as technology mandates, and other market-based instruments beyond taxes like emissions trading systems (ETSs), are widespread. Environmental taxes may be appropriate for environmental externalities where abatement costs are heterogeneous and pollutants are uniformly mixed,[1] such as with carbon dioxide (CO_2); however, for other environmental externalities, direct regulations may be more pragmatic and cost-effective.

Regulations may be more appropriate for localized environmental externalities, where tax revenues would be low and costs of administering Pigouvian taxes high. For example, reducing the environmental costs of plastic bags may be achieved by minimum pricing among retailers—such as in Ireland and several Organisation for Economic Co-operation and Development (OECD) countries—or by simply banning their use—as in Kenya, Tanzania, and parts of India. Such policies have also been applied to eliminate the use of toxic substances (like asbestos or polychlorinated biphenyls [PCBs]) or phasing out lead from gasoline in many OECD countries (through direct bans). In these cases, very steep marginal damage curves and high costs made outright bans more efficient given uncertain behavioral responses to tax instruments and high costs of compliance. Informational campaigns and behavioral "nudges" could also be applied at low cost, alongside or instead of tax incentives.

In addition, other instruments may be more appropriate where certainty over environmental impact is more important than economic impact. Environmental taxes may, ex ante, be efficient or cost-effective at achieving an environmental objective. As a *price instrument*, taxes can achieve environmental effect at the least cost, but the trade-off is that they leave some uncertainty as to what net environmental effect will be achieved. This uncertainty arises because the behavioral response of economic agents to price changes can be difficult to predict, and dynamically changes with tax rate over time.

By contrast, *quantity instruments*, such as ETSs, have inverse traits. ETSs can, in theory, guarantee that a specific environmental objective will be achieved (the "cap" in "cap and trade"), but they leave more uncertainty as to the net economic cost (because the prices of emission credits can fluctuate). A long-running debate questions the merits of price versus quantity instruments in general[2] and for environmental effectiveness.

An additional consideration when choosing among domestic environmental policies is the ability to link such policies internationally. International emissions trading (IET) constitutes an important part of previous international mitigation agreements. Under the Kyoto Protocol's hybrid, cap-and-trade-like design, countries with mitigation commitments (Annex I Parties) could trade emissions credits (assigned amount units, or AAUs) with each other. The Clean Development Mechanism (CDM) allowed non-Annex I parties (predominately developing countries) to generate credits that could be sold on the markets of Annex I country ETSs, such as New Zealand's or the European Union's ETS. Similar and new forms of international linking of environmental policies are allowed under the Paris Agreement's Article 6. Developing countries may want to make use of such links to lower mitigation costs or access international climate finance. Because the modalities and procedures of the Article 6 mechanisms have yet to be fully developed, it remains unclear what the effect of links under Article 6 will be on environmental effectiveness of domestic instruments. However, both environmental taxes and ETSs allow for such links in theory (Metcalf and Weisbach 2012).

Overall, ETR is generally desirable for addressing large-scale environmental problems. Although not appropriate in all contexts, ETR is particularly suited to uniformly dispersed pollutants, uncertain abatement costs, and a need for stimulating innovation.

CHANNELS AFFECTING OUTPUT AND EMPLOYMENT EFFECTS OF ETR

More than two decades of simulations of ETR's effects on developed countries have delivered broadly ambiguous results about whether ETR positively affects employment and output (the "double dividend"). These findings may understate the potential for a double dividend in general, and in developing countries specifically. Recent literature has identified a number of circumstances (channels) whereby positive effects of ETR on output and employment are more likely. Some of these channels, discussed below, are especially relevant for developing countries.

Imperfect labor markets

In assessing the economic effects of ETR, the double dividend literature focuses principally on labor markets. Switching from taxing labor to taxing pollution is said to raise employment, output, or welfare through reduced tax wedges, which increases labor supply (in the case of lowered income taxes paid by workers) or labor demand (for lowered payroll taxes falling on firms). But, by raising the price level, this tax switch also lowers real wages and therefore labor supply. The net effect on economic activity (the second dividend) could therefore be positive or negative.

However, many—but not all—simulations implicitly make an important simplifying assumption: the existence of perfect labor markets. With the assumption of full and transparent knowledge, no frictions (transactions or time costs), and perfect labor mobility, labor demand and supply are assumed to be in equilibrium (Boeri and Ours 2013) with no involuntary unemployment.[3] Perfect labor markets imply no excess labor supply or demand and therefore no involuntary unemployment. All those who would like to work are able to find a job, so there can be no involuntary unemployment, whether structural, classical, cyclical, or otherwise. This assumption is far from reality, even among developed countries. In the OECD, structural unemployment is the norm, ranging from 3.6 percent (in Japan in 2015), to 17.3 percent (in Greece).[4] The same is true for developing countries: notwithstanding differences in the quality of employment, involuntary unemployment remains a problem.

In the theoretical literature, deviations from full employment increase the likelihood of finding an employment dividend (see, for example, Carraro, Galeotti, and Gallow 1996; Bovenberg and van der Ploeg 1996; Schneider 1997; Bovenberg and van der Ploeg 1998; Schöb 2003; Markandya 2012). A cut in labor taxes paid by firms (such as social security contributions or other payroll taxes) would reduce the cost of labor and may therefore increase overall employment. Likewise, in the case of wage bargaining processes between firms and workers, a tax shift away from workers to nonworkers leads to wage moderation, reducing labor costs for firms (Anger, Böhringer, and Löschel 2010). A discrepancy therefore exists in the environmental taxation literature: the general acceptance of the importance of involuntary unemployment and the large number of studies that ignore this factor through the assumption of perfect labor markets.

Simulations also suggest that the employment dividend is less likely to emerge if the model assumes perfect labor markets. Anger, Böhringer, and Löschel (2010) use meta-regression analysis to isolate the effect of labor market structure on simulation estimates of the likely employment dividend from ETR in Europe. Figure A.1 shows the frequency of estimated effects on emissions (left side) and employment (right side), split between simulations assuming perfect or imperfect markets. The results of simulations assuming imperfect labor markets appear to skew toward a slightly stronger effect on emissions (left side) and a more positive employment dividend (right side). Statistically, the authors find that the assumption of perfect capital markets and more emissions stringency jointly reduce the likelihood of an employment dividend emerging from simulations. In other words, assuming perfect labor markets and stringent emissions reductions reduces the estimated employment dividend.[5]

FIGURE A.1

Perfect labor markets' assumption may affect double dividend estimates

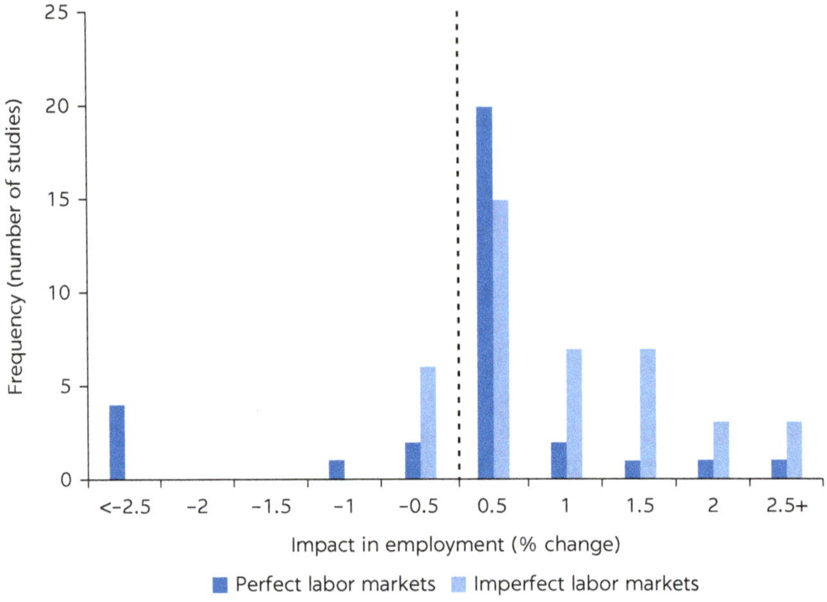

Source: Based on Anger, Böhringer, and Löschel 2010.
Note: Figure shows number of studies (y-axis) finding effects of ETR = Environmental Tax Reform on employment (x-axis) by assumption about labor markets. Total simulations numbered 73 from 43 studies, 15 of which had multiple simulations. Thirty-one simulations assumed perfect labor markets, 42 assumed imperfect labor markets, split between fixed real wages (30 simulations), bargaining process (7 simulations), and a wave curve mechanism (4 simulations). Dotted lines represent zero (no change). Emissions and output results are based against business-as-usual and organized into classes, for example, the "2.5+" class on output includes all simulations resulting in a 2.25 percent or greater positive effect on employment versus the business-as-usual case.

More recently, Pereira and Pereira (2016) find that "labor market conditions are a critical factor" in determining the possibility of a double dividend. By more precisely specifying labor market conditions—especially involuntary unemployment—they find much stronger, positive effects of ETR on the environment, economy, and government revenues. They argue that "ignoring labor supply responses, employment and unemployment effects leads to systematic underreporting" of the double dividend (Pereira and Pereira 2016).

Informal sector interactions

The informal sector, or "shadow economy," tends to be relatively untaxed compared with the formal sector. Agents in the informal sector avoid paying certain direct taxes like income taxes. In fact, avoidance of taxes is an important reason for informality (La Porta and Shleifer 2014). However, informal actors are nonetheless taxed indirectly: the prices of inputs purchased from the formal market include elements of taxation (for example, sales taxes, excises, and withholding taxes). The presence of the informal sector also increases the costs of generating revenue through traditional taxes (Piggott and Whalley 2001). The presence of the informal sector also increases the costs of generating revenue through direct taxes (Piggott and Whalley 2001). If a government has a fixed revenue requirement, informality—by reducing the overall tax base—increases the required rates of tax required on the formal sector. This exacerbates deadweight losses associated with the tax system.

The informal sector is a drag on growth. The disincentive from direct taxes for workers and firms to join the formal sector poses many challenges to countries' development. Informal firms face a disincentive to take on additional workers because doing so could attract the tax authorities' attention. Informality also prevents the effective use of liability systems, contract and property law, thus constraining business transactions—which in turn is a drag on output (for example, Acemoglu, Johnson, and Robinson 2000). Informality also prevents the economy from allocating resources optimally because, in the presence of informality, "allocation is determined not by productivity but by 'fiscally effective' productivity" (Markandya, González-Eguino, and Escapa 2013). Each of these factors means that there could be large gains from rebalancing the burden of taxation from the formal to the informal sector.

ETR creates the opportunity to shift the tax burden from the formal to the informal sector, thereby stimulating the relative growth of the formal sector and the economy. By increasing indirect taxes such as implementing an upstream environmental tax and using revenues to reduce direct taxes, the opportunity costs of a firm joining the formal sector (that is, higher rates of taxation) are reduced. In this way, a tax shift from direct taxes like income taxes to indirect taxes like carbon creates benefits for growth and poverty alleviation. Environmental taxation can reduce the informal economy and increase growth, through a variety of channels.

Better coverage

When imposed upstream where fuels enter the economy, environmental taxes can cover the informal sector (see "Tax base and rate" in chapter 1). A shift from traditional to environmental taxes can therefore broaden the tax base for raising revenue, and it can reduce the disincentive to join the formal sector for efficiency gains (Markandya, González-Eguino, and Escapa 2013). "Both the lessened dependence on a labor tax and the increased deployment of the energy tax cause substitution from the informal to the formal sector, increasing the size of the tax base and improving welfare" (Bento, Jacobsen, and Liu 2017).

VAT effects

Environmental taxation also boosts the ability of value added tax (VAT) systems to impose withholding taxes on the informal sector. As explained in box A.1, VAT functions as a tax on purchases of inputs by informal operators, including on imports (Keen 2008). An efficient VAT is imposed after any specific-rate taxes have been levied (Bodin et al. 2001). VAT is applied to the sum of the pre-tax product price plus the environmental tax.[6] When the environmental tax rate increases, the absolute amount of VAT collected per unit of the taxed product increases by the proportion of the VAT rate. This means that the larger the environmental tax the greater the implicit withholding tax that the VAT system imposes on firms in the informal sector.[7]

Upstream taxes with downstream rebates

For administrative simplicity, environmental fuel taxes should generally be levied "upstream" where the fuels enter the economy, rather than "downstream" where the fuels are burned. Adding tax rebates downstream for fuel users who install pollution control equipment can further protect competitiveness (at the cost of some added administrative complexity). For example, a company can be provided with a tax rebate when it installs highly efficient abatement

BOX A.1

VAT's role as a withholding tax on the informal sector

Like environmental taxes, VAT can tax the informal sector. Firms that dishonestly conceal themselves from the tax authorities are unable to recover VAT charged on inputs whether these informal firms import or purchase from VAT-compliant firms. A great advantage of VAT compared to other taxes is that, "while informal operators may be able to completely escape income tax, for example, the VAT may well reach them on their inputs" (Keen 2008).

VAT can also function as a tariff on importing informal firms. VAT is "charged even on imports by firms that are not registered for the VAT. But, whereas firms that are VAT-registered will be able to claim a credit or refund of that import VAT against the VAT they charge on their own sales, informal operators, who remit no output VAT, will not. For them, VAT at import stage is thus precisely equivalent to a tariff.... Broadly the same considerations apply to all inputs purchased by informal operators from the domestic formal sector. On these purchases, too, they will bear unrecovered VAT, just as they do on imports" (Keen 2008).

technologies like scrubbers for sulfur dioxide (SO_2), low nitrogen oxide (NO_x) burners, or electrostatic precipitators to capture dust particles. Where such tax rebates exist (such as those on the SO_2 tax in Sweden), requesting entities must provide proof that the applicable technology has been deployed and must be registered in the formal sector to receive the rebate. This environmental policy design provides firms in the informal sector with an increased incentive to formalize. Where these informal companies fail to make the switch, they cannot claim the tax rebate and face an increased tax burden.

Evidence from the computable general equilibrium literature

Even in developed countries with small informal markets, designing ETR so that it covers the informal sector alongside the rest of the economy can reduce the cost of the policy. In the United States, the informal market accounts for just 9 percent of gross domestic product (GDP). Even so, the cost of mitigation efforts to formal sector output is reduced by 62 percent when the environmental tax covers the informal sector compared to when it does not (or when the computable general equilibrium [CGE] model assumes that no informal sector exists) (Bento, Jacobsen, and Liu 2017). In Spain, which has an informal sector share of about 20 percent of GDP, introducing a carbon tax equivalent to a 15 percent emissions reduction would cause official GDP to rise by 7 percent and official unemployment to fall by 3 percent (Markandya, González-Eguino, and Escapa 2013).

In developing countries, which generally have larger informal markets, environmental taxation tends to have higher economic benefits. Country studies for China, India, and the Islamic Republic of Iran suggest that accounting for the existence of informal markets is sufficient for ETR to increase GDP (Carson, Jacobsen, and Liu 2014; Bento, Jacobsen, and Liu 2017; Mirhosseini, Mahmoudi, and Valokolaie 2017). These results continue to hold when controlling for any shift in the demand from taxed fuels to untaxed substitutes such as fuelwood. "Even when leakage to informal fuels is at its strongest, the impact of labor flows from the informal sector still dominates. This suggests that developing countries may be even better venues to deploy energy taxes in that energy taxes both correct environmental externalities and more efficiently collect revenue" (Bento, Jacobsen, and Liu 2017).

Tax system interactions

The literature on the economics of optimal taxation provides several channels that raise the potential for a positive second dividend from ETR, especially for developing countries. As this literature notes, arguments based on first-best assumptions (such as those prevalent among existent double dividend CGE studies) may give misleading results.[8] However, given the ubiquity of second-best tax policies, there is also "likely to be a large number of tax reforms that potentially raise welfare" (Atkinson and Stiglitz 1980).

ETR is one such reform that can raise welfare by improving the tax system. Two second-best considerations are notable, both of which are poorly reflected in the existing literature. First, the preponderance of preexisting tax distortions such as income tax deductions heighten costs of current tax policy. These distortions significantly raise the prospect for a double dividend. Second, numerous policy prescriptions and opportunities for optimizing tax systems arising from the second-best tax literature are relevant for ETR. These include the opportunity to broaden tax bases and reduce corruption, taxing Ricardian rents rather than entrepreneurship, taxing leisure rather than labor, ensuring VAT system neutrality, reducing compliance costs, and pursuing Ramsey efficiency. These considerations will be analyzed in turn.

Preexisting tax distortions

To the extent that current tax systems in developing countries are more distorted than in developed countries, the former have a greater chance of realizing a double dividend. In the United States, incorporating imperfections of the current tax system into the modeling of ETRs suggests there may in fact be net negative costs to output (Parry 2003). These costs occur because a more distortive existing tax burden (as is the case of systems with exemptions) means a bigger opportunity to reduce deadweight losses (the "excess burden") of the overall tax system. This effect is likely to be stronger in countries that have a more distorted tax system than the United States.

The opportunity to reduce preexisting distortions through ETR can converge with the opportunity to reduce the complexity of tax systems because distortions can be directly associated with tax system complexity.[9] Countries with distorted and complex existing tax systems can therefore realize gains through ETRs.

Broadening tax bases

Environmental tax shifts apply the general principle that growth-friendly tax policy should broaden tax bases and lower tax rates (see, for example, OECD 2010a, 2010b). Carbon represents a large, currently exempted tax base. As the deadweight loss of a tax rises in the square of the tax rate, the imposition of a small tax on a previously exempted tax base creates only little additional deadweight loss. Conversely, because the rates for more traditional taxes are much higher, their marginal deadweight loss is high. A tax shift can then reduce the overall deadweight loss caused by the tax system.

Implementing Ramsey efficiency

The optimal taxation literature also suggests higher taxation for tax bases that are supplied or demanded inelastically (*Ramsey taxation*). This argument favors environmental taxation because the price elasticity of demand for many polluting products is low, so they can be taxed significantly (the "inverse-elasticity rule" of Ramsey taxation). This advantage diminishes when other environmental regulations are equally imposed because those increase the elasticity of mitigating behavior. ETR creates the opportunity to implement Ramsey taxation, thereby increasing the efficiency of the tax system while overcoming two of the principal barriers to Ramsey taxation. The main two critiques of Ramsey taxation are that administration costs can be high and that tax incidence is potentially regressive (demand for necessities is inelastic compared to luxuries). But environmental taxes can be cheap to administer, and the revenues can be redistributed in a distributionally neutral or progressive way.

Taxing of Ricardian rents

ETR can help tax "pure" economic rents, thereby encouraging entrepreneurship over rent seeking. Economic rents (also known as *Ricardian rents*) refer to windfall gains received irrespective of risk taking and effort. By contrast, economic profit refers to the surplus income earned by choosing between risk-adjusted alternative economic activities. The impact of taxation on these two archetypes of income is different: a tax on profit may discourage effort, unlike a tax on rents, which have no effort to discourage. As a result, economists have long called on policy makers to lower the tax burden on profit to encourage entrepreneurship and to instead tax economic rents (for example, Quesnay 1768; Ricardo 1821; Tideman 1994; Eisenack, Edenhofer, and Kalkuhl 2012; Siegmeier, Mattauch, and Edenhofer 2018).

However, taxing Ricardian rents is a difficult policy to apply: it is hard to distinguish between pure rents and economic profits in practice, and earnings due to entrepreneurial activities may be a mix of economic profits and rents. As a result, many policy makers have chosen instead to tax both at a fixed rate, thereby increasing the distortionary effects of the tax system. In addition, even if rents could be identified, there is a risk that increased tax rates could simply be passed on to consumers (perfect pass-through of input costs to consumer prices).

The extraction of natural resources, including fuels, tends to generate a larger share of rents relative to profits than most other industries. Earnings in the fossil fuel extraction sector tend to exceed those in most other sectors. As a result, they are often classified as *resource rents* (Boadway and Flatters 1993; Bosquet 2002; Dankel, Keen, and McPherson 2010; Barma et al. 2011; Hamilton and Ley 2012).

Environmental taxes can extract a portion of these natural resource rents in the form of revenues, especially in developing countries. By imposing environmental taxes, for example, upstream on fossil fuel extraction or import or downstream on combustion, governments can capture a portion of the economic rents accruing to natural resource extraction. This capture is possible for two reasons. First, as noted above, the extraction of natural resources tends to generate a larger share of rents compared to other economic activities. Second, pass-through of the increase in input costs to consumer prices tends to be lower among fossil fuel consumption (particularly in developing countries). In the United States, for example, firms pass on a large proportion of motor fuel taxes to consumers (see, for example, Alm, Sennoga, and Skidmore 2009; Marion and Muehlegger 2011; Doyle and Samphantharak 2008; Harju, Kosonen, and Laukkanen 2016), so the government can capture only a low proportion of resource rents. However, the proportion passed on to consumers is smaller in poor areas and countries, (Parry et al. 2006; Sterner 2012; Stolper 2016) even when energy markets are liberalized, because fuel demand in developing countries is more elastic than in developed ones (demand responds more to changes in price).[10]

ETRs can therefore moderately shift the tax burden from profits to rents, without the need for complex rules for industry-specific tax rates. Environmental taxation can capture part of the natural resource extraction rents without the need for such special rules. For example, the same carbon tax applied across the economy would lead to a concentration of that tax in the fossil fuel extraction sector because its product is carbon intensive. Indeed, for net fossil fuel–importing countries, this means that environmental taxes such as carbon taxes can externalize the costs of mitigation (reduce negative economic effects or increase positive double dividend effects) by capturing rents on resource extraction overseas (Liski and Tahvonen 2004).

Evidence from simulations suggests that this tax shift, from profits to Ricardian rents, has the potential to raise output. Taking this into account, Bento and Jacobsen (2007) find that a revenue-neutral shift toward an environmental tax produces a double dividend: the overall costs for a moderately stringent ETR are negative, "suggesting that even if there is uncertainty about the benefits from the environmental policy, the environmental tax should be part of the tax system."

Reducing tax evasion

By raising the taxation of fuels while reducing reliance on harder-to-collect taxes, ETRs can reduce the overall burden of tax evasion, which tends to be widespread at the lower end of the income distribution (Johns and Slemrod 2010). Using an environmental tax to raise the income threshold beyond which individuals pay personal income tax (PIT) would therefore reduce the prevalence of tax evasion in society. This raised threshold would happen in conjunction with augmented incentives for labor supply and formal sector participation. Most important, these policies would more than compensate the poor for increased environmental taxes.

Countries in which tax evasion is more prevalent will see drastically lower costs of environmental taxation. For example, Liu (2013) finds the "tax evasion effect" reduces the estimated cost of environmental taxes by 28 percent in the United States, 89 percent in China, and 97 percent in India, so that, "in countries with high levels of preexisting tax evasion, a carbon tax will pay for itself through improvements in the efficiency of the tax system." Countries with pervasive tax evasion problems, including several developing countries, therefore have more potential to benefit from ETR.

Taxing leisure more than labor

The optimal taxation literature suggests that, when governments can identify a product or service that is consumed in leisure rather than work, they should tax that product at higher rates to reduce the negative effect of the PIT system on labor supply. Fuel is used in both leisure and production, whereas labor is used only in production. This suggestion in the literature contradicts the current practice to tax labor high and fuel low.[11]

Parry (1995) provides further caveats to this formulation, showing that an excess benefit will likely arise only if the polluting good is a relatively weak substitute for leisure. Otherwise, the negative labor-supply effects of increasing the costs of the polluting good will likely dominate the positive effects of reduced factor taxes. Parry (1997) later finds substantial costs for a number of reasonable parameters, but these may be partly or more than offset when preexisting distortions in the tax system are taken into account (Parry 2003).

In a related strategy, ETR can shift tax burdens from labor to pension incomes, with the reduction of labor taxes enabled by the revenues from environmental taxes paid for by all consumers, including retired ones. Through this channel, the incentives for generations that currently supply labor increase. As a result, output rises (Goulder 1995; Ligthart 1998; Chiroleu-Assouline and Fodha 2005, 2006). However, an intergenerational effect arises that may need to be managed: the young benefit from both the environmental improvement and the output rise, whereas the old face a larger tax burden.

Improving the tax neutrality of the VAT system

Environmental taxation can help ensure the principle of VAT neutrality. Heady et al. (2000) argue that, "although the focus of the policy discussion has been mainly on employment, it is important to note that a double dividend could arise without any change in employment, simply by reducing the distortions in consumer choice that result from sales taxes." A core principle for growth-friendly VAT is minimizing distortions in consumption choices, thus allowing the market to achieve allocative efficiency. However, if a polluting product is sold at lower prices because it can externalize part of its production cost, the absolute amount of VAT collected per unit of this product is artificially low. This reduces VAT neutrality, distorts competition, and prevents allocative efficiency. Environmental taxation, applied at the Pigouvian rate, can rectify this problem.

Minimizing compliance costs

ETR can reduce the overall compliance costs of the tax system by reducing the number of taxpayers charged. The burden of the tax system for taxpayers generally exceeds the amount of tax they pay because of the existence of transaction costs in complying with the tax system. Compliance costs rise with the number of taxpayers; a larger number of entities causes a larger overall burden. By contrast, an environmental tax collected "upstream" applies to only a small number of taxpayers. The revenues raised from upstream environmental taxation can finance an increase in the threshold for which personal income tax is collected. Such a tax shift would release masses of people from the burden of the income tax system (and especially poor ones for whom compliance may be particularly costly as a proportion of their income) and thus reduce overall compliance costs.

Induced technological change

ETR could also induce innovation. Taxes on pollution and polluting goods provide dynamic incentives that encourage innovation (see "Reason 1: Achieving market efficiency" in chapter 1) because, as 20th-century economist John Hicks argued, a "change in the relative prices of the factors of production is itself a spur to invention, and to invention of a particular kind" (Hicks 1932). These innovations are additional and, more controversially, may enhance firm productivity and international competitiveness (Porter and van der Linde 1995). ETR can induce firms to innovate that otherwise would not; in addition, this innovation can benefit from increasing returns to scale, improving productivity and competitiveness. These results are the so-called weak and strong versions of the "Porter hypothesis" on the link between environmental policy and innovation.

There is evidence for the weak Porter hypothesis. Although increased energy prices do appear to alter the mix of research and development (R&D) toward cleaner innovations within firms (Aghion et al. 2015), they do not crowd out other forms of R&D spending across sectors (Popp and Newell 2012). However, the evidence for the strong version of the Porter hypothesis—of productivity improvements among firms enhancing international competitiveness—is mixed (Lanoie et al. 2011; Ambec et al. 2013). For the European Union and China, for example, some studies find support for the strong version (Costantini and Mazzanti 2012; Xie, Yuan, and Huang 2017) whereas others do not (Rubashkina, Galeotti, and Verdolini 2015; Wang and Shen 2016). Additionally, productivity gains may diminish with distance from the global productivity frontier (Albrizio, Kozluk, and Zipperer 2017), implying that positive effects on competitiveness may be smaller in developing countries—although this also depends on firm strategies (Ramanathan et al. 2017).

The economic benefits of induced technological change (ITC) are likely to vary across countries but are not negligible. Historically, effects have been found to be positive but small. For example, one study suggests that ITC reduces mitigation costs by from 6 percent to 12 percent (Popp 2004). More recent studies have found even larger effects. Liu and Yamagami (2017) identify several important sensitivities in the results, notably the elasticity of knowledge to prices. When these assumptions are relaxed within reasonable parameters, savings from ITC rise to 40 percent or more (Liu and Yamagami 2017).

Notwithstanding these and similar findings, quantitative studies on the economic effects of environmental taxation have mostly ignored the benefits of ITC. It remains uncertain how large the effect will be across developing countries, but models that attribute a zero value to the benefits of ITC understate the potential economic benefits of ETR.

Imperfect competition in goods markets

Many ETR models assume perfect competition in goods markets. A corollary of this is perfect pass-through of input price increases—due, for example, to a new or increased environmental tax—to consumer prices. Perfect pass-through implies that welfare losses are entirely borne by consumers.

Despite this assumption, goods markets are rarely perfectly competitive, especially in developing countries. Goods markets in developing countries tend to be more concentrated, with lower levels of competition (Agénor and Montiel 2015), which confers the power on firms to set prices. In the extreme case of monopolistic markets, the monopoly firm chooses both the prices and the quantities that maximize profits. However, monopolist firms must consider the effect that changing prices have on demand. By contrast, firms in a competitive market make zero profits; when facing a common shock to input prices, these firms must therefore fully pass through costs or otherwise leave the market. Assuming demand is not too convex, pass-through should decrease as market competitiveness decreases (Muehlegger and Sweeney 2017).

Imperfect competition in goods markets may raise the prospect for a double dividend in two ways. First, any resulting imperfect pass-through to consumer prices means that the burden of environmental taxation is partly borne by the monopolistic firm. However, there is some evidence that the opposite can also be the case: that firms in imperfectly competitive markets pass on *more* than the increase in input costs ("overshifting"). For example, if demand for polluting goods is inelastic, firms can overshift to compensate themselves for the negative effect that price changes have on demand. In this case, a disproportionate burden may be borne by consumers compared with firms. Nerudová and Dobranschi

(2016) find overshifting of tax burdens for transport fuel in the Czech Republic. As a result, it is not clear ex ante whether tax incidence will be higher or lower for consumers than for producers in the case of imperfect competition.

Second, imperfect competition lowers economic activity through reduced output and employment. As a result, the relative sizes of tax bases for environmental levies on polluting goods and labor taxes are distorted. A smaller relative tax base on labor means that relatively more labor taxes can be cut using revenues from an environmental tax, yielding a higher output and employment dividend than in a situation with perfect competition. Several simulations have found this result (Marsiliani and Renström 2000; Chiroleu-Assouline 2001; Bayindir-Upmann 2004). One study in particular found, for a model calibrated on Italy, that welfare effects of ETR improve by 0.2 percentage points as firms' market power increases (Marsiliani and Renström 2000).

Overall, imperfect competition appears likely to raise the output and employment potential of ETR, but tax incidence renders welfare effects somewhat ambiguous. More empirical research is needed, especially to understand ETR's effects in developing countries.

Labor skills composition

An economy's mix of skilled and unskilled labor may also affect the likelihood of finding a positive second dividend, particularly for employment. This is because there are different relative demand elasticities between unskilled and skilled labor and the relative elasticities of the *wage curve*[12] (the extent to which increases in real wages are associated with unemployment) (Blanchflower and Oswald 2005; Markandya, González-Eguino, and Escapa 2012).[13] A developing country with a larger relative share of unskilled labor may see a more positive effect of ETR on employment because of elasticities on both the demand and supply sides of the labor market. On the demand side, unskilled labor tends to have higher demand elasticities than skilled labor (Markandya, González-Eguino, and Escapa 2012), which raises the prospect that preexisting labor taxes are distortionary. On the supply side, unskilled labor may have a more elastic wage curve (unemployment being more responsive to wages, implying that increases in real wages reduce unemployment by more) compared with skilled labor.[14]

Along with the related higher labor supply elasticities, these effects suggest that recycling the revenues from environmental taxes through broad wage tax reductions could therefore have stronger effects on employment in developing countries than in developed countries. The net effect from labor skills composition differences will vary across countries.[15] Developing countries with relatively higher proportions of unskilled labor, however, may have more scope for employment dividends than developed countries.

Improved energy efficiency

Energy use and economic growth have an interlinked relationship. Given its role as a major factor of production, energy affects broad swathes of the economy. Much of the macroeconomics of energy literature has therefore focused on identifying the causal effects between *aggregate energy consumption* and economic growth. Results remain mixed, however, with no consensus in the literature on direction or effect.

Studies have examined how *energy efficiency* among firms and households affects growth. Alongside sectoral factors like industry composition and social factors such as household preferences, energy efficiency affects the overall energy productivity (inverse of energy intensity) of an economy (figure A.2). These factors are themselves affected by energy prices, and therefore by ETR policies.

ETR promotes the energy efficiency of an economy. By raising the costs of energy, environmental taxation provides incentives to firms and households to increase energy efficiency. This effect—of prices on efficiency—has been demonstrated across sectors at the firm level and income groups at the household level (Rajbhandari and Zhang 2018). As a result, understanding the effects of energy efficiency on growth is important to fully account for the costs and benefits of ETR.

Early evidence suggests that improved energy efficiency promotes economic growth. Although no consensus has emerged on the causal effect between energy usage and growth, recent evidence suggests that firm-level energy efficiency improvements can encourage growth. More efficient use of energy reduces production costs, raising factor productivity and reducing domestic energy demand and prices.[16] Raising energy efficiency can help foster more cost-competitive industries. Efficiency is therefore likely to have a positive effect on economic growth. One empirical study found that a 10 percent increase in energy efficiency caused a 1 percentage point increase in GDP per capita growth rates among 28 OECD countries between 1979 and 2010 (Vivid Economics 2013).

Some developing countries have more potential for energy efficiency improvements, and therefore reap more of an economic benefit. Technologies in poorer countries are further away from maximum energy-efficiency levels (Vivid Economics 2013). As a result, poorer countries may have a stronger prospect for growth-enhancing effects of improved energy efficiency. There is some empirical evidence: one World Bank study of 56 economies between 1978 and 2012 found positive effects of energy efficiency on growth, especially for less developed and middle-income economies, the latter of which earned an "extra growth dividend from energy efficiency measures" compared to wealthier countries (Rajbhandari and Zhang 2018).

As with many aspects of energy economics, country circumstances matter. National energy systems are notoriously variable across numerous dimensions.

FIGURE A.2
Energy efficiency is a component of an economy's energy productivity

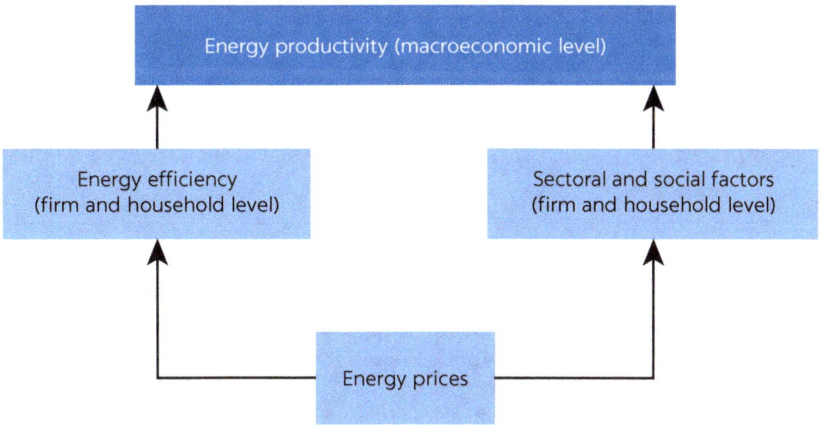

Source: Based on Vivid Economics 2013.

These dimensions include, but are not limited to, levels of energy access, state participation, concentration of ownership, market competitiveness, energy-import dependence, and domestic pricing structure. For the impact of energy efficiency on growth, a key factor affecting the magnitude is the availability of economically feasible energy efficiency measures. This frontier itself depends on factors such as domestic energy prices and the prevalence of energy-intensive industries like mining (Vivid Economics 2013). As a result, the effect of ETR on growth via energy efficiency may be strong for some countries but weak for others. Teasing out the overall effects requires country-specific analyses considering the various parameters that can determine growth effects, especially the opportunity for energy efficiency improvements. However, the effect is unlikely to be negative, so policy makers should consider this co-benefit.

ESTIMATED EFFECTS OF CHANNELS

Figure A.3 (seen in chapter 1 as figure 1.17) gives a first-pass attempt at comparing the potential effects of these various channels. Under a number of simplifying assumptions, it shows the range of estimates of the impact of these channels on welfare (blue bars) as well as a best-guess estimate of the likely average impact for developing countries. These estimations give a rough indication of the potential individual effects of these channels on welfare. Below are notes on how the chart was constructed.

FIGURE A.3

Channels that impact estimated welfare effects of ETR: Range of estimates from studies and possible effects for developing countries

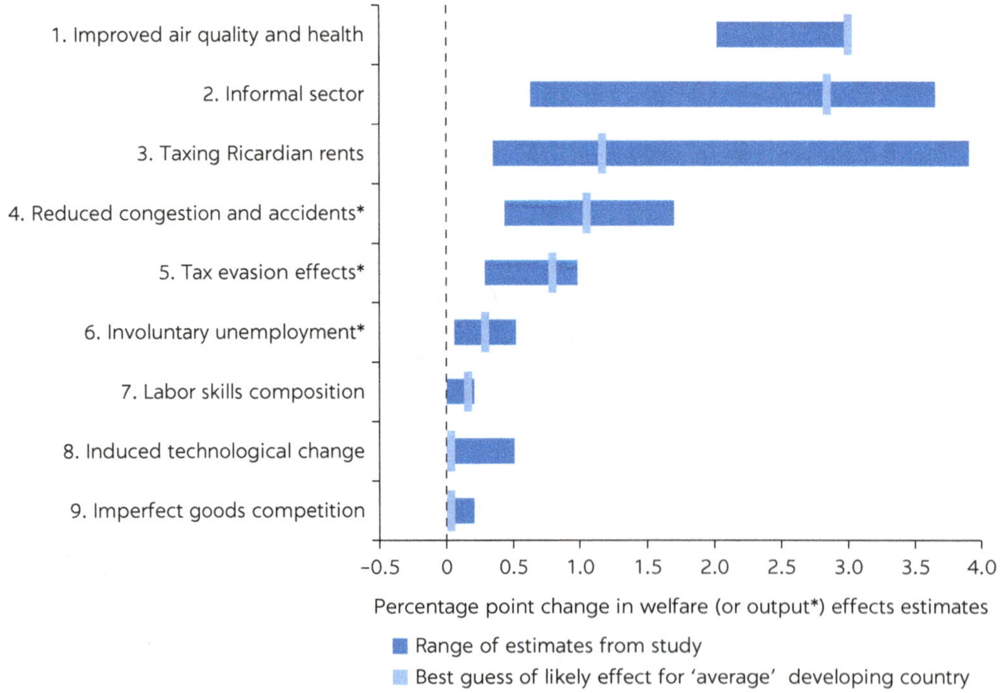

Sources: Based on data from Bento and Jacobsen 2007; Markandya, González-Eguino, and Escapa 2012; Liu 2013; Orlov, Grethe, and McDonald 2013; Burke and Nishitateno 2015; Pereira, Pereira, and Rodrigues 2016; Liu and Yamagami 2017; Bento, Jacobsen, and Liu 2017; World Bank Group 2017.

General notes on figure A.3:

- All estimates have a high degree of uncertainty. Blue bars display the range of estimated effects of channels discussed in chapter 1 of ETR on output or welfare (* indicates the effect is measured in output).
- Light blue bars give a rough indication (best guess) of the likely effect for an average developing country, depending on characteristics discussed in studies (such as size of informal sector).
- Another assumption is moderate environmental stringency of ETR policies, resulting in a 10–15 percent reduction in emissions against baseline.
- Where effects were stated as a proportion of mitigation costs (channels 1, 2, 3, 4, and 9), estimates have been converted assuming a 1 percent output or welfare cost of mitigation (broadly consistent with median findings in the early double dividend literature; above 1 percentage point can be interpreted as implying negative economic costs overall).

Notes on construction of channels:

- **Improved air quality and health:** Expressed as percentage point welfare change in equivalent variation terms due to improvements in air quality from ETR for a model calibrated to Spain (Markandya, González-Eguino, and Escapa 2012). Authors find either a small loss or gain in welfare that rises to a large increase (2–3 percent) in welfare when including the benefits of reduced local pollutants. Best guess for average developing country is that effects will be at the upper end of this range because co-benefits from pollution reduction tend to be higher.
- **Informal sector:** Lower bound is for low-informality case (for example, the United States at 8 percent), upper bound is for high-informality case (for example, Asia and Africa at 40 percent), assuming moderate emissions reduction of 10 percent (Bento, Jacobsen, and Liu 2017). Note, however, that savings will be above 100 percent for most countries: the OECD average is 15 percent informality with savings exceeding total mitigation costs (116 percent), and most developing countries have larger informal sectors. The potential effect for a developing country is based on estimates for countries whose informal economy represents 25–40 percent of GDP.
- **Taxing Ricardian rents:** Range of estimates based on varying size of polluting industry, fraction of fixed factors in polluting industry, size of preexisting taxes on fixed factors, and elasticity of substitution of production for a model calibrated on the United States (Bento and Jacobsen 2007). Best guess for average developing country is based on central case of a –0.17 ratio of second-best cost to primary cost for a 10 percent pollution reduction, that is, a savings of 117 percent of primary costs.
- **Reduced congestion and accidents:** Expressed as percentage point change in output due to road deaths saved from an assumed 10 percent increase in fuel costs (Burke and Nishitateno 2015). Evidence across countries is that a 10 percent increase in fuel costs reduces road deaths by 3 to 6 percent, and that halving road deaths over a period of 24 years would contribute to a 7 to 14 percent increase in GDP (Tanzania and India, respectively) (World Bank Group 2017). The best guess for representative developing country is the average effect.
- **Tax evasion effects:** Expressed as percentage point difference in output taking into account tax evasion effects on model calibrated to the United States and China: lower bound is for the United States, and upper is for China (Liu 2013). Tax evasion effects vary with ex ante tax evasion. Best guess for average developing country is that effects are closer to that of China than of the United States.

- **Involuntary unemployment:** Expressed in percentage point difference in output when including effects from endogenous involuntary unemployment. Based on range of estimates of the difference in model estimates of ETR's effect on output, assuming endogenous or exogenous involuntary unemployment (Pereira, Pereira, and Rodrigues 2016).
- **Labor skills composition:** Expressed as percent of welfare difference in equivalent variation terms assuming different labor supply elasticities for the Russian Federation (based on Orlov et al. 2013). Lower bound indicates a labor supply elasticity of 0.1; upper bound equals a labor supply elasticity of 0.9 (Orlov, Grethe, and McDonald 2013).
- **Imperfect goods competition**: Expressed as percentage point difference in welfare due to increase in market power of firms (less market competition) in Italy (Marsiliania and Renström 2000). Authors find that welfare rises by 0.2 percent if the firms' market power increases. The best-guess estimated effect for an average developing country is at the lower range of estimates given ambiguity on likely actual effects.
- **Induced technological change:** Expressed as percentage point change in welfare due to ITC from ETR, which varies from 6 to 51 percent of savings of mitigation costs (Lie and Yamagami 2017). The best guess for developing countries is at the lower end of the range given larger distance to the knowledge frontier.

LEARNING FROM EXPERIENCE: CASE STUDIES IN CARBON PRICING AND ENERGY PRICE REFORM

In implementing ETR, policy makers should draw on relevant experiences from other countries, including experience with environmental taxes like carbon taxes in general and specific policies that have near-identical effects such as fossil fuel subsidy reform.

Introducing carbon taxation and fuel tax reforms

A small number of developing countries have implemented ETRs in the form of carbon taxation and fuel tax reform:

- Turkey raised fuel taxes to increase tax revenues and cut its dependence on oil imports during its financial crisis of 1999–2001. Fuel taxes were favored because they were found to have low elasticities (Ramsey efficiency), were hard to evade (even accounting for increased border flows), and had a low administrative burden. Fuel taxes rose as a proportion of public revenues to a peak of 15 percent in 2008, compared to just 3–4 percent in most OECD countries. The taxes did not appear to hold back Turkey's economy: they became an important source of public funds, were largely pro-poor because of low levels of car ownership, and helped control car ownership levels despite rapid economic expansion from 2001 to 2015. Despite having among the highest taxes on gasoline, diesel, and heating oil in the OECD, the government faces limited political opposition. The economy is expected to continue to become more energy efficient while reducing its dependence on imported fuels; its current fuel account deficit is projected to shrink from 4.7 percent of GDP in 2015 to 3.9 percent of GDP by 2021 (IMF 2017a).

- Mexico became the first developing country to introduce an economy-wide carbon tax in 2014. Its motivations were partly to implement the planned emissions reductions under the 2012 Climate Change Law (later adapted as its Nationally Determined Contribution) and to diversify its energy supply toward renewables. The carbon tax was designed so that it would not impede international competitiveness. Fuels covered include natural gas, propane, butane, gasoline, diesel, jet fuel, turbosine and other kerosene, fuel oil, oil coke, and coal. The country did experience protests against rising fuel costs in 2017, and it remains too early to delineate economic effects.
- South Africa is also undertaking a carbon tax reform. This reform is designed to support the implementation of its Nationally Determined Contribution, reduce its dependence on fossil fuels, and develop a clean energy sector. The tax is part of a reform package that also involves several fiscal measures (including tax credits and rebates) to increase the provision of renewable energy (mainly wind and solar) and increase energy efficiency. To address concerns for the impact of selected sectors, South Africa has introduced tax-free allowances. A basic tax-free threshold covers 60 percent of preexisting emissions, an additional 10 percent for process emissions, 10 percent for trade-exposed sectors, and 10 percent for companies that opted in for voluntary emissions budgets. These allowances are to be gradually phased out. At the start of the policy, these allowances will provide a 90 percent exemption to some industries such as cement. South Africa undertook detailed impact assessments of alternative compensation methods. The tax is designed as revenue-neutral during the first few years. One option of revenue recycling considered is to decrease the existing electricity levy to neutralize the impact on electricity prices. The assessment process for preparing the tax was led by the National Treasury in collaboration with other ministries. It involved significant consultation of stakeholders and a wide range of economic modeling studies.

BOX A.2

FASTER principles for carbon pricing

Experiences with carbon and fuel taxes informed the World Bank–OECD FASTER principles for carbon pricing, jointly developed these as a normative framework for policy makers (World Bank and OECD 2015). Countries pursuing ETR, especially carbon pricing, should design and implement policies such that they ensure the following:

- **F**airness—distributing costs and benefits equitably, especially avoiding a disproportionate burden on low-income groups
- **A**lignment between objectives and policies—ensuring carbon pricing policies are a part of a package of measures that collectively align to objectives
- **S**tability and predictability—sending consistent and credible signals to the private sector
- **T**ransparency—clarity in design and implementation
- **E**fficiency and cost effectiveness—allowing private agents to adjust independently, and using raised revenues effectively
- **R**eliability and environmental integrity—aiming for measurable reductions in harmful activities

FIGURE A.4

Developing country experiences with raising energy prices vary

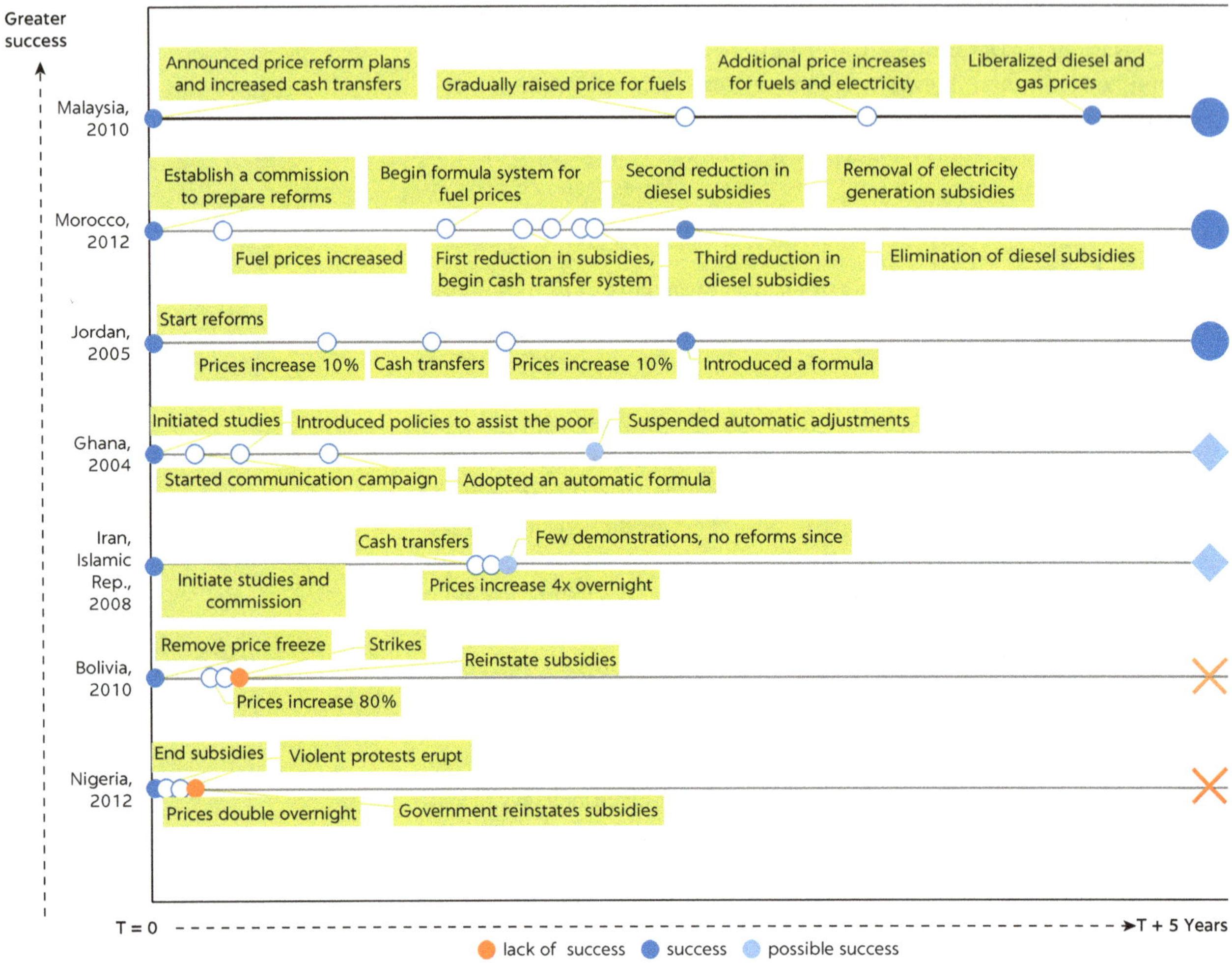

Source: IMF 2017a, Table 5, titled 'Energy reforms and steps timeline, by country'.
Note: T = time, defined as number of years since the start of the reform process, e.g. T = 0 means reform process has started, T + 5 means 5 years since the reform process was started. White circles = no judgments on the success of that stage.

Fossil fuel subsidy reform

Although few developing countries have experience with ETR implementation, several do have experience with energy price reform—raising energy prices by reducing energy subsidies. The tools are somewhat different (reducing subsidies versus raising or implementing environmental taxes), but the effect of raising prices on polluting sources of energy is similar. Developing country experiences with energy price reform have varied significantly (figure A.4). Successful examples include the following:

- Malaysia successfully reduced and then eliminated diesel and gas (pre-tax) subsidies from 2010 to 2015, assisted by numerous press statements from the prime minister on the need for reform and politicization that was limited to improving targeting of the poor.
- Morocco managed to eliminate (pre-tax) subsidies on fuel between 2012 and 2015. It established commissions to evaluate specific proposals, proceeded gradually with steady price increases, and used funds to expand spending in health, education, and transport.

- Jordan reformed subsidies gradually from 2005, eliminating fuel subsidies in 2012 and bringing its national utility back to full recovery of private operation costs. To compensate, the government increased public sector wages for low earners and put in place cash transfers if oil prices rise above US$100 per barrel, covering 70 percent of the population and a targeted food subsidy program. These measures were costly but generated public support for the program.

By contrast, some countries experienced mixed success in raising energy prices:

- Ghana embarked on a campaign of engagement, buttressed by a raft of compensatory measures across transport, education, and electrification that were ultimately followed by waning political support for automatic price adjustments in subsequent years.
- The Islamic Republic of Iran embarked on a bold reform program, increasing fuel prices by 400–2,000 percent in a short space of time. The sharp price increases, alongside sanctions, pushed inflation upward, while strongly decreasing inequality.
- Finally, two countries were notably unsuccessful in energy price reform:
- Bolivia increased fuel prices sharply (by 80 percent) in 2010. This rise led to strikes in major cities by unions, and the government quickly revoked the price hikes.
- Nigeria also increased fuel prices sharply in 2012. Facing fiscal pressure, it abruptly ended fuel subsidies, doubling gasoline prices overnight. This increase led to widespread protests, stoked by concerns about corruption and fears that interest groups were seizing control of natural resources.

BOX A.3

The International Monetary Fund's "rules of thumb" for energy price reform

The above experiences with energy price reform informed the International Monetary Fund's creation of five rules of thumb for reforming energy prices (IMF 2017b):

1. **Formulate an integrated reform strategy:** Consider all reform pieces holistically, tailored to the domestic policy making, including alignment and trajectory toward efficient prices, incentives, pace, support for consumers and producers who stand to lose, while maintaining appropriate monetary and fiscal policies to keep inflation expectations anchored.
2. **Protect the most vulnerable:** Prefer cash transfers over in-kind compensation; targeted cash transfers are ideal although universal cash transfers are easier to implement.
3. **Build public support:** Communicate costs and benefits of reform; use careful consultations and clear communication.
4. **Avoid piecemeal approaches:** Depoliticized and transparent rules that lead to automatic price changes are more durable than ad hoc, one-time adjustments.
5. **Reform gradually:** Avoid large adjustments when possible, allowing consumers and businesses time to steadily adjust to the new reality of higher prices.

Although designed for fossil fuel energy price reform, these rules also apply to ETRs that affect energy prices—that is, most ETRs. By following these rules of thumb, along with the FASTER Principles (box A.2), policy makers can increase the chances of success in pursuing ETRs.

BEHAVIORAL BARRIERS TO POLITICAL SUPPORT FOR ETR

Public support for ETRs can be low, and these low levels of support may force policy makers to maintain the status quo. Maintaining the status quo on the environment, however, could entail a state of the world in which climate change remains a significant threat to the long-term well-being of humanity. Addressing public support is therefore critical to ensuring that ETRs, such as those including carbon taxation, are both implemented and sustained. Numerous behavioral factors account for low levels of support for ETR. These are described below.

Concentration of losses and rational ignorance

Losses from ETRs tend to be more concentrated than benefits. As a result, "losers" have a stronger incentive to block change than "winners" to foster it (Stigler 1971; Buchanan and Tullock 1975; Trebilcock 2014). For carbon taxes, net beneficiaries include future generations and the young, who benefit from reduced climate risks, and most of existing generations, who gain from co-benefits and increased economic activity. These benefits, although tangible at the aggregate level, are spread out among a broad segment of the population. Conversely, the costs of ETRs are usually more concentrated on a smaller proportion of individuals, such as stakeholders of carbon-intense industries.

These smaller groups are easier to organize. Losers are therefore better able to have their voice heard in the policy process (Olson 1965; Stigler 1971; Peltzman, Levine, and Noll 1979; Vogt-Schilb and Hallegatte 2017). For example, although South Africa has long tried to introduce a carbon tax, progress has been slow, in part because of opposition from the influential and highly carbon-intense mining sector (Acosta 2015).[17]

As a result, losers may "rationally" decide to remain uninformed about the reform. And, when the costs of obtaining information about ETR are higher than the expected benefits of having this information, winners may prefer to remain "rationally ignorant" (Downs 1957).[18] The public may therefore remain rationally ignorant about ETR because its ability to affect policy making is weaker than that of vested interests. So, while the losers of reform become vocal and organized, winners remain uncoordinated and even rationally ignorant, reducing political support for ETR.

Discounting and poverty as a cognitive tax

Because its benefits are more spread out over time than its costs, overly high discount rates can reduce support for ETR. With carbon taxes, the benefits of reduced environmental risks from mitigation and welfare co-benefits, such as the reduction of traffic congestion and improvements in energy efficiency, do not materialize immediately whereas energy prices increase in the short term. These short-term increases make sense but may be socially undesirable if firms and individuals have discount rates above the social optimum. This can be further compounded if individuals discount future gains more than future costs because of, for example, risk aversion (Hardisty and Weber 2009).

Discount rates due to behavioral biases tend to be higher in developing countries for several reasons. Some of these reasons are rational: for example, developing countries with higher rates of GDP growth would logically have higher private discount rates. Other reasons may be irrational and due to contextual factors. Poverty, for example, acts as a cognitive tax that forces the poor to focus more on salient costs and benefits as well as on short-term outcomes (Mullainathan and Shafir 2013; World Bank 2015). Poor individuals may be more likely to miss or over-discount the benefits of ETR, while being overly sensitive to short-term energy price increases. Poverty has, in fact, been shown to correlate with, and cause, higher discount rates (Haushofer and Fehr, 2014).

Beliefs

The public may underestimate the benefits of environmental taxes. Citizens and businesses may believe that taxes are only revenue-generating measures (Dresner et al. 2006). The Pigouvian idea of using taxation to internalize external costs to reach a socially desirable competitive equilibrium may not be widely understood. Similarly, there may be skepticism about the effectiveness of environmental taxes. For example, many do not believe that environmental taxes can increase welfare or generate co-benefits like the alleviation of traffic congestion (Rienstra, Rietveld, and Verhoef 1999; Kallbekken, Kroll, and Cherry 2011).

Individuals may also be poorly informed about the merits of specific ETR designs. Individuals tend to prefer when revenues are earmarked for specific environmental projects, while fearing the financial consequences of ETR (Gevrek and Uyduranoglu 2015; Carattini, Carvalho, and Fankhauser 2017). By contrast, economists tend to prefer *tax shifts*—recycling of revenues through reduced taxes—for cost-effectiveness reasons, the logic of which can be lost on the public (Clinch, Dunne, and Dresner 2006; Carattini et al. 2017).

Worldviews affect perceptions of costs and benefits (World Bank 2015).[19] A *worldview* is a "socially constructed orientation that dictates how one interprets and interacts with reality" (Cherry, Kallbekken, and Kroll 2017). In the context of climate change risk perception, worldviews affect how climate change information is sought, perceived, and accepted. For example, worldviews affect the degree of acceptance of expert opinions on climate change (Kahan, Jenkins-Smith, and Braman 2011), and determine attitudes toward carbon taxation (Cherry, Kallbekken, and Kroll 2017).

Trust in government

A lack of trust in the government can be a significant source of opposition to ETRs (Clinch, Dunne, and Dresner 2006; Dresner et al. 2006). Citizens may fear that the increased fiscal pressure from ETR will not be followed by public spending that benefits them. A promise to compensate citizens for fuel price increases through cash transfers, for example, may have limited credibility (Inchauste and Victor 2017). This fear can be stronger when the perceived influence of vested interests on spending and the perceived corruption in the public sector are high. In these contexts, citizens may oppose ETR even if the planned use of revenues would benefit them.

Risk aversion

Risk aversion reduces support for ETR. Because environmental taxes are a new concept to most people, in the eyes of many citizens, ETRs have uncertain payoffs.

In these situations, risk-averse individuals prefer the status quo to the reform. Risk aversion may be a more significant impediment in developing countries than in developed countries because poorer people tend to be more risk averse than wealthy people (Heinemann 2008; Guiso and Paiella 2008; X. Liu, Yang, and Cai 2016; Ogaki and Zhang 2001).

Perceived coerciveness

ETR can be perceived as a coercive measure, and therefore opposed. Policies that are perceived as coercive, such as those limiting freedom or punishing negative activities like pollution, receive less support than measures perceived as rewarding positive behavior (Schuitema and Steg 2008; Schuitema, Steg, and Rothengatter 2010). This preference may account for why people opposed carbon taxes more than environmental policies (de Groot and Schuitema 2012).

Shame and stigmatization

Social stigmas associated with receiving public handouts may reduce support for ETR. The shame of being poor and the experience of being socially stigmatized can limit participation in programs destined to alleviate poverty (Shafir 2017). This general finding carries over to ETRs. When revenues from environmental taxes are earmarked to compensate low-income households, and the distribution of revenues is not carefully managed to safeguard anonymity, this shaming effect can reduce support for ETR. Compensation schemes explicitly named as compensation programs targeted to the poor can exacerbate this shaming effect and reduce support.

Distributional outcomes

People support tax reforms less when they view them as regressive. In 2015, more than 90 percent of Swiss voters rejected a proposal to substitute the national VAT with an energy tax. Distributional concerns were among the most prominent reasons (Baranzini et al. 2017). Distributional concerns also appear to have affected environmental taxation in Sweden and Turkey (Brannlund and Persson 2012; Gevrek and Uyduranoglu 2015).

Preexisting perceived inequalities among social groups can undermine support for ETR. After the introduction of the carbon tax in British Columbia, many in the rural north of the province felt that the reform imposed an unfairly high tax burden on them compared to those in the urban south. In reality, the opposite appears to have occurred (Beck, Rivers, and Yonezawa 2016; Beck, Rivers, and Yonezawa 2016). This experience shows that opposition to ETR can derive from preexisting tensions between regions (and other social groups), independent of the actual distribution of tax incidences.

Overall, these behavioral factors can be major barriers to public support for ETR. However, appropriate ETR designs and communications strategies can go a long way to overcoming them (see "Building political support" in chapter 1).

NOTES

1. Mixing refers to whether a pollutant's damage depends on the location of its source. The damage a uniformly mixed pollutant like CO_2 inflicts (for example, through increased climate risks) does not depend on the location of its source. One ton of CO_2 causes the same

impact on climate change no matter where it is emitted. By contrast, pollutants with non-uniform mixing that fall close to a source (for example, water pollutants, particulates, sulfur or nitrogen dioxides from low stack sources) have highly localized costs. The benefits of abatement for nonuniform mixing therefore vary by pollution source. Cost-effective policy in welfare terms may then entail requiring some firms (such as those with plants near major cities) to abate more than they would with a per-unit tax. Aggregate abatement costs may then be higher than in the uniform case, and uniform Pigouvian taxes may not be the efficient policy response.

2. Note that there is also an unresolved academic debate around efficiency and welfare effects (defined as achieving the environmental objective while minimizing deadweight losses) of price instruments like taxes versus quantity instruments like ETSs in the presence of uncertainty of marginal costs and benefits of pollution abatement. Weitzman (1974) argued that, when the damage costs are very high and uncertain while abatement costs are relatively low and predictable, restricting quantity through direct regulations or quantity instruments like ETSs can be more efficient. Alternatively, where marginal benefits of abatement are uncertain (as in the case for climate tipping points) and low (climate change is a stock problem, meaning each year's additional GHG emissions have a low marginal effect on temperature forcing), price instruments such as carbon taxes may be more appropriate. Last, correlation between costs and benefits further complicates instrument choice. Quantity instruments are preferred where marginal costs and benefits of abatement are positively correlated, whereas price instruments are preferred when these costs and benefits are negatively correlated (Stavins 1996).
3. Formally, the marginal worker's rent or surplus is the difference between the net wage received and his or her reservation wage. The surplus or rent for the firm is the difference between the value of a job and its costs. Under perfect labor markets, the market rate equals the marginal worker's reservation wage and the value of a job to the firm, so that the worker's and firm's surpluses are equal to zero. An imperfect labor market is one where rents are associated with any particular job (for example, because of imperfect information or low labor mobility), and hence total surpluses are positive. Imperfect labor markets are therefore characterized by informational asymmetries, frictions, or market power on at least one of the two sides of the labor market (Boeri and Ours 2013).
4. Structural employment data are from Economic Outlook No 102 - November 2017 (dataset), Organisation for Economic Co-operation and Development (accessed January 17, 2018), https://stats.oecd.org/Index.aspx?QueryId=51643.
5. However, when controlling for unobservable study characteristics (via a fixed-effects strategy, exploiting the fact some studies have multiple simulations, as described in Nelson and Kennedy 2009) the results are ambiguous on whether labor market structure assumptions individually affect simulations' estimated employment dividends (Anger, Böhringer, and Löschel 2010). Given the limited number of studies and simulations (41 and 73, respectively) and the period of publication (1995–2004 with a median year of 1997) augmenting this meta-analysis with more recent findings is warranted.
6. The post-tax price after the levying of the VAT and environmental taxation is equal to (1 + VAT rate)*(pre-tax price of one unit of the good + environmental tax per unit of the good), where the VAT rate is a percentage and the environmental tax is a set amount of currency per physical unit of the good.
7. This result can be illustrated with an example. First, we consider an imported product because "VAT collected at the border commonly accounts for more than half of gross VAT collections in developing countries" (Keen 2008). A liter of fuel is imported into the port of a country, and the customs agency applies the country's taxes before the fuel leaves the port for open circulation in the economy. Suppose the fuel costs $1.00 per liter, the VAT rate is 10 percent, and there is no environmental tax. In this case the post-tax consumer price is $1.10. After the fuel has been released into the market, if it is used by a company in the formal sector, that company will reclaim the absolute amount of VAT of $0.10. If, however, the fuel is used by a company in the informal sector, that company cannot reclaim the VAT and hence is effectively charged a withholding tax of $0.10. Suppose now an environmental tax is introduced at $0.05/liter. The absolute amount of VAT collected is now $0.15. Again, if a company in the informal sector consumes the fuel, that $0.15 becomes a withholding tax, whereas a formal sector company can reclaim that amount. Accordingly, the ability of the VAT system to undo some of the tax advantages of the informal sector has improved without any need to raise VAT rates in the country.

8. For a thorough treatment on tax efficiency in public economics, see Atkinson and Stiglitz (1980).
9. For example, the deductibility of certain consumption expenditure or loan interest payments from taxable income increases both the complexity and distortions of personal income taxes (Fullerton and Metcalf 2005).
10. Note that this pass-through effect can be further enhanced (that is, pass-through can be reduced leading to more capture of resource rents) using supplementary environmental policies. For example, if renewable energy shares are increased in electricity supplies, then fossil fuel sources need to compete more with renewable sources (Fabra and Reguant 2013; Hintermann 2014). Increases in input prices due to a tax could not as easily be passed on to consumers, and environmental taxes can capture a larger proportion of extraction rents. The same is true for public transport policies. Public investment in public transport, by increasing the alternatives to personal car transportation, makes fuel demand more elastic (Harju, Kosonen, and Laukkanen 2016), reducing pass-through and increasing the potential for taxing Ricardian rents from fuel extraction.
11. This argument for shifting tax burdens away from labor to fuel is weaker to the extent that fuels are important factor inputs of production—but that importance is less the case in poor countries.
12. The wage curve describes the empirically observed relationship between real wages and unemployment. Blanchflower and Oswald (1995, 2005) find a consistent pattern wage curve elasticity of −0.1 across developed countries: a doubling of the unemployment rate is associated with 10 percent decline in the level of the (real) wage. Note, however, that far fewer studies exist on wage curves in developing countries. One meta-analysis, for example, analyzed 208 estimates of wage curve elasticities, only 4 of which were for developing countries (Nijkamp and Poot 2005). The study identified significant heterogeneity across countries, but did not disaggregate between income groups or proportions of skilled and unskilled labor.
13. Other factors include the relative substitutability between unskilled and skilled labor types and relative substitutability between energy and labor types (Markandya, González-Eguino, and Escapa 2012), as well as the extent to which workers respond to lower unemployment by reducing effort (Schneider 1997).
14. At present, this is speculative (refer to the note above on wage curve elasticities). Baltagi and Blien (1998) find, for example, that wages of less skilled workers were more sensitive to local unemployment rates in Germany.
15. Note that there is also an interaction between relative skills in a labor market and levels of informality: in developing economies, workers in the informal sector "tend to be younger, have less education, and earn less than their counterparts in the formal sector" (Amaral and Quintin 2006). Policies like ETR that shift the tax burden to nonworkers and workers in the informal sector may have regressive short-run distributional consequences (between income groups and across generations), but may also increase the expected returns to education and skills, yielding more skilled workers in the long run. Little of the existing ETR literature has yet explored these dynamics.
16. Note that there is an ongoing debate about the "Jevons paradox," which suggests that increases in energy efficiency may actually increase energy use because of the reduction in energy prices. Theoretically, this rebound effect may more than compensate for the reduction in energy demand from increased efficiency (that is, the sum of substitution, income, and price effects results in rebound being greater than unity). For a summary of views on how the rebound might affect environmental objectives, see Sorrell (2009). For discussion of the potential effects on technological change and economic growth, see Madlener and Alcott (2009).
17. In 2015, a first tax bill was proposed. This carbon tax was expected to apply starting from January 1, 2017. However, the approval of the tax bill was significantly delayed and, in December 2017, a new tax bill has been put forward (Republic of South Africa 2017), and it is now expected to apply starting from January 1, 2019.
18. An individual is rationally ignorant when he chooses to refrain from acquiring knowledge about an issue when the cost of educating himself about it exceeds the potential benefit that the knowledge would provide.
19. Worldviews are a separate hurdle for climate policy than lack of knowledge: their influence on the perceived risks of climate change is not lower among individuals with higher levels of education in science and numeracy (Kahan, Jenkins-Smith, and Braman 2011).

REFERENCES

Acemoglu, Daron, Simon Johnson, and James Robinson. 2000. "The Colonial Origins of Comparative Development: An Empirical Investigation." *The American Economic Review* 91 (5): 1369–1401. https://doi.org/10.2139/ssrn.244582.

Acosta, Lilibeth A. 2015. "Political Economy in Climate Change Mitigation: The Case of Carbon Taxes." Case Study Prepared for the GIZ, German Development Institute, Bonn.

Agénor, P. R., and P. J. Montiel. 2015. *Development Macroeconomics*. Fourth Edition. Princeton, NJ: Princeton University Press. https://ideas.repec.org/b/pup/pbooks/10494.html.

Aghion, Philippe, Antoine Dechezleprêtre, David Hemous, Ralf Martin, and John Van Reenen. 2015. "Carbon Taxes, Path Dependency and Directed Technical Change: Evidence from the Auto Industry." NBER Working Paper No. 18596, National Bureau of Economic Research, Cambridge, MA. https://doi.org/10.3386/w18596.

Albrizio, Silvia, Tomasz Kozluk, and Vera Zipperer. 2017. "Environmental Policies and Productivity Growth: Evidence across Industries and Firms." *Journal of Environmental Economics and Management* 81 (January): 209–26. https://doi.org/10.1016/j.jeem.2016.06.002.

Alm, James, Edward Sennoga, and Mark Skidmore. 2009. "Perfect Competition, Urbanization, and Tax Incidence in the Retail Gasoline Market." *Economic Inquiry* 47 (1): 118–34. https://doi.org/10.1111/j.1465-7295.2008.00164.x.

Amaral, Pedro S., and Erwan Quintin. 2006. "A Competitive Model of the Informal Sector." *Journal of Monetary Economics* 53 (7): 1541–53. https://doi.org/10.1016/j.jmoneco.2005.07.016.

Ambec, S., M. A. Cohen, S. Elgie, and P. Lanoie. 2013. "The Porter Hypothesis at 20: Can Environmental Regulation Enhance Innovation and Competitiveness?" *Review of Environmental Economics and Policy* 7 (1): 2–22. https://doi.org/10.1093/reep/res016.

Anger, Niels, Christoph Böhringer, and Andreas Löschel. 2010. "Paying the Piper and Calling the Tune?. A Meta-Regression Analysis of the Double-Dividend Hypothesis." *Ecological Economics* 69 (7): 1495–1502. https://doi.org/10.1016/j.ecolecon.2010.02.003.

Atkinson, A. B., and Joseph Stiglitz. 1980. *Lectures on Public Economics*. Princeton, NJ: Princeton University Press.

Baltagi, Badi H,, and Uwe Blien. 1998. "The German Wage Curve: Evidence from the IAB Employment Sample." *Economics Letters* 61 (2): 135–42. https://doi.org/10.1016/S0165-1765(98)00166-9.

Baranzini, Andrea, Jeroen van den Bergh, Stefano Carattini, Richard Howarth, Emilio Padilla, and Jordi Roca. 2017. "Carbon Pricing in Climate Policy: Seven Reasons, Complementary Instruments, and Political Economy Considerations." *Wiley Interdisciplinary Reviews: Climate Change* 8 (4): 1–17. https://doi.org/10.1002/wcc.462.

Bayindir-Upmann, T. 2004. "On the Double Dividend under Imperfect Competition." *Environmental and Resource Economics* 28 (2): 169–94. https://doi.org/10.1023/B:EARE.0000029917.57621.df.

Barma, Naazneen, Kai Kaiser, Tuan Minh Le, and Lorena Viñuela, eds. 2011. *Rents to Riches?* Washington, DC: World Bank Group. https://elibrary.worldbank.org/doi/pdf/10.1596/978-0-8213-8480-0.

Beck, Marisa, Nicholas Rivers, and Hidemichi Yonezawa. 2016. "A Rural Myth? Sources and Implications of the Perceived Unfairness of Carbon Taxes in Rural Communities." *Ecological Economics* 124 (April): 124–34.

Bento, Antonio, and Mark Jacobsen. 2007. "Ricardian Rents, Environmental Policy and the 'Double-Dividend' Hypothesis." *Journal of Environmental Economics and Management* 53 (1): 17–31. https://doi.org/10.1016/j.jeem.2006.03.006.

Bento, Antonio, Mark Jacobsen, and Antung Liu. 2017. "Environmental Policy in the Presence of an Informal Sector." *The World Bank Economic Review* 9 (Suppl. 1): S126–34. https://doi.org/10.1093/wber/lhv026.

Blanchflower, David, and Andrew Oswald. 1995. "An Introduction to the Wage Curve." *Journal of Economic Perspectives* 9 (3): 153–67. https://doi.org/10.1257/jep.9.3.153.

——. 2005. "The Wage Curve Reloaded." NBER Working Paper No. 11338, National Bureau of Economic Research, Cambridge, MA. https://doi.org/10.3386/w11338.

Boadway, Robin, and Frank Flatters. 1993. "The Taxation of Natural Resources - Principles and Policy Issues." Policy Research Working Paper 1210, World Bank, Washington, DC.

Bodin, Jean-Paul, Liam Ebrill, Michael Keen, and Victoria Summers. 2001. *The Modern VAT*. Washington, DC: International Monetary Fund.

Boeri, Tito, and Jan Ours. 2013. *The Economics of Imperfect Labor Markets*. Second Edition. Princeton, NJ: Princeton University Press.

Bosquet, Benoît. 2002. "The Role of Natural Resources in Fundamental Tax Reform in the Russian Federation." Policy Research Working Paper 2807, World Bank, Washington, DC.

Bovenberg, Arij Lans, and Frederick van der Ploeg. 1996. "Optimal Taxation, Public Goods and Environmental Policy with Involuntary Unemployment." *Journal of Public Economics* 62 (1–2): 59–83. https://doi.org/10.1016/0047-2727(96)01574-5.

Bovenberg, Lans, and Frederick van der Ploeg. 1998. "Consequences of Environmental Tax Reform for Unemployment and Welfare." *Environmental and Resource Economics* 12 (2): 137–50. https://doi.org/10.1023/A:1016040327622.

Brannlund, R., and L. Persson. 2012. "To Tax, or Not To Tax: Preferences for Climate Policy Attributes." *Climate Policy* 12 (6): 704–21.

Buchanan, J., and G. Tullock. 1975. "Polluters' Profts and Political Response: Direct Controls versus Taxes." *The American Economic Review* 65 (1): 139–47.

Burke, Paul J., and Shuhei Nishitateno. 2015. "Gasoline Prices and Road Fatalities: International Evidence." *Economic Inquiry* 53 (3): 1437–50. https://doi.org/10.1111/ecin.12171.

Carattini, Stefano, Andrea Baranzini, Philippe Thalmann, Frédéric Varone, and Frank Vöhringer. 2017. "Green Taxes in a Post-Paris World: Are Millions of Nays Inevitable?" *Environmental and Resource Economics* 68 (1): 97–128. https://doi.org/10.1007/s10640-017-0133-8.

Carattini, Stefano, Maria Carvalho, and Sam Fankhauser. 2017. "How to Make Carbon Taxes More Acceptable." http://www.lse.ac.uk/GranthamInstitute/publication/make-carbon-taxes-acceptable/.

Cardenas, Juan Camilo, and Jeffrey Carpenter. 2008. "Behavioural Development Economics: Lessons from Field Labs in the Developing World." *Journal of Development Studies* 44 (3): 311–38. https://doi.org/10.1080/00220380701848327.

Carraro, Carlo, Marzio Galeotti, and Massimo Gallo. 1996. "Environmental Taxation and Unemployment: Some Evidence on the 'Double Dividend Hypothesis' in Europe." *Journal of Public Economics* 62 (1–2): 141–81. https://doi.org/10.1016/0047-2727(96)01577-0.

Carson, Richard, Mark Jacobsen, and Antung Liu. 2014. "Comparing the Cost of a Carbon Tax in China and the United States." American Economic Association. https://www.aeaweb.org/conference/2015/retrieve.php?pdfid=634&usg=%5CnAFQjCNGhW1bl9fFYsDXU3ujw-Wfyv7BW3A&sig2=DeUCH.

Cherry, Todd L., Steffen Kallbekken, and Stephan Kroll. 2017. "Accepting Market Failure: Cultural Worldviews and the Opposition to Corrective Environmental Policies." *Journal of Environmental Economics and Management* 85 (September): 193–204. https://doi.org/10.1016/j.jeem.2017.05.004.

Chiroleu-Assouline, M., and L. Lemiale. 2001. "Employment Double Dividend and Wage Determination." Université Paris1 Panthéon-Sorbonne (Post-Print and Working Papers), hal-00471276, HAL. http://ideas.repec.org/p/hal/cesptp/hal-00471276.html.

Chiroleu-Assouline, Mireille, and Mouez Fodha. 2005. "Double Dividend with Involuntary Unemployment: Efficiency and Intergenerational Equity." *Environmental & Resource Economics* 31 (4): 389–403. http://ideas.repec.org/a/kap/enreec/v31y2005i4p389-403.html.

——. 2006. "Double Dividend Hypothesis, Golden Rule and Welfare Distribution." *Journal of Environmental Economics and Management* 51 (3): 323–35. http://ideas.repec.org/a/eee/jeeman/v51y2006i3p323-335.html.

Clinch, J. Peter, Louise Dunne, and Simon Dresner. 2006. "Environmental and Wider Implications of Political Impediments to Environmental Tax Reform." *Energy Policy* 34 (8): 960–70. https://doi.org/10.1016/j.enpol.2004.08.048.

Costantini, Valeria, and Massimiliano Mazzanti. 2012. "On the Green and Innovative Side of Trade Competitiveness? The Impact of Environmental Policies and Innovation on EU Exports." *Research Policy* 41 (1): 132–53. https://doi.org/10.1016/j.respol.2011.08.004.

Daniel, Philip, Michael Keen, and Charles McPherson, eds. 2010. *The Taxation of Petroleum and Minerals*. Washington, DC: International Monetary Fund.

de Groot, J. I. M., and G. Schuitema. 2012. "How To Make the Unpopular Popular? Policy Characteristics, Social Norms and the Acceptability of Environmental Policies." *Environmental Science and Policy* 19–20 (May–June): 100–107. https://doi.org/10.1016/j.envsci.2012.03.004.

Downs, A. 1957. "An Economic Theory of Political Action in a Democracy." *The Journal of Political Economy* 65 (2): 135–50.

Doyle, Joseph J., and Krislert Samphantharak. 2008. "$2.00 Gas! Studying the Effects of a Gas Tax Moratorium." *Journal of Public Economics* 92 (3–4): 869–84. https://doi.org/10.1016/j.jpubeco.2007.05.011.

Dresner, Simon, Louise Dunne, Peter Clinch, and Christiane Beuermann. 2006. "Social and Political Responses to Ecological Tax Reform in Europe: An Introduction to the Special Issue." *Energy Policy* 34 (8): 895–904. https://doi.org/10.1016/j.enpol.2004.08.043.

Eisenack, Klaus, Ottmar Edenhofer, and Matthias Kalkuhl. 2012. "Resource Rents: The Effects of Energy Taxes and Quantity Instruments for Climate Protection." *Energy Policy* 48: 159–66. https://doi.org/10.1016/j.enpol.2012.05.001.

Fabra, Natalia, and Mar Reguant. 2013. "Pass-through of Emission Costs in Electricity Markets." *American Economic Review* 104 (9): 2872–99. https://doi.org/10.1257/aer.104.9.2872.

Fullerton, Don, and Gilbert Metcalf. 2005. "Tax Incidence." In *Handbook of Public Economics*, edited by Alan Auerbach and Martin Feldstein, II, 1–86. Amsterdam: Elsevier. https://doi.org/10.1017/CBO9781107415324.004.

Gevrek, Z. Eylem, and Ayse Uyduranoglu. 2015. "Public Preferences for Carbon Tax Attributes." *Ecological Economics* 118 (October): 186–97. https://doi.org/10.1016/j.ecolecon.2015.07.020.

Goulder, Lawrence. 1995. "Environmental Taxation and the Double Dividend: A Reader's Guide." *International Tax and Public Finance* 2 (2): 157–83. https://doi.org/10.1007/BF00877495.

Guiso, Luigi, and Monica Paiella. 2008. "Risk Aversion, Wealth, and Background Risk." *Journal of the European Economic Association* 6 (6): 1109–50. http://onlinelibrary.wiley.com/doi/10.1162/JEEA.2008.6.6.1109/abstract.

Hamilton, Kirk, and Eduardo Ley. 2012. "Fiscal Policy for Sustainable Development in Resource-Rich Low-Income Countries." In *Is Fiscal Policy the Answer? A Developing Country Perspective*, edited by Blanca Moreno-Dodson, 147–69. Washington, DC: World Bank Group. https://elibrary.worldbank.org/doi/book/10.1596/978-0-8213-9630-8.

Hardisty, David J., and Elke U. Weber. 2009. "Discounting Future Green: Money Versus the Environment." *Journal of Experimental Psychology: General* 138 (3): 329–40. https://doi.org/10.1037/a0016433.

Harju, Jarkko, Tuomas Kosonen, and Marita Laukkanen. 2016. "Tax Incidence in the Fuel Market: Evidence from Station-Level Data." Working paper, Helsinki.

Heady, C., J. Markandya, W. Blyth, J. Collingwood, and P. Taylor. 2000. "Study on the Relationship between Environmental/Energy Taxation and Employment Creation." Revised Final Report Prepared for the European Commission. http://ec.europa.eu/environment/enveco/taxation/pdf/entaxemp.pdf.

Heinemann, Frank. 2008. "Measuring Risk Aversion and the Wealth Effect." In *Research in Experimental Economics*, Volume 12, edited by James Cox and Glenn Harrison, 293–314. Bingley: JAI Press.

Hicks, J. R. 1932. *The Theory of Wages*. London: Macmillan.

Hintermann, Beat. 2014. "Pass-through of CO_2 Emission Costs to Hourly Electricity Prices in Germany." *Journal of the Association of Environmental and Resource Economists* 3 (4): 857–91.

IMF (International Monetary Fund). 2017a. "2017 Article IV Consultation: Turkey." Country Report No. 17, IMF, Washington, DC.

——. 2017b. "If Not Now, When? Energy Price Reform in Arab Countries." IMF Policy Paper, Washington, DC.

Inchauste, Gabriela, and David Victor. 2017. *The Political Economy of Subsidy Reform*. Washington, DC: World Bank Group. https://doi.org/10.1596/978-1-4648-1007-7.

Johns, Andrew, and Joel Slemrod. 2010. "The Distribution of Income Tax Nomcompliance." *National Tax Journal* 63 (3): 397–418. http://www.scopus.com/inward/record.url?eid=2-s2.0-83655207112&partnerID=tZOtx3y1.

Kahan, D., H. Jenkins-Smith, and D. Braman. 2011. "Cultural Cognition of Scientific Consensus." *Journal of Risk Research* 14 (2): 147–74.

Kallbekken, Steffen, Stephan Kroll, and Todd Cherry. 2011. "Do You Not like Pigou, or Do You Not Understand Him? Tax Aversion and Revenue Recycling in the Lab." *Journal of Environmental Economics and Management* 62 (1): 53–64.

Keen, Michael. 2008. "VAT, Tariffs, and Withholding: Border Taxes and Informality in Developing Countries." *Journal of Public Economics* 92 (10–11): 1892–1906. https://doi.org/10.1016/j.jpubeco.2008.05.006.

Lanoie, Paul, Jérémy Laurent-Lucchetti, Nick Johnstone, and Stefan Ambec. 2011. "Environmental Policy, Innovation and Performance: New Insights on the Porter Hypothesis." *Journal of Economics & Management Strategy* 20 (3): 803–42. https://doi.org/10.1111/j.1530-9134.2011.00301.x.

La Porta, Rafael, and Andrei Shleifer. 2014. "Informality and Development." *Journal of Economic Perspectives* 28 (3): 109–26. https://doi.org/10.1257/jep.28.3.109.

Ligthart, Jenny. 1998. "The Macroeconomic Effects of Environmental Taxes: A Closer Look At the Feasibility of Win-Win Outcomes." IMF Working Paper No. 98/75, IMF, Washington, DC.

Liski, Matti, and Olli Tahvonen. 2004. "Can Carbon Tax Eat OPEC's Rents?" *Journal of Environmental Economics and Management* 47 (1): 1–12. https://doi.org/10.1016/S0095-0696(03)00052-4.

Liu, Antung. 2013. "Tax Evasion and Optimal Environmental Taxes." *Journal of Environmental Economics and Management* 66 (3): 656–70. https://doi.org/10.1016/j.jeem.2013.06.004.

Liu, Antung, and Hiroaki Yamagami. 2017. "Environmental Policy in the Presence of Induced Technological Change." *Environmental and Resource Economics*, April 18. https://doi.org/10.1007/s10640-017-0150-7.

Liu, Xuan, Fang Yang, and Zongwu Cai. 2016. "Does Relative Risk Aversion Vary with Wealth? Evidence from Households' Portfolio Choice Data." *Journal of Economic Dynamics and Control* 69: 229–48. http://papers.ssrn.com/sol3/papers.cfm?abstract_id=2033427.

Madlener, R., and B. Alcott. 2009. "Energy Rebound and Economic Growth: A Review of the Main Issues and Research Needs." *Energy* 34 (3): 370–76. https://doi.org/10.1016/j.energy.2008.10.011.

Marion, Justin, and Erich Muehlegger. 2011. "Fuel Tax Incidence and Supply Conditions." *Journal of Public Economics* 95 (9–10): 1202–12. https://doi.org/10.1016/j.jpubeco.2011.04.003.

Markandya, Anil. 2012. "Environmental Taxation: What Have We Learnt in the Last 30 Years?" In *Environmental Taxes and Fiscal Reform*, edited by Laura Castellucci and Anil Markandya. Basingstoke: Macmillan. https://doi.org/10.1057/9780230392403.

Markandya, Anil, Mikel González-Eguino, and Marta Escapa. 2012. "Environmental Fiscal Reform and Unemployment in Spain." In *Carbon Pricing, Growth and the Environment*, edited by Lawrence Kreiser, Ana Sterling, Pedro Herrera, Janet Milne, and Hope Ashiabor, 3–15. Edward Elgar Publishing.

Markandya, Anil, Mikel González-Eguino, and Marta Escapa. 2013. "From Shadow to Green: Linking Environmental Fiscal Reforms and the Informal Economy." *Energy Economics* 40 (Supplement 1, December): S108–18. https://doi.org/10.1016/j.eneco.2013.09.014.

Marsiliani, Laura, and Thomas Renström. 2000. "Imperfect Competition, Labour Market Distortions, and the Double Dividend Hypothesis. Theory and Evidence from Italian Data." FEEM Working Paper 11.00, Fondazione Eni Enrico Mattei, Milan. https://papers.ssrn.com/sol3/papers.cfm?abstract_id=229157.

Metcalf, Gilbert E., and David Weisbach. 2012. "Linking Policies When Tastes Differ: Global Climate Policy in a Heterogeneous World." *Review of Environmental Economics and Policy* 6 (1): 110–29. https://doi.org/10.1093/reep/rer021.

Mirhosseini, Seyyedeh, Naman Mahmoudi, and Seyyedeh Valokolaie. 2017. "Investigating the Relationship between Green Tax Reforms and Shadow Economy Using a CGE Model—A Case Study in Iran." *Iranian Economic Review* 21 (1): 153–67.

Muehlegger, Erich, and Richard Sweeney. 2017. "Pass-Through of Input Cost Shocks Under Imperfect Competition: Evidence from the U.S. Fracking Boom." NBER Working Paper No. 24025, National Bureau of Economic Research, Cambridge, MA. https://doi.org/10.3386/w24025.

Mullainathan, Sendhil, and Eldar Shafir. 2013. *Scarcity: Why Having Too Little Means So Much.* Macmillan.

Nerudová, Danuše, and Marian Dobranschi. 2016. "The Impact of Tax Burden Overshifting on the Pigovian Taxation." *Procedia - Social and Behavioral Sciences* 220 (May): 302–11. https://doi.org/10.1016/j.sbspro.2016.05.503.

Nelson, Jon P., and Peter E. Kennedy. 2009. "The Use (and Abuse) of Meta-Analysis in Environmental and Natural Resource Economics: An Assessment." *Environmental and Resource Economics* 42 (3): 345–77. https://doi.org/10.1007/s10640-008-9253-5.

Nijkamp, Peter, and Jacques Poot. 2005. "The Last Word on the Wage Curve?" *Journal of Economic Surveys* 19 (3): 421–50. https://doi.org/10.1111/j.0950-0804.2005.00254.x.

OECD (Organisation for Economic Co-operation and Development). 2010a. *Tax Policy Reform and Economic Growth.* Paris: OECD Publishing.

——. 2010b. *Taxation, Innovation and the Environment.* Paris: OECD Publishing. https://doi.org/10.1787/9789264087637-en.

Ogaki, Masao, and Qiang Zhang. 2001. "Decreasing Relative Risk Aversion and Tests of Risk Sharing." *Econometrica* 69 (2): 515–26. http://onlinelibrary.wiley.com/doi/10.1111/1468-0262.00201/full.

Olson, M. 1965. *Logic of Collective Action: Public Goods and the Theory of Groups.* Cambridge, MA: Harvard University Press.

Orlov, Anton, Harald Grethe, and Scott McDonald. 2013. "Carbon Taxation in Russia: Prospects for a Double Dividend and Improved Energy Efficiency." *Energy Economics* 37 (May): 128–40. https://doi.org/10.1016/J.ENECO.2013.01.008.

Parry, Ian. 1995. "Pollution Taxes and Revenue Recycling." *Journal of Environmental Economics and Management* 29 (3): S64–S77. http://www.sciencedirect.com/science/article/pii/S0095069685710613.

——. 1997. "Environmental Taxes and Quotas in the Presence of Distorting Taxes in Factor Markets." *Resource and Energy Economics* 19 (3): 203–20. https://doi.org/10.1016/S0928-7655(96)00012-7.

——. 2003. "Fiscal Interactions and the Case for Carbon Taxes Over Grandfathered Carbon Permits." *Oxford Review of Economic Policy* 19 (3): 385–99. https://doi.org/10.1093/oxrep/19.3.385.

Parry, Ian, Hilary Sigman, Margaret Walls, and Roberton Williams III. 2006. "The Incidence of Pollution Control Policies." *The International Yearbook of Environmental and Resource Economics 2006/2007*, edited by Tom Tietenberg and Henk Folmer,1–42. Edward Elgar Publishing. https://doi.org/10.4337/9781847200235.00008.

Peltzman, S., M. Levine, and R. Noll. 1989. *The Economic Theory of Regulation after a Decade of Deregulation* (Brookings Papers on Economic Activity. Microeconomics). Washington, DC.

Pereira, Alfredo, and Rui Pereira. 2016. "On the Optimal Use of Revenues from a CO_2 Tax and the Importance of Labor Market Conditions." MPRA Paper No. 77630, Munich Personal RePEc Archive.

Pereira, Alfredo, Rui Pereira, and Pedro Rodrigues. 2016. "A New Carbon Tax in Portugal: A Missed Opportunity to Achieve the Triple Dividend?" *Energy Policy* 93 (June): 110–18. https://doi.org/10.1016/j.enpol.2016.03.002.

Piggott, John, and John Whalley. 2001. "VAT Base Broadening, Self Supply, and the Informal Sector." *American Economic Review* 91 (4): 1084–94.

Popp, David. 2004. "ENTICE: Endogenous Technological Change in the DICE Model of Global Warming." *Journal of Environmental Economics and Management* 48 (1): 742–68. https://doi.org/10.1016/J.JEEM.2003.09.002.

Popp, David, and Richard Newell. 2012. "Where Does Energy R&D Come from? Examining Crowding out from Energy R&D." *Energy Economics* 34 (4): 980–91. https://doi.org/10.1016/J.ENECO.2011.07.001.

Porter, Michael E, and Claas van der Linde. 1995. "Toward a New Conception of the Environment-Competitiveness Relationship." *Journal of Economic Perspectives* 9 (4): 97–118. https://doi.org/10.1257/jep.9.4.97.

Quesnay, F. 1768. "Analyse de la formule mathematique du tableau economique de la distribution des depenses annuelles d'une nation agricole." History of Economic Thought Chapters in *Physiocratie, ou Constitution naturelle du Gouvernement economique d'un royaume agricole*. McMaster University Archive for the History of Economic Thought.

Rajbhandari, Ashish, and Fan Zhang. 2018. "Does Energy Efficiency Promote Economic Growth? Evidence from a Multicountry and Multisectoral Panel Dataset." *Energy Economics* 69 (January): 128–39. https://doi.org/10.1016/j.eneco.2017.11.007.

Ramanathan, Ramakrishnan, Qile He, Andrew Black, Abby Ghobadian, and David Gallear. 2017. "Environmental Regulations, Innovation and Firm Performance: A Revisit of the Porter Hypothesis." *Journal of Cleaner Production* 155 (Part 2): 79–92. https://doi.org/10.1016/j.jclepro.2016.08.116.

Republic of South Africa. 2017. "Release of Carbon Tax Bill for Introduction in Parliament and Public Comment." Media Statement, National Treasury, December 14.

Ricardo, David. 1821. *On the Principles of Political Economy and Taxation*. Volume 1 of *The Works and Correspondence of David Ricardo*. Liberty Fund. https://doi.org/10.2307/2593726.

Rienstra, Sytze A., Piet Rietveld, and Erik T. Verhoef. 1999. "The Social Support for Policy Measures in Passenger Transport." *Transportation Research Part D: Transport and Environment* 4 (3): 181–200. https://doi.org/10.1016/S1361-9209(99)00005-X.

Rubashkina, Yana, Marzio Galeotti, and Elena Verdolini. 2015. "Environmental Regulation and Competitiveness: Empirical Evidence on the Porter Hypothesis from European Manufacturing Sectors." *Energy Policy* 83 (August): 288–300. https://doi.org/10.1016/j.enpol.2015.02.014.

Schneider, Kerstin. 1997. "Involuntary Unemployment and Environmental Policy: The Double Dividend Hypothesis." *The Scandinavian Journal of Economics* 99 (1): 45–59. http://onlinelibrary.wiley.com/doi/10.1111/1467-9442.00046/full.

Schöb, Ronnie. 2003. "The Double Dividend Hypothesis of Environmental Taxes: A Survey." FEEM Working Paper No. 60.2003, Fondazione Eni Enrico Mattei, Milan. https://papers.ssrn.com/sol3/papers.cfm?abstract_id=413866.

Schuitema, Geertje, and Linda Steg. 2008. "The Role of Revenue Use in the Acceptability of Transport Pricing Policies." *Transportation Research Part F: Traffic Psychology and Behaviour* 11 (3):221–31. https://doi.org/10.1016/j.trf.2007.11.003.

Schuitema, Geertje, Linda Steg, and J. Rothengatter. 2010. "The Acceptability, Personal Outcome Expectations, and Expected Effects of Transport Pricing Policies." *Journal of Environmental Psychology* 30 (4): 587–93. https://doi.org/10.1016/j.jenvp.2010.05.002.

Shafir, Eldar. 2017. "Decisions in Poverty Contexts." *Current Opinion in Psychology* 18 (December): 131–36. https://doi.org/10.1016/j.copsyc.2017.08.026.

Siegmeier, Jan, Linus Mattauch, and Ottmar Edenhofer. 2018. "Capital Beats Coal: How Collecting the Climate Rent Increases Aggregate Investment." *Journal of Environmental Economics and Management* 88 (March): 366–78. https://doi.org/10.1016/J.JEEM.2017.12.006.

Sorrell, Steve. 2009. "Jevons' Paradox Revisited: The Evidence for Backfire from Improved Energy Efficiency." *Energy Policy* 37 (4): 1456–69. https://doi.org/10.1016/j.enpol.2008.12.003.

Stavins, Robert. 1996. "Correlated Uncertainty and Policy Instrument Choice." *Journal of Environmental Economics and Management* 30 (2): 218–32.

Sterner, Thomas. 2012. "Distributional Effects of Taxing Transport Fuel." *Energy Policy* 41 (February): 75–83. https://doi.org/10.1016/j.enpol.2010.03.012.

Stigler, G. J. 1971. "The Theory of Economic Regulation." *The Bell Journal of Economics and Management Science* 2 (1): 3–21.

Stolper, Samuel. 2016. "Who Bears the Burden of Energy Taxes? The Critical Role of Pass-Through." Working Paper, Cambridge, MA. https://scholar.harvard.edu/sstolper/publications/who-bears-burden-energy-taxes-critical-role-pass-through.

Tideman, N. 1994. "Land and Taxation." https://scholar.google.com/scholar?hl=en&as_sdt=0%2C33&q=Land+and+taxation+-+Nicolaus+Tideman&btnG=.

Tomomi, Tanaka; Colin, Camerer; Quang, Nguyen. 2010. "Linking Experimental and Household Survey Data from Vietnam." *The American Economic Review* 100 (1): 557–71.

Trebilcock, M. 2014. *Dealing with Losers: the Political Economy of Policy Transitions.* Oxford University Press.

Vivid Economics. 2013. "Energy Efficiency and Economic Growth." Report Prepared for The Climate Institute, June.

Vogt-Schilb, A., and S. Hallegatte. 2017. *Climate Policies and NDCs: Reconciling the Needed Ambition with the Political Economy.* IDB Working Paper Series 818, International Development Bank, Washington, DC. https://publications.iadb.org/handle/11319/8319.

Wang, Yan, and Neng Shen. 2016. "Environmental Regulation and Environmental Productivity: The Case of China." *Renewable and Sustainable Energy Reviews* 62 (September): 758–66. https://doi.org/10.1016/j.rser.2016.05.048.

Weitzman, Martin. 1974. "Prices vs. Quantities." *The Review of Economic Studies* 41 (4): 477–91. http://www.jstor.org/stable/2296698.

World Bank and OECD (Organisation for Economic Co-operation and Development). 2015. "The FASTER Principles for Successful Carbon Pricing : An Approach Based on Initial Experience." World Bank, Washington, DC. http://documents.worldbank.org/curated/en/2015/09/25060584/faster-principles-successful-carbon-pricing-approach-based-initial-experience.

World Bank Group. 2017. *The High Toll of Traffic Injuries: Unacceptable and Preventable.* Washington, DC: World Bank Group. https://openknowledge.worldbank.org/bitstream/handle/10986/29129/HighTollofTrafficInjuries.pdf?sequence=5&isAllowed=y.

Xie, Rong hui, Yi jun Yuan, and Jing jing Huang. 2017. "Different Types of Environmental Regulations and Heterogeneous Influence on 'Green' Productivity: Evidence from China." *Ecological Economics* 132 (February): 104–12. https://doi.org/10.1016/j.ecolecon.2016.10.019.

Appendix B Staying Competitive: Productivity Effects of Environmental Taxes

CARBON PRICING MECHANISMS IN LOW- AND MIDDLE-INCOME COUNTRIES

TABLE B.1 **Carbon pricing mechanisms, select countries**

TYPE	COUNTRY	STATUS	YEAR	DESCRIPTION	GHGS COVERED	SECTORAL / FUEL COVERAGE	COMPETITIVENESS CONSIDERATIONS OR EXEMPTIONS	PRICE LEVEL
Carbon tax	Argentina	Under consideration		On October 31, 2017, the Argentina Ministry of Finance announced the introduction of a carbon tax as part of a comprehensive tax reform proposal.		If legislated, the carbon tax would apply to liquid fossil fuels from 2018 and expand to other fossil fuels by 2020.	To offset the fuel price increase by the carbon tax, the tax on liquid fossil fuels would be adjusted at the introduction.	n.a.
	Colombia	Implemented	2017	Carbon tax adopted as part of a structural tax reform.	24%	GHG emissions from all sectors with some minor exemptions; all liquid and gaseous fossil fuels used for combustion.	- Exemptions apply to natural gas consumers outside the petrochemical and refinery sectors. - Users certified to be carbon neutral are exempted (permit the use of offsets for projects within Colombia). - Income tax not due over costs incurred as a result of the carbon tax.	Col$15,000/$tCO_2e$ (US$5/$tCO_2e$). Tax recalculated annually to take inflation into account.
	Mexico	Implemented	2014	Excise tax on the additional CO_2 emission content compared to natural gas.	46%	CO_2 emissions from all sectors; all fossil fuels except natural gas.	Tax capped at 3% of the fuel sales price.	Upper: Mex$52/ tCO_2e (US$3/tCO_2e) Lower: Mex$6/ tCO_2e (US$0.36/ tCO_2e)
	South Africa	Scheduled		The implementation of the carbon tax has been delayed several times since 2015. A revised draft bill was submitted for public comment in December 2017. Implementation date to be announced in mid-2018 or in 2019 budget.	80%	GHG emissions from the industry, power, buildings, and transport sectors irrespective of the fossil fuel used, with partial exemptions for all these sectors	Tax-free thresholds ranging from 60 to 95% of emissions depending on various factors (such as trade exposure, emission performance, offset use) planned in the draft bill for many sectors.	R 120/tCO_2e (US$10/$tCO_2e$). To be adjusted in line with inflation + 2% each year until 2022.

(continued)

TABLE B.1, *continued*

TYPE	COUNTRY	STATUS	YEAR	DESCRIPTION	GHGS COVERED	SECTORAL / FUEL COVERAGE	COMPETITIVENESS CONSIDERATIONS OR EXEMPTIONS	PRICE LEVEL
ETS	Kazakhstan	Implemented / Suspended	2013	Scheme started in 2014 after a pilot covering emissions of large emitters in 2013. It was suspended for two years starting from January 1, 2016, to address imbalances in the system and reflect changes to the economy since ETS rules were designed.	50%	CO_2 emissions from the industry and power sectors.	All operators receive their allowances (largely) for free. Also, small emitters are exempt from the ETS.	n.a.
	Mexico	Under consideration		An ETS simulation was launched in 2016, with 80 companies from the transport, power, and industry sectors participating on a voluntary basis. An actual ETS pilot is expected for 2018.	n.a.	n.a.	n.a.	n.a.
	Colombia	Under consideration		Colombia is considering an ETS and has been part of dialogues in 2016 in the context of the Pacific Alliance to explore regional carbon pricing.	n.a.	n.a.	n.a.	n.a.
	Turkey	Under consideration		Turkey introduced a mandatory MRV system for many large industrial emitters in 2016 and is conducting several studies to evaluate its carbon pricing options. The studies are expected to be completed by June 2018.	n.a.	n.a.	n.a.	n.a.
	Thailand	Under consideration		Voluntary ETS launched at the end of 2014, with Phase 1 (2015–17) testing MRV system and Phase 2 (2018–20) testing the registry and allocation systems. Phase 2 will be an ETS simulation covering various industrial sectors.	n.a.	n.a.	n.a.	n.a.
	China	Scheduled		Several subnational ETS schemes have been piloted since 2013. A national ETS was approved in December 2017 and will be rolled out progressively over 2018–20.	34–39% initially	Power generation initially, later expended to other GHG-intensive industries	n.a.	n.a.

Sources: World Bank Carbon Pricing Dashboard at http://carbonpricingdashboard.worldbank.org (accessed April 16, 2018); PWC 2018; Timperley 2018.
Note: N.a. = not applicable; ETS = emissions trading system; GHG = greenhouse gas; MRV = measurement, reporting, and verification; tCO_2e = tonnes of carbon dioxide equivalent. Monetary units are the Colombian peso (Col$), the Mexican peso (Mex$), and the South African rand (R).

CROSS-COUNTRY ANALYSIS METHODOLOGY AND DATA

In this analysis, firm-level World Bank Enterprise Survey (WBES) data from various countries and over time are matched with time-varying national energy price data. The following benchmark specification, adapted from Sadath and Acharya (2015), is used:

$$Y_{it} = \pi_i + \alpha EP_{cs,t} + \beta EI_{it} + \gamma EI_{it} * EP_{cs,t} + \eta_{st} + \varepsilon_{it} \quad \text{(B.1)}$$

where Y represents a set of firm performance measures for firm i and year t; π_i is the firm fixed effect; $EP_{cs,t}$ are energy prices (two options by available data: in country c or sector s and year t); EI is firm-level energy intensity, measured as the share of energy expenditure over total output; and η_{st} are sector/year additional fixed effects that capture further heterogeneity. The interpretation of the interaction term is as follows: if γ is negative, a rise (decrease) in energy prices has a stronger negative (positive) effect on performance for more energy-intensive firms.

Endogeneity may be an issue to estimate specification (B.1), as unobserved firm-level shocks could be correlated both to energy intensity and firm performances (for example, a new manager). That possibility would generate biased estimates of our parameters of interest. Part of the endogeneity of energy intensity is addressed by including firm fixed effect that accounts for systematic differences in managerial ability, technology, and so on. As a result, the only countries and firms considered are those for which there are repeated observations over time in the WBES data. To the extent that there may be time-varying unobservables correlated with both energy intensity and Y variables, potential endogeneity is further addressed by exploiting a standard instrumental variable (IV) approach, instrumenting the firm-level energy intensity variable with the average sector-country energy intensity. A robustness check is also performed by using sectoral energy prices, and confirms the validity of the results (not shown here but available from the authors upon request). To account for specific country/sector shocks, country-, year-, and firm-specific dummies are also included.

The data to compute energy prices come from Sato et al. (2015), who provide both sector- and country-level data. Although sector-level data are preferable conceptually, their availability is more restricted: country coverage using the sector dataset for energy prices is limited to eight (mainly Eastern European) countries with observations in at least two years, whereas using national prices allows for the inclusion of twice as many countries (table B.2).[1] Table B3 presents

TABLE B.2 Country coverage with national-level energy prices

COUNTRY	WORLD BANK ENTERPRISE SURVEY YEAR (PANEL DATA)			
Brazil	2003	2009		
Czech Republic	2002	2005	2009	2013
Hungary	2002	2005	2009	2013
Kazakhstan	2002	2005	2009	
Mexico	2006	2010		
Poland	2002	2005	2009	2013
Romania	2002	2005	2009	
Russian Federation	2002	2005	2009	
Slovak Republic	2002	2005	2009	2013
Slovenia	2002	2005	2009	2013
Turkey	2005	2008	2013	

TABLE B.3 **Energy prices and firms' performance across countries (IV estimation), country-sector energy prices**

	(1)	(2)	(3)	(4)	(5)
	LOG (TOT EMP)	LOG (SALES/EMP)	LOG (VA/EMP)	RETURN ON SALES	EXPORT SHARE
Log (EP)	−0.131	1.708***	3.425	0.307**	0.113
	(0.355)	(0.591)	(3.903)	(0.147)	(0.0782)
Log (EP) x log (EI)	0.351	−25.93**	−31.22	−4.226	−0.891
	(6.782)	(11.21)	(62.82)	(2.933)	(1.842)
F test of excluded instruments	16.15	15.48	1.737	14.65	16.15
N	1016	869	166	774	1012
Effect at 10th percentile of EI	−0.129	1.513	2.944	0.275	0.107
Effect at 25th percentile of EI	−0.125	1.277	2.512	0.238	0.0983
Effect at 50th percentile of EI	−0.119	0.800	2.047	0.161	0.0816
Effect at 75th percentile of EI	−0.109	0.0843	1.308	0.0407	0.0576
Effect at 90th percentile of EI	−0.0967	−0.855	0.660	−0.109	0.0255

Note: Instrumental variable (IV)-fixed effect estimator. Robust standard errors in parenthesis. EI = energy intensity; EP = energy prices; N = number of firms; VA = value added; TOT EMP = total employment; SALES/EMP = sales per employee. * p<0.1, ** p<0.05, *** p<0.01. Additional controls: country-specific linear trends, year-specific size class dummies, year-specific dummy for foreign-owned firms.

the effect of energy prices on firms' performance using country-sector energy prices as the main regressor.

INDONESIA CASE STUDY METHODOLOGY

The main specification is the following:

$$Y_{ft} = \beta_0 + \beta_1 P_{ft}^{Elec} + \beta_2 P_{ft}^{Fuel} + D_{st} + \text{trend}_r + u_f + \varepsilon_{ft} \qquad \text{(B.2)}$$

where each plant is indexed by f. The dependent variable Y_{ft} is typically a performance indicator such as total factor productivity (TFP), value added per worker, and revenues. In some specifications, other plant-specific variables are used that define the plant's production function (for example, total employment, value of capital stock, capital purchases, sales), in order to investigate the channels through which energy prices affect performance. TFP is used as the main performance indicator.

The variable P_{ft}^{Elec} and P_{ft}^{Fuel} represent electricity and fuel prices, based on the implicit energy price paid by each plant. Fuels include gasoline, diesel, and lubricants, which together account for most fossil fuels used by the firms. The variable D_{st} represents a set of sector-year dummies; regional trends are included in all specifications; u_f is the plant fixed effect.

Because plant-level prices are likely to be endogenous to performance, prices are instrumented with the provincial exogenous variation in energy prices. The instrument captures the variation in energy prices that are purely due to location characteristics, which reflect differences in the distribution network across the archipelagoes. The geographical variation in energy prices is obtained by regressing implicit prices on province-year dummies, controlling for plants' characteristics. As an example, figure B.1 shows the estimated percentage departure of electricity prices from the national average in the provinces of Java. The figure

FIGURE B.1

Average electricity prices' deviation from national average across Java

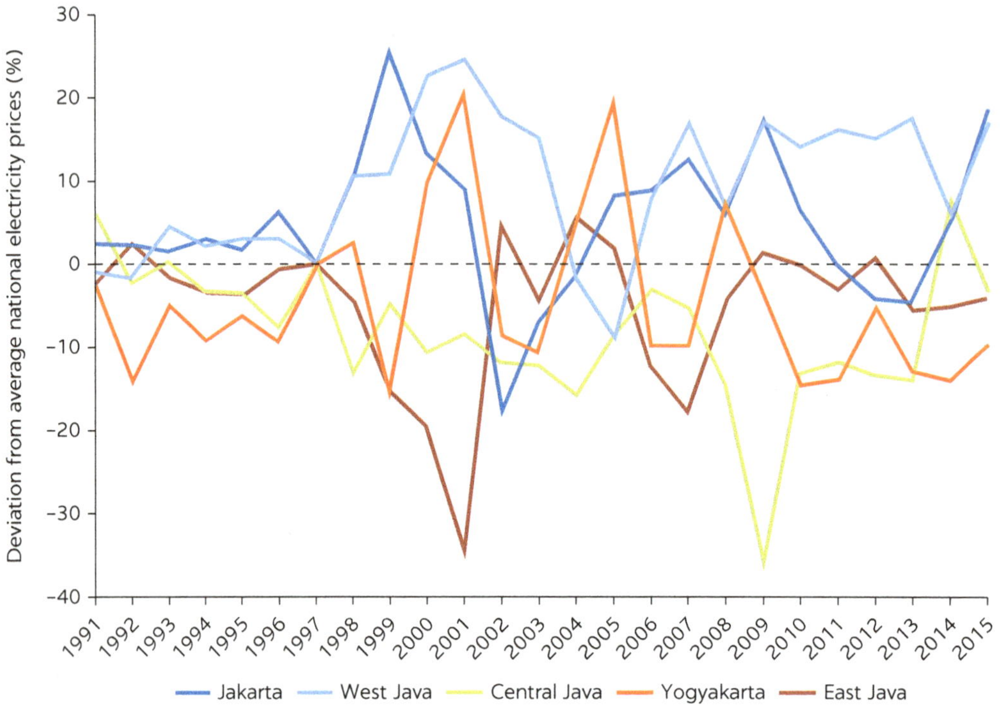

shows that significant and persistent differences exist even within the same island, which supports this strategy. Results are robust to an alternative measure of provincial variation, a simple province-average of the prices paid by the firms.

MEXICO CASE STUDY METHODOLOGY

The main specification is the following:

$$y_{it} = \beta_0 + \beta_1 P_{it} + \beta_2 EI_{it} + \beta_3 P_{it} * EI_{it} + \alpha_i + \gamma_t + u_{it} \quad \text{(B.3)}$$

where y_{it} represents *performance variables* $\left(\frac{VA}{worker}, \textit{Net profits, TFP index}\right)$; P_{it} is the energy price for firm i and time t; EI_{it} is energy intensity measured as electricity expenditure over total inputs; α_i represents firm fixed effects; and γ_t represents time effects.

For the electricity tariff calculation, the tariff schemes were obtained from Mexico's Federal Electricity Commission (*Comisión Federal de Electricidad* [CFE]), which yielded 32 tariffs with regional and seasonal differences. Four of these tariffs were selected: they apply to medium and large companies in the manufacturing sector, which depend on consumption levels, duration, and costs (fixed and variable). Using the information from CFE on sales and consumption, the analysis defined bill ranges at the municipal level to merge with the corresponding tariff.

In the case of other fuels, four specific fuels were selected that account for more than 85 percent of consumption of other fuels in the manufacturing

FIGURE B.2

Mexico: Average electricity prices, 2009–16

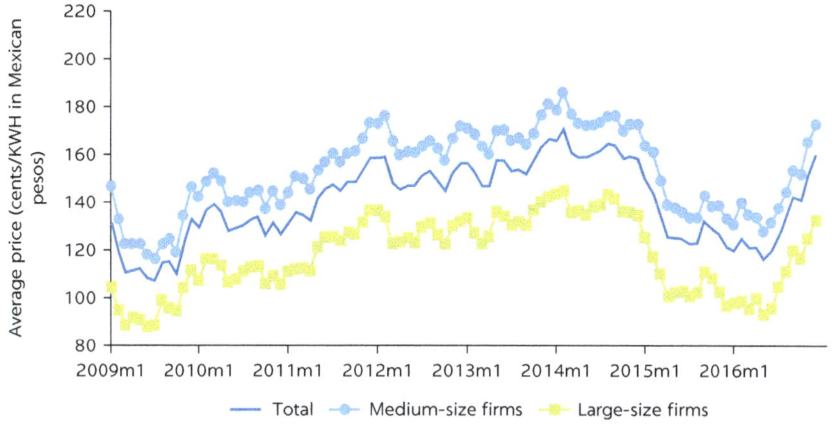

Source: Based on data from Ministry of Energy, Mexico, https://datos.gob.mx/busca/dataset/precios-medios-de-energia-electrica-por-tipo-de-tarifa.
Note: kWh = kilowatt-hours; m1 = January.

FIGURE B.3

Mexico: Energy intensity of electricity and fuels in 2015

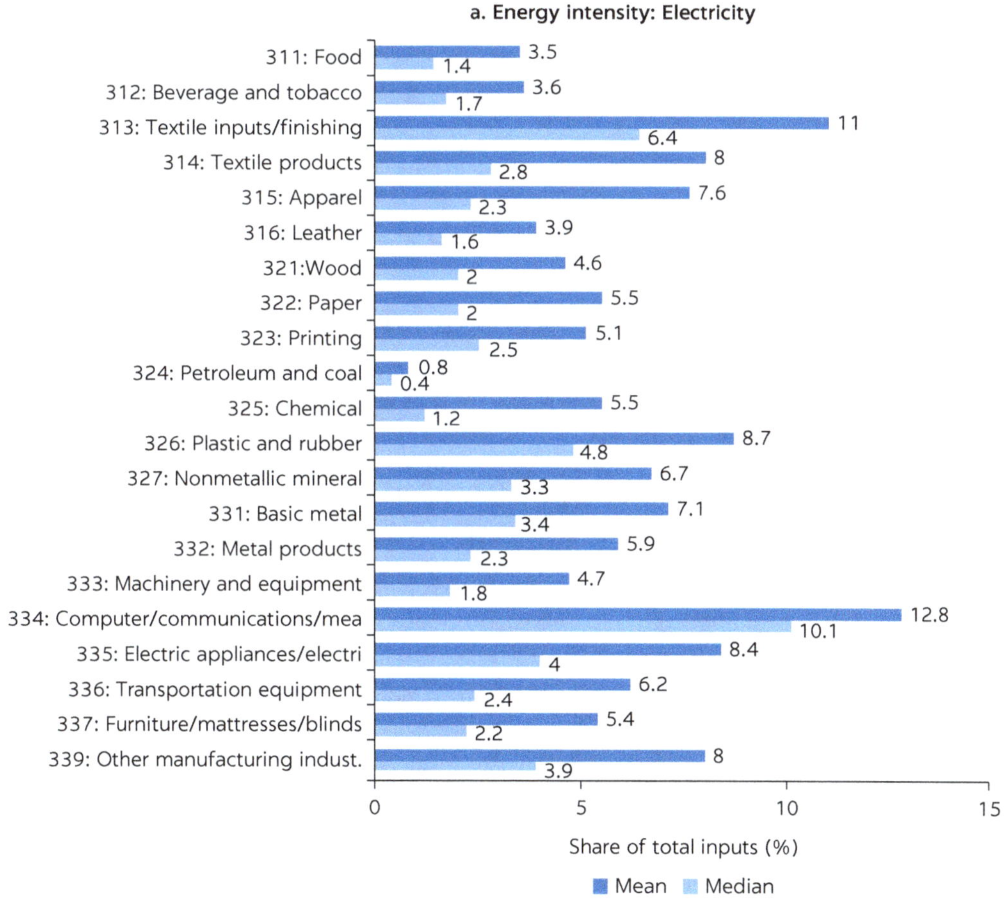

continued

FIGURE B.3, *Continued*

b. Energy intensity: Fuels

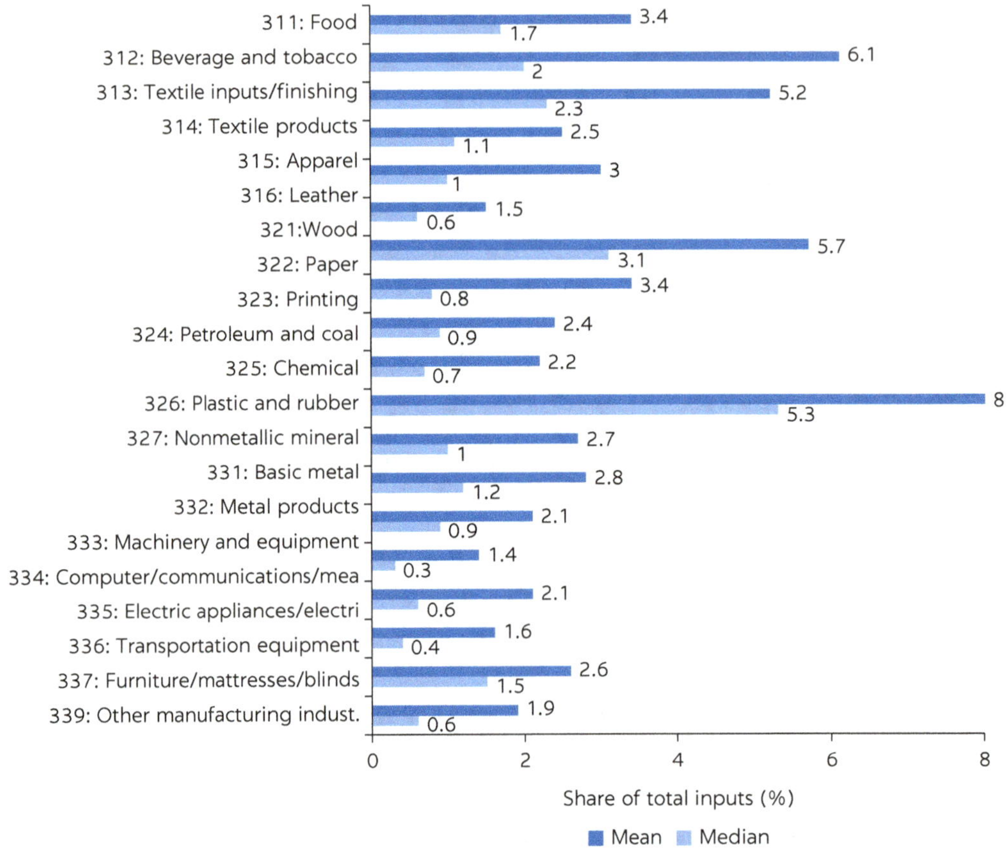

Source: Based on data from Instituto Nacional de Estadistica y Geografia's Encuesta Mensual de la Industria Manufacturera, 2009–15.
Note: Dark blue lines represent the arithmetic average, and light blue lines represent the median; Numbers on y axis are North American Industry Classification System (NAICS) 3-digit codes.

industry: coal, petroleum coke, diesel, and natural gas. Consumption shares by North American Industry Classification System (NAICS) sector for each type of fuel were obtained from the Ministry of Energy. Coal and petroleum coke prices were estimated with data on monthly production and value of production, and average monthly price data were obtained for fuels at the national level and for natural gas at the regional level. For diesel, nationwide prices through the period were obtained. Figure B2 reports the average prices of electricity during 2008–16. Figure B3 reports the energy intensity of different sectors of the economy in 2015.

The price for each energy input f is calculated as $P^f_{rkt} = \sum_{m=1}^{12}\sum_{r} P^{zm}_{rt} \left(E^z_{kt}/E_{kt}\right)\left(Y^m_i/Y_i\right)$, where P^{zm}_{rt} is the regional price of fuel z in month m at time t, which is weighted by the share of z in total fuels consumption (in petajouls or other energy units) for sector k and by the plant-specific share of output in month m in total output of the plant.

Due to the concern of endogeneity on the firm-level prices, three types of instruments were constructed for the composite energy price index: (i) average index within sector, tariff, and state; (ii) average index within tariff and state but excluding own sector; and (iii) average index within tariff and sector, but excluding own state. Each composite index is weighted by current monthly production variation; constant initial production variation in the first year; and last year production variation. The IV for energy intensity is constructed as the average index within sector at 6-digits and state, whereas for the interaction, the two individual instruments are interacted.

NOTE

1. Because of the limited availability of sector-country energy prices, the sample is reduced to the following countries: Croatia, Czech Republic, Hungary, Poland, Romania, Slovak Republic, and Slovenia.

REFERENCES

PWC (PriceWaterhouseCoopers). 2018. "Revised Carbon Tax Bill." Tax Alert, National Tax Technical, PWC, January 19. https://www.pwc.co.za/en/assets/pdf/carbon-tax-bill-alert.pdf.

Sadath, Anver C., and Rajesh H. Acharya. 2015. "Effects of Energy Price Rise on Investment: Firm Level Evidence from Indian Manufacturing Sector." *Energy Economics* 49 (May): 516–522.

Sato, Misato, Gregor Singer, Damien Dussaux, and Stefania Lovo. 2015. "International and Sectoral Variation in Energy Prices 1995-2011: How Does it Relate to Emissions Policy Stringency?" Working Paper No. 187, Grantham Research Institute on Climate Change and the Environment, London.

Timperley, Jocelyn. 2018. "Q&A: How Will China's New Carbon Trading Scheme Work?" *Carbon Brief*, January 29. https://www.carbonbrief.org/qa-how-will-chinas-new-carbon-trading-scheme-work.

Resilience: Fiscal
Climate Adaptation

MODEL DESCRIPTION

The model is a multicountry overlapping generations (OLG) economy, which includes long-term demographic and human capital projections to evaluate output growth. In the current application, we calibrate the model to represent two areas: the rest of the world and a single small open economy. The economy is small enough not to alter the world prices, interest rates, and incomes. In both the small economy and the rest of the world, the core sectors are households, firms, and government; and there are overlapping households with limited lifetime duration, each of them split into three education levels. To avoid computational complexity, we neglect endogenous human capital formation and build an exogenous measure of labor productivity based on education levels. We calculate the share of population with specific education level using data provided by Barro and Lee (2015). Households set the life-cycle saving decision without a voluntary bequest motive. The demographic setup of the model is based on the United Nations population projections 2016–2100; therefore, demography is taken as exogenous. All variables in the model are defined in real terms.

In the baseline scenario focused on gradual global warming, the government finances public investment for adaptation by increasing the government deficit. Alternatively, the government can finance the investment in adaptation by raising taxes or reducing transfers and other expenditures. In all cases, the goal is to increase the resilience of capital stock. In addition, the government can impose precautionary taxes to reduce public debt in the event of extreme events. In the latter case, the country can also count on the help of external grants. We assume that the government internalizes the likelihood of being cut off from the capital market in the event of an unexpected increase in capital demand from the domestic economy. In fact, the increase in debt level due to deterioration in fiscal revenue would trigger an inability to tap the capital market that could affect the ability of firms to finance the capital stock reconstruction. Therefore, to avoid this event, we assume that the government could anticipate such events by reducing the public debt stock and the likelihood of hitting the borrowing constraint and exacerbating the reconstruction costs.

HOUSEHOLDS

Each cohort is represented by one household that maximizes the disc… lifetime utility by choosing consumption and leisure over the life cycle fro… entry to the labor market (at earliest age 15) to death (age 101).

The households' life-cycle stream utility is given by

$$U=\sum_{t=s}^{s+T} q_{t-s} \frac{u[c_{t-s},(e_t-l_{t-s})]^{1-1/\xi}}{1-\frac{1}{\xi}} \frac{1}{(1+\rho)^{t-s}} \tag{C.1}$$

where T is longevity (101 years for all agents), ρ denotes the rate of time preference that is cohort invariant, and ξ defines the intertemporal elasticity of substitution. The variable q_{t-s} is the survival rate at age $t-s$, c denotes consumption goods, and l is the individual labor supply. Labor supply l is measured in efficiency units relative to the time endowment e. Households maximize utility in equation (C.1) with respect to consumption and leisure subject to the dynamic budget constraint:

$$\begin{aligned} a_{t+1-s} = & \frac{1}{q_{t-s}}(1+r_t)a_{t-s}+(1-\tau_{l,t})w_{t-s}h_{t-s}l_{t-s}+ \\ & -(1+\tau_{c,t})c_{t-s}-if_{t-s}+T_{t-s}, \end{aligned} \tag{C.2}$$

where a_{t-s} denotes the wealth at time t of the cohort born in the period s; r_t, $w_{t-s}h_{t-s}l_{t-s}$, T_{t-s} are respectively the interest rate, the post-tax labor income, and the social transfers at time t for the cohort aged $t-s$. The variables $\tau_{l,t}$ and $\tau_{c,t}$ respectively denote the exogenous tax contribution rate on labor and consumption, and if_t is a lump sum tax imposed by the government to reduce public debt as a precaution in expectation of extreme events.

The optimal labor/leisure choice gives the following first order condition:

$$\frac{u_{l,t-s}}{u_{c,t-s}}=\frac{(1-\tau_{l,t})}{(1+\tau_{c,t})}\omega_t h_t \tag{C.3}$$

The Euler equation for the intertemporal consumption choice is

$$\frac{u_{c,t+1-s}}{u_{c,t-s}}=\frac{q_{t-s}}{(1+\rho)(1-r_{t+1})}\frac{1+\tau_{c,t-s}}{(1+\tau_{c,t+1-s})} \tag{C.4}$$

where u_c and u_l are marginal utility from consumption and leisure.

Finally, we show the main aggregation for labor input (C.5), wealth (C.6), lump sum taxation (C.7), and public education expenditure (C.8).

$$L_t=\sum_{i\in I}\sum_{s=s_0,i}^{T_r} h_{t-s,i}l_{t-s,i}P_{t-s,i}, \tag{C.5}$$

$$A_t=\sum_{i\in I}\sum_{s=s_0}^{T} a_{t-s,i}P_{t-s,i}, \tag{C.6}$$

$$If_t=\sum_{i\in I}\sum_{s=s_0}^{T} if_{t-s,1}P_{t-s,i}, \tag{C.7}$$

$$SC_t = \sum_{i\in I}\sum_{s=s_0}^{T} sc_{t-s,i}P_{t-s,i}, \tag{C.8}$$

where $s_{0,i}$ is the year in which the cohort aged $t-s$ with education level i becomes employed; $P_{t-s,i}$ is the population aged $t-s$ in year t; T_r denotes the contribution years required in year t to obtain a pension benefit. The variable $h_{t-s,i}$ denotes the human capital for education level *I*. Aggregate and per capita education spending are, respectively, *SC* and *sc*. Equation (C.7) is used to get the per capita cohort invariant taxation level if_{t-s}.

FIRMS

The production sector is characterized by a representative firm that uses a Cobb–Douglas technology with increasing returns to scale, combining the capital stock K_t with the effective labor input L_t:

$$Y_t = TFP_t K_t^{\beta} L_t^{1-\beta} \tag{C.9}$$

where β is the capital share and TFP_t the endogenous total factor productivity.

Firm's profits are defined as

$$\pi_t = Y_t - (r_t + \tau_{k,t} + \delta_t)K_t - w_t L_t \tag{C.10}$$

where δ_t denotes the depreciation rate, which is endogenously affected by both gradual global warming and extreme events). The first order conditions from profit maximization give the following wage and interest rates:

$$r_t = TFP_t \beta f_K' - \tau_{k,t} - \delta_t \tag{C.11}$$

$$w_t = TFP_t(1-\beta)f_L', \tag{C.12}$$

where f_K' and f_L' are the marginal productivity of capital and labor, respectively. The economy is price taker—that is, $r_t = r_{rw,t}$—where *rw* denotes the rest of the world. This implies that equation (C.11) is used to determine the capital stock demand. Therefore, firms form their demand functions for capital and labor alike in the constant returns to scale framework, whereas TFP_t increases because of both capital/labor ratio and human capital per worker externalities, as follows:

$$TFP_t = \left(\frac{K_t}{N_t}\right)^g H_t^z, \tag{C.13}$$

where *g* and *z* denote the contribution of the production factors to TFP_t. In particular, *g* measures the capital-per-worker contribution in technology creation, and *z* is the contribution of human capital.

GOVERNMENT

The public sector consists of only three programs, namely social security, education, and adaptation to climate change. The government raises funds through public debt and taxes paid by households (at the exogenous labor income tax rate τ_l, VAT rate τ_c) and firms (at the capital tax rate).

In order to manage the climate change adaptation strategy, the government uses two instruments: (i) public investment I^{cc} to reduce capital value erosion due to climate change and (ii) lump sum tax on households' income If_t in order to raise funds that will be used specifically to reduce public debt in the event of extreme climate change. The government uses revenues to finance social transfers T_t to an audience of beneficiaries ζ of people aged 65+, education, and public investment for adaptation.

The government issues new debt in order to finance the deficit:

$$\Delta B_t = r_t B_t - \tau_{l,t} w_t L_t - \tau_{c,t} c_t - \tau_{k,t} K_t - \Delta RF_t + r_t RF_t + d_t + \zeta_t T_t + I_t^{cc} + SC_t. \quad \text{(C.14)}$$

where $r_t B_t$ denotes the interest repayment on public debt and $\Delta B_t = B_t - B_{t-1}$ denotes public debt change. The variables $\tau_{l,t} w_t L_t$, $\tau_{c,t} C_t$, and $\tau_{k,t} K_t$ denote revenues from labor, consumption, and capital, respectively. RF_t is the amount of revenue from households' income taxation used to build up a reserve fund to reduce public debt. $\zeta_t T_t$ and SC_t indicate respectively the expenditure for social transfers and the public spending on education. I_t^{cc} denotes the effective public investment to adapt to climate change, and d_t denotes the additional resources from grants needed to adapt to an extreme event. Because these resources are assumed to be earmarked to adaptation spending, they reduce the financing needs of the government and do not enter into households' and firms' budget constraints.

The financial constraint on the international market for the home country is given by

$$F_t < \overline{F}_t, \quad \text{(C.15)}$$

where $\overline{F}$ denotes a multiple of the net foreign asset (NFA) of the country in the gradual global warming case, without adaptation. The NFA position of the country affected by climate change is given by

$$F_t = A_t - K_t - B_t \quad \text{(C.16)}$$

We assume that $\overline{F}$ is 30 percent of gross domestic product (GDP), that is, 1.5 times the NFA in the baseline.

In order to manage future extreme events and to avoid borrowing constraint occurrence, the government chooses the optimal level of If_t by minimizing the following disutility function:

$$\min_{d_t, If_t, RF_{t+1}, B_{t+1}} -U = \sum_i \Lambda_{t+i} \left[\frac{If_{t+1}^{1+\sigma_b}}{1+\sigma_b} - \frac{d_{t+1}^{1-\sigma_d}}{1-\sigma_d} \right], \quad \text{(C.17)}$$

where grant funds d_t reduce the disutility associated with the climate event with the elasticity σ_d. The government discounts the future taking into account the average discount rate $\Lambda t = \frac{q_{t-s}}{1+\rho} \lambda_{t-s}$, where s = 50 years old. The disutility minimization is subject to the constraint (C.14) and the following:

$$RF_{t+1} = (1+r_{f,t})RF_t + If_t \quad \text{(C.18)}$$

$$F_t = A_t - K_t - B_t \quad \text{(C.19)}$$

$$F_t \geq \overline{F}_t \tag{C.20}$$

$$d_t \leq \overline{d_t} \tag{C.21}$$

where RF_t is the debt reduction amount and F_t is the NFA position of the small open economy. The reserve fund RF_t is collected through lump sum taxation. It is a liquid fund kept in the form of a numeraire good. It is assumed to be deposited abroad and to receive an interest rate equal to the prevailing global risk-free rate, net of a spread. The accumulated reserve fund RF is remunerated by an interest rate rf_t, which differs from the interest rate r_t prevailing on the financial markets by a spread depending on the deviation from the target level of the reserve fund $\frac{\overline{RF_t}}{Y_t}$ as follows:

$$r_{f,t} = r_t + i\left[\exp\left(\frac{RF_t}{Y_t} - \frac{\overline{RF_t}}{Y_t}\right) - 1\right] \tag{C.22}$$

$F_t \geq \overline{F_t}$ denotes an occasionally binding constraint on the international financial markets. This implies that the country cannot get into foreign debt beyond the threshold $\overline{F_t}$. Similarly, $d_t \leq \overline{d_t}$ denotes the constraint on the availability of external grants (limited budget). $\overline{d_t}$ is set to be equal to a certain percentage of GDP, $\overline{d_t} = \alpha idY_t$. This allows us to get the intertemporal optimal policy for taxation and donors:

$$If_t^{\sigma_b} = E_t \frac{1}{(1+r_{t+1})}\left[If_{t+1}^{\sigma_b}(1+r_{f,t+1}) + \theta_{1,t+1} - \theta_{2,t+1}\right] \tag{C.23}$$

$$d_t = \left[\theta_{1,t} + \theta_{2,t}\right]^{\frac{1}{\sigma_d}} \tag{C.24}$$

where $\vartheta_{1,t}$ and $\vartheta_{2,t}$ are the Lagrange multipliers associated with the international and grant constraints, respectively. Equation (C.23) shows the optimal policy given the expected value of taxation If_t. This depends intertemporally on the long-run target If_T that is fixed to the arbitrary target level of GDP. Solving equation (C.23) recursively gives the discounted tax stream

$$If_t = E_t\left[If_T \prod_{j=1}^{T} \frac{1+r_{f,t+1}}{1+r_{t+1}} + \sum_{k=0}^{T} \prod_{j=0}^{k} \left(\frac{1+r_{f,t+k}}{1+r_{t+k}}\right)^j \left(\frac{\theta_{1,t+k+1} - \theta_{2,t+k+1}}{1+r_{t+k+1}}\right)^{\frac{1}{\sigma_b}}\right] \tag{C.25}$$

Equation (C.24) describes the intertemporal optimal policy for grants demand. Equation (C.25) describes the optimal reserve fund policy. Precautionary savings depend on the expected present value of the net benefit of receiving external grants when the country is rationed on the credit market. When the marginal utility of grants exceeds the disutility of being rationed, the moral hazard mechanism reduces the incentive to accumulate saving funds. We use equation (C.24) as an intertemporal transmission channel in order to anticipate signal of borrowing constraint through Lagrange multipliers ϑ_1 and ϑ_2 in equation (C.23).

Whenever the constraint in equation (C.15) is binding—that is, the country cannot get all the needed financial resources (F_t)—grants intervene.

In particular, when (C.15) is binding, from equation (C.16) we get a binding level for the public debt $\overline{B}_t$; and from equation (C.14) we get the level d_t:

$$d_t \begin{cases} B_t - \overline{B_t} \text{ and } \theta_{1,t} = d_t^{-\sigma_d}, \theta_{2,t} = 0, \text{if } F_t < \overline{F_t} \text{ and } d_t < \overline{d_t} \\ \overline{d_t}, \text{and } \theta_{1,t} = \left(B_t - \overline{B_t}\right)^{-\sigma_d}, \theta_{2,t} = \overline{d_t}^{-\sigma_d}, \text{if } F_t < \overline{F_t} \text{ and } d_t > \overline{d_t} \\ 0 \text{ otherwise.} \end{cases} \tag{C.26}$$

GRADUAL IMPACTS OF CLIMATE CHANGE

Let's assume that the small open economy faces gradual global warming trends and extreme events. The impact of these trends/events is reflected in an increase in the depreciation rate of capital that, starting from its natural value, tends to increase over time. Gradual global warming trends define our baseline. In this scenario, in order to adapt to climate change, the government can increase public investment aimed at limiting the increase in the depreciation rate due to climate change. The gradual global warming process is modeled as follows:

$$m_t = \rho_{m,t} m_{t-1} + \varepsilon_{m,t}, \quad \rho_{m,t} > 1, \quad \varepsilon_{m,t} > 0 \tag{C.27}$$

where m_t represents all climate factors related to increasing global temperature that affect the economic activity. The target level of public investment to adapt to gradual global warming trends is exogenously fixed and given by

$$\overline{I_t^{cc}}_t = \alpha_{CC} Yt, \quad \alpha_{CC} = 1\%. \tag{C.28}$$

We assume that public investment in adaptation is an irreversible good—that is, once spent the full amount of targeted investment for the improvement in physical capital resilience to climate change is never lost (forgotten). Moreover, in order to simulate physical capital adjustment costs, we assume a certain degree of persistence meaning that actual investment takes time to reach the targeted level. In fact, actual level of investment $\hat{I}^{cc}$ is gradually adjusted to the target, implying residual current investment to be $I_t^{cc} = \overline{I}_t^{cc} - \hat{I}_t^{cc}$, thus reproducing the effect of the adjustment costs given by the persistence parameter $\rho_{cc,t}$:

$$\hat{I}_t^{cc} = \rho_{cc,t} \hat{I}_{t-1}^{cc} + (1 - \rho_{cc,t}) \overline{I}_t^{cc} \tag{C.29}$$

In the presence of gradual global warming trends, the depreciation rate of capital is assumed to follow a dynamic logistic equation

$$\delta_{t+1}(m) = \delta_t(m) + a_0 \delta_t(m) \frac{\delta_t^k(m) - \delta_t(m)}{\delta_t^k(m)} \tag{C.30}$$

whose solution used in the model is

$$\delta_t = \frac{\delta_t^k \delta_0}{\delta_0 + [\delta_t^k - \delta_0 exp(-a_0 m_t)],} \tag{C.31}$$

which allows the depreciation rate δ_t to range between δ_0 and $\delta_t^k = \overline{\delta} - B_k \overline{I}^{cc}$ over the observed period. The variable δ_0 is the natural depreciation rate (initial condition), $\overline{\delta}$ depends on the extent of the climate change that we assume to be moderate (10 percent) or high (20 percent), β_k is an adaptation resilience parameter, and α_0 is the damage transmission parameter.

The investment for adaptation is financed by gradually increasing public deficit:

$$\Delta B_t = \Delta \overline{B}_t + I_t^{cc,*}, \tag{C.32}$$

where $\Delta \overline{B}_t$ is the deficit level of the baseline. To balance the budget in equation (C.14), public transfers adjust.

EXTREME EVENTS

The *extreme event* is defined as a disaster that occurs suddenly causing a sharp increase in the depreciation rate of capital against the baseline (gradual global warming). In addition to domestic resources and international market financing, the country can use grants to deal with the damage caused by these events. Extreme events are important not only for the resulting sharp decline in GDP and consumption but also for a prolonged funding limitation period. When the intensity of extreme events is enough to financially constrain the economy, the real frictions in capital stock recovery could persist. The sharper the severity the higher the probability to be financially constrained and the higher the expected costs of capital recovery. This adverse causal loop could motivate a precautionary activation of fiscal policy to prevent such a nonlinearity. Similar to gradual global warming, the extreme event evolves according to the following:

$$m_t^f = \rho_{f,t} m_t^f + \epsilon_{f,t}, \quad \rho_{f,t} < 0.4, \quad \epsilon_{f,t} > 0 \tag{C.33}$$

The introduction of this event requires a change in the depreciation rate defined in (C.31) that becomes equal to the following:

$$\delta_t^k = \overline{\delta} - \beta_k \overline{I}_t^{cc} \tag{C.34}$$

Therefore, the new depreciation rate of capital is given by

$$\delta_t^f = \delta_t + m_t^f \tag{C.35}$$

Equation (C.35) implies that, when an extreme event occurs, the depreciation rate increases even more than in the baseline and leads to a further slowdown in the capital recovery.

CALIBRATION

In table C.1, we report the main parameters of the model.

Calibration of the model parameters is based on the literature and on some targets built to match data. We set the intratemporal elasticity of substitution ε to 1 in order to avoid trends in the labor-to-consumption ratio as in Auerbach and Kotlikoff (1987), and we set the intertemporal elasticity of substitution ξ to 0.5. We assume that total time endowment *e* grows at the human capital growth rate $\dot{h}$, that is, $e_{t+1} = e_t(1+\dot{h})$ as in Börsch-Supan, Ludwig, and Winter (2006). The human capital H_t is exogenous and computed as a Törnqvist index on the basis of ONU population projections and Barro and Lee (2015) education data (see Catalano and Pezzolla 2016 for details). Only when adaptation is financed through a cut in education spending is the human capital endogenously determined as follows:

$$H_t = H_{t-1}(1 + g_{h,t}), \tag{C.36}$$

where $g_{h,t}$ is a function of education spending. In line with Vogel, Ludwig, and Börsch-Supan (2014) we set ρ at 0.011 and the depreciation rate of physical capital δ at 0.03. We allow the capital share β to equal 0.3, in line with the values commonly assumed in the literature (0.3–0.4) (Börsch-Supan, Ludwig, and Winter 2006). For g and z we refer to the values used in Catalano and Pezzolla (2016) and based on the estimation of the long-run relation

$$\log(TFP) = g\log(K/N) + z\log(H) + \varepsilon_{tfp}. \tag{C.37}$$

In order to obtain a reasonable elasticity of the depreciation rate in response to adaptation policies, β_k and ρ_{cc} are set equal to 100 and 0.4, respectively. Accordingly, β_d is set to 0.1, ρ_f is equal to 0.7 to allow for extreme event

TABLE C.1 Parameters of the model

PARAMETER	VALUE	DESCRIPTION
ε	1.000	Labor-consumption elasticity of substitution
ξ	0.500	Intertemporal elasticity of substitution
ρ	0.011	Pure time impatience rate
δ	0.100–0.200	Final steady state depreciation rate
δ_0	0.030	Normal depreciation rate
β_k	100	Adaptation adoption rate
β_d	0.100	Capital adjustment cost
ρ_f	0.700	Extreme persistence shock
ρ_{cc}	0.400	Early action investment policy persistency
ρ_m	1.010	Exponential climate change rate
a_0	550	Damage transmission parameter
α_{cc}	0.010	Early action expenditure-to-GDP ratio
α_{id}	0.010	Grants-to-GDP ratio
σ_b	2.000	Reserve fund intertemporal elasticity of substitution
σ_d	2.000	Grants intertemporal elasticity of substitution
z	0.430	Human capital contribution to TFP
g	0.160	Capital-per-worker contribution to TFP
β	0.300	Capital share
τ_l	0.250	Labor tax rate
τ_c	0.200	VAT rate
τ_k	0.010	Tax rate on capital

Note: GDP = gross domestic product; TFP = total factor productivity; VAT = value added tax.

persistence, ρ_m is equal to 1.01 to get an exponential trend in the gradual factor of climate change, and α_0 is equal to 550 to allow for the desired depreciation rate.

REFERENCES

Auerbach, A., and L. Kotlikoff. 1987. *Dynamic Fiscal Policy*, Cambridge University Press.

Barro, Robert J., and Jong-Wha Lee. 2015. *Education Matters: Global Schooling Gains from the 19th to the 21st Century*. Oxford University Press.

Börsch-Supan Axel, Alexander Ludwig, and Joachim Winter. 2006. "Ageing, Pension Reform and Capital Flows: A Multi-country Simulation Model." *Economica* 73 (292): 625–58.

Catalano, Michele, and Emilia Pezzolla. 2016. "The Effects of Education and Aging in an OLG Model: Long-Run growth in France, Germany and Italy." *Empirica* 43 (4): 757–800.

Vogel, Edgar, Alexander Ludwig, and Axel Börsch-Supan. 2014. "Aging and Pension Reform: Extending the Retirement Age and Human Capital Formation." SAFE Working Paper No. 82, LOEWE Center, Sustainable Architecture for Finance in Europe, Frankfurt am Main.

www.ingramcontent.com/pod-product-compliance
Lightning Source LLC
LaVergne TN
LVHW080043210926
848481LV00011B/3268